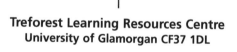

KOGAN
PAGE

First published in Great Britain and the United States in 2002 by Kogan Page Limited

120 Pentonville Road
London N1 9JN
UK
www.kogan-page.co.uk

22883 Quicksilver Drive
Sterling VA 20166–2012
USA

ISBN 0 7494 3808 8

British Library Cataloguing-in-Publication Data

A CIP record for this book is available from the British Library

---

Library of Congress Cataloging-in-Publication Data

Bennett, Roger, 1948 Apr. 9-
    International marketing: strategy planning, market entry and implementation / Roger Bennett, Jim Blythe.
        p. cm.
Includes bibliographical references and index.
    ISBN 0-7494-3808-8
    1. Export marketing. I. Blythe, Jim. II. Title.
    HF1416 .B466 2003
    658.8'48–dc21
                            2002014361

Typeset by Saxon Graphics Ltd, Derby
Printed and bound in Great Britain by Bell & Bain Ltd, Glasgow

Contents

Part I

The global approach to marketing

1

The nature of international marketing

INTRODUCTION TO INTERNATIONAL MARKETING

Readers already familiar with the rudiments of general marketing theory will know that marketing is far more than selling: profitability and added shareholder value are the ultimate aim of all marketing pursuits. Marketing is a collection of activities, including advertising, public relations and sales promotions, marketing research and new product development, package design and merchandising, personal selling and after-sales service, and the determination of selling prices. Readers who are less familiar with basic marketing theory should read one of the standard texts on the subject, such as Blythe (2000), Jobber (2001) or Lancaster and Massingham (1993). The term 'marketing mix' is frequently used to describe the combination of marketing elements applied in a given set of circumstances (Borden, 1965; McCarthy, 1981). Major components of the marketing mix can be listed under seven headings:

- **promotion** – including advertising, merchandising, public relations, and the control and deployment of sales staff;
- **product** – design and quality of output, assessment of consumer needs, choice of which products to offer for sale, after-sales service and policies for customer care;
- **price** – choice of pricing strategy, prediction of competitors' responses;
- **place** – selection of distribution channels, transport arrangements;
- **people** – the people who are in regular contact with the customers, and whose activities represent the company to the outside world;

- **process** – the sequence of events involved in delivering the product's benefits to the consumers;
- **physical evidence** – the tangible proof that the product has been delivered and consumed.

Table 1.1 Differences between domestic marketing and international marketing

Domestic	International
• Research data is available in a single language and is usually easily accessed	• Research data is generally in foreign languages and may be extremely difficult to obtain and interpret
• Business is transacted in a single currency	• Many currencies are involved, with wide exchange rate fluctuations
• Head office employees will normally possess detailed knowledge of the home market	• Head office employees might only possess an outline knowledge of the characteristics of foreign markets
• Promotional messages need to consider just a single national culture	• Numerous cultural differences must be taken into account
• Market segmentation occurs within a single country	• Market segments might be defined across the same type of consumer in many different countries
• Communication and control are immediate and direct	• International communication and control may be difficult
• Business laws and regulations are clearly understood	• Foreign laws and regulations might not be clear
• Business is conducted in a single language	• Multilingual communication is required
• Business risks can usually be identified and assessed	• Environments may be so unstable that it is extremely difficult to identify and assess risks
• Planning and organizational control systems can be simple and direct	• The complexity of international trade often necessitates the adoption of complex and sophisticated planning, organization and control systems
• Functional specialization within a marketing department is possible	• International marketing managers require a wide range of marketing skills
• Distribution and credit control are straightforward	• Distribution and credit control may be extremely complex
• Selling and delivery documentation is routine and easy to understand	• Documentation is often diverse and complicated due to meeting different border regulations
• Distribution channels are easy to monitor and control	• Distribution is often carried out by intermediaries, so is much harder to monitor
• Competitors' behaviour is easily predicted	• Competitors' behaviour is harder to observe, therefore less predictable
• New product development can be geared to the needs of the home market	• New product development must take account of all the markets the product will be sold in

Product adaptation and development for international markets

Packaging and labelling

Translation of technical literature

Quality management

Licensing and contract manufacturing

Choice of pricing strategy

Competitor analysis

Determination of discount structures

Credit management

Choice of delivery terms

Costing and budgeting

Product	Price
Place	Promotion

International distribution

Control of agents

Export documentation

Cargo insurance

Establishment of joint ventures and subsidiaries

International advertising, public relations and sales promotion

International direct marketing

Control of salespeople

Translation of sales literature

Exhibiting

Market research

Figure 1.1   Key elements of the international marketing mix

Domestic and international marketing

For international as well as domestic marketing the basic tools and concepts of marketing are applied in order to satisfy consumer demand, although the problems encountered in international marketing and the techniques used to overcome them can differ considerably. (See Bartels, 1968, for the classic discussion of this point.) Key elements of the international marketing mix are listed in Figure 1.1.

Marketing within a firm's home country is undertaken in a familiar environment, with known and accessible data sources and a single set of prices for advertising media, marketing services, printing of promotional materials, market research, and so on. For international marketing the environment differs substantially from country to country: services and facilities are priced differently and may not be available at all in some countries. Cultural, legal, political, economic and other environments differ markedly among nations (see Chapter 2). Essential differences are listed in Table 1.1.

Recent contributions to the academic literature regarding the marketing mix (see, for example, Gronroos, 1994) emphasize that its implementation must not be allowed to encourage narrow functional thinking where marketing is concerned. For example, customer service should not be confined to a company's 'distribution' department; customer service activities are so important that they need to suffuse *all* aspects of the enterprise's work. Further criticisms of the '7P' approach are that:

- It is naive and simplistic. Many variables in addition to those quoted are crucial to the success of a firm's marketing effort, and indeed to its wider success in a strategic sense.
- It tends to generate too many specialists (market researchers, media planners, sales promotions experts, etc) who lack a broad vision on the need to put the customer first.
- It is production orientated in that it implies that a customer is someone to be manipulated and 'worked upon', rather than a genuinely respected and valued partner of the supplying firm.

International marketing and exporting

Exporting means manufacturing a product in one country and selling it in another. International marketing is more than exporting, because it could involve any of the following:

- marketing products that have been manufactured or assembled in the target country;
- establishing a permanent presence in the foreign country to warehouse and distribute products;
- licensing and franchising of the firm's products to local businesses;
- sourcing components from foreign states.

Although governments encourage firms to export because exporting helps the balance of payments, exporting is not always the best route for the companies concerned. There is more on this in Chapter 11.

International and multinational marketing

A distinction is sometimes made between 'international' and 'multinational' marketing. International marketing means marketing across national frontiers, while multinational marketing means the integrated coordination of the firm's marketing activities throughout the world. Multinational marketing in practice is usually associated with the operations of multinational corporations (MNCs), which pursue *global* strategies in relation to production, investment and marketing, and derive significant proportions of their total revenues from foreign operations. (Indeed, some authorities define an MNC as any business that derives a minimum of 20 per cent of its net profits from operating abroad.) Thus an MNC will seek to maximize its revenues on the world rather than national level, locating its operations wherever conditions are most favourable and regardless of the country in which the company's head office is based. Trade liberalization, growth in the world economy, stable exchange rates for many years, and easier transnational transfer of tech-nologies and human and financial resources have greatly stimulated the expansion of MNC activities in the post Second World War era. Multinational corporations and global-ization are discussed further in Chapter 16.

The marketing concept and its international application

A common approach to marketing is to regard it as the function of finding customers for goods that the firm has already decided to supply. Thus, management selects products that are economical to put on the market relative to production costs and resource avail-abilities and then sets up a marketing department to persuade customers to purchase the goods. This approach, although fairly common, does not accord with the marketing concept.

The alternative approach is for the firm to evaluate marketing opportunities *before* it decides the product characteristics to offer, assesses potential demand for various items, determines the product attributes most needed and desired by consumers, predicts the prices consumers are willing to pay, and then supplies goods corresponding to these requirements. Firms that adopt the marketing concept are more likely to sell their prod-ucts because these will have been conceived and developed to satisfy *customer* demands. The marketing concept, then, is the proposition that the supply of goods and services should depend on the demands for them. Even the most vigorous advertising and other promotional campaigns will fail if people do not want the products.

The international marketing concept implies a shift away from looking for foreign customers who appreciate the firm's products and towards a focus on the supply of the goods that foreign consumers desire (Levitt, 1983). Manifestations of the latter approach include:

- Careful research into foreign consumer behaviour.
- Willingness to create new products and adapt existing products to satisfy the needs of *world* markets. Products may have to be adapted to suit the tastes, needs, purses and other characteristics of consumers in specific regions. Firms cannot assume that an item that sells well in one country will be equally successful in others.
- Integration of the international side of the company's business with all aspects of its operations.

International marketing considerations must be taken into account when designing and developing products, when selecting transport and distribution systems, when dealing with banks, advertising agencies and so on, and when structuring the overall organiza-tion of the firm. The international marketing manager needs to be involved in corporate planning, sales forecasting, the recruitment and training of marketing personnel, and the control of salespeople 'in the field'.

Adaptation of the marketing mix for international markets is difficult in view of the scale of the differences between some of the world's main economic regions. Major disparities occur in relation to economic development (manifest in income levels and lifestyles), social systems, technological environments, legal frameworks, competitive situation, business practices and cultural perspectives. All of these can affect how the marketing of goods and services in foreign countries needs to be executed.

Differentiated and undifferentiated international marketing strategies

International marketers might apply an identical (*undifferentiated*) marketing mix in all countries: examples include Coca-Cola and McDonald's. Conversely, they might modify products and promotional messages to take account of cultural, linguistic, legal and other national characteristics. The latter approach is called a *differentiated* marketing strategy, and normally involves higher costs than an undifferentiated strategy.

If an undifferentiated strategy is adopted, differences in market segments are ignored. Products are designed and advertised in order to appeal to the widest possible range of consumers. Although this saves costs for the company, it is not usually very effective in meeting consumer needs. In practice, even McDonald's and Coca-Cola have made some concessions to local tastes and culture: very few firms are able to provide a completely undifferentiated approach. There is more on this in Chapter 12.

REASONS FOR MARKETING ABROAD

Many factors induce firms to begin operating internationally. The most obvious, perhaps, are:

- economies of scale and scope (see Note 2 at the end of the chapter) and 'experience curve' effects (see below) resulting from increased outputs;
- the existence of lucrative markets in foreign countries that are not available at home (see Olson and Widersheim, 1978, for the pioneering empirical study into this subject);
- saturated markets in the home country;
- response to incoming competitive activity.

Scale economies might not be available if consumer tastes in the foreign markets necessitate numerous product modifications. Likewise, the costs of market entry (advertising and promotion, establishment of distribution networks and so on) could themselves outweigh production savings. Operating in foreign markets can also facilitate the 'experience curve' effect, ie cost reductions and efficiency increases attained in consequence of a business acquiring experience of certain types of activity, function or project. These effects differ from economies of scale in that they result from longer experience of doing something rather than producing a greater volume of output.

Doing business in foreign markets exposes a firm's management to fresh ideas and different approaches to solving problems. Individual executives develop their general management skills and personal effectiveness, become innovative and adopt broader horizons. The contacts and experience acquired through selling abroad can give a firm a competitive edge in its home country. Further reasons for firms becoming involved in international marketing include the following:

- Today, new product development typically requires so much expenditure that in many cases firms intending to introduce new products must adopt an international perspective.
- The higher turnover derived from international sales might enable a firm to initiate new product research and development that in the long term will give it a competitive edge.
- Corporate plans can be anchored against a wider range of (international) opportunities.
- There might be less competition in some foreign markets.
- A sudden collapse in market demand in one country may be offset by expansion in others.
- Opportunities may be afforded by new trade agreements between nations, or by the opening up of new markets in countries that were previously closed to imports. An example of this is the gradual opening up of trade with China.
- Consumers in some foreign markets might be wealthier than consumers in the firm's own country.

Firms are often forced to think global due to the entry of foreign competitors into the home markets. Foreign business accounts for a large proportion of the total Gross National Products of all major industrialized countries. As the world becomes 'smaller' in business terms, domestic customers are more likely to look abroad for suppliers.

A major reason for the increasing internationalization of business is that cross-border trade is today much easier to organize than in the past. The Internet revolution has actually been most noticeable and most successful in business-to-business markets: disappointing results in consumer markets have been widely publicized, but as a business tool the Net has been a resounding success. International telephone and fax facilities to 'remote' regions are today vastly better than they were just a few years ago; facilities for international business travel are more extensive; and business service firms (advertising agencies, market research companies, road hauliers, etc) now operate internationally. Hence it is simpler to visit and examine foreign markets, to select the best locations for operations and thereafter to control international activities.

EXPORTING

Technically, exporting means the sale in a foreign market of an item produced, stored or processed in the supplying firm's home country, as opposed to the supplier being involved in foreign manufacture or processing of goods. In practice, however, the distinction between pure 'exporting' on the one hand and wider foreign operations on the other has become increasingly blurred as businesses increasingly internationalize their activities. There is nevertheless a distinct set of commercial practices and techniques with which the would-be exporter has to become familiar. These techniques relate in particular to foreign trade documentation, transport and logistics, and methods for getting paid. They are considered further in Chapter 11.

Approaches to exporting

Some companies see exporting as little more than a convenient way of increasing overall sales; others regard the export function as a critical element of overall corporate strategy and accord exporting a status equivalent to any other field of operation within the firm. *Passive* exporting occurs when a firm receives orders from abroad without having canvassed them. *Active* exporting results from a business developing policies for setting up systems for organizing the export function and for dealing with export logistics, documentation and finance. Foreign demand for imports may arise from a variety of sources, including:

- non-availability of appropriate products from domestic producers;
- price differentials between imported and locally supplied items;
- exotic images attaching to foreign products;
- inefficiency in local distribution systems, political disruptions, industrial action, or other factors that prevent local firms from supplying goods.

A product that has reached the end of its life cycle at home may have a fresh lease of life if introduced to another country. There might be little competition in certain foreign nations, easy access to major customers (via centralized buying by government agencies or retail consortia, for example), and it may be possible to shift stock that is obsolescent in the home market but is nevertheless attractive to purchasers abroad. And, of course, exporting will increase turnover, hence spreading overheads over a greater number of units of output.

In practice...

Manchester United

Manchester United football club has an interesting distinction over most other football clubs – the vast majority of its fans have never seen the team play other than on television. This is because the majority of Manchester United's fans live outside the United Kingdom.

This huge international following has created a plethora of export marketing opportunities. Accordingly a subsidiary company, Manchester United Merchandising, was formed to sell Manchester United clothing, shoes, sports equipment, memorabilia and related items. In 1992 merchandising turnover was £2 million. This grew by 1,000 per cent over the next three years and in 1995, receipts from merchandising exceeded revenues from gate money and programme sales combined! Ninety per cent of 1995 turnover was domestic, but foreign interest was so intense that an export drive was initiated with the aim of increasing export turnover to UK levels. The monthly *Manchester United Magazine* spearheaded the campaign, together with the bi-monthly *Manchester United on Video*. More than 140,000 English language copies of the magazine are sold each month. A Thai language edition sells 25,000, and there are editions in Malay and Norwegian. Further foreign language editions are planned.

In 1996, the best markets for Manchester United merchandise were in Scandinavia, Ireland and Asia, regions where football is popular and watched extensively on TV and where there are strong national teams but few really big club sides. It followed that several other areas were ripe for targeting, notably Saudi Arabia and the Gulf States – where the additional desirable criteria of a very young population, the ability to watch football on TV three times a week, and high disposable income are also in evidence. South Africa was also targeted. As the world's best-known football club, Manchester United has a ready-made brand name powerful enough to rank its products alongside those of major sports equipment manufacturers. Since Manchester United Merchandising is currently in the early stages of internationalization it is exporting products directly rather than setting up licensing and/or local production arrangements. This provides the club with higher margins and total control over quality levels.

By 2002, the fan club membership was spread across 200 branches in 24 countries. The Internet had enabled MUFC fans to communicate through chat rooms on every continent on the planet. The club had its own TV channel, MUTV, available by subscription and pay-per-view. Even though membership of the US fan club costs $65 per person per annum, the membership lists had to be closed, and the club's allocation of tickets (held in the New York State branch and available to members travelling to the United Kingdom) were several hundred per cent oversubscribed. The vast majority of the club's income comes from sources other than playing football – a far cry from the days when players were part-timers with weekday jobs, and the club's only income was gate receipts.

Internationalization theories

The proposition that firms typically adapt to international marketing via an evolutionary series of sequential stages has a long and distinguished intellectual history (see Johanson and Vahlne, 1990; Andersen, 1993; and Calof and Beamish, 1995, for reviews of relevant literature), although it is known that businesses do not necessarily internationalize in this manner (Turnbull, 1987; Millington and Bayliss, 1990). Of particular interest here is the highly influential 'Uppsala model' (Johanson and Vahlne, 1990), which sees internationalization as a process whereby firms gradually increase their international involvement as, on the one hand, they develop knowledge of foreign markets and operations, and on the other commit more and more resources to foreign sales.

Businesses are said to change their institutional arrangements for foreign operations as they gain knowledge and experience of cross-border trade, moving from passive to active and from indirect to direct exporting. Eventually, the firm establishes foreign branches and other more capital-intensive forms of involvement with markets abroad. Market knowledge, according to the Uppsala model, derives predominantly from experience of operating in the foreign nation concerned. Experience is said to be country-specific and not easily generalized to other foreign markets. However, the experience gained generates further business opportunities, reduced market uncertainty, and hence an incentive to increase the firm's international operations. The model suggests that the only circumstances in which additional commitment to internationalization will occur other than in small incremental stages is when:

- firms have very large resources and the downside consequences are small;
- market conditions are stable;
- relevant market knowledge can be obtained in ways other than through experience.

According to the Uppsala model, firms go through the following stages:

1. exporting, usually indirectly and often opportunistically or passively;
2. active exporting;
3. direct exporting;
4. establishing a sales office in the overseas country;
5. establishing warehouse facilities in the overseas country;
6. assembly or manufacture overseas;
7. establishing a subsidiary overseas;
8. full multinational status, with autonomous branches in other countries;
9. global status, sourcing raw materials wherever convenient, manufacturing where most convenient, and seeking out market segments that cross national boundaries.

A number of studies have challenged these propositions (Turnbull, 1987; Millington and Bayliss, 1990). In reality, it is alleged, firms often jump straight into (extensive) foreign operations as a strategic choice, contingent on market conditions. Dunning's Eclectic Theory of Internationalization is an example of this school of thought: according to Dunning, firms take account of all the factors when deciding their entry method into foreign markets, and choose an approach that is appropriate in all the circumstances.

Nevertheless, the stages hypothesis continues to command substantial support from empirical investigations (see Calof and Beamish, 1995). In fact, it seems likely that some firms take the Uppsala route, while others take the Dunning route. For example, it is almost inconceivable that glass manufacturers (such as Pilkington) would adopt the stages-of-development approach, since glass is too fragile to export on any large scale. Pilkington therefore went the route of licensing its float-glass technique internationally. McDonald's could clearly not have expanded worldwide by exporting hamburgers – the business can only be conducted by sourcing and manufacturing locally.

Notes
1. The UK Chartered Institute of Marketing defines marketing as 'the management process responsible for identifying, anticipating and satisfying customers' requirements profitably'.
2. Economies of scale are reductions in unit production costs resulting from large-scale operations. Common examples are discounts obtained on bulk purchases, benefits from the application of the division of labour, integration of processes, the ability to attract high-calibre labour and the capacity to establish research and development facilities. Similar benefits might occur from 'economies of scope', ie unit cost reductions resulting from a firm undertaking a wide range of activities, and hence being able to provide common services and inputs useful for each activity.

2

Strategic considerations in international marketing

STRATEGY

The nature of strategy

The *Concise Oxford Dictionary* defines 'strategy' in militaristic terms. Strategy, it asserts, is 'the imposition upon an enemy of a place and time and conditions for fighting preferred by oneself'. Business strategy may be similarly described. It means choosing a general direction for the firm, together with organizational designs, policies, systems and a style of management best suited for beating the competition 'in the field'. Adoption of correct strategies causes the firm to offer the right products to the right markets at the right time with the right quality and at the right price. Examples of strategic decisions relevant to international marketing are:

- The products the firm will supply, in terms of positioning the firm against competition that already exists or is likely to exist in the overseas market.
- The markets in which the business is to operate, in terms of both target countries and market segments within those countries.
- Quality and price levels, based on available market niches.
- Legal forms of the parent enterprise and its subsidiaries (public company, private company, partnership, etc) and how many departments and divisions to have within the firm. This will be relative both to the overall corporate strategy of the parent company and the local regulatory systems in the target country.

- Financing of international operations, and policy on repatriation and reinvestment of profits.

Strategy differs from 'tactics' in that, whereas strategy involves the formulation of general and wide-ranging policies, tactics concern practical methods for implementing strategic decisions. Examples of tactical management in the international marketing field are decisions concerning the choice of an advertising agent, selection of distributors or the determination of advertising budgets for particular international markets. Tactical objectives within each national market are likely to include target sales by product and market sector, timescales for entry to a certain number of new distribution systems, attaining brand awareness among a specified proportion of consumers, and the completion of ad hoc projects involving the introduction of new models, analysing the results of research exercises, etc.

Strategies define the major overall goals of the organization. Plans state how these goals are to be accomplished. Strategy concerns ideas, creativity and grand conceptions; plans involve instrumental measures for the efficient allocation of resources.

Why have strategies?

Some businesses do not bother formulating strategies, preferring instead to *respond* to situations as they arise. Several reasons might be advanced for this line of approach: inaccuracy of forecasts, sudden and unforeseeable changes in laws, regulations and technical and market environments, the costs and inconveniences of long-range planning, and so on. There are nevertheless many real and significant advantages to having coherent and well-prepared strategies. Diverse activities can be better coordinated, resources allocated more effectively, and activities monitored and controlled. Special benefits include the following:

- The firm is compelled to recognize its strengths and weaknesses and to assess critically the feasibilities of its goals.
- Reactions to changes in competitors' behaviour can be decided in advance.
- Results may be compared against logically predetermined targets.
- Foreseeable pitfalls can be avoided. Indeed, the systematic consideration of likely environments could even lead to the discovery of fresh opportunities.
- The administrative processes of strategy formulation themselves require people and departments to meet, discuss issues, exchange ideas and cooperate. This should motivate employees (since the staff who participate in devising a strategy will want it to succeed), encourage initiative, avoid the duplication of effort and help eliminate unnecessary waste.
- The existence of a strategy provides a focal point towards which all the company's promotional efforts may be directed.

The clearer the strategy, the more obvious the objectives (in terms of target market share, revenues and net profits, establishment of market position, etc) that need to be attained for its successful implementation. It is particularly important not to neglect strategy matters until forced to do so by an unexpected catastrophe (loss of major customers, failure to penetrate a lucrative new market, collapse of an expensive campaign, etc) that indicates that the firm's current activities and approaches are inadequate. Otherwise the firm will be forced into taking important decisions in chaotic situations without proper information or the time necessary to consider all relevant factors. A firm without a strategy is ill-prepared to adapt its activities to meet the demands of rapid environmental change.

Corporate strategy and international marketing strategy

International marketing strategy derives from the firm's overall corporate strategy and concerns such matters as product positioning (see Chapter 12), branding strategies, choice of target countries and methods for entering them (see Chapters 10 and 4), whether to use national or international media for promotional campaigns, and so on. An international marketing strategy is a route map for guiding the overall direction of international campaigns. It needs to encompass decisions concerning media mixes, whether to use an advertising agency and, if so, for which purposes and to what extent, and whether to confront or avoid competitors when operating in foreign markets. Corporate and international marketing strategies are intimately intertwined (Brown, 1994). Examples of specific linkages are as follows:

- Operating in multiple markets affects the risk configuration of the company's operations as a whole, thus creating numerous implications for capital investment decisions.
- Product development strategies in firms selling internationally will depend critically on *international* consumer characteristics and on likely imitative behaviour by rival firms in foreign markets.
- Organization structure will be determined at least in part by the need to control international operations.
- Accumulation of foreign currency balances will affect how the firm is financed, and hence its debt/equity structure.
- For multinational corporations the recruitment of senior managers in several different countries and their subsequent deployment around the world (including the head office country) help determine who will take or influence strategic decisions.

Strategy formulation

The process of formulating and implementing strategies can be viewed as a continuous cycle, as shown in Figure 2.1.

This begins with a statement of the *mission* of the business, ie its fundamental purpose, why it exists and – in the broadest terms – what it wishes to do. Mission statements cover five components (Campbell and Tawadey, 1990):

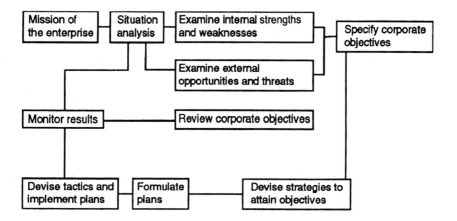

Figure 2.1   Formulating and implementing strategies

- **purpose** – the organization's reason for existing;
- **strategic goals** – what it wishes to achieve;
- **values** – how it relates to its stakeholders;
- **standards** – organizational policies and norms of behaviour;
- **strategic pathway** – the means it will use to achieve its goals.

In the context of a firm that is striving to becoming global, the international context will affect each of these strategy components. For example, a haulage firm's reason for existing might move from 'Providing an effective and efficient road haulage service within the United Kingdom' to 'Providing an effective and efficient international logistics service to UK exporters'. This is no mere shift of words: the latter statement implies that the firm will not only provide trucking services, but will also sort out international export documentation and provide all the other services of an international logistics service.

The next step is to establish the firm's present situation: where it is, the business it is in, its internal strengths and weaknesses and the external opportunities and threats it faces. This situation analysis also needs to include a marketing audit of the usefulness of current activities and the attractiveness of existing markets. Table 2.1 outlines some of the major variables involved.

Situation analysis seeks to answer the question 'Where are we now?' It assesses the conditions in each of the firm's foreign markets at a particular moment in time and the company's capacity to meet its international marketing objectives. The analysis should indicate the direction in which the company needs to move (the markets in which it ought to be operating, whether it needs to diversify its product range, etc) and what precisely it has to do to get to where it wants to be. Plans are formulated and implemented and the consequences observed. Feedback on the results might cause the firm's management to look again at the feasibility of its core objectives, the adequacy of its resources, and environmental opportunities and threats.

Table 2.1 Situation analysis

Internal strengths and weaknesses	Environmental opportunities and threats	Marketing audit
• Customer care	• Competitor behaviour	• Effectiveness of advertising
• Product efficiency	• Legal threats	• Responsiveness of sales to price
• Staff resources and skills	• Market stagnation	• Behaviour of competitors
• Delivery periods	• Technological advances	• Efficiency of distributors
• Ability to manage change	• Product obsolescence	• Length of trading cycle
• Supply of components and raw materials	• Entry barriers to markets	• Market trends
• Ability to raise capital	• Changes in consumer tastes and preferences	• Frequency and cause of stockouts
• Tangible resources: plant and machinery	• Declining profitability per unit of sales	• Identification of slow-moving products
• Internal efficiency between departments	• Lengthening credit periods	• Stockholding costs
• Suitability of premises	• Stability of demand	• Sales force effectiveness
• Quality control	• Counterfeiting	• Product knowledge of staff
• Operational effectiveness of distribution	• Socio-cultural change	• Corporate image and PR
• Control of information	• Legal and political changes	• Effectiveness of advertisin
		• Relationships with intermediaries

COMPETITIVE ADVANTAGE

Firms obtain a competitive edge in world markets via their possession of particular assets, abilities or characteristics. The elements of competitive advantage are the critical offer, the significant operating factors, and the firm's strategic resources. The relationship between these is shown in Figure 2.2.

The critical offer is the bundle of benefits the product provides that outstrip those of the other products in the market segment. Significant operating factors are often industry-specific: for example, access to raw materials supply is crucial in the food industry, so firms go to great lengths to ensure continuity of supply. Securing the supply of raw materials is often a strong motivator for going international, and it is obvious that oil companies, aluminium manufacturers, and food processors such as chocolate manufacturers could not exist without internationalizing: many have taken the natural next step of going global. The key area of strategic resources is often one in which marketing expertise comes to the forefront.

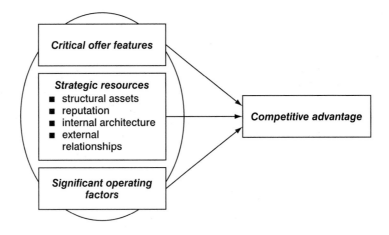

Figure 2.2 Sources of competitive advantage

Competitive *strategy* means the development of those elements of the firm's overall corporate activities that relate to beating the competition in the field. Some businesses choose to develop just one source of competitive advantage and allocate company resources accordingly. More commonly firms identify a combination of areas in which they need to excel and address these as a whole.

Formulation of a competitive strategy involves an analysis of the strengths and weaknesses of the firm in question and of its rivals, identification of key success factors in the markets in which the business is to operate, and definition of consumer attributes, demands, attitudes and behaviour. Figure 2.3 outlines the process of formulating a competitive strategy. 'Critical success factors' are the variables that determine whether a company can beat its rivals in the market concerned. Some common critical success factors are listed in Table 2.2.

Porter's model of competitive advantage

According to Michael Porter, a successful competitive strategy needs to contain measures for attaining at least one of the following (Porter, 1980):

- **cost leadership** – resulting from super-efficient organization and/or production methods or from the economies made possible by producing on a large scale;
- **differentiation** – making the firm's brands stand out from those of competitors;
- **specialization** – finding profitable niches not serviced by other firms.

These basic strategic options are mutually exclusive. It is not possible to be the cost leader while also investing heavily in building a differentiated brand: nor is it possible to specialize and still maintain cost leadership, because economies of scale will be lacking.

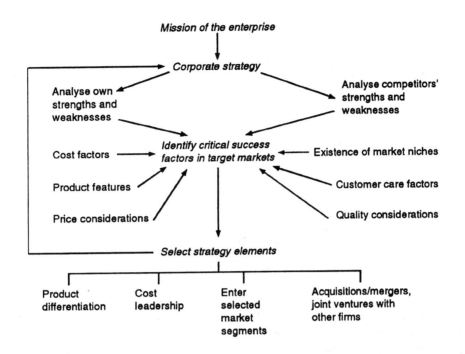

Figure 2.3 Formulating a competitive strategy

Table 2.2 Critical success factors

The *product*:
- Fulfils a clear need
- Has many uses
- Has unique features
- Is psychologically appealing
- Can be modified easily
- Is the right quality
- Performs better than that of competitors

Delivery is:
- Fast
- Reliable
- Followed by excellent customer care
- Accompanied by attractive warranties
- Competitively priced

Demand for the product is:
- Growing rapidly
- Expected to continue to expand
- Concentrated in high-spending consumers
- Concentrated in high-involvement consumers
- Concentrated in easily-accessible areas

Promotion is:
- The right mix for the product's life cycle stage within its market, the market segment itself, and corporate strategic needs
- Geared to local tastes and preferences
- Based on a positive brand image

Therefore Porter postulates a fourth strategic position, which is an attempt to achieve all three of the other positions at once: this is the strategy that is always doomed to failure.

Market conditions usually determine the specific strategies that businesses adopt. A firm in a newly established industry, for instance, will probably be more concerned with product differentiation, whereas companies in older industries might be especially interested in cutting costs. Firms in highly competitive markets may embark on a train of acquisitions in order to eliminate competition and/or establish a large organization able to obtain economies of scale, while firms in declining industries will probably want to disinvest and concentrate on profitable market niches.

The competitive environment

Porter defines competitive strategy as 'the art of relating a company to the economic environment within which it exists'. According to Porter, five major factors determine this environment, as follows:

- **Ease of entry by competitors into the market.**
- **The bargaining power of customers**. Customers are powerful if they are few in number, if they know all about the product and about competitors' prices, and if they can quickly switch between supplying firms.
- **The bargaining power of suppliers**. Suppliers have power when their output is unique and the purchasing company must design its own product system to accommodate the product supplied.
- **Availability of substitutes**. If many substitute products are available, the firm loses its ability to raise its prices by significant amounts since a price increase would merely cause customers to switch to other brands.
- **Level of existing competitive pressure**.

Porter asserts that the following general principles of inter-firm competition normally apply:

- Rivalry between companies increases as the market share of existing firms becomes more equal. Severe competition is unlikely in 'market-leader/market-follower' situations.
- Competition intensifies as the rate of growth of the market as a whole slows down.
- Since goods that are difficult to store or are perishable must be sold quickly, there will be great competition in the industries supplying such goods.
- Firms will compete more aggressively when they have much to lose from the activities of competing businesses (eg because of extremely large investments in plant and equipment).
- Competition becomes fierce when competing products acquire more and more similar characteristics and is greatest in industries supplying products that are virtually the same.

These factors affect a firm's profitability, market power, and the nature of its competitive advantage, as summarized in Figure 2.4.

Criticisms of the approach are as follows:

- Firms often change the 'industry' in which they operate. The criteria defining a particular industry sector are likely to alter (eg through technical innovation) and as the firm finds itself in new competitive environments, so its dynamic strategies will need to change. Industry structures are dynamic, so that the basic unit of analysis is constantly shifting.
- Businesses that rate highly in terms of Porter's model (ie that face few rivals, substitute products, threats from new entrants, etc) often fail, and vice versa. Many organizational and efficiency factors determine whether a firm succeeds.
- Although the model describes situations at a particular moment in time (rather like a snapshot of the early part of a horse race), its ability to predict outcomes is questionable.
- Porter's model implies that firms should choose a specific strategy route. Yet businesses that simply react to current events can be more flexible, responsive to change and profitable than firms with distinct (and perhaps rigid) strategies. Mintzberg (1983) has called this approach the 'adhocracy'.

Competition between nations

Traditional economic theories (which focus on currency exchange rates, unit labour costs, factor endowments, interest rates, etc) fail to explain why certain countries have succeeded in the post-Second World War era (Porter, 1985). Companies today are increasingly global in outlook and able to shift operations from country to country at will. The capacity to automate complete production processes means that workforce costs and competencies are not as critically important to successful operations as they once were.

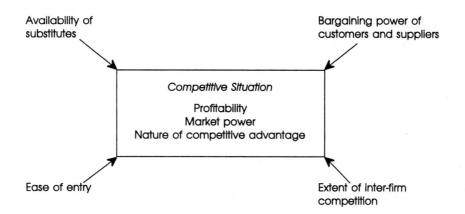

Figure 2.4 The Porter model

The rise of the multinational corporation has broken the link between corporate efficiency and the quality and availability of resources (labour, capital, etc) within the firm's
own country. A global corporation is not dependent on the resource base of just one
country; it operates wherever and whenever conditions are favourable. The workforces
and capital market arrangements of many industrialized countries are today broadly
comparable, so that companies have greater choice over where they can locate activities
(Porter, 1990). Hence the pressures of supply and demand will tend in the long term to
equalize the costs of skilled labour and capital in these countries. Today, automated
equipment can easily be substituted for labour, and modern technology enables the
creation of synthetic substitutes for expensive raw materials. Against this background,
firms need constantly to seek new sources of competitive advantage. In particular they
need to operate internationally in order to fine-tune their competitive strengths and to
identify and then remove weaknesses. Selling to the most demanding consumers causes
a firm to achieve quality and service levels it would not otherwise attain.

In this context, the rapid growth of multinational service organizations such as
McDonald's restaurants and global hotel chains has meant that local wage rates, business practices, cultural norms and so forth have been successfully subsumed into the
overall global strategy of the firms concerned. In some cases, these global service organizations have tried to act as if the local differences do not exist (for example,
Disneyland Paris in its early days), whereas in other cases the firm has made some
concessions (McDonald's burgers are made of lamb in India, where the cow is sacred).
Training local staff to provide the same service throughout the world has sometimes
been problematical, but has not been impossible – the Hotel Intercontinental in Lusaka,
Zambia provides the same service level as the Hotel Intercontinental at Hyde Park
Corner in London, although of course it is easier to have breakfast outdoors in Lusaka.
The key determinant of contemporary national competitive advantage, Porter argues,
is product and process innovation – not cheap labour or an abundance of natural
resources. Indeed, lack of the latter can spur a country to a high level of technological
innovation.

The Porter diamond

Porter summarized his argument in a diagram (see Figure 2.5) suggesting that four major
things determine a country's ability to compete internationally, namely:

- **factor conditions** – skilled labour, road and rail infrastructure, natural resources, and
  so forth;
- **demand conditions** – the strength and nature of domestic demand, consumer
  desires, perceptions and levels of sophistication;
- **related and supporting industries** – extent of supply industries, ancillary business
  services, input component manufacturers and so on;
- **firm strategy, structure and rivalry** – the organization and management of companies and the extent of domestic competition.

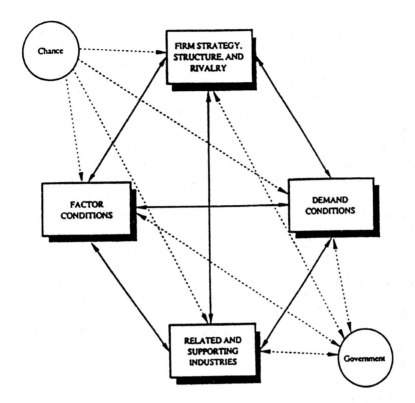

Figure 2.5 The national diamond (reprinted with the permission of The Free Press, a division of Simon and Schuster, from *The Competitive Advantage of Nations* by Michael E. Porter, copyright © 1990 by Michael E. Porter).

Other important influences on how an industry develops in a particular country are the policies of its government, opportunity, and luck. Government policies include rules on business competition, state intervention in industry, regional development, health and education, and (importantly) vocational training. Porter concludes that to be successful countries must move from having a factor-driven to having an investment-driven economy, followed by a further move to an innovation-driven economy. The latter contrasts with the 'wealth-driven' economies of some countries, which have complacent businesses and are in decline despite per capita GDP continuing to rise. According to Porter:

- Countries with governments that have been heavily involved with industries have generally been the least successful.
- The creation of domestic monopolies through mergers and takeovers creates moribund economic environments that are not conducive to innovation, even though domestic monopolies may have to compete fiercely on the international level.
- Lack of national resources (eg oil, labour, minerals, etc) can spur a country to a high level of innovation.

The value chain

Another notable contribution attributable to Michael Porter is 'value chain analysis', ie the examination of the relationships between activities that add value to a company's inputs through to final outputs (Porter, 1985). Value chain analysis helps determine how well a firm's resources are being utilized. Porter distinguished between 'primary activities' and 'support activities'. The former are as follows:

- **Inbound logistics** – activities involving the receipt, storage and handling of inputs, including warehousing, stock control, transport and so on. Relevant factors to be examined here include procurement costs, supply sources of funds, and relationships with suppliers.
- **Operations** – the conversion of inputs into products. This can include both manufacturing and the provision of services. Examples of operational decisions are plant location, production control, labour management, investments in new equipment, training and employee development.
- **Outbound logistics** – which concern distribution to customers, packaging, outward transport, storage, etc.
- **Marketing and sales** – ie all those activities connected with informing customers about the product and persuading them to buy. Each of the '7Ps' of marketing is involved (see Chapter 1).
- **Service activities** – which cover customer care, after-sales service, installation, provision of spare parts, maintenance of equipment, and so on.

Support activities provide the inputs, human resources, technology and infrastructure that underpin primary activities. **Procurement** means the acquisition of materials, subcomponents and other material resources. **Technology development** refers to work organization, R&D, product design, and the improvement of processes for resource utilization. **Human resource** management involves recruitment, training, motivation and the reward systems of the company. **Infrastructure** concerns planning mechanisms, finance, quality management, and so on.

Value may be added directly or indirectly. Examples of indirect value-adding activities are maintenance and sales force administration. Additionally, firms undertake *quality assurance* activities such as auditing, inspection, product quality control and appraisal. All activities need to be linked together, and the linkages require coordination in order to secure a smooth transition of inputs into delivered output. Note the existence of tradeoffs between specific activities: greater expenditure on quality control, for instance, may reduce the need to spend money on after-sales service. The value chains of individual firms connect to form the *value system* of an economy. Companies could gain competitive advantage by harmonizing their value chains with those of suppliers and customers. The 'margin' in a firm's value chain is the surplus of the price paid by the customer over and above the costs of resource inputs and value-adding activities.

INVESTMENT IN PRODUCTS AND MARKETS

Assessing the international marketplace: Ansoff's matrix

Strategies can be classified into two general categories: those seeking to maintain present markets and those designed to facilitate entry to fresh markets. H I Ansoff suggested a two-dimensional tabulation of strategy options for proposed and existing products in intended and current markets (Ansoff, 1957). An Ansoff matrix for a particular company might look something like that depicted in Figure 2.6.

Companies with numerous opportunities and few problems in present markets are likely to focus on maintenance and development strategies. For example, a firm in this position might seek to expand its distribution outlets, local offices and warehousing facilities, or might seek to expand business through increased promotional effort or introducing further products to the market. Lack of growth in existing markets and/or the availability of profitable new markets abroad may lead a firm to look for foreign partners in these latter unexplored markets, to adapt existing products to satisfy the needs of new market segments, and to diversify the product range to encompass completely new items.

Product portfolio analysis

The problem is deciding whether to develop or abandon specific products, since heavy expenditures on a product that sells in a low-growth market sector can drain the company of cash. One of the earliest analyses of the issue was by the Boston Consulting Group, which classified products according to two variables: the product's share of its total market, and rate of the market's growth. The best products, obviously, were those with high market shares of buoyant markets experiencing high rates of growth, and the firm's strategy should be directed, therefore, to promoting these.

A development of this approach, the 'Business Screen' method, uses market attractiveness and organizational strength to categorize products and activities. Market attractiveness depends on the size, growth rate, profitability and competitive intensity of the

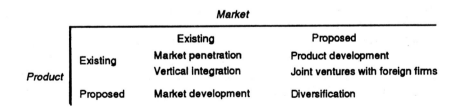

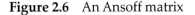

Figure 2.6   An Ansoff matrix

market and on how easily it can be served. Organizational strength involves the quality of the firm's product, the firm's efficiency and the effectiveness of its marketing.

Figure 2.7 illustrates the approach, showing a firm with three products, A, B and C. The area of the circles indicates the relative sizes of the markets for each product, while the wedge in each circle shows the firm's share of that particular market. It can be seen that although the market for product A is large and highly attractive, the company lacks the necessary competences to serve this potentially lucrative segment, implying the need for further investment in this field.

Product B should probably be discarded, while product C presents a 'question mark' about how to proceed. There is a large market for product C, the firm can supply it easily and the company already has a large market share. But the market for C is stagnant and profit margins are low.

Problems with portfolio analysis

The main limitation of portfolio analysis is its concentration on the composition of the firm's activities rather than on how the business should be run. Other problems include the measurement of market size and how to define market segments (a broad definition of a

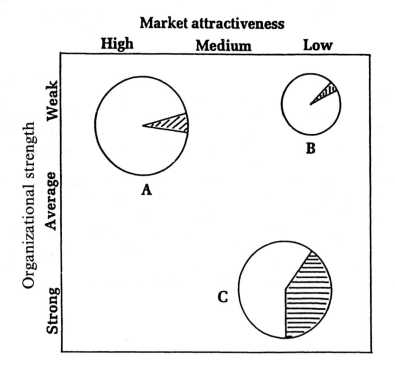

Figure 2.7   Business screen method of portfolio analysis

market will give the firm a relatively low market share and vice versa). Also, the list of factors potentially contributing to 'organizational strength' and to 'market attraction' is extremely long, so great skill is needed to sort out which are important in any given situation.

A further variant on the product portfolio approach is to classify products according to *market profitability* on one axis and *competitive capacity* on the other. Again the evaluation of these variables is subjective and, for international markets, extremely problematic. Note, moreover, that:

- National markets exhibiting low growth (even stagnation) overall can still be profitable.
- The model can become a self-fulfilling prophesy in that once a product is perceived to be in decline, resources will be withdrawn from promoting it and sales will collapse still further. In fact the product might have had a long and healthy life had the marketing mix been varied in an appropriate manner.
- Sometimes the various models in a firm's product range complement each other to the extent that withdrawal of one will adversely affect the others. The promotional images of the models might be interdependent, or the production and distribution of a particular item could involve skills the maintenance and development of which are crucial for the supply of the firm's other products.
- In a global marketplace, declining sales in one country might be accompanied by increasing sales in another. More importantly, a product that is in decline might be introduced into a new market where it begins a new product life cycle – an example is McDonald's, which is facing decline in the United States but rapid growth in the Third World. Cigarette sales are also declining in the industrialized world, but increasing in the Third World.

Nevertheless, the portfolio model is a simple, logical and convenient device for taking a bird's-eye view of the firm's activities, for varying the marketing mix applied to specific products, for corporate planning and departmental structuring of the firm, and for deciding which individuals shall assume responsibility for which products (managing a rapidly developing product requires skills different from those needed merely to maintain a stable situation).

Portfolio thinking is perhaps more appropriate for a firm serving particular country markets rather than marketing globally using an undifferentiated approach. Market attractiveness might be measured in terms of population size, GDP per head of population, some index of economic stability, percentage of the population in a certain age group, etc. Organizational strength would relate to the company's capacity to cope with the marketing problems of the country concerned in terms of such matters as language, business methods, distribution structure, agency contacts, and so on.

INTERNATIONAL MARKETING PLANNING

The nature of planning

Planning means looking into the future and deciding today what to do in the future given predicted or intended circumstances. The process of planning is troublesome and expensive – troublesome because it requires forecasts of the future, expensive because it absorbs large amounts of time. Nevertheless, planning is usually worthwhile. It forces management to prepare for unforeseen eventualities, to clarify objectives, to develop criteria for monitoring performance and to think ahead systematically. Also, it demands the conscious coordination of projects and the active participation and cooperation of several departments in the formation and execution of planned activities. Duplications of effort might be revealed, foreseeable pitfalls avoided, and opportunities for greater efficiency identified. Further benefits are that:

- Decisions concerning future activities can be taken in advance, unhurriedly, using all the data that is available and considering all possible options. This avoids decision-making in crisis situations with management unable to study all relevant issues judiciously and at length.
- The organization will be ready to adapt future activities to meet changing circumstances.
- Managements are forced to recognize their own strengths and weaknesses.
- Allowance can be made for some of the extra difficulties inherent in international trade, for example the longer periods needed to repatriate profits, or revenues in the case of exporting.

The international planning process

International marketing plans derive from international marketing strategies. Frameworks for international marketing planning necessarily involve:

- **Objective setting** – this is the quantification and precise specification of targets.
- **Resource planning** – the examination of available resources and the determination of additional resources necessary to attain objectives.
- **Environmental auditing** – situation analysis and the assessment of the firm's competitive position.
- **Risk assessment** – relating the probabilities of the success of various courses of action to the firm's overall objectives and activities. An essential component of such an assessment is an analysis of the firm's assumptions about the stability and prospects of the markets in which it plans to operate: it is obviously essential to cross-refer the risk assessments to minimize the risks of several projects failing at the same time.
- **Sales and profit forecasts**.

- **Budgeting** – including both expenditures and incomes for all of the markets the company expects to be involved in. Again, cross-referencing needs to take place so that budget deficits do not coincide too much.
- **Tactical planning** – operational plans for each component of the marketing mix should be drawn up.

The problems involved

International marketing planning is intrinsically problematic, in consequence of the complexities created by diverse national distribution systems, cultural factors that impinge upon promotional methods, information-gathering difficulties and the uncertainties surrounding competitors' responses in foreign markets. Variables taken as given for domestic marketing may need complete reassessment when marketing abroad; legal and tax issues are important examples. All the difficulties associated with domestic business planning are intensified at the international level, in particular:

- the need to consider the implications of environmental change in several different countries;
- lack of reliable market information, particularly on what constitutes realistic targets for the development of foreign markets;
- possible misinterpretation of foreign statistics, which may have been collected in a different way from home country statistics or which may use different definitions;
- different perspectives on the planning process adopted by head office managers and staff in local subsidiary units.

A more general criticism is that adherence to plans places the firm into a straitjacket, denying it the flexibility needed to respond quickly to changing international market environments. Also, many senior managers are unable to cope with the volume and complexity of the information generated in corporate planning processes. They receive so much information in such diverse forms (sales forecasts, written reports, efficiency audits, bar charts, etc) that they cannot identify clear priorities for action. The quality of information may be suspect and the system for providing it might be extremely expensive. Flexibility needs to be woven into the master strategy, with a variety of fallback options ready for quick implementation.

A number of empirical studies have claimed that there are few long-term relations between particular approaches to corporate planning and company profitability (see Stacey, 1993; Mintzberg, 1994). The rankings of the most successful businesses in each of the world's major countries change dramatically over five-year periods, with firms that pay little attention to formal strategic planning procedures sometimes achieving enormous success. Arguably, the competitive business environment of the modern world is so turbulent that it is unreasonable to expect any plan to be valid for anything but a short period. Situations change, and fresh targets may have to be adopted. Hence, the absence of rigid plans might actually help management adopt a flexible approach and improve overall performance.

A not uncommon experience is for firms to begin international marketing planning in earnest as their foreign operations multiply, to introduce highly sophisticated planning systems, and then to abandon the entire activity in consequence of unforeseen changes, making a nonsense of projections and hence bringing the process into disrepute. Management realizes that all its plans are constructed on a handful of key assumptions (constant competitor prices, absence of state intervention in industry, political stability in foreign markets, etc), and panic when these assumptions collapse. Yet the relinquishment of planning means the sacrifice of all the benefits previously outlined. What is needed therefore is a pragmatic and realistic approach that recognizes the problems involved and sets out a number of options and a series of time horizons, with contingency arrangements for events not completed on schedule.

Planning methods

Three overall approaches to planning are available: 'top-down' planning, which means that senior management plans and establishes targets for all levels and subsidiary units within the firm; 'bottom-up' planning, whereby each division and subsidiary prepares an estimate of what it believes it can achieve and submits this to higher management for approval; and a third (and common) method whereby senior management imposes general objectives, leaving individual subsidiary units to devise plans for attaining them.

Top-down planning

Here, head office plays the major role in the planning process, and acts as the focal point for generating fresh ideas and for coordinating and integrating activity. The major point in its favour is the inexperience of junior and/or local subsidiary managers in policy-making. They might not be familiar with the work of other units, so that their judgments may be short-sighted and might conflict with the needs of other aspects of the organization. Headquarters staff, conversely, can adopt a broader perspective on the company's overall operations, and can facilitate the efficient use of worldwide corporate resources with central control to avoid each local unit 'doing its own thing'. Foreign operations can be integrated into the company's global strategies.

Bottom-up planning

This utilizes the local knowledge and skills of managers in subsidiary units and should ensure that local conditions are properly considered when company plans are being formulated. Managers of subsidiaries develop their planning competencies and, through their involvement, may be better motivated and committed to the implementation of resulting policies. A problem, however, is that local subsidiaries are likely to put forward plans aimed at furthering the subsidiary's interests rather than the interests of the entire company. Bottom-up approaches might be put into effect via the establishment of regional planning offices responsible for coordinating individual country programmes in various areas. The regional office will support local subsidiaries, but itself report to international headquarters.

The case for bottom-up planning is more powerful in decentralized organizations. In a decentralized international company, local subsidiaries will already be responsible for selecting promotional programmes, choosing and controlling distributors, managing local sales representatives, conducting research, and so on.

Criteria for successful planning

Plans should be as detailed as expenditure constraints allow, but should not extend too far into the future since accurate prediction of the distant future is impossible. All alternative courses of action should be considered, not just some of them, and the side-effects and implications of the actions envisaged should be examined. Instructions to individuals and departments must be incorporated into the body of the plan. As the plan is executed, its effectiveness in achieving stated objectives must be monitored and this will be facilitated if the plan is concise and easy to understand. Note the importance of setting reasonable initial targets; over-ambitious objectives lead to disillusion and cynicism when they are not achieved. Equally, targets that are too low have little operational significance.

Plans cannot be successfully implemented unless there is full commitment to them at the top of the organization. Senior management must be willing to take the firm's international operations seriously and to devote proper resources to fulfilling their needs.

International sales forecasting

All sales forecasting is difficult, international sales forecasting especially so. Political and legal superstructures can change overnight, foreign taxes can alter and consumer tastes can alter suddenly and in seemingly unpredictable ways. Competing firms may change their prices, new firms might enter the market, new production techniques could become available that require complete re-estimation of future output constraints. The process of international sales forecasting is outlined in Figure 2.8. Forecasts need to move from the general to the particular, beginning from an overall assessment of the economy and business environment of the country in question, followed by a forecast by aggregate sales in a specific industrial sector or market segment, and finally to a prediction of the company's sales in the market and its market share.

Most forecasting techniques extrapolate past trends into the future. They assume consistency and continuity, and cannot cope with trend breaks and environmental turbulence. Long-range forecasts in particular are as much acts of faith as they are statistical predictions. A long-range forecast is a statement of intent, not a prognostication. Accordingly, some organizations establish special committees to prepare long-range forecasts and plans and to inaugurate the policies needed to achieve long-run objectives. Such committees meet periodically to speculate about the future. Their membership usually consists of senior managers who are not concerned with routine company administration but rather

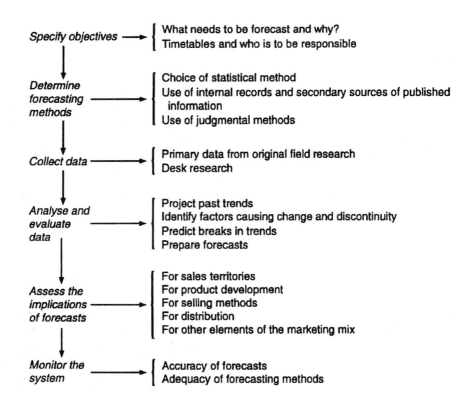

Figure 2.8 International sales forecasting

with diagnostic and organizational activities. Hopefully, such individuals will possess a broad outlook and be able to assess objectively the future prospects of the firm. Special problems applying to international sales forecasting include:

- The expense of collecting and analysing data on numerous countries and market segments within them.
- The diversity of economic and social conditions around the world, with income and lifestyle differences being so great that many separate forecasts need to be undertaken, each with its own unique set of causal variables.
- The paucity and inaccuracy of the data used for forecasting in some countries. Problems caused by gaps in data for foreign markets are made worse by the fact that it is difficult to make 'intelligent guesses' about missing data for a foreign country with which the forecaster is totally unfamiliar.
- The turbulent political, social and financial environments of some countries renders long-term predictions unreliable. Forecasts need to be completed more frequently and evaluated more critically for these countries, and contingency plans need to be more numerous.

- The difficulty of comparing forecasts for different countries.
- The lack of information on the likely behaviour of current and potential competitors in distant foreign markets.

Also, a wider range of factors can disrupt a firm's foreign sales than might reduce sales in the domestic market. Currency exchange rate fluctuations, imposition of extra tariffs or import controls, government interference with a foreign country's trade policies, and transport difficulties are all likely to create problems. 'Scientific' approaches to planning and forecasting can lead to predetermined conclusions, since they often assume there is 'one best way' and a single route map to guide the business. The problem is that, in business, the map itself is likely to change constantly, and how travellers read the map depends on varying perceptions and interpretations.

'What if' analysis

This involves asking a series of questions to establish the various outcomes likely to result from different future environments. Outcomes are quantified in terms of expected sales, costs, expenditures, asset structures, flows of funds and other operational variables. The idea is to help management prepare for the future by describing various possible future worlds and how they may come about. Rather than asking the question 'Will it happen?', as occurs in forecasting, management asks the question 'What will we need to do if it happens?' and hence makes sure that the firm is adequately prepared for environmental change. 'What if' analysis recognizes the complexities, discontinuities and uncertainties of the real world and, by implication, the limited value of extrapolating past information. It is more concerned with possibilities than with probabilities, and has a qualitative rather than quantitative orientation. Opposing possibilities can be considered simultaneously. The process is illustrated in Figure 2.9.

CONTROL AND COORDINATION

Processes for controlling international marketing activities involve:

1. establishing standards and targets;
2. monitoring activities and comparing actual with target performance; and
3. implementing measures to remedy deficiencies.

Control links inputs to outputs and provides feedback to the people in charge. An effective control system will enable the rapid deployment of resources to their most efficient uses, will transmit management expertise throughout the organization, and will generate comprehensive information on the activities of subsidiary units.

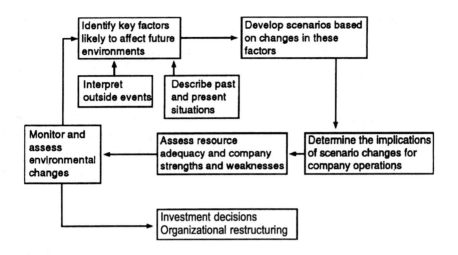

Figure 2.9 'What if' analysis

Selecting a control mechanism

The essential issue is whether to centralize decision-taking at head office or allow local subsidiary units to control local operations. Factors affecting this decision might include the extent of the company's foreign business, ease of communications with local units, and the extent of the information on local market conditions available in the head office country. Other factors influencing the decision of whether or not to centralize include the following:

- **Degree of interdependence among subsidiaries**. If units in some countries require inputs from subsidiaries in others, then close central control and coordination will be needed.
- **Nature, extent and intensity of local competition**. Highly competitive environments require immediate responses at the local level, without having constantly to refer back to head office for direction.
- **Size and complexity of the enterprise**. Large companies with extensive activities need centralized units to coordinate worldwide operations.
- **Ownership of the firm**. If a company is largely owned by one or just a handful of shareholders, then its management may feel obliged to centralize its administration. Diverse shareholding – especially if large shareholders are to be found in host countries – could favour decentralization.
- **Opportunities for achieving production and administration economies of scale through centralization**.
- **Value of capital assets**. Head office may be reluctant to delegate authority to local units if extremely expensive capital equipment is involved.

- **Volatility of local trading conditions**. The more volatile the trading environment, the greater the need for instant on-the-spot decisions.
- **Cultural divergence**. The greater the cultural divergence between the overseas market and the home market, the greater the degree to which local control must be delegated.

A two-tier control mechanism might be feasible with tight and centralized monitoring and control of agents, distributors and subsidiary units in some countries and the adoption of an arm's length approach elsewhere. Whichever method is adopted, head office needs to be well informed of local activities, problems and prospects. Factors relevant to the choice of system include:

- how easily it can be adjusted as circumstances change;
- its cost and the amount of detailed supervision involved;
- the quality of the reports it generates and how quickly operating errors are revealed;
- whether it is clear and fully understood by all concerned.

Coordination

Coordination means the unification of effort, ie ensuring that everyone within the enterprise is working towards a common goal. Effective coordination requires efficient control, which itself presupposes the existence within the firm of sound information-gathering and reporting procedures, an effective appraisal system, and an efficient system for rapid intervention to deal with shortcomings. Coordination may be achieved in of two main ways: either by mechanistic systems of control, or by developing an overall corporate culture coordinated by a vision of where the corporation should be going. Mechanistic systems of control might include the following:

- Standardization of administrative procedures in all the company's establishments at head office and abroad. Consequently a uniform and simplified set of policies can be applied 'across the board' to all the firm's foreign operations and be subsequently monitored. Standards could relate to reporting methods, after-sales service and customer care procedures, determination of selling prices and discount structures, decisions concerning promotional expenditures and techniques, etc.
- Feedback systems involving frequent reports (possibly on a daily basis) to a central control. Normally, reports will be restricted to key data and to unexpected occurrences (including deviations from targets) since otherwise head office becomes overloaded with information.
- Regular face-to-face meetings of managers of the firm's operations in various countries. Note the costs and time involved, and the possibility that discussions at meetings may be trivial.
- Appointment of a full-time liaison manager whose main duty is the coordination of the work of several subsidiary units. The problem here is deciding to whom this

person should report. If the coordinator outranks each of the heads of participating units, the status of these units might be lowered. If, conversely, the liaison manager is accountable to the head of department (for example, of an international division), then that department may be seen by others as occupying a special and undeservedly privileged position.

Cultural systems of control include the following:

- ensuring that there is a clear corporate vision and mission;
- free-flowing communication between the workforce and the management;
- good internal PR and internal marketing;
- good induction procedures for new staff to inculcate the corporate culture at an early stage;
- 'loose–tight' management structures in which boundaries are clearly laid down, but with enough leeway within them to allow for empowerment of staff at the 'sharp end' of decision-making.

Given the diverse nature of doing business in international markets, control by corporate culture is likely to be more effective, and certainly has more flexibility. The drawback is that cultural norms within the overseas countries might contaminate the corporate culture and create differences between countries – although in practice this is likely to happen anyway.

THE ENVIRONMENTS OF INTERNATIONAL MARKETING

All marketing activities occur within legal, economic, cultural, political and other environments to which strategies and policies must relate. Marketers need to operate within the constraints of this environment, and in the case of international marketing there will be more than one environment constraining the company at any one time.

Figure 2.10 indicates some of the forces involved. The problem in international as opposed to domestic marketing is that the environments confronted are vastly more complex and extensive than for domestic operations. Each country has its own legal system, culture, socio-economic infrastructure, and so on.

Coping with environmental change

Most of the firm's environments have to be taken as they are and cannot be controlled, yet they have profound consequences for marketing management. Thus procedures are needed for the speedy identification of fresh market opportunities resulting from environmental change. A two-step procedure for scanning environments and coping with environmental change is necessary. First, the firm should predict the external changes that might occur and then detail: how the organization would be affected by them and how it should respond.

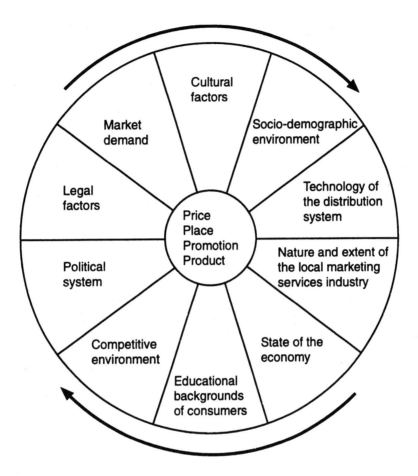

Figure 2.10   Environments and the marketing mix

Second, it should list the business's major functions, followed by an outline of all environmental factors likely to affect these functions. Unfortunately there is a huge number of external variables that might affect a firm's operations, creating the danger that some important variables may be overlooked.

Very large companies might attempt to influence the governments and institutions that help determine environments in the first place. Lobbying of governments, the media, international organizations, etc, can occur via trade associations, chambers of commerce, industry trade missions to foreign countries and similar organizations.

THE ECONOMIC AND POLITICAL ENVIRONMENT

Key factors in the economic environment of a country in which a firm is doing business are the nature and extent of competition, growth rates and living standards, tax regimes, import controls and market opportunities as a whole. International marketing managers need to take an interest in both the economic structures of the countries in which they wish to do business and the international economy as a whole in order to establish the sizes and characteristics of various markets, identify high-growth sectors, assess the degree of risk attached to operating in specific countries, and deploy resources effectively.

If the company is operating a centralized system of control, the foreign subsidiaries will collect information on national economies. Headquarters staff may then interpret the information (possibly in liaison with local subsidiary managers) and make cross-national comparisons using standard criteria. Important variables to be examined include Gross Domestic Product (GDP) in total and per head of population, the regional distribution of GDP, levels of capital investment, consumer expenditures, labour costs, inflation rates and levels of unemployment. Comparison of the economic conditions prevailing in many disparate countries is a formidable task. There are problems of data comparability, unreliability of information on certain economies, differences in data collection periods, and so on. Each firm will of course be interested in a particular set of economic variables specifically relevant to its operations.

If the firm has a decentralized system of control, information will be collected and acted on locally, with the home-country management kept in the picture in order for them to retain an overall view of the company's progress. In many cases, global corporations allow their overseas subsidiaries considerable leeway – even allowing them to compete with each other. For example, Volkswagen ceased production of the Beetle in Germany, but the firm's Mexican and Brazilian subsidiaries continued to make the car – and even exported them back to Germany. Companies need to look beyond the obvious, and use economic indicators to predict what governments might do. For example, the balance of payments indicates the following:

● the overall economic health of the country;
● the likelihood of the country's government imposing foreign exchange controls, import restrictions and deflationary economic policies such as tax increases and interest rate rises; and
● whether a devaluation of the national currency against other currencies might occur.

Political considerations affect the laws and hence the business practices of the country, restrictions on entry to the market (tariff levels and controls over the foreign ownership of enterprises for example), the prices a firm can charge its customers and the ability to repatriate profits. The political superstructure defines the legal environment in which business operates, particularly with respect to the law of contract (see below) and rules on advertising and consumer protection. Economic and political environments interrelate: political factors influence the economy, while economic hardship may trigger political upheaval. Political instability can arise from internal revolution and insurgency, involvement in foreign wars, frequent changes of government (peacefully or through violence), bad international relations, falling national income and living standards, high inflation and rising foreign debt. Further indices are:

- how much capital is leaving the country and the attitudes towards the country of international organizations such as the World Bank and the IMF;
- the roles of opposition political parties;
- widespread bribery and corruption among government officials;
- industrial relations, including the legality of strikes and trade unions;
- incidence of terrorism.

Political risk needs to be assessed systematically and monitored on a continuous basis: there are many examples of previously stable countries collapsing into anarchy, with foreign firms losing all their investments. Terrorist acts can happen at any time, with far-reaching economic consequences, as the destruction of the World Trade Center in New York on 11 September 2001 showed.

Micro risk and macro risk

Macro political risk affects all foreign firms operating in the country to an equal extent. Examples include the imposition of exchange controls, special taxes on foreign firms, 'local content' rules, etc. Micro risk, conversely, applies to a particular company, industry or project, eg import restrictions on a specific category of product, the compulsory breaking up of a very large firm into smaller units, cancellation of contracts, etc. There exist consultancies that specialize in political risk assessment, usually by focusing on analysis of the following issues:

Domestic politics

- whether there is a peaceful mechanism for transferring political leadership;
- the extent to which the population shares common values;
- relations with other countries;
- ethnic divisions within the country and whether ethnic minorities are properly represented in government;
- incidence and severity of terrorism and/or violent political demonstrations;
- whether fundamental political issues are openly debated;
- responsiveness of the government to changes in public opinion and/or to pressure group influences.

Economic factors

- distributions of wealth and income;
- labour relations, the incidence of strikes and whether there exist orderly procedures for resolving industrial relations disputes;
- the effectiveness of public administration;
- rates of economic growth and inflation;
- the level of unemployment;

- balance of payments situation;
- ratio of foreign debt to national income.

A major problem with political risk assessment is that the information on which it is based is likely to be biased, to rely on hearsay, and to be incomplete, quantitatively unmeasurable, contradictory and difficult to verify. Choice of the factors upon which an analysis should be based is necessarily subjective, and a huge range of variables may be relevant to the country concerned. The interpretation of information is also subjective. It is of course much easier to evaluate political risk in a democratic country wherein the views of the government and opposition may be monitored via the press, parliamentary debates, party manifestos and similar documents. Much censorship occurs in undemocratic countries, and it can be extremely difficult (perhaps impossible) to establish the true situation.

THE CULTURAL ENVIRONMENT

Culture is easier to recognize than to define, involving as it does a complex set of inter-relating beliefs and ways of living. A nation's culture represents a collective frame of reference through which a wide range of issues and problems are interpreted. It determines how symbols, sounds, pictures and behaviour are perceived by individuals and affects socialization, friendship patterns, social institutions, aesthetics and language (Deyliner, 1990; Ferraro, 1990; Usunier, 1993). Culture consists of the following main elements:

- **Religion**. Even if the bulk of the population is non-practising, the prevailing religion permeates the culture: this is the case with Christianity in Britain, and with Islam in Turkey.
- **Language**. The language shapes the nation's thought, because some concepts are difficult to express in some languages, while others are easily expressed. For example, Eskimos have a large number of words for 'snow' but few words to express 'fighting'. In English the reverse is the case.
- **Social structure**. This may range from the rigid caste structure of India through to the so-called 'classless society' of Australia. Social structure also includes gender roles and family patterns.
- **Shared beliefs and ethics**. Beliefs about what is and is not acceptable behaviour are essentially cultural.
- **Non-verbal language**. This includes gestures and body language: while some gestures are universal (for example, smiling), most are not. Even nodding the head changes its meaning across cultural boundaries.

Culture helps individuals to define concepts. A 'concept' is a conscious linking together of images, objects, stimuli or events. Individuals receive huge numbers of messages, so the brain needs a system for classifying them into groups, which can then be dealt with efficiently. For instance, apples, oranges and bananas are all separate and unique items, but the brain will categorize them into a single concept of 'fruit'. Conceptualization helps the individual to manage data, identify relations among events and objects, and to discover similarities and differences that enable the comparison of items of information. This is vitally important for the design of advertising images because culturally based conceptualizations can determine how a message is interpreted (as good or bad, conservative or risqué, etc) and *how* the message recipient responds to its contents. National media that carry advertisements are themselves influenced by a country's culture in terms of:

- the spoken and written language used – even within a country, these may differ according to social class;
- whether a country has a tabloid press;
- the editorial content of magazines, newspapers, and radio and television programmes;
- attitudes expressed by the media towards national issues (manifest in non-coverage of 'taboo' subjects, adoption of ideological 'lines', etc).

Culture affects what people buy (taboos, local tastes, historical traditions, etc), when they buy (eg the spending boom around Christmas in Christian countries), who does the purchasing (men or women) and the overall pattern of consumer buying behaviour. Culture can also affect consumer behaviour in relation to:

- which consumer needs are felt more intensively;
- which family members take which purchasing decisions;
- attitudes towards foreign supplied products;
- the numbers of people who will purchase an item during the introductory phase of its life cycle;
- the segmentation of national markets.

On a wider level, cultural influences are evident in some aspects of a country's demographic make-up (eg household size, kinship patterns, social mobility and social stratification) and in authority and status systems that emerge from the management styles of firms. Some important cultural influences are listed in Table 2.3. The absence of a certain type of product or the fact that certain styles of advertising are not used in a particular market might not be indicative of gaps available for them, but rather that such products or advertising styles are culturally unacceptable in the country concerned. At the same time it is important to realize that culture represents just one of several environments within which a company operates. Political considerations and/or economic laws of supply and demand frequently outweigh cultural effects (Bangeman, 1992).

in practice...

Cultural gaffes

Tales of cultural gaffes are common in marketing circles: brand names that translate poorly, meetings that went wildly wrong, and so forth. Many of these stories are likely to be apocryphal, but

Table 2.3　Cultural influences

On attitudes towards:	On advertising:
• Work • Material possessions • Sexuality • The upbringing and education of children • Social class • The role of women in society • Morality • Respect for the law and social institutions • The underpriveleged • Religion • Politics • Entrepreneurship • Willingness to accept risk • Wealth	• How local customers perceive the market • Positions of various products • How the female form may be used in advertising • The acceptability of nudity and/or what parts of the human body may be shown • The extent of an advertisement's display of physical contact between people (of the same or differing sexes) • The degree of elegance, quality, urbanity, etc, expected of advertisements • Advertising style

On business protocols:	On business environments:
• Conduct of meetings • Negotiating style • Degree of formality of relationships • Manner of greeting • Buyer/seller relationships	• Communication systems • Participation in management decisions • Role of government in business affairs • Employment conditions • Relationships between trade union confederations and employers' associations

anyone who travels regularly becomes aware of brand names that seem inappropriate, or of misunderstandings brought about by cultural differences. Here are some examples:

- An exporter of soft drinks to Africa promoted one of its products via a poster depicting a father and son drinking from a bottle in full sunshine in the middle of a lake. Sales plummeted. It turned out that the agency preparing the poster had used Black models from New York whose ethnic origins were different from the major tribal groups in the country concerned, and that only an imbecile would sit out under a full sun in that part of the world.
- McDonald's restaurants' 'Ronald McDonald' character failed in Japan, where the white makeup on the face of the character is a symbol of death.
- It is considered rude in Thailand to show people the soles of your feet.
- Ford's Pinto car sold poorly in certain parts of Latin America, where the word 'pinto' is slang for 'small male sexual organ'.
- Crest toothpaste initially failed in Mexico because it used a pre-existing campaign strategy based on 'scientifically tested' properties of the product. Scientifically orientated promotional messages meant little to the typical Mexican consumer.
- Japanese executives dislike saying 'no' in face-to-face negotiations: often they will say 'yes' meaning 'yes, I understand what you mean' rather than 'yes, I agree'. Foreign business people

sometimes leave meetings with Japanese buyers thinking they have clinched a deal when this is not actually the case.

- Sales of a highly successful brand of canned beer suddenly dropped in a certain part of Central Africa, coinciding with a change in the size and shape of the can containing the beer. It emerged that the old cans were widely used as oil lamps and for a variety of other strange purposes. The new cans could not be adapted in these ways.

Models of culture

Three main approaches to the analysis of culture and of the consequences of cultural influences have been developed as follows:

- **Taxonomies of cultures**. Dividing them into different levels and/or into high-context/low-context categories (see below).
- **Lifestyle analysis**.
- **Identification of *cultural universals***. These are aspects of culture supposedly found in all societies. To the extent that cultural universals exist, societies can be regarded as essentially the same and cultural differences between them relatively unimportant. Examples of cultural universals are interest in sport, bodily adornment, courtship, household hygiene, sexual taboos, gift giving, and status differentiation (Murdock, 1945).

Group norms

A group norm is a shared perception of how things should be done, or a common attitude, feeling or belief. Individuals within a group will behave according to how they feel other group members expect them to behave. Norms facilitate the integration of an individual into a group: initially, an entrant into an existing group will feel isolated and insecure, and will seek out established norms that will act as a guide to behaviour. Certain group norms will be regarded by organization members as applicable in all circumstances at all times. Such norms (or values) are referred to as *cultural absolutes*. A *cultural imperative* is something that an individual must do in order to fit in with group norms and a firm's organizational culture. This contrasts with a *cultural exclusive*, ie something that must not be done for the maintenance of cultural harmony, and a cultural *adiaphora*, which is an act without cultural implications. Cultural norms are *learned* by new entrants to a group. The processes whereby an individual acquires cultural norms via learning is known as *enculturation*.

Social values

These are moral principles or standards against which the desirability of behaviour may be assessed. Values help determine what an individual considers important, personal priorities, and how they assess other people's worth. Values influence perspectives on a variety of matters: the work ethic, honesty, social responsibility, choice of career, and so on.

Values change over time; some may disappear entirely as environmental circumstances alter. Also, values may vary across industries and from country to country (Japanese and British values, for instance, differ significantly).

High-context culture and low-context culture

High-context culture is that which is internalized and/or embedded within the person and not expressed in an explicit manner (Hofstede, 1980). Persons sharing the same high-context culture do not feel any need to explain their thoughts or behaviour to each other. Hence high-context culture relies heavily on non-verbal communication. Characteristics of high-context culture are as follows:

- communication *within* the high-context group is fast and efficient, but can break down in relation to outsiders who may not be able to comprehend what the high-context group believes or is talking about;
- behaviour within a high-context culture is stable and predictable;
- the nature of a particular high-context culture might be understood by outsiders in consequence of the latter's stereotyping of the former's members;
- for effective communication to occur, all parties need to share the same perceptual field.

These points are clearly important for international marketing as it is necessary to understand consumer groups in high-context cultures in order to design marketing campaigns and promotional messages that will appeal to them. Low-context culture is explicit: words, signs, symbols, and rituals are used to rationalize, communicate and explain cultural norms and social activities. When dealing with a low-context culture, it is necessary to argue and persuade and to present propositions (eg appeals to purchase particular products) in a clear and precise manner. Features of low-context cultures are that:

- they are individualistic rather than collectivistic;
- members communicate using clearly coded messages;
- members' values, attitudes, perceptions and patterns of behaviour are diverse and liable to change quickly.

It is sometimes suggested that Japan is an example of a high-context culture, the United States of a low-context culture.

Language and non-linguistic influences

There are around 3,000 distinct languages and about 10,000 dialects in the modern world. Many countries have more than one language. Canada, for example, recognizes English and French; Belgium has Flemish in the north, French in the south, and German in the south-east. India has 15 main languages and around 800 dialects; around 200 dialects were spoken in the former USSR. Some ex-colonies of Western countries have an 'official' language used for public administration, government communications and the administration of justice, which is taught in schools alongside the local language or dialect. Typically the official language is English or French (according to the former occupying power) and is used to maintain the unity of the country in the face of numerous regional languages, dialects and (often) ethnic groups. An interesting development has been the adoption of English as the official 'corporate language' of a number of multinational firms that are not based in English-speaking nations (Philips in the Netherlands, for instance). Hence intra-firm communications between branches, subsidiaries, etc, in various parts of the world are conducted in English, with company executives being expected to be able to communicate in English as a matter of course.

Many aspects of a community's culture are reflected in the language it uses, and a detailed knowledge of that language provides illuminative insights into the relevant culture. Equally, ignorance of the nuances of a particular language creates boundless opportunities for absurdities in translation, mistaken messages and ambiguity. Note how linguistic communities have extensive vocabularies to describe activities and surroundings important to them (eg industry and commerce in some cultures, aspects of the weather, agriculture, etc, in others). Culture affects how people think, quite independently of what they do or the words they utter (Hofstede, 1980). Social values (see above) are an example. Other examples are:

- Whether people approach issues analytically rather than intuitively.
- Concepts of time, in the sense that some societies are more prone to set deadlines for completion of activities than are others (attitudes towards punctuality also differ).
- Whether individuals inwardly feel they should be organized and methodical, rather than 'taking life as it comes'.
- How people use space. Physical nearness to other people is regarded as correct in Middle Eastern cultures but rude (representing a violation of 'personal space') in the United States. Handholding and other forms of physical contact have different meanings in different societies.

Use of body language and how this is interpreted also differs from country to country. For example, disagreement is indicated by shaking the head from side to side in some countries (the United Kingdom, for example), or by nodding the head or perhaps by waving a hand in front of the face in certain parts of the world. Showing the soles of the feet to another person (as when putting feet on a desk or placing a foot on the knee) is considered a grave insult in Thailand. Further examples of culturally sensitive body language are joining together the thumb and index finger (which means 'everything's perfect' in the United States, but something a great deal ruder in Brazil), the 'thumbs up' sign (which means 'Good' in the United Kingdom, but 'One' in France), and a small toss of the head, which symbolizes frustration in the United Kingdom but simply means 'No' in Greece.

The biggest problem with this type of communication is that people tend to believe that gestures are universal, and thus tend to attribute misunderstandings to the stupidity, craziness or rudeness of the other person. While mistakes in grammar or pronunciation of a spoken language are forgiven, mistakes in body language or other non-verbal cues are unlikely to be so easily accepted. This is because of the self-referential nature of cultural interchanges.

Self-referencing

Most of us are captives of our own cultural assumptions about the rest of the world. We assess other people's attitudes and behaviour against our *own* cultural values and miss the true meaning of the signals we receive. This is called ethnocentrism, and is probably one of the few features that virtually all cultures have in common.

It is necessary therefore to look at problems from *foreign* as well as home country norms and perspectives, and identify clearly the differences between the two. Local nationals should be consulted, as they will be sensitive to local cultural influences and will understand the 'inner logic' of the local way of life. Ethnocentrism can cost an exporting company dear. Ethnocentrism is the tendency to regard one's own country, group or culture as superior and to compare the standards of other countries, groups or cultures against this belief. Ethnocentrism contrasts with polycentrism, which regards other countries, groups and cultures as different but of equal value, and with geocentrism, that sees some but not all countries, groups and cultures as being of equal status.

Assessment of cultural differences

This is a difficult task because a thorough understanding of another country's culture can only be obtained by learning its language (and becoming aware of the significance of differences in regional dialects), knowing its history, mixing with host nationals socially as well as in working situations, and living in the country for several years. These are obviously impossible tasks for the great majority of managers of international businesses. But it is feasible to identify those cultural influences most likely to cause problems for the firm. One approach to this task is to take an overall view of the cultures of particular countries; another is to focus on just a handful of key variables. The problem with the former method is the enormous number of cultural influences that could be considered. In practice it is more common to seek to identify a handful of key variables believed critically relevant to the firm's operations in each of the countries in which is does business and to examine their implications in great depth.

The variables involved might relate to material culture (attitudes towards the possession of objects, accumulation of wealth, etc), motivation to work, social institutions and social structure, and so on. Studies of the factors that cause local customers to be attracted to a specific category of goods might be undertaken; as might research designed to describe a typical day in the life of a local customer of a certain type of product. The difficulty with partial cultural assessment is that although it might identify critical variables relevant to an issue at a particular moment, these variables might change very quickly. Culture depends in large part on the interrelations between such variables as well as on the elements themselves. Also, regional and social class distinctions exist within the country that outweigh the effects of dissimilarities between the culture of that particular nation and others. People undertaking the same occupation in disparate countries may share more in common with each other in terms of attitude, lifestyle, housing conditions and so on than they share with fellow nationals. Indeed, some analysts have suggested that the influence of culture on customer preferences is over-exaggerated. Theodore Levitt, for example, contended that provided a company supplies reliable, high-quality products at attractive prices, then customers throughout the world will be happy to purchase them in a standardized form (Levitt, 1983). He suggested moreover that to the extent that international firms do modify their output for local markets, this results more from managerial presumptions that differences in local preferences exist than from actual variations in national preferences. Many factors cause national cultures to change over time. Examples include:

- Economic destabilization (as occurred in Eastern Europe in the early 1990s, for example).
- Improvements in state welfare provision: old age pensions, child support, national health services, and so on.
- Immigration and emigration, especially if the people coming in have a different religion and lifestyle from members of the existing population. Returning migrants will also affect the national culture: this has been apparent in Ireland during the last years of the 20th century and the first years of the 21st century.
- Improvements in education systems, with consequent increases in the proportion of the population that is literate.
- Changes in the extent of government control of an economy. This is apparent in China, as the Communist government allow more Western and Taiwanese entrepreneurs to set up businesses in the country.
- Urbanization of populations. The drift away from agriculture and towards the cities has wrought remarkable changes. This is exemplified by the culture of Bombay, where women have careers and a Western approach to their lives, which would be unthinkable elsewhere in India.
- Increased opportunities for consumption (a wider range of products, shorter working hours, longer holidays, etc).
- Opening up of foreign trade and the influx of new ideas from other countries.

Cultural convergence

Arguably there is a convergence of the cultures of many countries, brought about by:

- similarities in the tastes and consumption patterns of young people;
- improvements in transport and communications and a huge increase in the number of people who visit foreign countries;

- adoption of similar technologies in numerous countries, creating common work experiences and working methods;
- globalization of the media, with similar television programmes, newspaper and magazine articles, etc, appearing in all countries, eg MTV, CNN and the *Financial Times*;
- a seemingly worldwide increase in consumers' willingness to accept fresh ideas and to try new products;
- the operations of global businesses across the world, supplying standardized products and frequently using undifferentiated marketing strategies.

Some transnational market segments have been identified, notably the youth market (driven by MTV, McDonald's, and Hollywood), and the international executive market, driven by world travel, standardized working practices, and Microsoft software.

LEGAL ASPECTS OF INTERNATIONAL MARKETING

Local laws determine marketing practice. Legislation may exist regarding product characteristics (safety, physical contents, dimensions, etc), packaging and labelling, brand names, length of guarantees, pricing and promotion, and many other issues. Moreover, international legal considerations impinge upon the ways in which contracts of sale are drafted, the carriage of goods, insurance of payments and of consignments, and the means for financing transactions. Disputes concerning these matters must be resolved, ultimately, through the courts. Unfortunately, different laws, interpretations and legal methods apply to commercial litigation within each country, and conflicts between the legal systems of specific countries frequently occur.

There is no uniform law governing international trade, only the application of a country's domestic law to international transactions. On the plus side, the domestic commercial laws of many countries adhere to rules established via international conventions, and it is also possible to specify the country under whose laws a contract will be interpreted. This has proved invaluable for firms dealing in Eastern Europe, where the former Communist legal system lacked any form of commercial law. Many contracts within these countries are decided under English or German law, even when UK and German companies are not involved in the contract.

Legal systems

Three types of legal system predominate in the modern world: common law, civil codes and Islamic law. Common law approaches apply in English-speaking countries and rely on historical precedent, on judgments in specific cases and on ad hoc legislation to create and interpret statutes. Countries with civil codes, conversely, have written rules intended to cover all eventualities, so that 'the law' on a particular issue can be looked up in the appropriate article of the country's civil code. Islamic law derives directly from the Koran and typically is mixed in with the pre-existing common law or civil code provisions of the country. Many countries implementing Islamic law are ex-colonial territories that inherited foreign-imposed legal systems on independence. There are no fundamental differences between Islamic and other legal systems where international trade is concerned.

Conflict of laws

International business inevitably involves clashes between differing legal systems. Examples of conflict of laws include the following:

- The intervals beyond which cases become 'statute barred' (so that no one can sue for compensation) differ among countries. In Britain, for example, the period for most classes of contract is six years; in France it can be up to 30 years, while in Germany it depends on whether the case concerns a commercial transaction and, if so, whether both the parties to the contract are traders.
- Laws concerning the circumstances in which an offer may be withdrawn without penalty vary in detail between countries. Normally the law of the country in which obligations arising from a contract were intended to be *performed* will apply to this matter, although many disputes arise over the question of where exactly the performance was supposed to take place.
- Consideration does not *necessarily* have to be proven prior to suing for breach of contract in certain countries. Examples of 'consideration' are the price paid for goods, the wages of employees (as consideration for providing labour), the hire fee paid for a lease of equipment, etc. Under English law a contract *cannot exist* without consideration.
- Exemption clauses and penalty clauses included in contracts may be acceptable in some countries, but illegal in others. This is particularly true in agency contracts, where agents may have much greater protection in some countries (for example, France) than they do in others (for example, the United Kingdom).
- Some countries (especially in continental Europe) draw important distinctions between 'commercial' and 'non-commercial' contracts, with a lower burden of proof being necessary to establish the existence of the former, and disputes arising from commercial contracts being heard in special commercial courts (Dicey and Morris, 1993).
- The US government sometimes penalizes the US subsidiaries of foreign firms, the parents of which have supplied goods to countries the United States is attempting to embargo, even though no prohibitions on such exports apply within the parent's own country.

Another important aspect of the legal system of certain countries is the need formally to 'protest' unpaid debts prior to suing for payment. This means getting a notary public (ie a local person legally qualified to attest and certify documents) to ask the customer for payment or for reason for non-payment. The latter are put into a formal deed of protest, which is then placed before a local court as evidence of refusal to pay.

Jurisdiction

Legal action occurs in the country of the party that is being sued. Thus, for example, a UK exporter alleging breach of contract by a Taiwanese customer must instigate legal proceedings in Taiwan. Note that if the contract of sale specified that the laws of England would apply to the deal, then the Taiwanese court hearing the case would have to interpret the contract according to English rather than Taiwanese law, leading to many delays and much complexity.

Jurisdictional issues within the European Union are covered by the Brussels Convention of 1982 and the Rome Convention of 1990, which establish the (sometimes complex) circumstances in which cases will be heard in particular EU countries. Either the contract of sale will name a country, or the country with 'the closest connection' with the contract must be chosen (see Crabtree *et al*, 1991). The Lugano Convention of 1988 established jurisdictional rules for disputes involving EU and (the then) EFTA countries.

Rules covering the transport of goods

The Hague-Visby Rules cover carriage by sea and are incorporated into the domestic laws of the majority of the world's trading nations. Notwithstanding this, nearly all bills of lading include clauses explicitly stating that at least some of these rules will apply. The Hague Rules were drafted in 1921 and subsequently extended (to become the Hague-Visby Rules) via the 1968 Brussels Protocol. The Hague-Visby rules formally determine the legal status of the bill of lading and specify upper limits and a formula for calculating the carrier's liability for damage to cargoes. Claims must be lodged within one year of delivery or the date a cargo was lost.

Air transport is covered by the Warsaw Convention 1929 (subsequently amended), which sets maximum limits of liability for negligence and regulates the legal carrier relationships between air carriers and consignees. Conditions and performance of contracts for rail transport are governed by the 1985 Convention Relative aux Transports Internationaux Ferroviaires (COTIF).

European road haulage is most governed by the 1956 Convention de Marchandises part Route, which lays down standard international contractual conditions for road transport, covering liability for loss or damage to goods and the maximum value for insurance claims against the haulier. The Convention has eight chapters, as outlined in Table 2.4.

These Uniform Laws were reconsidered, extended and developed by the United Nations Commission on International Trade Law (UNCITRAL), which organized a 'Vienna Convention' to draft a commercial code for use in all international transactions. The resulting code included a clearly defined procedure for arbitration. The intention of the Hague and Vienna Conventions was that agreed Uniform Laws be incorporated into the domestic law of all United Nations countries. This has indeed occurred in many countries, including the United States, France, Italy, the Netherlands and in Scandinavia. In countries that have not acceded to the Convention (Britain, for example) the Uniform Laws only apply if both parties agree to this happening.

Table 2.4 The CMR Convention

Chapter	Purpose
1	Defines the contracts covered by the Convention, including contracts involving joint road, sea, air and rail transport
2	Makes the carrier responsible for the acts and omissions of employees and agents
3	Specifies the documentation to be used for road haulage contracts
4	Defines the extent of a road haulier's liability for loss, damage or delay to consignments
5	Gives time limits for claims against hauliers and specifies where claims may be pursued*
6	Defines the liabilities of individual carriers where several carriers are party to the contract (ie 'successive' carriers)
7 & 8	Technical provisions concerning the implementation of the Convention in signatory states

* This can be the courts of the country in which the defendant's head office is situated, or those of the country in which the contract was made, or the goods were accepted or delivered.

The key requirements for the existence of a contract in virtually every legal system in the world are that there be an offer and an acceptance, an intention to create a legal relationship between the parties, and clear consent to the terms of the agreement. Also the contract must be legal and technically capable of being completed, and, in some countries (including the United Kingdom), there has to be consideration, which means some form of value exchanged. National laws on these matters are similar in most respects, but with notable exceptions. Use of UNCITRAL Uniform Laws is extremely valuable, therefore, as a means for dealing with such exceptions, since the differences in national approach can be enormous. Specific UNCITRAL rules are as follows:

- An offer must be addressed to one or more particular people or organizations. Otherwise, proposals not addressed to specific persons are not 'offers' but merely invitations to members of the public themselves to make offers to buy the goods. Examples of offers not addressed to specific persons include catalogues, circularized price lists, advertisements, etc. This does not contradict English law, but does reverse the rules on these matters in certain countries.
- If the party making an offer says it will remain open for a period, then it *cannot* be withdrawn during that period once the offer has been received by the other side (a reversal of English law, which states that an offer may be withdrawn at any time *before acceptance*).
- Consideration is not necessary for the existence of a contract.
- An offer that is accepted is deemed to have been accepted at the moment of receipt and not the moment the offer was transmitted (as is the case under English law).

Resolution of disputes

The commonest procedures for resolving disputes involving the conflict of national laws are: to specify explicitly in the initial contract that the law of a particular country shall apply to the deal; or to insert an arbitration clause into the contract under which an international body will resolve the issue (see Schmitthoff, 1990, for a discussion of the available options).

UNCITRAL does not itself provide arbitration facilities; rather it lays down a model set of rules and procedures, which other bodies (the International Chamber of Commerce [ICC], the American Arbitration Association, the London Court of Arbitration or the International Centre for Settlement of Investment Disputes, for example) can apply (Dore, 1993). The ICC is the most commonly used arbitration organization. It is based in Paris and offers arbitration facilities both to members and to non-member companies. ICC proceedings begin with an attempt at conciliation by a panel of three persons nominated by the President of the ICC, followed by the appointment of an arbitration tribunal whose members are nationals of countries not involved in the dispute.

If the parties to a contract agree to arbitration, then the arbitrator's decision becomes legally binding under their domestic laws via the 1958 New York Convention of the Recognition and Enforcement of Foreign Arbitral Awards, the rules of which the overwhelming majority of the world's countries have accepted.

ORGANIZATION OF MNCS

The organizational structure of an MNC needs to integrate the firm's worldwide operations within a single administrative system that optimizes the use of company resources and enables it to take full advantage of opportunities wherever they arise. A common feature of an MNC organization is that senior managers have worldwide responsibilities. Thereafter, however, a range of organizational models may be applied, namely:

- geographic structure;
- subsidiary structure;
- product structure;
- divisional structure;
- matrix structure.

Some of the special problems connected with the construction of a sound organizational system for international management and marketing are as follows:

- the difficulties of coordinating the activities of units in many geographically distant countries;
- understanding the cultural orientations of employees, distributors, etc, in foreign countries;
- turbulence in the economic and political environments of certain world markets;

- the multiplicity of interest groups (governments, consumers, local representatives, intermediaries and so on) that need to be appeased in each state;
- possible wide discrepancies in the motivations of staff in various subsidiaries;
- the complexity of managing a worldwide management information system.

The major structural alternatives for an MNC are discussed below.

Geographic structure

In this case the firm sets up regional divisions, each responsible for a certain part of the globe (Europe, South America, Asia Pacific, etc). Strategies are determined at headquarters, leaving regional managements in day-to-day control. Operations can be specifically designed to suit regional conditions. Geographic structure is commonest when the countries covered by a division are in close proximity and the same product is being marketed in the area concerned. The system is clear, logical and easy to apply. There is close coordination between production and marketing, and local needs are taken into account. However, it becomes difficult for managers to adopt a totally international perspective on the enterprise's worldwide activities and there could be insufficient emphasis on new product development. Another problem with geographic structures is the determination of boundaries for each region. (NAFTA, for example, is a single trading bloc, but there are big differences in the cultures and market structures of its three members.) Also, it places heavy demands on the managers in charge of each geographic division, who need to acquire a wide range of general management skills.

An example of a geographic structure for an MNC is given in Figure 2.11. Here there exist head office advisory departments providing staff support for personnel, marking, etc, leaving day-to-day line management in the hands of managers of regional departments. The latter have total responsibility for secondary activities (contract manufacturing and so on) in the relevant region. There is no distinction between domestic and foreign operations. Geographic organization is especially suitable, perhaps, where:

- firms have technically simple products and operate in a stable environment;
- regional customer groups have different needs and/or special difficulties (complex documentation and distribution arrangements, for example) apply to the area;
- product modification, different packaging and pricing policies, and different customer service activities are needed for each geographic market.

Duplication of activities in geographic departments is inevitable if they are located in distant regional centres. If, conversely, they share premises with head office, then an administrative support unit can be set up to serve all departments in the building, and functional and product specialists can simultaneously assist several geographic departments with their work. Note, however, that in the latter situation the departments can lose touch with events 'in the field' within the relevant region.

A major argument for organizing on a geographical basis is the increasing economic integration of the world's main regions (NAFTA, the EU, etc). As business methods and

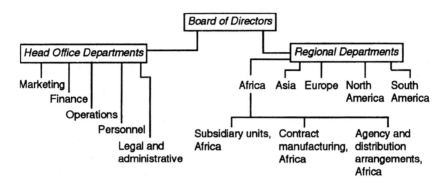

Figure 2.11   Geographic organization for an MNC

consumer behaviour harmonize within these trading blocs it makes sense to regard each region as a single unit. Staff within a regional department acquire extensive knowledge about its characteristics, the nature of the competition, customer preferences, local business norms and cultures, etc.

International subsidiary structure

A couple of foreign subsidiaries can be managed directly from head office, but as soon as a company has established a permanent presence in a substantial number of countries it will need a formal organization system for monitoring and controlling subsidiary operations. One solution (technically known as the international subsidiary structure) is for the parent firm to retain responsibility for its subsidiaries' functional activities, while setting up a board of management for each subsidiary to oversee local operations and to develop the local market. This is a simple and inexpensive approach to international organization, which provides for local responses to changes in local conditions while maintaining effective central control. It is moreover, useful, for the training and development of managers within subsidiary boards.

Problems with the approach include the need for extensive liaison and coordination, and the tendency for subsidiary boards to mirror (perhaps inappropriately) the structure of the main company. Incorrect strategies might be imposed on subsidiaries, and local managers could lose sight of the global objectives of the organization. Also the system becomes complicated and unwieldy as the number of subsidiaries increases. Conflicts between subsidiary boards and head office functional specialists might develop.

Product structure

Businesses already organized according to products might decide to create international functions within each of their product divisions (see Figure 2.12). The system is appropri-

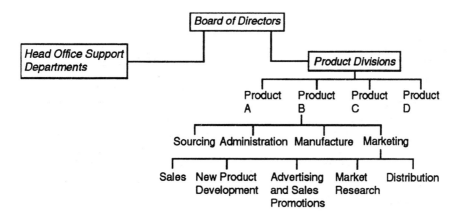

Figure 2.12   A product structure for an MNC

ate for organizations that supply several unrelated types of product or where significant product modifications for various markets are required. Product structure is useful for management development. Problems are that the importance of marketing might not be properly recognized, and that important regions could be overlooked. Moreover, coordination across product divisions may be difficult.

Further potential difficulties are that since each product division has to assume an international dimension, and international activities have to compete with other elements of the division for attention and resources, then important opportunities for developing international sales might be missed. Also, product managers may be knowledgeable about the item and about general marketing, but lack the expertise necessary to make decisions concerning international distribution, selection of foreign advertising media, etc.

Product organization enables the firm to quickly add or discard departments as new products emerge or existing ones disappear. It is most likely to be found in firms with several technically complex and unrelated product lines and serving a limited number of countries.

Divisional structure

As a business becomes genuinely international it might upgrade its existing export department to become the 'international division' of the firm. This international division assumes full control of all foreign operations and perhaps takes over some functions previously undertaken by the company's marketing department. Expertise in all aspects of international business is concentrated in the division, and it takes significant decisions about product and distribution policy and is increasingly involved in the firm's strategic affairs. International divisions provide the firm with a convenient device for developing a multinational strategy, and decisions on international matters are taken at the heart of the enterprise. Divisions acquire experience in international business. Disadvantages to this form of organization are its possible inability to handle extremely diverse international operations, the potential for conflict between domestic and international divisions, and the risk that senior management at head office will not take the international division seriously.

in practice...

Levi Strauss

The Levi Strauss company, manufacturer of jeans and leisure clothing, sells in over 70 countries, sometimes via licensees and joint ventures with foreign firms. International operations are organized on a divisional basis. The continental Europe division (based in Brussels) arose from modest beginnings as the company's export sales office, which was established in 1965. Today it controls nearly 20 manufacturing plants across 12 continental European countries. The Northern European division has headquarters in London and serves the United Kingdom and Scandinavia. Further divisions exist for Latin America, Canada and Asia. Divisions explore market opportunities, control local manufacture and coordinate marketing in the relevant area. A separate division has been set up to arrange joint ventures with companies in China and Eastern Europe.

Appraising divisions

An important task when creating divisions is to ensure that their performance can be easily measured and appraised, as sometimes one or more divisions subsidize others without anyone being aware of the fact. Problems attached to devising an appraisal scheme for divisions include:

- deciding whether each division is to be regarded as a cost centre in its own right ('buying in' materials and services from other divisions);
- choice of criteria for measuring profitability (absolute money values, rates of return on capital employed, etc);
- assessing the effects of company policies on the profits made by a particular division (eg the effects of artificially low input prices from other divisions);
- overhead allocations vis-à-vis shared common services (administrative premises for instance) and relating these to estimates for divisional rates of return on capital employed;
- deciding whether divisions should manage their own idle cash balances or turn them over to a central treasury for investment outside the division (externally or elsewhere in the company).

Other difficulties potentially confronting an international division are that its relationship with the marketing department may be unclear, that it might take decisions its staff are not properly qualified to implement, and that it may lack the authority needed to influence significantly the other major decisions of the firm.

Functional orientation

A firm based on a core technology producing a few basic products needs an organization suitable for maximizing scale economies and for adapting these products for markets throughout the world. It has to identify market opportunities and satisfy them in the shortest possible time. Such a business may seek to accommodate its international marketing activities *within* its existing functional structure, so that departments responsible for sales, market research, promotion, etc, generally would handle international aspects as well. Although functional organization is used by a number of important companies with significant international operations (especially companies based in France and Germany), it is not normally considered appropriate for genuinely multinational operations because each functional department has to deal with several diverse territories (each possessing unique problems and characteristics) as well as with the international dimension (documentation, need for special packaging, etc) of its work. Functional organization may be appropriate, however, for firms with just a handful of technically simple products that sell in a limited number of countries, with few prospects for international expansion.

Strategic business units

A device adopted by some international businesses for planning and controlling worldwide operations is that of the strategic business unit (SBU). SBUs are groupings of a business's activities that are then treated as self-contained entities for the purposes of strategic planning and control. An SBU could be a division of a company, a department, a collection of departments, a subsidiary or a function undertaken within the firm (eg all the firm's marketing activities might be regarded as an independent SBU). Often SBUs cut across existing divisional, functional and departmental boundaries. Having defined SBUs, management then gives each unit a budget and the authority to administer its own resources.

The idea was conceived by the US General Electric Company, which, dissatisfied with its existing divisional structure, rearranged all the enterprise's activities into SBUs, some of which bore little relation to traditional departments, divisions or profit centres. Thus, for example, a number of food preparation appliances previously manufactured and sold through several independent divisions were merged into a single 'housewares' SBU.

Similarly, a firm might produce television sets in one division, radios in the next and car stereo systems in another. Yet for strategy and planning purposes all three activities could be conveniently lumped together into a self-contained administrative unit. To make sense, an SBU should:

- comprise compatible elements, each possessing a direct and identifiable link with the unit as a whole;
- be easy to appraise (which requires that its performance can be compared with something similar within or outside the organization);
- contribute significantly towards the attainment of the organization's goals.

The main problems with SBUs are how to coordinate many disparate activities simultaneously and how to assess the financial and other contributions of various activities to a particular unit.

Matrix organization

Frustrations arising from the rigidities imposed by formal product, geographical or other conventional organization structures have caused a number of firms to experiment with the matrix approach to organizational structure. Matrix organization is a means for creating project teams that cut across departmental boundaries. Individuals are seconded from their 'home' departments onto various project committees and thus have a number of bosses – their head of department and the team leaders of the groups to which they are temporarily attached. This can create problems, of course, in that individuals may receive conflicting instructions from different bosses, each insisting that the work of their particular team be given top priority. Teams cut across product, geographical market and functional lines. They are multi-disciplinary and provide numerous opportunities for employee participation in decision-taking and the rapid development of general managerial skills. The system is extremely flexible (teams can be set up and disbanded at will). Matrix structures are especially useful for dealing with complex problems where immediate access to several highly specialized professional skills is required.

The aim of matrix organization is to relate company organization to the needs of internal decision-making processes, ensuring that every section that ought to be involved in a particular decision is adequately represented. Matrix organization is useful where several sections are grouped together into an international division. Interdepartmental communications are enhanced and duplication of effort can be avoided. Further advantages are that:

- Team members develop broad perspectives on problems and issues.
- It encourages interdisciplinary cooperation and flexible attitudes.
- Departmental boundaries do not interfere with the completion of projects.
- Teams that have outlived their usefulness can be quickly disbanded.

The essential problem with the matrix approach is perhaps its sophistication and complexity, leading to the need for managers who are trained and competent in the system and committed to making it work. Other difficulties are the duplication of effort created, the time spent in committees (with consequent effects on the speed of decision-making), and possible disputes regarding who should do what and who is in charge of whom. Conflicts may occur between the decisions of individual line managers and the collective decisions of project teams (which normally are given their own budgets and authority to implement decisions). Also matrix structures might encourage managers to develop their political and negotiating skills at the expense of their managerial abilities.

SELECTING THE BEST STRUCTURE

In selecting a structure (see Figure 2.13) an MNC needs to ensure that the organization has an unambiguous chain of command, is capable of coordinating worldwide activities, can take decisions quickly at the most appropriate level, and provides for fast and effective communication between units. The structure chosen needs to motivate and develop employees, facilitate international communications, planning, decision-making and control, create a clearly defined accountability and delegation system, and make it as easy as possible for the company to satisfy customer demand. It is particularly important that managers of all units (subsidiaries, divisions, product groupings or whatever) have a common perception of the firm's overall goals and how they should be pursued.

There is no single 'best way' to organize for international business, since much depends on company and industry characteristics, the product and the markets the enterprise serves. Indeed, an ideal structure will be sufficiently flexible to allow the firm quickly to alter its organizational form as circumstances change. Note, moreover, that there is no reason in principle why a business's structure should not be an ad hoc mixture

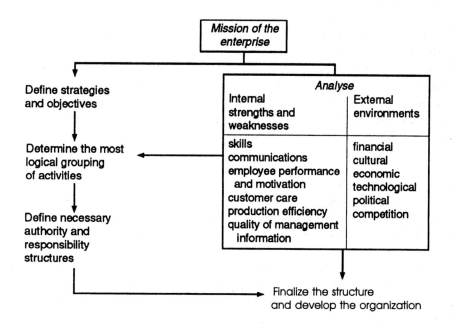

Figure 2.13   Procedure for determining an organization structure for an MNC

of product, geographic and other systems. This leads to complex communication and accountability procedures but could be just what the company in question actually needs. Factors influencing the choice of organizational form should include the extent of the company's foreign operations and experience of international markets, the size of the business, the number and technical nature of its products, and its aspirations regarding further international expansion. Other factors to be considered are:

- the ability levels and experience of the MNC's staff in each country, especially their capacities to think strategically and plan for the long term;
- the stability of local markets (the more uncertain the local market, the greater the need for local control);
- the availability and calibre of local business services;
- the number, types and complexity of operating units in various countries;
- how well the structure will serve the business's customers and generate concern and facilities for customer care.

Centralization versus decentralization

Effective implementation of a global strategy obviously requires the careful coordination of the company's activities throughout the world. This might be achieved through tight centralization of decision-making and control at the apex of the organization, but in this case the benefits of decentralization of management to local units are foregone (Gates and Engelhoff, 1986). Advantages of decentralization are the encouragement of local initiative and that local circumstances are taken into account when policies are determined. Senior executives can devote their time to strategic planning, while leaving operational matters to expert local managers. Those at the top can take an overall bird's-eye view of the situation. The word 'local' in this context need not refer to geographical location. Rather it means nearness to operations and to the units where the decisions taken have to be applied. There ought to be less red tape and hence faster decision-making, and the organization as a whole should become more responsive to conditions in various foreign markets.

On the other hand, centralization of decision-making means that all the firm's activities are subject to direct and immediate control, correct working methods can be imposed on all parts of the organization, and the coordination of operations may be enhanced. There are no possibilities for disagreements and haggling among different decentralized units. All major decisions can be directly related to the core objectives of the enterprise. Further advantages to centralization are the avoidance of duplication of effort and the unambiguous nature of decision-making systems and procedures.

Centralization of decision-making at head office is encouraged by the need to adopt a global approach to the allocation of resources and where decisions detrimental to the interests of local units might be required. It is particularly appropriate for a firm supplying a simple and standardized product from an integrated manufacturing system and which sells the (unmodified) product in multiple markets using the same promotional messages and techniques. International fax and other communication developments have of course significantly improved communication between head office and subsidiary units in foreign countries, thus facilitating the potential for tight central control over worldwide operations.

Problems with centralization are its tendency to create inflexible attitudes and possibly the inability to adapt to change, the potential for missing lucrative opportunities at the local level, and that senior executives at the core of the organization might receive so much complicated information from subsidiary units that important matters may be overlooked. Also there is no guarantee that instructions emanating from the top of the organization will in practice be implemented by local units.

Decentralization and divisionalization

There is a difference between divisionalization and decentralization in that the latter simply means passing authority to others – perhaps to the bottom levels of a conventional line and staff system – whereas the former is the consequence of growth and diversification and involves the creation of new and quasi-autonomous organizational units. The advantages of divisionalization, apart from the general benefits of decentralization already mentioned, relate to:

- its value as a training medium for the development of divisional managers for top-level posts in the parent organization;
- the relative ease with which divisional activities can be integrated at higher levels of control;
- the motivation afforded to local managers who are encouraged to use individual initiative involving local problems.

Note, however, that total decentralization of an organization by divisionalization is impossible, since any decision arising at the divisional level that has policy implications for the organization as a whole must be endorsed by central control.

Note
The term 'transnational enterprise' is sometimes used to describe a company with significant parts of its share capital owned by the nationals of at least two countries.

Part II

The trading environment

This section comprises five chapters that look at the background against which global business is conducted. Trade is subject to a set of international laws and local trading conditions that provide constraints and opportunities under which the global firm must operate.

International trade is conducted against a raft of international regulations, treaties, trade agreements, alliances and enmities. Chapter 3 looks at these in some detail, and gives the historical background to much of these in order to provide a framework against which future developments might be predicted.

Different regions of the world can be grouped in terms of their economic and cultural similarities. In the same way as customers can be grouped in segments, this type of grouping enables global marketers to apply similar marketing approaches. Chapter 4 outlines some approaches to assessing the potential of different regions of the world in international trade terms, and offers some macro-segmentation ideas.

Chapters 5, 6 and 7 provide background information on the three main regional types: the North Atlantic countries, which include Europe and the United States, the Asia Pacific countries, which include Japan and the Far East and Oceania, and the Third World, which includes Africa, India and South America. These distinctions are, of course, somewhat arbitrary and some countries will exhibit characteristics of each, but there is a broad commonality of cultures and trading needs within those regions. This group of chapters is intended to provide the framework within which the tactical approaches to global trading can be applied. These are covered in the third section of the book.

3

International trade

THE BALANCE OF PAYMENTS

A country's balance of payments is the total of all the transactions that occur between residents of that country and foreigners over a specified period of time. Receipts resulting from exports or inflows of capital are recorded as credit items; payments for imports and capital outflows appear as debits.

Most countries publish their balance of payments figures monthly, quarterly and annually. The accounts themselves show the structure of a country's external trade, its net position as an international lender or borrower, and trends in the direction of its economic relationships with the rest of the world. Balance of payments accounts attempt to identify the reasons behind various categories of international receipts and payments. Hopefully, therefore, it becomes possible to establish the values of total payments by domestic residents to foreigners (and vice versa) for such purposes as the purchase of imports, the use of services (shipping, for example), short- and long-term lending, and direct foreign investment.

Balance of payments accounts are constructed on the principle of double-entry book-keeping, meaning that each receipt and payment is recorded twice, once in each of two columns (debit and credit), so that the two columns should add up to the same amount. In practice, measurement errors and delays in the reporting of transactions prevent this, so that a 'balancing item' has to be inserted in order to reconcile the two sides of the account. A country's balance of payments accounts can be presented in several ways. There is a standard United Nations recommended layout that all countries apply in order to make international comparisons possible. Additionally, each country typically drafts its accounts in a number of other formats so as to highlight particular features of its international trading situation. Distinctions that have the most analytical significance are those between:

- transactions involving goods and services and movements in financial capital;
- long-term and short-term financial transactions;
- transactions initiated by the national monetary authorities and all other monetary movements;
- unilateral transfers (such as gifts or wages sent by workers in one country to their relatives in others) and payments for goods, services or financial assets.

Since the 'balance of payments' always balances in consequence of how the accounts are prepared, how is it possible to speak of 'deficits' or 'surpluses' in a country's balance of payments? The answer to this question is that the people who analyse balance of payments information select particular groupings of transactions *within* the body of the accounts and examine surpluses or shortfalls in relation to just these specific groupings. The most widely reported grouping is perhaps the 'current account' of the balance of payments, which records physical imports and exports plus international transactions in 'invisibles', ie non-physical items such as residents' receipts of pensions, interest and royalties from abroad (and payments of such items to foreign countries), domestic firms' fees for arranging the transportation of goods belonging to firms in other countries, private gifts (foreign workers sending part of their wages to families in other countries for example), and so on. The 'balance of trade' within the current account is the balance on visible (physical) imports and exports.

A country's 'capital account' shows the balance on its transactions in financial assets, including direct portfolio investments in foreign shares and debentures (and foreigners' purchases of these assets within the country concerned), movements in short-term financial assets such as Treasury bills and other short-dated stock, intergovernmental loans, and changes in the country's official gold and foreign exchange reserves. The last will decline if, for example, there is a current account deficit but no offsetting inflow of capital account funds. This is because residents' demands for foreign exchange to pay for imports will exceed foreigners' demands for the deficit country's currency, so that a deficit country's currency exchange rate will fall via the forces of supply and demand for foreign exchange.

To prevent the exchange rate dropping too far, deficit countries governments used to sell part of their stock of foreign exchange reserves on the open market in order to satisfy the excess demand for foreign currency. The growth of international trade in the last 10 years or so, however, has become so large that very few governments carry sufficient reserves to be able to do this. The approach now is, typically, to adjust interest rates. This affects the flow of short-term capital deposits by multinationals, which in turn affects the value of the currency. For example, a firm such as IBM has huge cash reserves on hand: the payroll bill alone runs to billions of dollars a month. This cash could be deposited in any of the countries where IBM does business, and firms of that size find it worthwhile to employ analysts who move the money to where it will earn the most interest. Even an extra thousandth of a per cent interest on the money more than covers the salaries of the analysts. This 'hot money' is sufficient to affect the value of the currency in which it is deposited, because it increases demand for the currency in the short term.

Problems of interpretation

Global marketers take an interest in the balance of payments accounts of the countries in which they do business because they indicate for each country:

- its overall economic health;
- the extent of competition likely to be encountered from other imported products;
- the likelihood of internal deflationary government polices and/or imposition of trade and exchange controls.

Equally, analysts need to appreciate the extent of the difficulties associated with the interpretation of balance of payments statements, which include the following:

- Groupings of transactions within the accounts are to some extent arbitrary. A 'deficit' becomes a surplus if certain items are removed and others inserted in a particular category.
- Current account deficits only become a problem if there is no corresponding inflow of private capital. Indeed, a number of countries operate in near-perpetual current account deficit, this being offset by capital account transactions.
- The magnitude of the balancing item can be enormous compared to other elements of the accounts. Sometimes the balancing item exceeds the total value of a country's current account deficit or surplus.
- Accounts for the same period can change radically over time as more data becomes available. For example, the current account for the first quarter of a certain year might show a deficit when first published, but a surplus when subsequently revised in about 12 months' time. Yet media attention (and stock exchange reaction) focuses on the preliminary figures as they appear.
- Not all transactions are included. In some countries, smuggling is a significant activity, but not one that is recorded in the country's balance of payments. Also there might be innocent non-recording or under-recording of some consignments of imported or exported items. Agents might conduct business on behalf of foreigners but not be aware that this is the case, companies might engage in transfer pricing (selling products to their own overseas subsidiary in order to avoid tax) and so forth.
- A country's balance of payments accounts represent a statement of its external trade position over a particular period. They do not indicate the causes of the underlying forces that led to the results.

BARRIERS TO INTERNATIONAL TRADE

Trade is generally regarded as a way of increasing welfare for all. Whenever an exchange takes place, both parties are better off as a result: if this were not the case, trade would be impossible since one or other party would not agree to the terms. Therefore governments have sought to free up trade.

The worldwide liberalization of international trade practices and procedures has been an outstanding feature of the post-Second World War era. Overall, tariffs have tumbled since 1945, and are beginning to fall in the former Communist countries. Governments increasingly recognize the benefits of free trade: more jobs, a wider choice of goods for consumers, wider markets for businesses, economic growth and improved living standards, closer political links, etc. Yet despite their notional support for free trade, many countries continue to use restrictive measures in order to improve their balance of payments. All countries have import tariffs that, apart from their impact on the level of imports, also represent a valuable source of state revenue. Some have exchange controls and non-tariff restrictions (import quotas, for example); a few operate a variety of hidden import barriers.

The reasons for this vary. Some countries seek to protect fledgling industries from cheap imports from established firms in other countries: others try to protect their balance of payments position by restricting imports and encouraging exports. Still others impose barriers for political reasons – trade embargoes are a popular way of bringing rogue administrations into line. Whatever the reasons, restricting trade damages welfare.

Exchange controls

These restrict importers' abilities to obtain the foreign currency needed to pay for imports, either via direct prohibition or through the government artificially increasing the exchange rate prices of certain foreign currencies (eg by limiting the supply of these currencies available for importers to purchase). Administration of exchange controls is problematic for the authorities of the country in question and may involve any or all of the following:

- legal requirements that firms hand over to the national central bank all the foreign exchange they acquire;
- government rules that different exchange rates apply to different types of transaction (although this is extremely rare, following a long-standing international agreement that prohibits the use of multiple exchange rates for normal import/export activity);
- restriction of foreign exchange availability to the import of certain specified products;
- selection of particular firms that may obtain foreign exchange;
- imposition of foreign exchange queues and waiting lists;
- issue of foreign exchange licences and quotas;
- only allowing foreign exchange to importers who enter into joint venture domestic manufacturing arrangements with exporting companies.

Exchange controls are becoming rarer as governments are better able to use the interest rate mechanism to maintain the value of their currencies. They are still common in Third World countries, however, and can cause problems for global firms who wish to repatriate profits from those countries.

Tariffs

A tariff is a tax or customs duty imposed on goods crossing international frontiers. It could be calculated as a specific amount of money per item imported or as a percentage of the value of the imported goods. The latter form is known as an *ad valorem* tariff. A combination of specific and *ad valorem* duties applied to an import is called a 'compound' tariff. Specific duties discourage lower-priced imports of a class item. For example, a specific duty of £5 per pair of shoes will be felt more keenly on bottom end of the market shoes imported at, say, £15 per pair than on luxury shoes imported at £160 a pair. Percentage tariffs, conversely, make higher-priced imports relatively more expensive. Tariff systems may be 'single column' or 'double column'. The former apply the same duty to imports of a particular product no matter where the goods come from; the latter allow for the imposition of different tariff rates on imports of the same item from different countries.

Sometimes goods are imported, pay a tariff, and are then re-exported to other countries with all or part of the initial tariff payment being refunded by the government of the importing country. Such reimbursements are known as 'drawbacks' and frequently arise when imports are used as inputs into other goods destined for export to foreign countries.

Common external tariffs

An important phenomenon of recent decades has of course been the development of regional common markets operating common external tariffs. Although it may be expensive and troublesome to enter a regional trading bloc from outside, once entry has been effected the goods face no further tariffs and minimal control over cross-border movement within the area. Uniform documentation and trading procedures will apply, thus simplifying regional distribution and selling. Also regional trade blocs typically have numerous ad hoc agreements with external countries. The European Union (EU), for example, has numerous trade agreements with other countries. Preferential rates of tariff apply to less developed countries in Latin America, various African, Caribbean and Pacific (ACP) states, and with Eastern European countries.

Former colonies of the founder members of the European Common Market negotiated the Yaoundé Convention, which provided for special trading arrangements with these newly independent states. Following the United Kingdom's accession to the Common Market this was replaced by the first Lomé Convention, which extended the Yaoundé agreement to 20 other developing countries. The Convention is updated every few years and currently covers around 70 ACP countries plus the EU 15. Collectively the Lomé countries have trade agreements with Mediterranean and Latin American states, effectively taking in half the countries of the world. All the signatories to the Convention itself are eligible for EU technical and financial help plus tariff-free and quota-free access to EU countries, without reciprocity, except for a handful of agricultural products.

Many Third World countries not party to the Lomé Convention receive preferential treatment by the EU under a special scheme monitored by the United Nations Conference on Trade Aid and Development (UNCTAD). The latter has also arranged a tariff preference system whereby exports of manufactured goods from less developed to developed countries receive favourable treatment.

Transit duties and export

Transit duties are taxes levied by national governments on foreign goods passing through their territory en route for another. They are rare in international trade since most countries adhere to the 1921 Barcelona Agreement on Freedom of Transit, which abolished such duties within signatory countries. Export taxes are also rare, but do apply to the export of primary commodities from less developed countries, especially where transfer pricing by global companies might occur. Apart from raising revenue for the government of the exporting country, export taxes might encourage domestic processing of raw materials and the general economic development of the exporting country. Equally, however, they may stimulate foreign importers to seek alternative sources of supply.

Non-tariff barriers

Non-tariff barriers are restrictions placed on trade that do not involve a financial penalty. They include import quotas imposed on particular firms or types of goods (motor cars, for example), anti-dumping laws and regulations, special technical or health and safety requirements for imported goods, insistence on complex and expensive pre-shipment inspection, special documentation requirements, the need for unusual packaging and labelling, or the demand that certain products contain a minimum input of locally produced materials.

Non-tariff barriers are often used to restrict imports when trade agreements limiting tariffs are in place. Examples include French refusal to import British beef following the BSE crisis (even though there was a lower incidence of BSE in British beef than in French beef at the time) and British insistence on type approval for imported cars.

Quantitative controls

Quantitative restrictions impose physical limits on the amount of imports to a country. Quotas are the commonest example, followed perhaps by the practice of issuing licences to certain companies, allowing only these businesses to import certain products up to a specified amount. Note how the latter policy typically generates a flurry of merger and takeover activity in countries where it is applied, with firms acquiring others simply in order to obtain their import licences. Further devices for avoiding quota restrictions are the modification and redefinition of goods into non-quota categories, routing consignments through countries with which the importing country has special trading arrangements, or through joint ventures with local manufacturers (which practice may give exemption from quota restrictions). Other non-tariff deficits include 'import deposits' whereby importers have to deposit with their country's central bank a significant proportion (eg 50 per cent) of the price of the goods imported, the money being repaid only after a lengthy period (hence tying up the firm's working capital), and 'import surcharges', ie ad hoc levies on particular imported goods.

Hidden barriers

There is a seemingly endless variety of ways in which a government can make life diffi-cult for foreign firms wishing to sell in its territory. Japan is particularly subject to criti-cism in these respects. The following are examples of the numerous complaints lodged by exporters to the Japanese market:

- requirements that certain goods be imported into Japan via ports a long distance from their final destinations;
- prohibitions on containers of imported goods over a certain size travelling on Japanese roads;
- lengthy customs procedures;
- insistence that imported products undergo several safety checks, each one having to be conducted by an official from a different government department;
- application of separate customs, importation and other documentation procedures to imports of the same product of the same company but which enter Japan via differ-ent subsidiaries of the supplying company.

Further hidden barriers adopted by various countries include the following:

- **Local content rules**. This is a requirement that a proportion of a product's inputs have to be sourced locally rather than being imported. The supposed objective is to prevent the establishment of 'screwdriver' plants that exist merely to assemble imported components and hence circumvent anti-dumping taxes and tariffs. Disputes frequently arise concerning the measurement of domestically sourced inputs (numbers, monetary values, etc) and the accuracy of the firm's declarations of the extent of their use of locally supplied items.
- **State subsidies**. These apply to domestic companies to help them compete with imported goods.
- **Complex rules on packing and labelling**. A country's customs authorities might require that imported products bear a brand name, country of origin, the importer's tax identity number, etc.
- **Restrictive specification of technical product standards**. Much politics is involved in the determination of technical standards, since the introduction of mandatory rules for all suppliers means that firms already satisfying the new standard have an initial advantage over their rivals. Note how the European Union is helping many develop-ing and underdeveloped countries establish their own international standards based on EU norms. As these standards become compulsory, EU firms will be able to satisfy them ahead of US or Pacific Rim companies.
- **Barriers created by national customs authorities**, which might include:
  - imposition of arbitrary short periods in which buyers may apply for import licences;
  - deliberate delays in processing documentation by customs officers;
  - customs authorities vexatiously valuing imported goods at prices much higher than those (fairly) stated on invoices, or classifying products into inappropriate high-tariff categories so that the exporter has to initiate a time-consuming and expensive appeal.

THE WORLD TRADE ORGANIZATION

The World Trade Organization (WTO, formerly the General Agreement on Tariffs and Trade) is a Geneva-based institution founded in 1947 (under the name of 'General Agreement on Tariffs and Trade' [GATT]) to encourage multilateral (as opposed to bilateral) trade and to minimize tariff levels and non-tariff trade barriers. Its 116 members include all the industrialized countries, over 70 developing countries, and a number of developing Eastern European states. To date there have been eight rounds of negotiation (the eighth being referred to as the 'Uruguay Round'), resulting in 180 treaties. WTO rules now cover 90 per cent of world trade, and are based on the following principles:

1. **non-discrimination**, meaning that each WTO country must apply the same rates of tariff to imports from all member countries, although customs unions and free-trade areas are permitted and special arrangements apply to underdeveloped countries;
2. **resolution of disputes via consultation**, though note that dumping (selling goods below the cost of manufacture) may be counteracted by retaliatory measures targeted at the offending country;
3. **non-legality of quantitative restrictions** on imports, *unless* a country is 'underdeveloped', is experiencing severe balance of payments difficulties, or an agricultural or fisheries product is involved.

Countries in dispute first try to settle their problems bilaterally. If this fails a WTO working party investigates the matter and makes a recommendation. Should the offending country ignore the recommendation, the aggrieved country is permitted to retaliate.

A number of countries (notably the United States) have indicated their willingness to reduce tariffs significantly on a range of products in return for worldwide binding rules on protection for patents, trade marks, computer software and other intellectual property. Unfortunately the 1989 Uruguay Round ran into difficulties in consequence of bitter arguments between the United States and the European Union over the extent and effect on international trade of each party's method for subsidizing agricultural goods. The European Union's agricultural price support mechanism – whereby its market price falls below a predetermined (and artificially high) level – has led to enormous surpluses of EU-supplied food products. Hence the EU has not been prepared to make tariff concessions on agricultural items either to crop-dependent underdeveloped countries or to the United States. Instead, non-EU agricultural produce must pay import duties to bring its selling prices up to internal EU levels. The United States (itself a major agricultural producer) objected strongly to this state of affairs as it wished its farmers to have free access to the (lucrative) European market. In reply, the EU argued that the United States *itself* pays huge subsidies to its farmers, hence enabling them to export food at artificially low prices.

The basis of the US objection is that EU surpluses are dumped onto the world agricultural market at low prices, thus forcing down the world rate. Since the United States supports its farmers by making up the difference between a notional 'fair' price and the actual price obtained, EU policy is costing the US taxpayer billions in subsidies. The EU, on the other hand, operates by intervening in the market, either buying up surpluses to maintain the prices or releasing stored produce to reduce prices and even out supply. This frequently results in oversupply, with consequent dumping.

The Uruguay settlement

Conclusion of the Uruguay Round in December 1993 created the most significant trade agreement in GATT's history, estimated by the OECD to be sure to increase world income by at least US$250 billion annually. The United States and the EU each cut tariffs on the other's products by 50 per cent immediately, with more cuts to follow. GATT itself was restructured, renamed as the World Trade Organization, and its powers extended.

Under the settlement, agricultural subsidies were cut over six years. Domestic farm support has been reduced by 20 per cent, export subsidies by 36 per cent (by value). Tariffs are now the only permitted barrier to the import of agricultural goods. Restrictions have been placed on countries' abilities to dump subsidized food exports on the rest of the world. Adjustments on the European side are occurring under the EU's own plans for common agricultural policy reform. Note how, despite its political importance, agriculture accounts for less than 3 per cent of EU GDP and only 6 per cent of the Union's workforce, so that losses (if any) to the EU in this connection will be small. The Uruguay deal provides for the following in relation to intellectual property:

- Patent protection for 20 years regardless of where an item is invented or whether it is imported or locally produced.
- Limitations on the use of compulsory licensing (see Chapter 12) for patented products (licences are easily obtained in some underdeveloped countries).
- Copyright protection for at least 50 years from the creator's death. This is to include computer software and compiled databases.
- All countries will have to introduce laws to prevent the unauthorized disclosure of trade secrets.
- Provision of equal treatment for domestic and foreign intellectual property holders.

Developed countries had one year in which to introduce appropriate legislation, less developed countries five years and the poorest countries 10 years. However, the last were required to allow the filing of patents from 1995 and their implementation 10 years following the date they were filed. Europe in particular will benefit enormously from the Uruguay agreement in a number of areas, including:

- The extension of the WTO to cover trade in services (notably banking, insurance and telecommunications), which today accounts for 20 per cent of all international trade by value. Private sector services now contribute just under 50 per cent of the EU's aggregate GDP and employ 42 per cent of all EU workers. Industry, conversely, provides just a third of total GDP and 32 per cent of employment.

- The opening-up of world markets (especially in North America and Australia) to European exports of agricultural products, natural resources, and textiles originating in Italy, Greece and Portugal.
- Significant international tariff reductions for chemicals, pharmaceuticals, scientific equipment and spirits – all of which the European Union exports in large quantity.
- The limits that are being placed on national governments' capacities to subsidize inefficient local industries.

Despite its occasional difficulties, there can be no doubt that since 1947, GATT has reduced tariff levels significantly across a wide range of products throughout the world, has encouraged 'good behaviour' in international trade practice and has led to much useful dialogue and communication among countries. Fresh measures prejudicial to international trade (other than a number of hidden non-tariff barriers) have not been initiated since the first GATT negotiations. Problems with the WTO are that:

- Rule changes require a two-thirds majority of members. There is 'one vote, one country' regardless of the size of the voting countries.
- Policing the use of hidden non-tariff barriers has proven difficult. As soon as one variety of hidden barrier is outlawed, another might be invented.
- An increasing number of governments outside the major trade blocs are currently advocating *bilateral* trade treaties as a means for counteracting the power of the regional trade groupings. To the extent that bilateral agreements are concluded, they undermine the WTO's position and influence.
- The wording of the main WTO agreement is vague and complicated, making it quite easy to circumvent commitments.
- The WTO cannot *itself* impose sanctions.
- Underdeveloped countries have been as unwilling to renounce excessively protectionist import controls as economically advanced countries have been to accept more Third World imports.

The WTO and UNCTAD

Tariffs on manufactured items have fallen by far more than tariffs on primary commodities. Hence previous tariff-cutting agreements have greatly expanded trade among industrialized countries, but *not* between them and poorer countries. Because the share in total world trade of the less developed countries has declined, the benefits of trade have not been felt as keenly in those countries: put simply, the rich countries have grown richer, and the poor have grown poorer. In order to confront this problem the United Nations set up in 1964 the UN Conference on Trade and Development (UNCTAD) with the goal of improving the returns to exports of primary products. UNCTAD established a system whereby GATT countries apply preferential tariff rates to imports of primary and manufactured goods from developing countries. At the same time, the underdeveloped countries were allowed to maintain high import tariffs against other countries in order to protect their own industries.

COUNTERTRADE

Countertrade means the direct or indirect exchange of goods for other goods across national frontiers. It is found in situations where one or more of the parties is unable to pay for imports using foreign currency, either because its central bank has insufficient stocks of foreign exchange or in consequence of government restrictions on the availability of foreign exchange imposed for political reasons.

Countertrade has greatly diminished in importance since the collapse of Communism and the implementation of the Uruguay Round recommendations, because fewer countries restrict the free movement of currencies. It still flourishes in dealings with China and much of the Third World, and in fact has distinct advantages for firms who are prepared to take the trouble to deal with it. The main difficulty in exchanging a shipment of truck engines for a shipment of cabbages is that a firm in the truck industry has no knowledge of how to dispose of cabbages. Intermediaries are crucial in countertrading operations.

Countertrade as a marketing tool

Countertrade can assist technology transfer from advanced to developing countries and facilitate economic growth in the latter. Importantly it can be used to circumvent protectionist government policies in certain countries.

Countertrade can also be used by exporters to offer favourable 'prices' to potential customers in countries where there is fierce local competition. It may well be the case that a customer in a country where there are *no* foreign exchange controls or shortages will prefer to countertrade, perhaps because of having access to a supply of a suitable local export item.

Application of conventional anti-dumping levies to countertrade transactions may be difficult. Thus national tax authorities, which suspect that countertrade deals are in reality a form of disguised dumping, might impose countervailing duties on the export side of the transaction. To avoid such accusations and to ensure that all local anti-dumping rules are complied with, the exporter might record all details of the intended deal in a separate document (known as an 'evidence account'), which is formally deposited with the appropriate government department of the importer's country.

Countertrade methods

Countertrade typically involves dealings in product categories unfamiliar to the supplying company (machine oil in exchange for foodstuffs, for example) so that the services of an expert intermediary are normally required. Countertrade intermediaries will store and process goods and advertise and otherwise promote the items on offer. The intermediary will act either as an agent or a principal, charging between 3 and 15 per cent commission for its services. Today the countertrade industry is worldwide, with firms operating in all major trading centres.

Barter

The simplest form of countertrade is barter, ie the straightforward exchange of item for item (so many barrels of oil for so many units of machinery, for example). Deals are usually transacted at the prevailing world market prices of the products involved. Barter arrangements are also known as 'contra-trading' or 'reciprocal trading'.

A situation wherein the exporter (or an intermediary) arranges for the disposal of the barter goods to a third party is called a 'switch deal'. Switch trading via intermediaries originally developed in Austria, where banks have traditionally been prepared to advance cash to exporters prior to finding third-party customers for the goods. Many Austrian banks have subsidiaries that directly engage in international trade and so may actually buy the products offered by importers (enabling importers to make cash payments to suppliers).

In risky situations the exporter might insist on receiving the barter goods before dispatching the export consignment. The exporter sells these goods, the money received being paid to an independent third party (usually a bank), which holds it 'in escrow' (meaning that the money is held in trust until certain conditions have been fulfilled). As soon as sales revenues are sufficient to finance the deal, the exporter sends off the goods and presents shipping documents to the third party, who pays the money into the exporter's account.

Compensation dealing

Here the exporting firm receives part payment in its own currency and the remainder in goods.

Buyback

This occurs when a firm supplies plant and equipment in exchange for a share of the future output of the equipment. For example, mining equipment might be supplied to a mining company in exchange for payment in ore, to be supplied over a number of years.

If wages and other non-capital production costs are lower in the importing country, then the plant and equipment supplier can obtain finished output at highly competitive prices. The problem is finding buyers for the output received: ores such as coal or bauxite can sometimes be sold on the futures markets for ready cash, but manufactured goods might be more problematical. This could lead to the exporter entering into competition with its own domestic customers (to whom the firm might have supplied similar plant and equipment to produce the same type of item). Buyback contracts need to specify the quality level and delivery schedule of the buyback products.

It is sometimes the case that a government will sanction the import of major capital goods only on condition that they contain a specified proportion of local inputs or that the exporter agrees to purchase locally produced items of at least a certain value. This is known as an 'offset' arrangement, and might include a buyback element.

McDonnell Douglas and Thailand

In 1995 the government of Thailand introduced a new set of countertrade regulations designed to help reduce its current account balance of payments deficit (which at the time was running at 8.1 per cent of GDP). For larger contracts, the law now required that locally produced raw materials, finished products and/or processed agricultural goods be exchanged for 20 to 50 per cent of the value of a countertrade contract. This rule applied to the Thai government's purchase of eight F/A-18 fighter aircraft from McDonnell Douglas of the United States. Hence fourth-fifths of the $578 million cost was paid in cash, and the remainder in a 'lucky dip' of locally supplied items including Thai rubber, ceramics, furniture, frozen chicken and canned fruit. McDonnell retailed most of the products in Thailand itself, and the rest internationally via facilities provided by a large Japanese trading company. Such countertrade deals are increasingly common in the fiercely competitive arms industry, where individual contracts can run into billions of pounds.

Counterpurchase

With a counterpurchase arrangement the exporting firm receives part payment in its own currency or a hard foreign currency (ie one that is freely exchangeable into any other currency) and the balance in the currency of the importer's country. The exporter then uses the latter currency to buy whatever products in the importer's country happen to be available.

McDonnell Douglas and Finland

Offset arrangements are particularly common in situations where military equipment is being bought or sold, in view of the high monetary value of the goods involved and consequent potential for national trade imbalances, foreign currency problems and other adverse economic consequences. In 1992 the McDonnell Aircraft Company sold 64 F/A-18 twin-engine tactical aircraft to the Finnish government under an offset agreement, delivery to take place between 1995 and 2000. A major beneficiary of the deal was Finland's only aircraft manufacturer, Valmet, which was awarded a contract for assembling 57 of the 64 F/A-18s within Finland. This deal gave Valmet access to McDonnell's international marketing systems for the distribution of its Redigo trainer aircraft. Additionally McDonnell purchased a variety of products (ranging from tableware to cheese manufacturing plants) from Hackman, a leading Finnish metal products company. McDonnell also bought disinfecting machines and food processing equipment from Finnish enterprises. This was possible because of McDonnell's interests in the hospital and construction sectors.

Advantages and criticisms of countertrade

Arguably countertrade arrangements have greatly facilitated the expansion of world trade in the post-Second World War years. Business is transacted without the need for hard foreign currency and less developed countries are able to import high-technology products and pay for them using items they might not otherwise have been able to market internationally. Exporters can sell their outputs in a wider range of countries, and some of the countries in which countertrade is common represent large and fast-growing markets (Eastern European countries, for example).

There are, however, a number of problems with countertrade, including its administrative cost, the possibility of a sudden collapse in the world market price of the goods received as payment, and the scarcity of potential third-party buyers for certain types of item. Further criticisms are that:

- There is little evidence that countertrade actually improves the foreign exchange positions of the countries in which it is common.
- Foreign customers might be more interested in having unpaid distributors for their outputs than in the imported goods per se.
- It distorts the normal competitive mechanisms of price adjustment via supply and demand in relevant markets. Only a minority of exporters have the knowledge or capacity to engage in countertrade, so that the number of firms competing within certain countries is diminished.
- Disputes can arise over the acceptability of the level of quality of the barter goods actually delivered, especially if no precise quality specification for the goods has been agreed. The exporter could be landed with poor-quality goods that are difficult to sell. Slow-moving products impose warehousing costs on the exporter receiving them and cause a deterioration in the firm's liquidity position.

Countertrade is, in any event, reducing as more countries either join big trading blocs such as the European Union, or at least free up the exchange of their currencies. Global trade is running at such a high level that very few countries feel able to remain outside the mainstream: a refusal to trade one's currency freely is certainly a major barrier to reaping the benefits of world trade.

4

Regional analysis techniques

REGIONAL ANALYSIS OF WORLD MARKETS

The world today is dominated economically by a triad comprising the European Union, the North American Free Trade Agreement (NAFTA), and Asia Pacific. Within each region there is a concentration of economic activity, affluent consumer markets and extensive manufacturing potential. The European element of the triad is based on the EU, the North American element on the United States and the Pacific Rim element on Japan. Lucrative markets exist in all three pillars of the triad, but more importantly these areas control the economic welfare of the rest of the world.

There are examples of relatively homogeneous market segments, which cut across all three regions, so that the same products can be sold across the world in a similar way. For larger technologically advanced companies, operating in certain 'lead markets' is a must, since new trends, product characteristics and changes in consumer preference occur in these countries prior to their transfer abroad. Such firms need to be 'where the action is', if only to observe current developments at first hand and to monitor the activities of rival firms.

This restructuring of the world economy makes it essential for businesses to look at potential markets in a *regional* context rather than country by country. Of course, each country has its own idiosyncratic features, and is characterized by a particular set of historical, cultural and behavioural factors.

REGIONAL ECONOMIC GROUPINGS

The development of regional trade and economic groupings has been one of the outstanding phenomena of the post-Second World War period, with the European Union leading the way. Regional alliances create huge markets, facilitate cross-border transactions and enable companies based in the region to obtain economies of scale sufficient to make them competitive in the global market.

Customs unions and free trade areas

A free trade area is a grouping of nations that remove trade barriers against each other, but with each member country continuing to determine and apply its own unique set of barriers (tariffs, quotas, etc) to the entry of imports from other countries that do not belong to the free trade area. An example of this is the North American Free Trade Area (NAFTA), comprising Canada, the United States and Mexico.

With a 'customs union', conversely, there is free trade within the union and a *common* external tariff is applied to imports from the rest of the world. An example is CARICOM, the Caribbean customs union, which includes 14 island states. Quotas and other non-tariff barriers are determined by and for the union as a whole, not by individual members. The next highest stage is the 'common market', wherein business methods, procedures, rules on competition, etc, are harmonized among member states and there is free movement within the market of capital and labour as well as goods. Commercial laws drafted by the authorities of the common market override domestic national legislation. CARICOM is currently in the process of moving towards single-market status, and is deeply involved in discussions with the European Union.

Regional cooperation groups

With a regional cooperation group (RCG), several governments participate in a scheme for developing certain industries across their national frontiers, usually in conjunction with private sector businesses. Each country contributes to the cost and undertakes to purchase a specific amount of the outputs of the industries being developed.

Major regional trading groupings

Currently there exist around 30 organizations of nation states intended to foster economic cooperation. NAFTA and the European Union are perhaps the best known. For South-East Asia there is ASEAN (the Association of South-East Asian Nations): a free-trade area comprising Brunei, Myanmar (Burma), Cambodia, Indonesia, Laos, Malaysia, the Philippines, Singapore, Thailand and Vietnam. ASEAN's aims are to remove internal tariffs and trade barriers, guarantee free access for members' products into any ASEAN market, and harmonize national investment incentives. The ASEAN Vison declaration adopted in 1997 aims to create a complete single market by 2020. ASEAN countries are characterized by deregulated private enterprise economies and diverse industrial capacity. They export much to Japan and receive large amounts of foreign investment from that country.

South and Central America have two common markets: MERCOSUR (the Mercado Comundel Cono Sur) made up of Brazil, Argentina, Paraguay, and Uruguay, and ANCOM (the Andean Common Market) composed of Colombia, Venezuela, Peru, Bolivia and Ecuador. MERCOSUR has a bilateral trade agreement with the United States, and has already eliminated immigration formalities between member states. This means that any citizen of the member states can cross the borders using only an identity card.

In the Middle East there is an Arab Common Market comprising Jordan, Iraq, Libya, Kuwait, Syria and Egypt, with headquarters in Amman. Its activities are supervised by a Council of Arab Economic Unity, also based in Jordan. Additionally, there is the Gulf Cooperation Council, which operates a common external tariff and has free internal movement of goods, capital and labour within certain Arabian Gulf countries.

Most Caribbean countries belong to the Caribbean Community and Common Market (CARICOM), which was established in 1973 to eliminate customs duties and import restrictions among member states and to coordinate economic policies and development within the area. A common external tariff applies to imports entering CARICOM from the rest of the world. The external tariff is high for finished manufactured items but negligible for capital goods and raw materials destined for local industries. CARICOM faces the problems of:

- large disparities in the per capita national income of member states (leading to conflicts of interest in relation to foreign trade policy);
- geographically fragmented markets; and
- heavy dependence on the export of a limited range of commodities.

Nearly all CARICOM countries have signed the Lomé Convention.

Africa

Kenya, Uganda and Tanzania formed a trade bloc called the East African Community (EAC) in January 2001. The trade bloc aims to work towards economic policies that are pro-market, pro-private sector and pro-liberalization. COMESA, the Southern and Eastern African Common Market, was established in 1995 with 21 members, but progress to date has been slow: political instability often hampers attempts to rationalize procedures, and there may be too many member states for a reasonable concensus to be arrived at.

COMESA has been designated a pillar of the African Economic Community. The other pillars are the Southern African Development Community (SADC), the Economic Community of West African States (ECOWAS), the Economic Community of Central African States (ECCAS/CEEAC), and the Arab Maghreb Union (AMU/UMA). Further problems are that for many African States, national borders are the consequence of agreements between former colonial powers and in no way relate to tribal and ethnic divisions, which exert powerful influences on patterns of trade between African nations. Also, the frequency of coups d'état in certain states has caused neighbours to be reluctant to enter into long-term agreements with any one government.

Sub-Saharan Africa in general has such serious economic problems that cooperation between states is likely to remain subservient to cooperation with the wealthier countries of the world, at least for the foreseeable future.

The Commonwealth of Independent States (CIS)

This currently comprises 10 republics of the former Soviet Union (Azerbaijan Republic, Republic of Armenia, Republic of Belarus, Republic of Kazakhstan, Kyrgyz Republic, Republic of Moldova, Russian Federation, Republic of Tajikistan, Republic of Uzbekistan and Ukraine). It was formed in 1991, but has an unstable membership: political upheavals in member states regularly call into question its long-term viability. Also the national boundaries of members are liable to change.

Originally the Russian Republic comprised 15 separate units (each with its own legislature) plus 20 homelands ('autonomous republics') for specific ethnic groups. However, fresh alliances and ethnic movements may alter the domains of various 'states'. What could occur are closer ties between the Slavic republics on the one hand, and the Central Asian republics on the other. Equally, some of the latter might be more at home forming economic alliances with 'Western' Islamic countries such as Turkey. Belarus has much in common with Poland, Kazakhstan might gravitate towards China, and so on.

The main attraction of the CIS from the marketing perspective, is that it has a large population *and* a technologically sophisticated industrial infrastructure in many areas. The CIS's far east has low population density and low per capita incomes, but is enormously rich in mineral deposits, timber and agricultural products. The potential for development is huge; what is lacking is an economic and social infrastructure – roads, dwellings, schools, business services, etc.

China and Japan

The glaring omissions from all these regional trade groupings are China and Japan. Political considerations have in the past prevented these countries from forming customs unions with regional neighbours. The implications of a possible grouping of either country with (say) the United States or the newly industrialized nations of the Pacific Rim are awesome.

Implications for marketing

The majority of countries in Asia, Africa, Latin America and Eastern Europe now belong to a regional grouping or are planning to join one. To some extent, therefore, larger economic groupings are replacing nation states as the main focus of attention for international business. Increasingly, marketing decisions have to relate to (at least) several countries as a whole and not just to individual ones. Long-term implications of the emergence of regional economic blocs include the following:

- The larger blocs will have the economic and political power to force trade liberalization on previously protectionist countries. Tariffs and so on will fall on a reciprocal basis, leading to *more* rather than less international competition.
- Countries not belonging to a bloc will be driven towards joining one.
- The overall pattern of international trade might shift towards a greater volume of transactions *within* regions rather than between individual countries and the triad of Europe, the United States and Japan.
- Decisions concerning the extent and location of the subsidiary activities of international businesses will be affected by the need to:
  - avoid high common external tariffs;
  - obtain local investment grants and subsidies; and
  - satisfy the requirements of region-wide (rather than national) consumer segments.

5

North Atlantic countries

THE AMERICAS

NAFTA

The North American Free Trade Agreement (NAFTA) took effect on 1 January 1994 and
will eliminate all tariffs and trade obstacles between member countries by 2009. Internal
tariffs on a large number of product categories were removed immediately. NAFTA is
unique as a trading bloc in that it brings together two of the world's most affluent countries (Canada and the United States) with Mexico, a poor and economically underdeveloped country. A free trade agreement between the United States and Canada was signed
in 1989. Its extension to Mexico presents Canada (a small population economy that is
nevertheless resource-rich and highly industrial) and the United States with a large
consumer goods market, while the United States is a major importer of Mexican manufactures and oil. NAFTA is one of the most important economic trading areas in the
world, clearly able to compete effectively against Europe and Asia Pacific. The arguments
behind the formation of NAFTA were that it should:

- create fresh business opportunities in expanding national markets (especially
  Mexico, which is developing rapidly);
- enhance the competitive advantage of NAFTA-based firms operating in wider international markets;
- reduce consumer prices through extending competition;
- increase employment throughout the region;
- create a stable and predictable environment for investors;

- decrease the flow of emigration from Mexico to the United States by providing job opportunities 'south of the border';
- help Mexico earn additional foreign exchange to meet its foreign debt burden;
- improve and consolidate political relationships among member nations.

Government procurement markets in each member state are opened up to suppliers from other NAFTA countries, subject to minimum values for the contracts involved. Residents of any NAFTA country may freely invest in any member state. The agreement sets out specific requirements regarding the protection of intellectual property within each member state. Further measures include:

- Simplification and harmonization of product standards across the region.
- Easy border crossings for business personnel.
- Application of stringent local content rules to prevent non-NAFTA firms assembling goods in Mexico and hence avoiding US and Canadian tariffs and quotas. Third-country products imported into one country cannot be re-exported to other members as if they were domestically produced goods, unless a certain minimum percentage of their manufacturing costs have been incurred in the importing country. For Canada and the United States the figure is 50 per cent; for Mexico the local content requirement can be as high as 80 per cent. Each country continues to operate its own system of tariffs against non-NAFTA states.
- Regulations to control pollution along the Mexico/US border.

Criticisms of NAFTA have emerged predominantly from US labour representatives and concern competition between the United States and Mexico. The main complaints are that Mexico has fewer and less stringent (and hence less costly) environmental protection and health and safety legislation than the United States. This will encourage US businesses to shift their operations to Mexico. Also that the NAFTA treaty is being implemented too quickly. It could result in little more than the direct assimilation by the United States of the Mexican economy.

US Republican presidential candidate Ross Perot is famously quoted as saying the NAFTA would be followed by 'a loud sucking sound as American jobs move to Mexico'. There is some evidence that this has happened, with some sources stating that over 350,000 jobs have been lost as a direct result of NAFTA (http://www.citizen.org/trade/nafta/jobs/).

From 1999 to 2000, US farm and food exports to Mexico climbed by $916 million to $6.5 billion – the highest level ever and the fifth record in five years under NAFTA. US exports of soybeans, cotton and rice all set new records. By value, more US agricultural products went to Mexico in 2001 than to China, Hong Kong, and Russia combined.

In the years immediately prior to NAFTA, US agricultural products lost market share in Mexico as competition for the Mexican market increased. NAFTA reversed this trend. The United States now supplies more than 75 per cent of Mexico's total agricultural imports, due in part to the price advantage and preferential access that US products now enjoy. For example, Mexico's imports of US red meat and poultry have grown rapidly, exceeding pre-NAFTA levels and reaching the highest level ever in 2000.

The United States

The United States of America has a population of about 285 million, and covers a geographical area nearly twice that of the 15 EU countries combined. It is the world's largest import market. The United States stretches from Hawaii in the tropics, through to the Arctic Circle (Alaska). Twenty-five US conurbations have populations in excess of 1.5 million. New York (including northern New Jersey) has 18 million people and Los Angeles 14.5 million. Three-quarters of the US's population live in cities. The US's population can be roughly categorized as 20 per cent poor and 20 per cent affluent, with the rest in the middle.

Unemployment is unevenly distributed. Black people, Hispanics and the poorly educated experience the highest rates of unemployment (around 30 per cent for Black youths). As in other Western countries, the proportion of the US labour force employed in manufacturing has declined, while the proportion engaged in services is continuously increasing. The new jobs created over the last 20 years have tended to be in office administration and catering, and are frequently low paid and part-time. Jobs lost have been in well-paid skilled and semi-skilled manual occupations. In the 1970s only 20 per cent on average of the new jobs created each year fell within the Federal Department of Labour's lowest category of income. Through the 1980s the figure was 60 per cent, and one-third were part-time.

Despite these changes, the United States retains an enormous manufacturing capacity, and in most years the country's GDP per head of population ranks the sixth or seventh highest in the world. Major US corporations are huge and exercise enormous economic power. Many of them have turnovers well in excess of the national incomes of most countries. Also the United States possesses vast natural resources. Public administration and services employ three-quarters of all US workers. Major service sectors are retailing (18 per cent of all employment), finance and insurance (6 per cent), and wholesaling and transportation (5 per cent).

Economic growth and structure

The US government carries out an economic census every five years. Among the key findings of the 1997 Economic Census were:

- The nation's information sector, including publishing, motion pictures, broadcasting, telecommunications, and information and data processing services, generates 3.2 million jobs, a $135 billion annual payroll and $642 billion in receipts at 115,000 locations.
- The health care/social assistance sector generates 13.6 million jobs, a $379 billion annual payroll and $890 billion in receipts at 645,000 locations.
- The professional/scientific/technical services sector, including scientists, engineers, architects, programmers and designers, generates 5.4 million jobs, a $233 billion annual payroll and $609 billion in receipts at 622,000 locations.

- The administrative/support services subsector, including employment agencies, employee leasing services, phone centres, telemarketing bureaus and travel agencies, generates 7.2 million jobs, a $129 billion annual payroll and $262 billion in receipts at 260,000 locations.
- The computer/electronic manufacturing sector generates 1.7 million jobs, a $71 billion annual payroll and $431 billion in shipments at 17,000 locations.
- The arts/entertainment/recreation sector generates 1.6 million jobs, a $32 billion annual payroll and $103 billion in receipts at 100,000 locations.
- The manufacturing sector employs the most people at 17 million employees, followed by the retail trade at 14 million employees and health care/social assistance at 14 million employees.
- The top five manufacturing subsectors by shipment value are transportation equipment ($578 billion), computers/electronic products ($431 billion), food ($425 billion), chemicals ($418 billion) and machinery ($272 billion).
- The top five retail subsectors by sales are motor vehicle/parts dealers ($648) billion, food/beverage stores ($401 billion), general merchandise stores ($330 billion), building material/garden equipment stores ($230 billion) and gas stations ($198 billion).

The 1997 census was the first to use the new NAICS system for classifying businesses. The NAICS system replaced the Standard Industrial Classification (SIC) system begun in the 1930s, and is regarded as a better measure for the 21st century economy by highlighting businesses that contribute the most to the US economy and classifying businesses consistently by production process. Jointly developed with Canada and Mexico as part of the NAFTA agreement, the system makes possible comparisons with these major trading partners.

The NAICS system provides 1,170 detailed US industry classifications, or 15 per cent more than were available under the old system. This includes 358 new industries and 390 revised industry classifications. Only 422 industries will continue to be measured in the old way.

Large corporations, the top 50 of which account for three-quarters of all the nation's business revenues, dominate the US economy. Otherwise there are at least 3 million companies, 1.5 million partnerships and 11 million sole traders, a huge potential market for foreign exporters. Machinery and transport equipment constitute the country's biggest category of both imports and exports. Other main exports and imports are manufactures and foodstuffs. Large amounts of oil and raw materials are also imported. Canada, Japan, Mexico, the United Kingdom and Germany are the United States's major customers, in that rank order. The country's main suppliers are Canada, Mexico, Germany and Taiwan.

The population

Three-quarters of all Americans live in urban conurbations, the largest 40 of which contain over half the population. California is the most populous state, New York the second. There are 94 million households, with an average household size of 2.6.

Each US region has its own distinct climate, industrial structure and pattern of consumer preferences. Twelve per cent of US residents are Black, and nearly 10 per cent Hispanic. In California about 10 per cent of the population are of Asian extraction, and 25 per cent Hispanic. In total there are around 20 million 'Hispanic' US citizens and their numbers are growing. Hispanics could be the biggest US minority group by the end of the decade. Large numbers of Spanish-speaking Americans live in New York, Los Angeles, Chicago, Miami and California. Spanish-language advertising is common in these cities. It should be noted that in Texas, New Mexico and California large numbers of Hispanics are descended from the original Spanish settlers, and were there before the Anglo-Saxons arrived from Europe: this accounts for some of the resentment some of these people feel at being treated as second-class citizens in their own country.

The United States is a nation of immigrants, and the overwhelming bulk of the population can trace their origins to a specific foreign country within the last half dozen generations. A survey conducted in 1990 (see DTI, 1994) suggested that about 23 per cent of all Americans would claim their ancestry to be German, 16 per cent Irish, 13 per cent English, 10 per cent African and 6 per cent Italian. Other significant groupings were Mexican (5 per cent) and French, Polish and Native American (4 per cent each). Note the extensive immigration that has occurred over the last quarter of a century (the highest since the 1890s). Fifteen million immigrants entered the United States legally over the period 1965–90, plus perhaps 2 or 3 million entering illegally. Most of the newcomers are Hispanic or Asian. Foreign-born Americans now constitute nearly 9 per cent of the population, and nearly 50 per cent of all Americans entering the labour force will have been born outside the United States. Immigration from South-East Asia (especially the Philippines and Korea) is swelling the American-Asian community.

Americans are well educated. Full-time education is compulsory to the age of 16, although the majority stay at school until 18, with two-thirds of all high school graduates moving on to university education. Drop-out rates in US higher education are high by international standards.

Six in 10 US citizens belong to an organized religious group. About half of these people are Protestant, 40 per cent Roman Catholic. All versions of Protestantism are represented. Important social and economic trends in the United States include:

- An increasing divorce rate and smaller household sizes. In 1960 about 75 per cent of all American families were headed by married couples – today the figure is barely 50 per cent.
- Continuing expansion of the service economy at the expense of manufacturing.
- Public concern for environmental issues and hence greater demand for environmentally friendly products.
- Increasing interest in health care and health-related foodstuffs, pharmaceuticals and fitness items.
- A proliferation of high-discount retail outlets.
- Growing demand for technology products imported from Pacific Rim countries.

Doing business in the United States

Each of the United States's 50 states, plus the District of Columbia, has its own set of commercial laws. Additionally there are federal laws that apply throughout the country. This results in great complexity and the need to take full account of legal factors when planning business operations. Note, moreover, that the United States is the world's most litigious country. There are more lawyers per 1,000 population than in any other country, and lawyers are prepared to work on a 'no-win, no-fee' basis, thus creating incentives for aggrieved parties to seek legal redress. State and federal laws extend to product safety and quality requirements, competition, advertising and sales promotion, and banking and finance. Laws relating to tort (ie civil wrongs such as negligence), company incorporation and management, partnerships and insurance are mainly determined at the state level. The supplier's liability for product safety is strict in this country. Distributors are jointly liable with importers and original manufacturers for damages resulting from defective products, but they typically include clauses in their contracts with suppliers that explicitly pass back liability.

US anti-trust law prohibits *any* contract, combination or 'conspiracy in restraint of trade or commerce' and any attempt to monopolize trade or commerce. What this means in practice is a highly contentious issue, and there has been much litigation in the field. US courts apply the 'rule of reason' to such matters, ie the court will ask itself whether the act in question will have an anti-competitive effect. Note that operations in small niche markets involving distribution or licensing agreements are just as vulnerable to anti-trust legislation as are unreasonable restraints on competition by large enterprises selling across the country.

US patent law seeks to protect and reward inventors. Patent applications are secret and adjudicated within two years. Grant of a patent gives protection for 17 years. Importantly, the United States is one of the very few countries in the world where a patent can be held for its entire duration without being worked. Trade marks can but need not be registered in order to enjoy legal protection. All that is required is positive proof of first use. A registered trade mark that is dormant for two years can be challenged by a competing business.

Regulation of US advertising is the responsibility of the Federal Trade Commission, which is mandated by the US Congress to prevent 'deceptive acts or practices'. Misleading advertising is illegal under federal law. This means 'false representations' (express or implied) and/or failing to disclose misleading facts. The rules are stringent, so that liability arises even if there is no proof that any consumers were actually deceived by a false representation; and literal truth is no defence to an accusation of misleading advertising if the overall representation conveys a false impression, nor is it a defence to argue that the advertiser was not aware of the deception.

However, insignificant false representations unlikely to affect purchasing decisions are not actionable. Also, the use of exaggerations, superlatives and subjective opinions to describe an item are perfectly acceptable. Rules on the acceptability of comparative advertising vary from state to state, and expert advice is necessary on this matter.

Agents and distributors

Although many products sell equally well throughout the country (industrial goods, for example), a regional approach to selling in the United States is generally required – with variations in consumer tastes following a distinct regional pattern. It is extremely unlikely that a single representative will have the expertise and/or capability to handle a product throughout the entire US market. Most exporters to the United States find they need to engage regional rather than national agreements in consequence of the great size and regional diversity of the country. The general law of contract governs agency agreements; there is no federal legislation on the subject although many states have particular rules on agency termination and compensation. Great care is needed when drafting agency or distribution agreements, since any contract to fix resale prices, impose territorial restrictions or handle competing products has the potential to fall foul of US anti-trust legislation. Aggrieved parties are permitted to sue for three times the level of actual damages incurred.

Branches and subsidiaries

A subsidiary company can be incorporated in any state under the incorporation laws of that state or the laws of the District of Columbia (there are no federal laws on incorporation). The state of registration need not be the state in which a subsidiary operates and, once it has been incorporated, it may trade across the country. If it sets up permanent establishments in other states it needs to declare this fact to the authorities of these states and pay annual fees. New York, Maryland and Delaware have the most liberal rules on company formation. Delaware is particularly attractive because its incorporation laws do not require any of a company's founders to be US citizens or for the company to hold formal meetings. Regardless of where a company is incorporated the process is straightforward and rarely takes longer than a week. Foreign-owned companies may be set up at will and in exactly the same way as those owned by US citizens. A foreign business may freely repatriate its profits.

Branches are established under state laws, or the laws of the District of Columbia. Registration of a branch involves a one-off fee, which varies from state to state. Branch employees are, of course, subject to US equal opportunity and other civil rights legislation.

External trade

The United States is the world's biggest trading nation and the extent of its foreign trade is increasing. Overall, the pattern of the United States's trade has shifted away from Europe and towards Asia Pacific, notably Japan, Taiwan and South Korea. Nevertheless, the European Union remains a critically important trading partner, taking about 20 per cent of US exports and furnishing nearly the same percentage of its imports. Japan is the United States's biggest supplier (providing nearly 20 per cent of all imports – slightly more than Canada). However, the US trade deficit with Japan is enormous, causing much displeasure to successive US governments. Particular concern has been expressed about the *structure* of the deficit, which is mostly in manufactured goods (especially high-technology products). Main imports are automotive products, machinery, clothing and footwear, and foodstuffs. The most accessible and fastest growing import sectors include automotive products; clothing, textiles, cosmetics, toiletries and fashion accessories; agricultural equipment; giftware; sports and leisure goods; furniture and home furnishings; and healthcare items.

Public procurement is important, contributing nearly 20 per cent to GDP. Fifteen per cent of the labour force works for the government. However, it is difficult to sell to US federal government agencies because of restrictions imposed by the 'Buy America Act', which prohibits federal bodies from purchasing foreign goods if local substitutes are available at no more than 6 per cent above the cost of the imports (12 per cent for small businesses or suppliers in areas of high unemployment). Local government is not subject to the Act, but many states have comparable legislation. Big department and chain stores purchase large quantities of imports, as do the major mail-order houses. All have buying offices in other countries.

Customs entry

Most items can enter the United States freely, although quotas apply to some products. Quotas may specify an absolute upper limit, or impose higher rates of tariff once a certain volume of imports of the goods has been exceeded. Anti-dumping rules are stringent and countervailing duties are imposed on items imported at less than a 'fair market price'. There are over 150 freezones across the country. Although there are no general import restrictions per se, critics sometimes allege that technical product safety standards and food and drug legislation are used as de facto non-tariff barriers for certain types of goods. All imported items must be marked with the country of origin unless such marking would physically damage the product. A useful facility available to the owner of a registered trade mark in the United States is that it can be recorded with the US Customs Service, which will then seize and confiscate all imports that violate the trade mark.

Mexico

Mexico is a geographically diverse country with swamps and deserts, lowland jungles and high alpine areas. It has a population exceeding 98 million, 40 per cent of which are below 18 years of age. There are 14 million households with an average household size of seven (extremely high by international standards). Ninety per cent of Mexicans are literate. Most of the population is of mixed European and Indian ancestry. About one in five Mexicans lives in Mexico City. The official language is Spanish, although English is widely spoken. Ninety-five per cent of all Mexicans are Roman Catholic. Half of all Mexicans live below the poverty line (defined as in the income level 15 per cent lower than the national minimum wage). Of these poor people, about 40 per cent live in extreme poverty and cannot afford adequate nourishment.

Manufacturing accounts for a quarter of the country's GDP, services for 60 per cent and agriculture for 7 per cent. Important components of Mexico's manufactured output are textiles and clothing (15 per cent), machinery and transport (12 per cent) and food processing (20 per cent). Manufactured items contribute 60 per cent of all exports. The main destinations for Mexico's exports are the United States (75 per cent) and Canada and Japan (5 per cent each). Eighty-five per cent of Mexico's imports are industrial supplies and capital equipment. Consumer goods account for the remaining 15 per cent. Agriculture contributes just 8 per cent to GDP, but employs 23 per cent of the working population, typically on small and inefficient farms. Industry accounts for 16 per cent of GDP and 20 per cent of employment.

Historically, inflation has been high, averaging 48 per cent annually in the late 1980s and early 1990s. However, growth accelerated in the 1990s and inflation fell considerably (to 7 per cent in 1994), rising again in the mid-90s and falling somewhat in the early 21st century. A further encouraging sign is that although the country has a large balance of payments deficit, most of the growth in imports in the 1990s was in capital equipment and industrial goods, which eventually will increase the country's manufacturing capacity. This is largely as a result of US firms moving operations south: growth at this rate may well not continue. Mexico led the way in relation to privatization of industry in Latin America, including all the country's banks, its entire telecommunications system, the state airline and most of the steel and mining industries.

Membership of NAFTA is attracting foreign capital and creating new jobs, especially among the poorer sections of the population. Communications in Mexico have yet to attain First World standards. Letter delivery takes two to three days in the main cities, longer in rural areas. Half the country's roads are without paving. However, there are international airports in Mexico City, Guadalajara, Acapulco and Monterrey, plus an excellent system of internal daily scheduled services between commercial centres. There is an extensive rail network linking all major towns in the country. Note the extent of the dependence of the Mexican companies on US importers and 50 per cent of Mexican government Treasury bills are held by US investors. Exporters to the country typically quote CIF export prices in US dollars rather than Mexican currency.

Many firms selling to Mexico open a 'representative office', which can be set up at will provided the country's Foreign Investment Commission is notified within 30 days of establishment. Otherwise much import business is conducted through agents, the majority of which are based in Mexico City. There is no specific legislation on agency. Individuals (rather than limited companies) appointed as agents are entitled to regard themselves as employees, and hence to claim the protection of Mexican employment law and severance pay. Debt collection in Mexico is problematic. Non-accepted bills of exchange have to be protested before a notary public within two days of presentation. Unpaid accepted bills must also be protested within two days of maturity. Failure to protest results in long delays in subsequent legal proceedings.

Canada

As the world's largest country, Canada covers an area of nearly 10 million square kilometres, but has a population of just 31 million. The country ranges from the polar ice cap in the north to the wheat regions of the central plains and the industrial areas of the south-east. Forty per cent of the country is forest. The country comprises 10 provinces and two 'territories'. Provinces have their own local legislatures; territories are subject to central control. Canada is the seventh-largest exporter and importer in the world, and has an extremely high standard of living and immense natural resources. Half the country's agricultural output is sold abroad. Eighteen per cent of Canada's GDP is attributable to manufacturing, two-thirds to services and a meagre 5 per cent to agriculture, although agriculture and forestry provide 22 per cent of all Canada's exports. In 2001, the United States accounted for seven-eighths of Canada's trade, with Japan coming second. Trade with the United States showed a huge balance of payments surplus, but there was a deficit in trade with Japan and the European Union (http://www.statcan.ca/english/Pgdb/Economy/International/gblec02a.htm).

Canada is a bilingual country (English and French). About 45 per cent of the population are Roman Catholic, 30 per cent Protestant. A fifth of Canadians are under 15 years of age; 12 per cent are over 65. There are 10 million households with an average household size of 2.5 persons. Forty per cent of Canadians claim British or Irish ancestry, 27 per cent French, 5 per cent German, 3 per cent Italian and a further 8 per cent from more than one ethnic or national grouping. Native Indians and Inuits represent just over 1 per cent.

French-speaking Quebec has its own distinct society. It is on the eastern seaboard of the country, with coasts on the Hudson and James Bays and the St Lawrence seaway. Quebec covers an enormous area (1,356,790 square kilometres) and has a population of 6.75 million. A million of the latter can speak English as well as French. Eighty-five per cent of Canadians live within 320 kilometres of the US border. Although Canada is a vast country, internal communications are good. There is no national daily newspaper as such, although the *Toronto Globe and Mail* has a nationwide distribution. Regional newspapers have a large circulation. French-language dailies are published in seven Canadian cities. Satellite and radio communications with remote areas are highly developed. Accordingly, Canadian consumers are knowledgeable, discerning and demand high-quality products, regardless of their geographical location.

The country has three major regional airlines plus around 75 local air services. The road network is extensive and covers vast distances (the west–east Trans-Canada Highway is 8,000 kilometres long). Goods can normally be transported to any major Canadian city by road within three days of importation at a sea port, or within five hours' flying time by air. Rail traffic is declining; certain services have disappeared entirely and others now only run on a weekly or twice-weekly basis. Canada has thousands of kilometres of navigable canals, rivers and seaways and water transport remains a common means for shifting consignments. There are no free ports or zones, although extensive bonded warehouse facilities are available.

Canada has no specific agency legislation. Agency agreements are regulated by normal contract law, which itself is based on English law. Branches of foreign (and domestic) companies must be registered in each of the provinces in which they do business, and a Canadian resident must be authorized to enter into contracts on behalf of the branch. Canada should gain from NAFTA through the overall expansion of the North American market that it involves, and because Mexico's tariffs against Canada have in the past been higher than vice versa. Problems resulting from Canada's membership of NAFTA include:

- intense competition from low-cost Mexican production of automobiles;
- the likelihood of more imports of Mexican fruit and vegetables;
- possible relocation of some Canadian low-skill assembly enterprises in Mexico.

Otherwise, Canada's main difficulty relates perhaps to the possibility of it breaking up into separate and politically independent French and English speaking countries, although with the implementation of NAFTA this should not affect business and trade. Other problems facing Canada include:

- a low rate of growth of industrial productivity compared to rival countries;
- large budget deficits;
- wages and manufacturing costs higher than the average for the United States.

EUROPE

West European integration

The West European market is dominated by the European Union and, in particular, by a 'golden triangle' (roughly within the area enclosed by Liverpool, Cologne and Paris) that contains 60 per cent of the entire EU population, but with a land mass smaller than the United Kingdom. The Union itself consists of 15 countries, which together represent one of the largest and most affluent integrated trading groups in the developed world. It began in 1956 when six of the current European Union member states formed an internal free trade area by removing all tariff barriers amongst themselves, while imposing a common external tariff on imports coming from outside. Also the six countries decided to harmonize (ie standardize and coordinate) their internal business laws and practices (eg laws on business competition, company accounts, patent and trade mark regulations) and to set up a special court, the European Court of Justice, to interpret the agreement (known as the Treaty of Rome), which legally established the system.

In 1986, the scope of the Treaty of Rome was greatly extended via the Single European Act, which transformed the European Community (as it was then known) from being little more than a customs union into a genuine single market with complete freedom for Community businesses to set up anywhere in the EC and to engage in cross-border intra-Community trade as if they were doing business within a single country.

The Maastricht Agreement and the European Economic Area

Further progress towards West European economic union occurred in 1991/92 via the Maastricht Agreement, by which the majority of EC members committed themselves to the introduction of a common currency (the euro) and the formation of the European Economic Area (EAA), which included the European Free Trade Association states. In fact, EFTA broke up shortly afterwards because Austria, Sweden and Finland joined the EU, and Switzerland and Liechtenstein refused to join the EEA. This left Iceland isolated. The European Community became known as the European Union in 1993 when the Maastricht Treaty was finally ratified.

The formulation of European business regulations

Decisions taken at the EU level pass into Union law (which is binding on all member states) through one of the following devices:

- **regulations**, ie laws that apply immediately and equally in all member states;
- **directives**, which specify a necessary outcome (eg to prevent misleading advertising) but then allow the government of each member country to introduce its own particular legislation to achieve the desired objective;
- **decisions** of the European Court of Justice, which have the same effect as regulations.

Additionally, the European Commission issues 'recommendations' which are not legally binding but express the Commission's considered opinions about how certain matters should be dealt with. Today, EU directives, regulations, etc, affect most aspects of European business. There are directives on consumer protection, advertising and cross-border broadcasting, company administration, intellectual property, agency and distribution arrangements, business mergers and acquisitions, working conditions, health and safety, gender equal opportunities in employment, and on numerous other facets of business life.

The West European market

The EU has four really large markets: Germany, France, Italy and the United Kingdom. Germany has West Europe's highest population, and is the dominant economic power. Other West European countries have smaller populations but many are, nevertheless, *extremely* affluent and represent lucrative markets for foreign firms (Wallace, 1991). The outstanding demographic feel pertaining to the EU is the low (or zero) rate of growth of population in most countries. This has caused a significant increase in the average age of the West European population and (in consequence) changing attitudes and spending patterns among European consumers. At the same time, younger Europeans are increasingly well educated, with nearly a quarter of the West European population now in some kind of full-time education.

Living standards

European Union countries can be categorized into three groups according to their per capita Gross Domestic Product. There are the rich countries, Denmark, Germany, Austria, Sweden, Luxembourg and France (in that rank order); the middling countries, ie the

Netherlands, Belgium, Finland, Italy and the United Kingdom; and the less prosperous states of Spain, Ireland, Portugal and Greece (although the recent economic development of Spain has been extremely rapid). All European Union countries, however, are well off compared to the majority of the world's countries, and even the poorer members are experiencing steady long-term economic growth. Importantly, moreover, all the lower-income EU countries contain substantial groups of consumers whose tastes, living standards and lifestyles are virtually identical to those of equivalent consumers in the richer EU states. The European Union is the largest single international trader in the world, accounting for more than a fifth of global imports and exports (compared with about 15 per cent for the United States and 10 per cent for Japan).

Affluent Europeans

Virtually all EU households possess a television set and telephone, and more than 90 per cent have a refrigerator. Rates of ownership of other key consumer durables are high. An important consequence of West European prosperity is the low number of people per average household in EU countries compared to other states. Typical household size varies between 2.1 and 3 for all EU countries except Ireland, where the average is 3.8. There are 60 United Nations member countries with an average household size of 5 or more.

Cultural differences

Post-Second World War Western Europe has seen the emergence of comparable fashions, music, television programmes and (importantly) a broadly similar youth culture in all industrially developed countries. The fact that more Europeans visit other countries than at any time in history has greatly contributed to this trend, as have the activities of large multinational corporations that offer near identical products in all European states. Note, however, that European economic integration does *not* mean that Germans will cease to be German, that the Dutch will no longer be Dutch or that the French will not be French. The Single Market has in no way created 'grey uniformity' among national consumer populations. Indeed, regional cultures appear, if anything, to have been reinforced, with the consequence that small but significant niche markets are flourishing throughout the EU.

Economic performance

The combined national income of the 15 EU countries exceeds that of the United States by about 14 per cent and is more than two-and-a-half times that of Japan. Germany has Western Europe's highest level of industrial production, followed by France, Italy and the United Kingdom. Spain's industrial production was 42 per cent that of France. The Netherlands and Belgium have an industrial output of 26 per cent and 16 per cent respectively of the French figure. Today Germany accounts for nearly 20 per cent of European consumer spending (including EFTA nations and Eastern bloc countries as well as the EU). France accounts for 13 per cent, and Italy and Britain for 12 per cent each.

Despite rises in unemployment occurring in 1997, the European Commission is generally optimistic about the EU's economic prospects for the forthcoming decade. Forecasts prepared by the Directorate-General for Economic and Financial Affairs (and published quarterly in Supplement A of the Commission's journal *European Economy*) predict overall EU growth of between 2.3 per cent and 2.8 per cent per annum, supported by 'healthy fundamentals' (the Commission's own phrase) and a favourable international environment. The Commission cites the monetary and fiscal measures introduced by a number of EU countries in preparation for their membership of the single European currency as one of the main reasons for the Union's underlying economic health. Employment should increase and the average EU inflation rate fall towards the end of the decade. The average budget deficit/GDP ratio in the EU fell from 4.4 per cent in 1996 to 3 per cent in 1997 and is expected to decline still further. Levels of national debt are also falling. These favourable projections, the Commission notes, are contingent on the continuation of existing economic policies and of substantial external demand for European products. (The latter supported the upturn in the EU growth rate that began in the mid-1990s.) In principle, current national approaches to economic management ought not to alter significantly in coming years, since *all* member states formally agreed at the 1996 Florence summit to develop a macroeconomic framework involving:

- stability-orientated monetary policies not undermined by excessive government spending;
- attempting to restrict real wage increases to below the increase in productivity in order to enhance the profitability of employment-creating investment;
- a commitment to reducing the EU's unacceptably high level of unemployment;
- ensuring the lasting success of economic and monetary union via meaningful attempts at converging the core objectives of member states' economic policies;
- redirecting, wherever possible, government spending towards infrastructure investment and the improvement of human capital.

Marketing in the new Europe

West European integration presents numerous marketing opportunities and threats for the individual firm. Among the benefits of the new situation are:

- new ideas and fresh thinking generated by the process of analysing and evaluating fresh possibilities in the wider European market;
- the competitive edge in the world markets outside Europe that a firm might develop from the contacts and experience it acquires through trading on a pan-European basis;
- EU-wide technical product standards, the compulsory application of which enables small enterprises to compete in foreign EU states;
- faster transmission of innovative marketing methods across national frontiers.

Problems and threats to a firm arising from the opening up of the pan-European market include the wider choice of products available to local customers, who may opt to purchase items supplied from other European countries, plus the possibilities that:

- Harmonization of product standards may compel (costly) alterations in the size, shape, ingredients, safety features and other characteristics of a firm's products.
- Markets could fragment into many more sub-units than exist at present, with intense competition to dominate these smaller market segments, particularly in relation to control over distribution channels and outlets.
- Translations of existing promotional literature might not be suitable for European markets, so that substantial modification may be required.
- Enhanced business communications between West European countries might increase the likelihood of a company's products, ideas or trade marks being pirated and sold by other businesses. Hence the firm may need to implement new measures for protecting its intellectual property.

The proposed single currency

This was introduced to the EU's core economies at the end of 2001. Britain and Denmark have negotiated opt-out clauses, but even without their participation, the creation of a common European currency will alter fundamentally and forever the extent and pattern of European trade.

A single European currency will require firms to quote prices in a common unit and will enable consumers readily to compare the prices of similar items sold in various EU countries. It means pan-European price labelling and packaging, easier product position- ing in national markets, and the absence of currency conversion costs for businesses in countries that are members of the scheme. Firms outside the common currency area, conversely, will need separate prices, packaging and labelling for domestic and European markets, and must incur the (substantial) expense of currency conversion. A common currency removes *entirely* the currency exchange risk associated with international trans- actions. However, such risks – and the consequent need to hedge against them via the forward currency exchange markets – will continue to apply to non-common currency area enterprises.

The average levels of cash held within firms engaged in cross-border EU trade will fall as the need to accumulate temporary foreign exchange balances disappears. A common currency will enable cash received from several different countries to be lumped together instantly and without conversion and to be deposited in the highest interest-earning country. Businesses will be able to record and compare all accounting values in one unit, making for easy identification of the most costly and the most profitable activities in various markets. Cross-border cash transactions will be executed much faster on average than in the past. A major advantage will be the clearer and better information made avail- able on input costs and competitors' prices. The assessment of potential customers' credit worthiness should be facilitated.

Competition law

Restrictions on entry to specific EU industries and/or markets are generally forbidden, as are price-fixing agreements, 'concerted practices' whereby firms rig markets through their behaviour but without entering explicit agreements, exclusive distributorship arrangements, and mergers or acquisitions that give rise to monopoly power. EU rules on competition derive from Articles 85 and 86 of the Treaty of Rome. Article 85 prohibits trade practices that prevent, restrict or distort competition. Agreements by firms to carve up the European market among themselves are void and thus unenforceable in the courts of member states. Article 86 prohibits firms that already occupy a dominant position in an EU market from abusing that position. A dominant position is defined as a position of economic strength that enables an enterprise to prevent effective competition by being able to operate independently of its competitors and customers. There have been cases in the European Court where abuse has occurred through firms increasing their market share by taking over competitors, or through gaining control over the supply of raw materials and then cutting off supplies to competing businesses. Additionally, the Treaty of Rome defines the following business practices as abuses of a dominant position:

- imposition of unfair prices for purchases of raw materials or sale of final goods;
- restrictions on production;
- restrictions on distribution;
- holding back technological development;
- charging different prices to different customers.

This is a formidable list. And Articles 85 and 86 are directly enforceable via the laws of member countries and/or the European Commission. Note, however, that in practice the Commission's stance on the enforcement of free business competition has been somewhat ambivalent. On the one hand it wishes to prevent firms from exploiting consumers through restrictive agreements and/or their domination of markets, while on the other the Commission recognizes the need for Europe to possess large economic units able to achieve economies of scale and compete effectively in the rest of the world. Thus in recent years new regulations have been introduced that allow cross-frontier amalgamations enabling large firms to organize themselves on a Europe-wide basis, and many situations and practices have been exempted from the regulations. The current trend is towards interpreting Article 85 as covering *only* restrictions that have a significant effect on the market. Yet it remains unclear what precisely will and will not be allowed. The main factors considered appear to be the maintenance of freedom of choice for consumers, open market entry for businesses, access to distribution channels for all suppliers, and whether price levels will continue to be determined by market forces. Note that Article 85 does not apply to transactions between a parent company and its subsidiaries, which are all regarded as part of the same economic unit.

Position of small firms

Despite its concerns regarding dominant positions, the Commission has been extremely anxious to encourage cooperation among smaller firms in order to enable them to compete with bigger companies. Accordingly, the Commission does not regard certain types of agreement as violating Articles 85 and 86, notably the exchange of 'opinion or experience', joint research, or the joint provision of credit or collection of debts. Also the Commission has issued block exemptions covering small firms that enter into exclusive dealership, licensing, materials supply and certain other business arrangements.

A wide range of practices common among small firms could be caught by EU competition law. In particular, the licensing of intellectual property rights, franchising, joint ventures and exclusive dealership arrangements could all be regarded as unlawful. In recognition of the fact that cooperation between small firms will not distort competition appreciably, the Commission has issued a Notice on Minor Agreements exempting from Articles 85 and 86 all situations where: the goods or services covered by an agreement represent less than 5 per cent of the total market for these goods or services; and (additionally) the aggregate turnover of the parties to the agreement is less than a certain threshold (currently 200 million Euros). Even if these criteria are not satisfied the Commission may exempt agreements that:

1. contribute to improving the methods of producing or distributing goods or to the promotion of technical or economic progress; and
2. give consumers a fair share of resulting benefits; and
3. will not significantly reduce competition across the entire Single European Market.

Applications for exemption must be submitted to the Commission unless the following are involved, in which case an automatic bloc exemption applies and no formal application is needed (provided, of course, that points 1 to 3 above are met):

1. exclusive distribution or purchasing agreements;
2. patent and (unpatented) know-how licensing;
3. research and development agreements;
4. motor vehicle agreements;
5. franchising.

Larger firms engaging in restrictive agreements may apply for 'individual exemptions', which, if approved, must be registered with the Commission. Unfortunately the period taken to obtain an individual exemption (referred to as a 'negative clearance') is so long that, in order to avoid chaos within applicant businesses, the Commission is prepared to issue informal 'comfort letters', which express the view that (initially at least) the Commission can see no reason to intervene. In consequence, the firm cannot be fined during the period the matter is awaiting formal resolution.

Another device for relieving the Commission's administrative burdens is the 'opposition procedure' whereby, if an agreement that falls just partly outside a block exemption is *not* challenged by the Commission within six months of its notification, the agreement automatically becomes valid.

Public procurement

The public sector is an important customer for many European companies. Completion of the Single Market has been accompanied by the opening up of public sector contracts to competitive bidding by any EU firm, regardless of its geographical location. It is intended that within a few years, all public procurement will be subject to competitive tendering. Meanwhile, however, certain restrictions continue. At the time of writing, there are three types of tendering procedure (open, restricted and negotiated) available for use by EU public bodies. 'Open' tendering means that any company may enter a bid. 'Restricted' tendering requires bidding companies to satisfy certain pre-qualifications set by the purchaser (eg providing evidence of their technical expertise and/or financial standing) 'Negotiated' procedures relate to direct discussions between the purchaser and chosen suppliers, without any competition. This may only occur:

- if no tenders have been received using the other procedures; or
- in consequence of the highly technical nature of the goods (eg the need for compatibility with existing stocks); or
- for reasons of extreme urgency.

Purchasers can be forced to justify a decision to use negotiated procedures to the European Commission. Only contracts with values exceeding certain thresholds are covered by the legislation.

Eastern European disintegration

Although the liberalization of the economies of the former Communist countries of Central and Eastern Europe has generated enormous commercial energy and demands for imported products, numerous problems remain for businesses wishing to sell in these markets. Key facts on the major countries in Eastern Europe (1998 figures) are provided in Tables 5.1 and 5.2.

Advantages to selling in Eastern Europe

On the positive side it is true to say that progress achieved towards privatization and modernization has been astounding, and that once the transition to a well-organized mixed economy is complete Eastern Europe will constitute one of the most attractive business environments in the world (Zanis and Semler, 1992). Business laws, rules and practices in Eastern European countries will soon be identical to those in the West, and it is easy to investigate markets first hand. Most Eastern European countries have extensive engineering industries capable of manufacturing virtually all categories of item (over a

Table 5.1 Eastern Europe: key demographic facts

Country	Population (millions)	Area (sq. km)	Density[1]	Capital city & population (millions)	Languages	Religions	Literacy[2] %	Life expectancy (M)	(F)
Albania	3.37	28.748	117	Tirana 0.3	Albanian Greek	70% Muslim	95.0	70	76
Bulgaria	8.5	100.994	80	Sofia 1.1	Bulgarian Turkish Macedonian	75% Eastern Orthodox 15% Muslim	94.0	68	75
Czech & Slovak Republics	10.3	78.900 49.000	131	Prague 1.26 Bratislava 0.44	Czech Slovak	Rom. Catholic Protestant	99.0	68 67	75 75
Estonia	1.55	45.100	34	Tallinn 0.44	Estonian Russian	Protestant	99.0	65	75
Hungary	10.3	93.031	111	Budapest 2.1	Magyar German	Rom. Catholic Protestant	99.0	65	74
Latvia	2.59	64.589	40	Riga 0.87	Latvian	Protestant Lutheran	99.0	65	74
Lithuania	3.75	65.200	58	Vilnius 0.58	Lithuanian (2 forms) Russian	Rom. Catholic	99.0	67	76
Poland	38.5	312.683	124	Warsaw 1.7	Polish German	95% Roman Catholic	99.0	67	76
Romania	22.8	237.500	99	Bucharest 2.3	Romanian Hungarian Greek	95% Greek Othodox	96.9	67	73
Russian Federation	148.5	17.075.400	9	Moscow 9	Russian	Russian Orthodox	98.7	62	74
Ukraine	52.1	603.700	86	Kiev 3	Ukranian Russian	Russian Orthodox	95.0	64	74

1. Density – number of people per square kilometre
2. Literacy – percentage of adults able to read in the main native language.

quarter of all output in Hungary, Poland, Russia and the Czech and Slovak Republics consists of manufactured goods), and the local availability of such items greatly enhances the possibilities for barter trade (Engholm, 1993). Free ports and free trade zones now exist in Bulgaria, Hungary, the Czech Republic, Romania, Belarus, Estonia and the Ukraine.

Problems involved in selling in Eastern Europe

Economic problems in Eastern Europe, however, are huge. Unemployment rocketed as grossly inefficient enterprises closed down; inflation soared as cheap sources of energy

Table 5.2 Eastern Europe: key economic facts

Country	GDP per capita ($US)	Main industries	Main exports	Main imports	Main suppliers	Main customers
Albania	790	Chromium, copper, nickel, pyrites, oil, agriculture	Chrome, copper wire, ferro-nickel ore, bitumen, oil, hydroelectricity	Chemicals, machinery, textiles, vehicles, lubricants, consumer goods	Former Yugoslavia Greece Bulgaria China Czech and Slovak Republics	Former Yugoslavia Greece Bulgaria China France Hungary
Bulgaria	1,555	Agriculture, engineering, chemicals, metals, biotechnology	Minerals, fuels & chemicals, agriculture & food products, machinery & equipment	Minerals, fuels & chemicals, machinery & equipment, agriculture & food	CIS Germany Italy Greece	CIS Turkey Germany Macedonia Greece
Czech & Slovak Republics	2,732 1,896	Metal products & machinery	Manufactured goods, machinery & industrial equipment, chemicals, food products	Machinery & industrial equipment, chemicals & products, raw materials, agricultural products & foodstuffs	CIS Germany EU Other Eastern Europe	Germany CIS EU Other Eastern Europe
Estonia	3,034	Wood, leather, fur, oil, electrical & electronic components	Textiles, timber, shipping, food, furniture, fertilizers	Raw materials, machinery & metalworking, chemicals & products, light industry, food	CIS Finland Sweden Netherlands Germany	CIS Finland Sweden Netherlands Germany
Hungary	3,332	Telecommun-ications, mining, agriculture, pharmaceuticals, fertilizers	Raw materials, consumer goods, food products, capital equipment, fuels & electricity	Raw materials, capital equipment, consumer goods, fuel & electricity, food products	CIS Germany EU Eastern Europe	Germany CIS EU Eastern Europe
Latvia	2,030	Vehicles & railway equipment, timber, fertilizers, light machinery	Electrical energy, rolled steel, mineral fertilizers, varnishes & paints, railway passenger cars, buses	Electricity, fuel oil, natural gas, liquefied natural gas, coal	Russia Ukraine Other Eastern Europe	Russia Ukraine Other Eastern Europe EU
Lithuania	1,304	Electrical goods, optical goods, food processing, fishing, farming	Machinery & metal working, light industry, chemicals & products, food	Fuel & energy, chemicals & products, oil & gas, food	CIS Other Eastern Europe EU	CIS Other Eastern Europe EU
Poland	2,271	Shipbuilding, textiles, steel, cement, chemicals, livestock	Machinery, chemicals, food & agricultural products, copper, steel	Machinery, chemicals, oil, food & agricultural products, light industry, metals	Germany Ex-Soviet Union Italy UK, USA Netherlands France	Germany Netherlands Ex-Soviet Union Italy, UK France USA

continued overleaf

Table 5.2 continued

Country	GDP per capita ($US)	Main industries	Main exports	Main imports	Main suppliers	Main customers
Romania	1,117	Agriculture, livestock, industrial equipment, natural gas, oil & products	Basic metals & products, textiles & footwear, machinery & equipment, oil products	Fuels, minerals & metals, machinery & equipment, food products, chemicals	Germany Russia Italy France Iran	Germany China Italy Turkey Netherlands France
Russia	2,346	Energy, oil & natural gas, minerals, timber, paper & cellulose, fish & fish products	Fuels & raw materials, machinery & equipment chemicals & rubber, timber & paper, food	Machinery & equipment, food products, textiles, fuels & raw materials, chemicals & rubber	Germany Bulgaria Czech Republic Poland Hungary	Germany Poland Czech & Slovak Republics Hungary Bulgaria Cuba
Ukraine	1,912	Agriculture, minerals	Machinery & metalworking, ferrous metallurgy, food, chemicals & products, light industry	Machinery & metal working, light industry, chemicals & products, food industry, oil & gas	Germany Poland Ex-Czecho-slovakia Other EU Other Eastern Europe	Other EU Germany Bulgaria Ex-Czecho-slovakia Other Eastern Europe

and raw materials disappeared; governments were compelled to implement economic austerity measures, including severe cutbacks in welfare subsidies. This led to consumers' inability to finance desired purchases and to increasingly uneven distributions of incomes.

Exports to Western markets have been low, causing chronic shortages of the foreign exchange necessary to pay for imported goods. Devaluation of local currencies is commonplace. These devaluations increase the prices of imports, including imports of much needed capital equipment. Foreign firms have to compete against state-owned local enterprises that continue to receive massive government subsidies. And Western companies establishing a permanent presence in East European countries complain that working methods in many industries are so out of date that employees' attitudes may have been adversely affected, leading perhaps to an unwillingness to accept the latest business techniques. In Poland and Romania, foreign companies may dismiss workers in manners analogous to those used in the West. Elsewhere, however, local rules on labour lay-offs apply, and can make dismissal procedures extremely problematic. Further difficulties include:

- Underdevelopment of East European commercial banking systems (with the consequence that many consumers do not use cheques).
- Delays and frustrations arising from having to deal with numerous (well-meaning) state officials who do not possess the authority to take significant decisions.

- The fact that English (the international language of business) is not as widely spoken in Eastern Europe as in the West.
- Lack of formal business procedures. These countries have yet to develop proper legal frameworks for consumer and employee protection, contract, business insolvency, etc, within a private enterprise system.
- Absence of the cost and financial accounting procedures commonplace in Western businesses.

Some of the major advantages and problems associated with doing business in Eastern Europe are summarized in Table 5.3.

Eastern European markets

Central and Eastern Europe has a population of 400 million (including the former USSR) and there is excess demand for nearly every type of product. Consumers are well educated and as such are responsive to advertising and other promotional campaigns. Literacy levels are among the highest in the world, and many workers possess top-class industrial skills. The region has 100 million households and purchases a wide variety of imported goods. Major consumer import markets have arisen for food items (consequent

Table 5.3   Doing business in Eastern Europe

Advantages	Problems
• Large population • Unsatisfied demand • Numerous opportunities for counter-trade • Need for imports of capital goods for infrastructure improvement • Enthusiasm for business and trade • Highly skilled and educated workforce • Low-cost labour • Extensive natural resources • Much technological know-how in certain industrial sectors • Potential for rapid economic growth • Absence of competing firms in many sectors • Desires to pursue Western lifestyle • Numerous market niches • Commitment to introducing currency convertibility in the long term • Minimal restrictions on joint ventures or licensing systems • Eastern European governments are genuinely committed to reform	• Political instability and uncertainty • Falling national income in some countries • High levels of inflation • Shortages of foreign exchange • Lack of market data • Lack of business services (market research agencies, management consultancies, etc) • May be difficult for Western exporters to obtain payments insurance • Confused business legal systems • Inefficient distribution systems • Environmental problems • Low incomes and high unemployment • Relatively few small- to medium-sized companies • High tariffs and quota restrictions against certain categories of imports • Lack of an experienced commercial banking system • Persistence of complex state bureaucracies and lack of managerial and commercial skills

to the removal of price controls and hence the uncompetitiveness of certain locally produced items), house and home improvement goods (resulting from the pressing need to renovate dilapidated housing), clothing and footwear, and computer hardware and software of all kinds. Sales of automotive products, video and other electronic equipment, toys and health care items are also increasing. Equipment for business and industrial modernization is in particularly heavy demand. The sale of automotive products is sure to increase sharply as road systems improve.

An important characteristic of Eastern European consumers is that most of them live in cities and have a lifestyle essentially similar to urban dwellers in the West, although rates of ownership of consumer goods and other household items are well below those for advanced Western states. There is internal currency convertibility in most Eastern European countries. The Eastern European consumer is familiar with Western products, advertisements and selling methods and wishes to purchase Western exports. Unfortunately, wages are low (on average barely 10 per cent of Western European and US levels, but rising in the newly established private sectors), so that consumers do not have the cash to satisfy their requirements. The population of Eastern European countries is generally younger than in the West, and there are some large rural populations, eg 40 per cent of the total population of Poland and Hungary live in rural areas (compared to 12 per cent in the United Kingdom).

An essential feature of Eastern Europe is its ethnic diversity. There are substantial numbers of people of German descent living in Poland, Romania and Russia. Bulgaria has a large Turkish minority; there are Russians and Hungarians in Romania, Croats in Hungary, Poles in Russia, Ukrainians in the Slovak Republic, and so on. Often, diverse local cultures and languages coexist within the same national frontiers. This gives rise to the need for extensive research into national markets. The problem is that market research data and facilities are extremely limited in these countries.

Entry barriers

Import tariffs are generally high, and many Eastern European countries apply protectionist foreign policies. Tariff rates very enormously between Eastern European countries and among product groups, and rates themselves are subject to sudden and unpredictable alteration. Quota and import licensing systems are common. Tariff rates will fall in consequence of the conclusion of the Uruguay Round of the GATT negotiations, and through the Association Agreements that have been signed between the EU and certain Eastern European countries. These Association Agreements (also known as Europe Agreements) provide for reciprocal trade concessions between the EU and relevant states, plus the setting up of a legal framework for political dialogue among the parties. EU Association Agreements with Poland, Hungary and the Czech and Slovak Republics became effective on 1 May 1992; an Association Agreement with Romania was implemented on 1 May 1993 and with Bulgaria on 1 July 1993. At the time of writing four other countries (Estonia, Latvia, Lithuania and Slovenia) were negotiating Association Agreements. Quotas on many Eastern European goods entering the EU have been abolished and EU import tariffs greatly reduced. The Central European Free Trade

Agreement countries have removed quotas and tariffs. Only goods with at least 60 per cent Eastern European local content will qualify for duty-free EU entry.

Success in Eastern European markets requires the adoption of a long-term view, as living standards in several Eastern European countries will almost certainly fall still further before they eventually begin to improve. Eastern Europe does most of its Western trading with Germany, Austria, Finland, the United States and Japan.

Advertising in Eastern Europe

Advertising agencies and consultancies serving Eastern Europe tend to be based in Austria or Germany rather than in the Eastern European countries they cover. Eastern Europeans react positively to advertising and direct marketing (DM) since, to them, they are relatively new and interesting phenomena. Television and press advertising are especially important (nearly all the populations of Eastern European countries have access to a television set). Note the overspill of Western TV stations (including satellite services) into Eastern European countries. Media space is cheap but there is minimal audience audit data, so that customer targeting is difficult. Response rates to direct mail promotions are high compared to Western countries (DM is still something of a novelty in Eastern Europe), but the technical difficulties associated with implementing DM campaigns are substantial. Compiled lists of DM prospects are few and far between and frequently unreliable. A major problem has been the extensive renaming of streets in Eastern European countries to remove names with Communist or certain other connotations.

Prospects for business in Eastern Europe

Privatization of industry lies at the heart of the process of economic liberalization, but is proving extremely difficult. Many of the firms offered for sale are simply not worth buying at any price, and face immediate closure. Others require drastic reorganization and labour redundancies to bring them up to scratch. Poland, Hungary and the Czech and Slovak Republics have adopted a 'big bang' approach to the transition process, with Russia (at the time of writing) following suit. For example, the former Czechoslovakia denationalized many state-run firms via a voucher system. Each resident could obtain a book of vouchers, the contents of which could be converted into shares in companies that were put up for auction. Shares were then traded on a stock exchange. Privatization has been severely hindered by disputes over the ownership of land and property nationalized in 1948.

Russia and Lithuania are implementing voucher systems on the Czech and Slovak model. Bulgaria and Romania have been more cautious in privatizing their economies than most other Eastern European states, preferring to encourage new start-ups of private businesses rather than the wholesale selling off of state-owned firms. Romania is privatizing 30 per cent of its industries by transferring their ownership to five investment trusts, which in turn will administer enterprises as joint stock companies. The remaining 70 per cent is to be available to international investors. Hungary has privatized enterprises by converting them into private limited companies, which were then offered for sale to the highest bidder. In Poland, management buyouts have been a common device for shifting enterprise ownership into private hands. Otherwise businesses have been handed over to local authorities, which then become responsible for their privatization.

The transition to a market economy has several dimensions: privatization, removal of price controls, abolition of state subsidies and industry control, the opening up of foreign trade and investment, making the local currency internally and externally convertible, and the establishment of business services and institutions (banks, insurance companies, stock exchanges, etc.) At best the recent reforms will improve the efficiency of enterprises and create economic growth in the longer period. At worst they will pauperize Eastern European countries, generate social discontent and exacerbate existing ethnic divisions. Poland, Hungary and the Czech Republic seem to have turned the corner in economic terms, but significant problems remain for all three countries. Unemployment is rising in the Czech Republic and will continue to do so as privatization is implemented. Russia stands at the crossroads between rapid business development and massive economic failure. The country is rich in natural and human resources and possesses a strong scientific and technical base. At the same time, Russia has the potential for political instability and could easily fragment into smaller units. There is mass unemployment, falling living standards, rampant inflation and accusations that government has lost control. Growth rates have differed substantially between, on the one hand, the countries of the former Soviet Union and, on the other, the 10 Central and Eastern European countries that have, or are in the process of negotiating, EU Association Agreements (see above). The latter have experienced strong positive growth (of around 5 per cent per annum on average) since 1995, sustained mostly by domestic demand. Exports from these countries are increasing, especially to each other. Within the former Soviet Union, conversely, economic activity was stagnant in the mid-1990s, and only turned significantly positive at the end of 1997. Ukraine suffered some of the most severe economic problems.

A number of Eastern European countries have stated their intention to apply for full membership of the European Union, although many factors militate against such an eventuality in the foreseeable future. Note in particular that all Eastern European countries depend heavily on agriculture and hence would immediately qualify for huge amounts of EU agricultural subsidies and support. It has been alleged, moreover, that the low wage cost of Eastern European enterprises could give them a competitive advantage against EU firms. Average per capita income of Bulgaria, Hungary, Poland, Romania and the Czech and Slovak Republics is about 12 per cent of the average for the EU 15, and just 60 per cent of the per capita GDP of Portugal – the Union's poorest member state. Extension of free movement of labour (a key principle of the European Union) to Eastern countries would almost certainly lead to large-scale migration of technically well-qualified workers from East to West, causing stresses and strains in both Eastern and Western European labour markets. At least 85 per cent of all workers in Poland and Hungary have completed some form of industrial training, a higher percentage than for any European Union country. Note how the combination of low wages and a highly skilled industrial workforce could lead to Western manufacturers locating just inside the Western borders of Eastern European countries, in order to serve Western European markets.

Note

In 2002, the EU countries were: Austria, Belgium, Denmark, Finland, France, Germany, Greece, Ireland, Italy, Luxembourg, the Netherlands, Portugal, Spain, Sweden and the United Kingdom. The European Fair Trade Association (EFTA) is now a network of 12 Fair Trade organizations in nine European countries, which import Fair Trade products from some 575 economically disadvantaged producer groups in Africa, Asia and Latin America. EFTA's members are based in Austria, Belgium, France, Germany, Italy, the Netherlands, Spain, Switzerland and the United Kingdom.

6

China, Asia Pacific, Japan and Oceania

CHINA

China is a vast country both in terms of its geographical area (9,571,300 square kilometres) and population (1.2 billion, which is almost a quarter of the population of the entire world). Shanghai, the country's largest city, has at least 7.5 million residents; Beijing (the capital) has about 10.9 million. The country comprises 23 provinces, five autonomous regions and three municipalities subject to central government control. Only 10 per cent of China is suitable for agriculture, yet the country is entirely self-sufficient in food. There are around 220 million households, with an estimated household size of 5.5 (very high by international standards). Although there is a single *official* language (Mandarin, of which there are several dialects), large numbers of southern Chinese people speak Cantonese, and there are six other widely spoken local languages. China is home to numerous religions. There are at least 100 million Buddhists, 20 million Muslims, at least 5 million Protestants (various denominations) and the same number of Roman Catholics. Confucianism and Taoism are the other main religions. Barely 75 per cent of the population is literate. Despite the best efforts of the Beijing government, China's population has expanded at an average 1.5 per cent per annum over the last 15 years. Twenty-seven per cent of the population are under 15 years of age, 6 per cent are over 65. Two-thirds of the population are employed on the land. China is the world's biggest producer of rice, a major producer of grain and cereals and is rich in mineral deposits. Three-quarters of China's industrial output is attributable to about 100,000 state-owned enterprises located in urban areas. Most of the remainder comes from 8 million rural collectives.

China began to introduce capitalist business methods in 1978, but made them subject to central government control. Each year the state authorities draw up a foreign trade plan which prioritizes imports of goods that cannot be produced at home in adequate quantity, and items required for key government projects. The privatization of certain state-run companies began in 1984, although Chinese industry continues to be overwhelmingly state-owned. Legal protection of intellectual property was introduced in 1988. During the late 1990s, following the handover of Hong Kong to the Communist government of China, considerable liberalization of Chinese industry has taken place, with business people coming in from Taiwan and Hong Kong to set up modern, capitalist-style enterprises. While many of these enterprises have been factories (taking advantage of the low labour costs in China), financial services firms have also entered the market, much to the consternation of the state-owned banks, which now have to compete.

According to the World Bank, virtually all China's recent economic growth has been concentrated in the private sector, especially in Guangdong Province (the per capita GDP of which the World Bank estimates to be well above the average for developing countries). China's economic reforms are proceeding without vast publicity, and are unlikely to be reversed. Note, however, that the country's extensive state welfare benefits would not be tenable in a privatized free enterprise system.

The 1980s saw unprecedented rates of economic growth (averaging 8 per cent annually – the second highest in the world after South Korea). This led to severe overheating of the economy, a short recession in the early 1990s, followed by a recovery that continues to the present day. Inflation averaged nearly 10 per cent per annum over the period 1987–91, but then fell to 3 per cent per annum in the early 1990s, rising to 14.8 per cent in 1995. Prospects for Guangdong are especially bright. Its Cantonese-speaking people have numerous business contacts outside China (in Singapore, for example); the province has one of the world's best natural harbours, cheap land and labour (less than a quarter of the costs in Hong Kong), and instant access to the extensive and sophisticated international trading and financial services facilities of Hong Kong.

The Chinese economy itself is enormous. Industry accounts for 41 per cent of Gross National Product, agriculture for 24 per cent. Major manufacturing industries include machinery and metal products (77 per cent of total manufacturing output), textiles and clothing (13 per cent) and agricultural equipment and food processing (10 per cent). Industrial output grew by an average 12.5 per cent per annum throughout the 1980s and early 1990s. China is not a trade-dependent country, accounting for less than 2 per cent of total world exports. Exports break down as follows: United States 21 per cent, Hong Kong 18 per cent, Japan 17 per cent, the remainder going to South Korea, Germany, the Netherlands, United Kingdom, Singapore and Taiwan (estimated figures for 2000). Principal exports are clothing and textiles, petroleum and agricultural products and telecommunications equipment. The main imports are of light industrial and metal products.

The Special Economic Zones

The Special Economic Zones (SEZs) have played a critical role in China's rapid economic development and are attracting the great bulk of foreign investments in the country. The first and most successful was established in 1979 in Shenzen in Guangdong Province, which borders Hong Kong. Guangdong itself has achieved levels of economic growth and development comparable to those of South Korea and Taiwan. Several more large SEZs were set up in the 1980s, including the entire island of Hainan. In 1984, the SEZs were supplemented by 14 Economic and Technical Department Zones (ETDZs) in towns and cities along China's coast. SEZs and ETDZs are essentially freezones, have very low tax rates for local businesses, and may accept any amount of foreign investment. The latter can supply goods or services, purchase land, operate electricity generation and telecommunications systems, and are generally allowed to conduct business without red tape. Each zone has a special regulatory authority to oversee joint venture agreements between foreigners and local firms, and special tax reductions are available for ventures exporting most of their output or introducing completely new technology. The experiment was highly successful and the economies of these regions prospered. Growth rates in the SEZs reached 20 per cent per annum, living standards on average rose well above those in the rest of China, and SEZ involvement in international trade increased substantially. This led to the setting-up of hundreds of small unofficial 'copycat' enterprise zones by city governments throughout China. These did well initially, but faltered during the recession of 1991/92 when most were closed down.

Foreign investment

Three-quarters of all foreign investment in China derives from companies owned by Chinese people based in Hong Kong, Taiwan, Singapore and other countries in the Pacific Rim. Typically the owners and managers of these businesses have family or historical links with the regions and cities in which they are investing, giving them an obvious advantage over Western firms. Note the extent of the overseas Chinese population: 7.5 million people of Chinese descent live in Indonesia, 5.8 million in Thailand, 5.5 million in Malaysia, 1.5 million in Burma and nearly 2 million in the United States. An estimated 6 million Chinese live in other countries outside China, ignoring Taiwan, Hong Kong and Singapore. Each year more than a million visitors a year travel to China from Taiwan, and despite continuing political differences, business between the two countries is booming. China is keen to attract foreign investment as this is seen as a means for:

- generating hard currency earnings;
- training the Chinese workforce in new methods; and
- generally accelerating the learning curve of Chinese business.

A number of Western firms have operated wholly owned subsidiaries in China for decades. Usually these firms are involved in buying local products (especially low-cost textiles, plastics and machine parts) and selling abroad. Otherwise joint ventures with state-owned Chinese enterprises are the primary means for doing business in the country. A recent development has been the entry of foreign firms to China's emerging marketing and business services industries; advertising agencies; law and accountancy firms, etc. Ventures involving technology transfer are especially welcome. Problems associated with establishing and running Chinese joint ventures include the following:

- Foreign investors are still required to obtain approval for their intended projects from the Chinese government authorities and to deal with the state bureaucracy. Registration procedures are complex, and it is sometimes alleged that the government officials dealing with foreign firms have ulterior political motives unrelated to business factors.
- Staff with business skills are difficult to obtain.
- A foreign venture's ability to supply local domestic markets is restricted.
- Enterprises must have foreign exchange incomes exceeding their local currency incomes.
- The government insists that Chinese law must apply to all joint venture agreements.

The Chinese market

The average Chinese household has an extremely low income (80 per cent of which is spent on food, clothing and accommodation), although living standards are improving. For example, in 1991 the average Chinese family consumed 20 per cent more grain, 200 per cent more seafood and pork, three times the number of eggs and four times the amount of poultry consumed in 1978. For every 1,000 urban Chinese households in 1978 there were 60 washing machines, nine televisions and two refrigerators. In 1991 the figures had increased to 800, 700 and 500 respectively (see Rafferty and Bird, 1993). Also the Chinese government is keen to modernize industry, creating many demands for advanced technology industrial goods.

China is a difficult market to enter, and a long-term view is required. Imports into China are subject to tight quota and licensing arrangements, and usually have to go through the state Foreign Trade Corporation (which takes care of all customs formalities). Chinese currency is convertible to Western currencies, but the Chinese government often introduces restrictions, and there is a permanent shortage of foreign exchange. Hence countertrade is often necessary to balance an export deal. Currently about 40 per cent of all exports to China are paid for at least in part in goods. Further characteristics of the Chinese market are as follows:

- Ancillary business services (advertising agencies for example) are few and far between, and usually foreign owned. There is widespread ignorance of commercial business methods among the general population.
- Outside the main cities, marketing in China is severely hampered by inadequate distribution systems. Only about a quarter of the rural population has access to imported consumer goods.
- Once a foothold in the market has been secured, demand is likely to be extremely high. The volume of orders may exceed the supplier's capacity to provide the goods (or willingness, given the uncertainties and payment difficulties likely to be encoun-

tered), leading to cancellation of all existing contracts by current buyers. In China, marketing is frequently supply driven, the problem being to distribute a restricted amount of goods to customers lucky enough to be able to purchase them.

- Selling prices need to be extremely low.
- There is a lack of uniform technical product standards upon which to base the design of products.
- It is extremely difficult to estimate consumer demand, as government statistics based on national economic plans are frequently inaccurate.
- Commercial laws were only drafted in the 1980s, and are frequently imprecise. Contracts and obligations often have to rely on trust and the goodwill of the parties rather than the legal enforceability of the government. Many business disputes are settled via conciliation, and a government body (the Beijing Conciliation Centre) exists to facilitate this. Contracts commonly provide for compulsory conciliation prior to the appointment of an arbitrator if conciliation fails.

Advertising

This can be undertaken via commercial television, newspapers and magazines, and posters. The main national newspapers are the *People's Daily* and *Guangming's Daily*. Many of China's provinces have their own newspapers with huge circulations. At the time of writing, Chinese TV and other media charged higher rates to foreign than to domestic advertisers. The major problem with advertising in China is the lack of information on consumer characteristics and preferences, so that it is not possible to segment consumer markets precisely and hence customize advertising messages to attract specific consumer groups. And despite its enormous size, China has fewer than 1,500 advertising agencies (see Besher, 1991), plus around 10,000 media companies with advertising departments that offer services to client firms. It is common for advertisers to deal directly with media firms rather than with agencies.

ASIA PACIFIC

The Pacific Ocean touches so many countries, including all of Oceania, Southern Asia, China, the West Coast of the United States and, of course, Japan. This section, however, briefly considers markets and business conditions in 'the four dragons' of Hong Kong, Singapore, South Korea and Taiwan, and in the currently emerging industrial countries of Indonesia, Malaysia, the Philippines and Thailand, plus Vietnam.

Rates of economic growth attained by these places (excluding Vietnam) were without parallel anywhere else in the world until the late 1990s, when a major economic collapse occurred throughout the region. During the early part of the 21st century growth rates began to rise again, and it seems likely that these 'tiger' economies will return to rapid growth.

High rates of economic growth are perhaps the only common features uniting places on the Pacific Rim. Otherwise they exhibit a variety of characteristics. Political systems range from democracy through monarchies to single-party states. Some places practise genuine free trade; others are highly protectionist. Living standards vary enormously. A few areas on the Pacific Rim have vast natural resources; some depend on trading and manufacture. Dozens of languages are spoken in the region and there are many religions. Further notable features of the region are as follows:

- High rates of inflation are seemingly endemic in many places on the Pacific Rim, fuelled by high levels of demand created by 7 to 9 per cent annual GDP rates of growth. Governments have been committed to private-enterprise free-market economic principles and are reluctant therefore to apply deflationary economic measures intended to combat inflationary trends.
- On average, Pacific Rim consumers currently spend less of their income on health care than in Europe or North or South America. This is partly due to the younger population, but also the consequence of national preferences, as the proportion of income devoted to health care is higher in a number of regions that are poorer than the Asian Pacific Rim.
- According to United Nations statistics, the size of the industrial sector of the places in question has expanded enormously and now accounts for on average 35 per cent of national GDP. Agriculture, conversely, contributes just 12 per cent to the aggregate GDP, less than half the figure for 1970.
- There have been vast improvements in transport and communications in the (geographically huge) area.
- Beneficiaries from regional economic growth are spending their money on a wide range of imported consumer goods.

A significant consequence of increased government revenues has been a big increase in military spending in the Pacific region. There are (literally) several million armed soldiers in the area (2 million in Korea alone), a number of large navies, and sophisticated air forces. China's defence budget increased 50 per cent between 1988 and 1993, and the country has 3 million men under arms. Taiwan, Singapore, Malaysia and Japan are purchasing large amounts of modern and sophisticated weaponry (much of it from the countries of the former USSR) and there has been a proliferation of territorial disputes. This creates the potential for political instability, but also generates a huge market for defence-related goods.

The 'four dragons'

These comprise the former British colonies of Hong Kong and Singapore, which are essentially *trading* areas with a strong manufacturing base, and Taiwan and South Korea, which today are major industrial countries in their own right. All four are becoming important consumer markets, and their businesses increasingly invest in other Asian countries that possess lower labour and other costs. South Korea, Taiwan and Singapore have large numbers of well-trained technicians able to support their consumer electronics, electrical components and other sophisticated high-technology industries.

Hong Kong

Initially a trading port, Hong Kong has developed into a significant manufacturing territory, with about a quarter of its GDP deriving from industry (especially textiles, machinery, plastics and consumer electronics). Hong Kong was formerly a British colony, but was handed back to mainland China on 1 July 1997 for administrative purposes. However, the Hong Kong government still maintains complete control of almost all aspects of life in the colony, so that (in effect) Hong Kong is an independent state.

The Hong Kong government levies no import tariffs. However, domestic consumption taxes (referred to as duties in Hong Kong) are imposed on certain goods, such as tobacco (including cigarettes), alcoholic beverages, methyl alcohol and some fuels. These taxes are levied equally on local manufactures and imports. In addition, a steep tax, called a 'First Registration Tax,' which ranges from 40 to 60 per cent of the price, is levied on new car purchases.

The Hong Kong government imposes restrictions on the import and export of high-technology products, mirroring the control lists of the multilateral export control regimes (Wassenaar, MTCR, Australia Group). This includes restrictions on unlicensed re-exports to the People's Republic of China. Textiles are subject to import and export licensing because of Hong Kong's obligations under agreements with the United States and other countries. Hong Kong's export control system has not changed as a result of reversion to Chinese sovereignty. Additionally, Hong Kong's status with regard to access to controlled US technologies has not been altered as a result of reversion.

Business practices are Anglo-American in nature, open and highly competitive. The whole territory is, effectively, a free trade zone with very few controls on imports or exports. Today, Hong Kong workers are among the most productive in the world. Note, however, that many important companies exporting to Hong Kong chose not to establish a local office there, in view of the extremely high cost of premises and staff accommodation. The Territory is well endowed with agents and distributors able to act on a foreign company's behalf.

Most of Hong Kong's trade is with China, which takes 36 per cent of the Territory's exports and provides nearly one-third of its imports. Note, moreover, that about 80 per cent of Hong Kong's exported goods are in reality re-exports from China, and that much foreign investment in China is channelled through Hong Kong. Entrepreneurs based in the Territory are estimated to employ up to 3 million workers in Guangdong Province alone.

The return of Hong Kong to China has resulted in two major consequences: an exodus of manufacturing across the border to China's Guangdong Province (employment in Hong Kong manufacturing fell from 900,000 to 500,000 between 1988 and 1993), and a huge increase in the value of Hong Kong trade with the mainland. It is important, nevertheless, not to assume that Guangdong and Hong Kong are *culturally* the same. On average, Hong Kong consumers are no wealthier than many others in Guangdong, but their tastes are essentially Western, and they are totally familiar with the Western approach to sales promotion and the presentation of goods.

Singapore

Singapore's population is predominantly Chinese (78 per cent), with 14 per cent Malay and 6 per cent Indian. About 250,000 foreigners work in the country, mostly employed in low-wage jobs. Singaporeans have the second highest per capita income in Asia following Japan, and living standards are rising steadily. Singapore is the world's largest container port, is a major oil-refining centre and has extensive electronics, shipbuilding and pharmaceuticals industries. Five million tourists visit Singapore annually. There is full employment and a highly skilled workforce. The opening up of the Chinese market presents huge possibilities for this country. Note the extensive public investment that occurs in Singapore, and that state-owned companies account for a quarter of the country's GDP.

Companies that have goods to be imported into Singapore or exported from Singapore, whether commercial or non-commercial, are required to register with the Imports & Exports Office as an importer, exporter, common carrier or other. The I&E Office issues a Central Registration Number (CR No). The registration also applies to local companies/organizations. Companies can apply for registration through the Internet.

In per capita terms Singapore is one of the world's highest importing countries, and is a major hub of Pacific Rim communication and re-export transactions. It is a self-contained business centre with state-of-the-art facilities and ancillary business services: many joint venture and distributorship arrangements in neighbouring countries are organized from the territory. Business is conducted in the English language. A big problem for Singapore is its heavy dependence on external trade, especially with the United States, which takes 60 per cent of the country's exports and provides 40 per cent of all inward foreign investment. The country's exports typically exceed 150 per cent of its GDP, making it extremely vulnerable to foreign recessions. Singapore, moreover, is host to 3,000 foreign companies, which account for the majority of the country's exports. If these firms decide that Singapore is not the best place to locate their South-East Asian operations, then the country will face acute difficulties. The future of manufacturing in Singapore is likely to depend on the country's ability to foster high-tech industrial sectors. Industrial productivity growth rates have declined, while real wages have risen. Hence, Singapore's costs relative to other Pacific Rim areas have the potential to make its manufacturing businesses uncompetitive.

South Korea

South Korea has a population of about 48 million, 40 per cent of whom live in the country's four main industrial cities. This is due in part to land reforms, which forced large numbers of workers from agriculture to the cities, thus creating a large pool of low-wage labour. South Korea's drive for industrialization has made it one of the strongest newly industrialized countries on the Pacific Rim, with an average growth rate exceeding 6 per cent per annum since 1965: the financial crisis of 1997–99 proved to be a temporary setback, and growth during 2000 was estimated at 9 per cent. Unemployment is and has been low, at an estimated 4.1 per cent for 2000.

Note in particular that South Korea has experienced the highest rate of increase of per capita disposable income in the entire Pacific Rim over recent years, albeit from a relatively low base. Hence consumer spending is increasing and there are growing demands for imported goods, especially machinery and industrial equipment. Growing prosperity is reflected in the ownership of cellular telephones: the population of 47 million people owns 27 million mobile telephones. There are only 24 million landline telephones in the country.

The South Korean economy is one of the most open in the world, with a 75 per cent ratio of trade to national income. In the past, however, the country has tended towards protectionism, and despite recent tariff reductions and the phasing out of import quotas, non-tariff barriers are common. The latter include lengthy import clearance requirements, rules on product testing, package marking and declarations of origin, and general lack of transparency in the regulatory system. All imports require individual licences, which may only be obtained by registered traders. Tariffs on imported manufactured goods have been exceptionally heavy. Also, there is a ceiling on the share of a Stock Exchange listed South Korean company that may be owned by foreigners, foreign currency restrictions, and controls over South Korean companies' abilities to borrow overseas. The country is dominated by a small number of very large enterprises, the top 30 of which account for more than three-quarters of South Korea's GDP.

Reunification with the north will happen eventually, generating enormous market opportunities for southern businesses. Note, moreover, that South Korea's wage costs are the second highest in Asia (after Japan) and that reunification will provide southern industrialists with immediate access to an abundance of cheap northern labour.

Exports from South Korea go to the United States (20.5 per cent), Japan (11 per cent), China (9.5 per cent), Hong Kong (6.3 per cent), and Taiwan (4.4 per cent). Imports come from the United States (20.8 per cent), Japan (20.2 per cent), China (7.4 per cent), Saudi Arabia (4.7 per cent) and Australia (3.9 per cent). During 2000, exports were $172.6 billion, compared with imports of $160.5 billion.

South Korea has a young population: 21 per cent of the population is aged under 14, while only 7 per cent are aged over 65. This is a reflection of the relatively high fertility rate rather than a low life expectancy.

Taiwan

Taiwan is the world's twelfth largest trading country and has the twentieth biggest aggregate Gross Domestic Product. Manufacturing contributes 35 per cent of GDP, services 55 per cent. Wages are rising, causing the Taiwanese government to promote high-tech industrial developments for which wage costs are not such a critical factor. Export industries are also encouraged, with generous tax and credit incentives being offered to exporting businesses. Taiwan is perhaps one of the more difficult export markets to enter; tariffs are relatively high, and more than half of all import items are subject to licensing. Also the country is notorious as a haven for the production of counterfeit goods, and exporters to Taiwan must not be surprised if their products are quickly and illicitly copied by local enterprises.

One of the difficulties facing Taiwan is the country's dubious international status. For many years the Communist government of mainland China was not recognized internationally, and the Taiwanese were regarded as the government in exile of the whole of China. International recognition of China has left Taiwan with the dilemma of either seeking to join up with the mainland (presumably as a capitalist state) or of becoming an independent country. The current limbo in which Taiwan finds itself means that the country has signed up to very few international agreements, and is therefore a haven for polluting industries, counterfeit manufacturing and trading in endangered species.

Taiwanese exports are shifting away from the United States (which in the 1970s and 1980s took over half the country's exports and now takes only 23 per cent) towards mainland China. These exports go through Hong Kong, and amounted to $31 billion in 2000. China's Fujian Province is fast becoming a Taiwanese economic satellite as Taiwanese business people take advantage of the lower wages on the mainland. Indeed, the Taiwanese government is actively encouraging domestic and foreign companies to extend their operations to China's coastal provinces. Fears have been expressed within Taiwan that the strengthening business links between the two countries (Taiwan is populated predominantly by overseas Chinese) is leaving Taiwan highly vulnerable to a change in Chinese foreign policy, and that the country will have insufficient alternative markets if these links collapse.

The newly industrialized countries

Indonesia, Malaysia, the Philippines and Thailand have much lower per capita incomes than 'the four dragons' but, at the time of writing, higher rates of growth. Malaysia (the wealthiest of the four) has a per capita GDP a fifth that of Singapore. Indonesia's per capita GDP (which is the lowest of the group) is barely 7 per cent of the Singapore level. The four countries are major importers of industrial equipment, machinery and other capital goods in consequence of their wide-ranging industrialization programmes. Some of the heaviest demands are for telecommunications equipment, and computer hardware and software.

Exporters to these countries need to be aware of the possibility (indeed likelihood) of the local counterfeiting of brands. Indeed, critics have alleged that some of the intellectual property laws of these countries, especially in relation to computer software and pharmaceuticals, are so imprecise that the copying of certain items is actually encouraged. Note also how (at the time of writing) all four countries impose significant restrictions on the proportion of a quoted company's equity capital that may be owned by foreigners (49 per cent maximum, sometimes 40 per cent). Similar restrictions might apply to the ownership of real estate: foreigners are not allowed to buy real estate in Thailand, for example.

Indonesia

Indonesia faces severe economic problems, stemming from secessionist movements and the low level of security in the region, the lack of reliable legal recourse in contract disputes, corruption, weaknesses in the banking system, and strained relations with the IMF. Investor confidence will remain low and few new jobs will be created under these circumstances. Growth of 4.8 per cent in 2000 is not sustainable: it is only attributable to short-term factors, including high world oil prices, a surge in non-oil exports, and increased domestic demand for consumer durables.

Export partners are Japan (21 per cent), the United States (14 per cent), Singapore (10 per cent), South Korea (7 per cent), the Netherlands (3 per cent), Australia (3 per cent), Hong Kong, China and Taiwan (1999 estimates). Imports come from Japan (12 per cent), the United States (12 per cent), Singapore (10 per cent), Germany (6 per cent), Australia (6 per cent), South Korea (6 per cent), Taiwan and China (1999 estimates).

Indonesia's 16,000 islands stretch for 5,120 kilometres and contain over 300 ethnic groups, although most Indonesians are ethnic Malays. There is a single common language. The country has a huge population (194 million) but a low per capita income, making it a large potential market for low-cost basic consumer products. Eighty-seven per cent of Indonesians are nominally Muslims, and there are significant Buddhist, Hindu and Christian minorities. Several versions of Islam are practised, and the Hindu and Buddhist religions appear in a number of different forms. Four million Indonesians are of Chinese origin. The country is rich in oil and other natural resources, and is developing rapidly. Forty per cent of GDP derives from industry, 20 per cent from agriculture.

Indonesia has average wage costs 15 times lower than in South Korea and 20 times lower than in Japan. Against this, however, is the fact that the country's workforce is not well educated and generally unskilled. There are vast differences in lifestyle within the country, ranging from affluence in some of the major cities to subsistence village dwelling in Java and the itinerant jungle life of certain groups in Irian Jaya. Foreign investment is substantial (mainly from Japan, Taiwan, Singapore and South Korea) but focuses on labour-intensive low-skill assembly operations. The share of manufacturing in Indonesia's GDP is steadily increasing. Per capita incomes are growing, creating huge potential for consumer markets in this high-population country.

Problems confronting firms wishing to do business in Indonesia include transportation and communication difficulties, the cultural diversity of consumers and lack of commercial services. Tariffs are high, and there are limits on the foreign ownership of Indonesian enterprises. Also there is political unrest within the country, bad industrial relations at times, and occasional conflict between Muslims and Indonesia's Chinese residents.

Malaysia

Malaysia's GDP grew at 8.6 per cent in 2000, mainly on the strength of double-digit export growth and continued government fiscal stimulus. As an oil exporter, Malaysia also benefited from higher petroleum prices. Higher export revenues allowed the country to register a current account surplus, but foreign exchange reserves have been declining – from a peak of $34.5 billion in April 2000 to $29.7 billion by December – as foreign investors pulled money out of the country. An economic slowdown in key Western markets, especially the United States, and lower world demand for electronics products is likely to reduce this growth in GDP, according to private forecasters. Over the longer term, Malaysia's failure to make substantial progress on key reforms of the corporate and financial sectors clouds prospects for sustained growth and the return of critical foreign investment.

Malaysia's export markets are as follows: the United States (21 per cent), Singapore (18 per cent), Japan (13 per cent), Hong Kong (5 per cent), the Netherlands (4 per cent), Taiwan (4 per cent) and Thailand (3 per cent) (2000 estimates). Malaysia's import partners are Japan (21 per cent), the United States (17 per cent), Singapore (14 per cent), Taiwan (6 per cent), South Korea (5 per cent), Thailand (4 per cent) and China (4 per cent) (2000 estimates).

Malaysia is ethnically diverse, with Malays forming a bare majority of the population. Thirty-five per cent of Malaysians are ethnic Chinese, 10 per cent are Indian. The province of Sabah has 50 ethnic groups, and a ruling party consisting mainly of Christians. Each ethnic group predominates in certain parts of the country. Eighty per cent of the population lives on the Malay Peninsula. The country is rich in natural resources. There is a national language (Bahasa Malay) but about half the population can speak and write English (the United Kingdom being the former colonial power).

Manufactured goods account for 30 per cent of GDP and 65 per cent of exports; there is virtually full employment and living standards are rising. Malaysia's government is committed to a policy of industrialization and there are many developing markets for industrial goods. This has involved big increases in government spending and hence in budget deficits. Problems facing firms wishing to do business in Malaysia include:

- lack of industrial infrastructure and general commercial services;
- the possibility of acute foreign exchange shortages as a consequence of the country's persistent balance of payments difficulties;
- political risk resulting from ethnic tensions, which have been the source of much instability over the years and are likely to continue.

Distribution within Malaysia is dominated by a handful of large (and mostly foreign-owned) trading companies that own retail and other outlets in Malaysian cities.

The Philippines

The Philippines has been one of Asia's economically less successful countries over recent decades (though it was once the most prosperous country in the region). Pressing problems include a huge foreign debt (the servicing of which takes a quarter of each year's export earnings), plus high levels of unemployment and inflation. Political instability, extensive regulations and poor business infrastructure have discouraged foreign investment, which in the 1980s and early 1990s was about half that of rival countries. The Philippines is the only South-East Asian country with a Christian majority (85 per cent of the population are Roman Catholic, the remainder mostly Muslims). English is the dominant language of business and government. American influence and culture is very pronounced in many aspects of life. Problems with doing business in the Philippines include high import tariffs, underdeveloped transport and distribution infrastructures, and much civil unrest, with frequent outbursts of fighting.

Thailand

Thailand has a diverse economy, with high growth in nearly all sectors. There is much new investment, including extensive public sector infrastructure development. Manufacturing is growing rapidly, especially in textiles, electronics, domestic appliances, footwear, toys and furniture. Three-quarters of the country's exports consist of manufactured items. Thailand's government is the least interventionist in the Pacific Rim, spending less than 15 per cent of annual Gross Domestic Product.

Ninety per cent of the population are ethnic Thais, the remainder mostly Chinese. Eighty per cent of the population live in rural areas. The distribution of income and wealth is extremely uneven in this country, as are economic growth rates between regions. Bangkok, for example, has an average per capita income around eight times higher than in the north-east. Also the country's population is not particularly well educated: three-quarters of all Thais have received only a primary education. English is used for international business in the main cities, but not in other areas.

Thailand's international trade is being greatly facilitated by the completion of two deep-water docks around Bangkok plus associated container facilities. However, import tariffs are high and there are many quantitative restrictions on imports. A problem for Thailand is its heavy dependence on trade with the United States and Japan, making it extremely vulnerable to downturns in these markets.

Vietnam

At present Vietnam is a very poor country, but it has great potential for future development. It is self-sufficient in agriculture, has extremely cheap labour, abundant natural resources (including off-shore oil), and may well be poised to experience massive growth and industrial expansion. Despite political unification, North and South Vietnam are effectively two different economies. Most industry in the North is state-owned (although some attempts at privatization have been initiated) and is losing money, while private businesses persist in the South (especially in food production and retailing) and contribute much to state revenues. Trade with and inside Vietnam remains subject to bureaucratic regulations, and the country's commercial infrastructure is negligible. Northern provinces are pitifully poor and there is much regional rivalry.

Economic reform is under way: state-owned firms now have to fend for themselves, and prices are set by the market. Foreign investment is beginning to arrive from Taiwan, Japan, Hong Kong, France and Australia. Links with China (a long-standing adversary – China invaded Vietnam in 1979) are developing. Vietnam's biggest economic problem has been the US trade embargo, which greatly impeded the country's attempts to improve its war-damaged infrastructure. Other difficulties are an inadequate transport system and a workforce that is generally lacking in technical competencies.

JAPAN

Japan has a population of 126.8 million, about 18 per cent of whom are under 15 years of age. The population growth rate is modest and, in consequence, average age is rising. About 60 per cent of Japanese males aged 60–64 are in employment, as are around a third of those aged 65–69. There are 38 million households with an average household size of three persons. The latter figure is high for an industrially developed country, and due in large part to a general shortage of space for dwellings and hence the high cost of urban land. Housing is very expensive. Most Japanese people cannot afford to buy a house until they are in their early 40s. Despite this, the average size of Japanese households is decreasing and the number of single-person households increasing. There is a large and growing market for single-person household items: convenience foods, light furniture, small domestic appliances, etc. An important consequence of the housing shortage is that Japanese families frequently look for luxury consumption opportunities outside the home: cars, holidays in expensive hotels, and so on. Japan's population is well educated (hardly anyone leaves school until they are at least 18 years old) and there is an excellent health care system. The main religions are Shinto, Buddhism and Christianity in that order.

Apart from the four main islands of Japan, the country covers over 3,000 small islands and islets extending over 3,000 kilometres from north to south. Much of the terrain of the four large islands is mountainous, volcanic and subject to frequent earthquakes (especially around Tokyo). Population and industrial development are concentrated on the eastern coast, particularly in the conurbations around Osaka and Tokyo (population 12 million). A 900-kilometre coastal region running south-west from Tokyo contains half Japan's total population and 80 per cent of its manufacturing capacity. The population of provincial cities is growing, creating lucrative markets for consumer goods. Another trend is for more people to live on city outskirts, thus expanding the suburban consumer market.

Industry contributes about 42 per cent to GDP and employs a third of the workforce. All manufacturing sectors are to be found in Japan, plus a steel industry (dependent on imported iron ore) and shipbuilding. Japan plunged into recession in 1993, with the Japanese stock market falling to just 40 per cent of its all-time high during the year. The 1990s had started badly for this country, with several leading companies recording big losses (some for the first time ever) and domestic investment slowing down. Land prices in Tokyo fell by 20 per cent in the early 1990s. Nevertheless, trade surpluses continued and the country's export industries continued to do well. Note, however, that Japanese labour and other business costs are much higher than in other Asian countries, and that long-term prospects for the Japanese economy remain unclear.

Unemployment is rising, but Japan continues to be a low unemployment country by international standards. A quarter of the workforce is engaged in manufacturing (supplying over 10 per cent of all goods manufactured in the entire world); 7 per cent are employed in agriculture (the country is self-sufficient in food); the remainder are mainly involved in services. An important current trend is for fewer people to be engaged in primary industry and many more in high-technology light engineering and services. Automation is highly-developed: Japan has 410,000 of the world's 720,000 factory robots. More than a third of the workforce is female. Inflation has been low, recently averaging just under 2 per cent per annum.

The country's main export is motor vehicles, followed by office equipment, chemicals, iron and steel, and scientific equipment. Its major customer is the United States (which takes nearly 30 per cent of all Japanese exports), followed by South Korea, Taiwan and Hong Kong (which take around 6 per cent each). Japan has no indigenous oil, and energy is by far the highest-value import. Eighty per cent of energy needs are met by imported fuel. The second largest import category is foodstuffs and agricultural products, followed by chemical and textiles. Twenty-two per cent of Japan's imports come from the United States, followed by China, which takes 11 per cent, and South Korea and Taiwan, which provide around 4 per cent each of total imports.

Role of women

Only 30 per cent of Japanese university students are female, although women form a majority on lower-level higher education courses. Many young women begin work immediately they leave school and are expected by a large number of firms to resign as soon as they marry (typically in their late 20s) or have children. Prior to marriage the great majority of females live with their parents and have a high disposable income. Young women spend large amounts on clothing, leisure goods and travel. However, less than 30 per cent of women aged 20–29 own a car, compared with 65 per cent of males. About three-quarters of all Japanese women re-enter the workforce after they have had children; many work part-time. Japan's direct marketing industry may be expected to grow in line with the increase in the number of working women currently occurring within the country.

The Japanese market

The Japanese market is large and (despite the Asian financial collapse of the 1990s) prosperous. Per capita GDP is among the highest in the world and, importantly, Japanese consumers are today spending a bigger proportion of national income than ever before. Debt levels are growing, although the Japanese remain a frugal people compared to most others in the developed world. The yen is one of the strongest international currencies, so that imports are an attractive buy. Increasing affluence is reflected in a shift in spending patterns towards luxury consumer goods, high-tech products, fashion clothing, health care and financial services. The Japanese market is remarkably homogeneous, partly due to almost non-existent immigration.

Japanese people are educated in a similar manner, are influenced by the same media and have similar lifestyles – even in small towns. All socio-economic groups buy household goods in great quantity, except for the lowest-income families. Rates of ownership of particular consumer durables do not vary significantly between regions. Spending on clothing is also similar throughout Japan. Japanese households spend a larger percentage of their income on foodstuffs than in other developed countries (16 per cent compared with 13 per cent in, for example, the United States), as a consequence of high prices both for luxury and basic food items (this resulting from inefficient domestic food production and high tariffs on food imports).

Trends in consumer spending

High per capita GDP has enabled Japan's households to purchase large quantities of consumer durables and other domestic items to the extent that only the highest-quality and most original products are in demand. An interesting characteristic of Japanese consumers is their propensity to dispose of consumer durables faster than in the West, and not to purchase second-hand items. The biggest expansions of sales are in consumer services (insurance, legal services, investment advice, etc), fashion goods and designer items. Affluence is also creating demands for sports and leisure equipment, health and fitness facilities, cultural pursuits and related products, and educational materials. The Japanese government has announced its intention to reduce the male average working year to 1,800 hours (from its current 2,100 hours) by the end of the decade and to have a five-day working week for everyone. This will greatly increase the demand for leisure products. One of the problems facing Japan in this regard is the scarcity of land available for developing sports facilities: there is a total national ban on creating new golf courses, for example, which means that most of Japan's 7 million golfers are restricted to driving ranges.

Recent trends in the structure of Japanese imports suggest that major markets for imported goods are developing in the fields of computer software, telecommunications equipment, construction equipment and supplies, medical technology, fashion goods (especially clothing), and gourmet foods. Japan imports 60 per cent of its food and is the world's largest importer of food products. Note that international trade has always represented a smaller proportion of GDP (never more than 13 per cent) than for many competing countries.

Japan's total spending on advertising is second only to the United States. Television takes about 30 per cent of the aggregate adspend, followed by newspapers (25 per cent), magazines (6 per cent) and radio (5 per cent). Two Japanese agencies dominate the market: Deitsu, which accounts for a quarter of all national advertising expenditure; and Hakuhodo, which has a 10 per cent market share. All the multinational advertising agencies operate in Japan. Food and beverages are the most heavily advertised products, absorbing nearly a fifth of total spending. Services and leisure take 12 per cent, and retail outlets and cosmetics/toiletries 7 per cent. Advertising rates are generally expensive compared with other industrialized countries.

The 'silver' market

Japan has an unusual demographic structure in that it has large proportions in both the young and old age brackets relative to other countries. The country has the highest life expectancy in the world (77 for men and 83 for women), due perhaps to the Japanese lifestyle and diet. There are nearly 35 million people aged over 55, representing a large and lucrative 'silver market'. Note, moreover, that the number of Japanese citizens aged 65 or over is predicted to reach about 30 million by the year 2025. Characteristics of the Japanese silver market are that:

- Older Japanese people are relatively free-spending compared to the rest of the population, owing substantially to savings habits and the widespread operation of occupational pension schemes, resulting in very few Japanese senior citizens having to rely on their children for financial support (less than 3 per cent of those aged 65 or over according to the Japanese Statistical Bureau), although over half of them share premises with their children.
- Senior citizens are big spenders on travel and leisure goods (about 15 per cent of all foreign holidays taken by Japanese residents are taken by those aged over 65).
- Despite the stock market crashes of 1992 and 1997, the average level of savings of people over 55 continues to grow, creating a large market for financial services.

Problems of marketing to Japan

Specific problems attached to selling in Japan include the following:

- Japanese consumers are perhaps the most demanding in the world, expecting the highest standards of product quality and customer care.
- The bottom end of the import market (which is considerable in consequence of the uneven distribution of wealth within the country) is already saturated with low-price items from South Korea, Hong Kong and Taiwan.
- Business etiquette is highly formal and salespeople approaching Japanese buyers need to be fully knowledgeable about these matters: when to bow, the use of business cards, etc.
- Government procurement policies discriminate in favour of local Japanese suppliers, giving them scale economies and other competitive advantages in the local market.
- The country has domestic distribution systems that, critics allege, respond to Japanese suppliers' pressures to discriminate against non-Japanese goods.
- Certain mandatory technical standards exactly replicate the characteristics of whatever locally produced Japanese goods happen to be on the market. Items have to conform to these specialized Japanese standards rather than international norms.

For some products (notably pharmaceuticals) Japanese rules insist that safety tests be completed within Japan prior to their being marketed, even though the items have already satisfied the more rigorous foreign safety standards. Hence extra money has to be spent on replicating previous tests within Japanese territory. Not only must pharmaceutical products developed and tested on patients in other (reputable) countries be retested in Japan, but also the *pre-clinical* tests have to be repeated (eg the initial experiments undertaken on animals). The basic technical standard required of items selling in Japan is the JIS (Japan Industrial Standard), which lays down minimum quality levels (themselves updated every five years) for various products and provides certification for goods that satisfy JIS specifications. Certification (which usually takes from three to six months) enables the supplying firm to mark its output to this effect. Foreign firms may be certificated, and will usually increase their sales as a result.

Japanese companies' success in world markets can be attributed to their ability to supply high-quality goods at reasonable prices and their mastery of physical distribution and of distribution channels. Note how Japanese goods are sold throughout the Pacific Islands, Central Africa and parts of inland Latin America considered remote and inaccessible by many European and US firms. This success in international markets has led, perhaps inevitably, to frictions between Japan and its trading partners, some of which allege that the pattern of trade is too much in Japan's favour. The country's balance of payments surpluses have been massive, causing acute foreign exchange difficulties for some other parts of the world. Japan was a highly protectionist country in the 1950s and 1960s. Its industries sheltered behind high external tariffs and received much direct government support. Further devices encompassed the provision of tax rebates, investment incentives, etc, to carefully targeted Japanese companies, and making available to these firms the results of publicly funded research and technical development. Over the years tariffs have fallen to quite low levels compared to many other trading countries (lower than corresponding tariffs in the United States in many instances), but non-tariff barriers allegedly continue, including:

- Complex safety testing procedures, with the need to test excessively large samples under excessively arduous conditions. Pre-shipment testing was not allowed for many products: testing had to be completed in Japan and the shortage of qualified inspectors led to long delays in the testing process.
- The practice of giving product safety acceptance certificates to local Japanese agents rather than to foreign manufacturers, so that if the latter changed their agents the entire testing process had to be repeated.
- Modification of product standards at very short notice.
- The issuing of guidelines on product standards to Japanese firms but not to foreigners; and then insisting that the latter meet exactly the same conditions.
- Customs officers refusing to give reasons for rejecting the import of specific consignments.

A further cause of complaint by foreign companies attempting to enter the Japanese market is the extent to which large Japanese firms collaborate in a manner that would create difficulties under the monopoly and competition laws of many other countries. Groupings of firms (called *keiretsu*) occur via financial links, sharing common suppliers or through joint control of distribution outlets. These *keiretsu* exert a powerful influence on the Japanese economy. Arguably it would be easier to export to Japan if there were a bigger number of genuinely independent buying firms. Within a *keiretsu* there will be dominant companies, with material supplies and services being exchanged within the group. The system is supplemented by extensive and close-knit subcontracting networks. Arguably the members of a *keiretsu* do too much business with each other and not enough with the outside world.

Another criticism is that the share of consumer goods in total imports is significantly lower for Japan than for other industrialized countries, meaning that many imports are in fact capital items that help Japan increase its exports still further. A major international political problem now facing the Japanese government is that the country's manufacturing capacity has been built up to such a high level that any fall in domestic demand will (apart from reducing imports) cause Japanese firms to attack foreign markets even more aggressively – leading to further embarrassment in relations with deficit countries.

Intellectual property

A simple and inexpensive trade mark registration scheme operates, and it is wise to register trade marks in order to obtain legal protection. Evidence of prior use of a trade mark does not confer legal rights. Trade mark registrations last for 10 years, but are renewable at the end of each period. Trade marks similar to the original should also be registered in order to prevent imitation. The procedure for patenting an invention is more complex and can be costly. Note, moreover, that Japanese patent systems have the *opposite* purpose to those of many other countries, seeking to spread technological know-how rather than protect it. All patent applications are immediately made public, and the adjudication process is long and bureaucratic. Examination of the patent application typically occurs about 18 months after the filing date, although it can take a staggering four to six years. During this period, anyone can inspect the application and perhaps copy the invention, making marginal alterations in order to keep within the law. Hence it is wise simultaneously to lodge applications for a variety of similar inventions so as to make imitations difficult. Patent applications that are not from Japanese residents have to be made through a local patent attorney. The patent period is 15 or 20 years from the time the application was first registered, depending on the type of product. These lax rules on intellectual property have been a source of criticism by foreign companies for many years. Note, however, that domestic Japanese firms also suffer from the system, with many local enterprises experiencing patent violation.

The import promotion scheme

International pressure on Japan to reduce its trade surplus has caused the country's government to encourage imports in certain sectors. 'Buy foreign' campaigns have been initiated among both industrial buyers and final consumers, and import missions and trade fairs have been organized to help foreigners enter the market. In 1989, the government imposed a special consumption tax intended to discriminate in favour of foreign imported luxury products (including furniture, jewellery and high-performance motor vehicles). It also encouraged local agents to handle imports and requested exporters to purchase more foreign items. In 1990, the Japanese government introduced a package of measures intended to boost the import of manufactured goods, including the abolition of tariffs on imported machinery and several hundred other types of product, plus 10 per cent corporation tax credits for firms increasing the value of their imports of manufactures by more than 10 per cent per year. Wholesalers and retailers were permitted to create tax-free reserves set aside for the development of markets for manufactured items. Low-interest loans were offered to importing firms. The subsidies were substantial and covered a wide range of product categories (especially machinery and high-tech items).

An Office of Trade ombudsman was appointed to investigate complaints of unfair discrimination against imported products. Cases can be initiated via foreign chambers of commerce or made direct to the Japan External Trade Organization (JETRO), which has over 80 offices in 60 countries around the world. JETRO publishes a variety of booklets on such matters as using Japanese distribution systems, contact points for business partners within the country, product sector reports and (importantly) the addresses and details of Japanese wholesalers and large retailing companies. Exporters of manufactured goods can obtain similar but more specialized advice from the Japanese Manufactured Imports Promotion Organizer (MIPRO). Further import promotion measures introduced in 1993 include a large increase in the budget of JETRO (enabling it to set up more offices in other countries), the provision of loan guarantees to importers and the establishment of 10 Foreign Access Zones near to ports and airports set up in order to facilitate the entry of imports. Local firms providing help to foreign suppliers using Foreign Access Zones qualify for subsidies and tax incentives. Zones themselves have bonded warehouses and processing facilities.

Doing business in Japan

Foreigners can open branches, subsidiaries or 'representative offices' in Japan at will, and may purchase land and buildings. Branches must be registered with the appropriate District Legal Affairs Bureau and a Japanese resident appointed as branch representative. Representative offices do not have to register but cannot engage directly in manufacturing or other operational functions; rather they are restricted to supplying auxiliary services such as advertising, market research, information gathering, etc. Joint ventures with local Japanese firms are somewhat different from joint ventures in other countries. Japanese partners expect total commitment from the foreign firm and a long-term contractual relationship. Foreigners might be expected to accept low rates of return during the first years of the operation, and to exercise the same degree of quality assurance as the Japanese firm would demand of one of its own domestic suppliers, agents or distributors. Maximization of market share is invariably seen as more important than increasing the level of short-term profit.

Japan is not a litigious country. There is less than one-tenth the number of lawyers per 1,000 population in Japan than in the United States: this is largely because the Japanese legal system requires firms to make very large cash deposits with the courts in order to cover any settlements and legal fees. This makes litigation prohibitively expensive, and since the courts generally have long waiting lists of cases to decide, there is a strong bias against litigation.

Business is therefore conducted predominantly on the basis of trust rather than litigation, and contract law is far less strict than in the West. The country has a Civil Code, but this has little to say about business relationships other than when home selling or credit transactions are involved. There is a Fair Trade Commission that is empowered to impose fines on firms engaging in unfair business practices. Contracts are governed essentially by provisions agreed between the parties, and disputes are normally resolved without legal action. This 'custom and practice' approach to the regulations of commerce can lead to imprecision regarding the rights and duties of buyer and seller, and rules on agency are vague. Agents are perceived as long-term partners of the principal's business rather than as people engaged to supply ad hoc services. Agents normally operate on 10 per cent commission. Contracts can be terminated without indemnity provided a provision to this effect is written into the initial agreement.

Note how the Japanese tradition of lifetime employment with a single company means that Japanese executives undergo many horizontal transfers during their careers and acquire first-hand experience of several business functions. Hence a company's buying department will almost certainly be managed by people with extensive knowledge of marketing, production, company finance and general operations, as well as purchasing per se. Japanese company buyers, moreover, expect the same reliability, commitment and quality standards from foreign suppliers as is the norm among local Japanese firms.

The distribution system

Japan's distribution system is estimated to account for up to 20 per cent of the total labour force and to contribute 15 per cent to Gross National Product (see Shiotani, 1988). It is intensive (there are twice as many retailers per 1,000 population as in the United States), complex, costly and unwieldy, and arguably a barrier to entry to the Japanese market by foreign suppliers. There are several levels in the distribution chain, each link in the chain taking a substantial margin. Specific problems are that:

- Japanese buyers have taken the just-in-time philosophy to the extreme and demand a continuous flow of very small deliveries on short deadlines, thus preventing suppliers obtaining economies of scale from bulk transportation. Suppliers are expected to carry the costs of the stockholding needed to ensure prompt and full deliveries.
- Retailers routinely purchase on a 'sale or return' basis.
- Intermediaries charge higher commission to new suppliers (domestic or foreign) than to firms with which they have a long-standing relationship. This necessarily discriminates against would-be exporters to the market.
- Compared to other developed countries, a relatively high proportion of distribution outlets are partially or wholly owned by suppliers.

A number of reasons explain the diverse nature of Japanese distribution methods:

- Prior to industrialization Japan was governed through a large number of small and essentially self-contained provinces, each with its own peculiar business system. Firms wishing to trade across the entire country had to set up separate distribution networks in each area.
- Many Japanese men retire at 55 and are paid a substantial lump sum rather than an ongoing pension. Opening a small retail outlet is a popular investment for such people.
- There is obvious consumer demand for a large number of small retail stores.
- The layout and architecture of Japanese cities sometimes prevents the construction of large integrated retail units.

The *sogo shosha*

Giant trading houses (*sogo shoshas*) have assumed critical importance for Japanese foreign trade. They have offices throughout the world (Marubeni alone has over 150) and deal in a huge variety of products, providing economies of scale that enable them to offer to suppliers extremely low commissions. A trading house will lend money to foreign exporters in exchange for agency rights, and will also lend to importing customers. *Sogo shoshas* developed in the early years of the post-Second World War period, when Japanese businesses needed to export but possessed little knowledge of foreign markets or export procedures, gradually extending their roles from that of simple intermediary to one of direct involvement with exporting firms. Current activities include:

- joint ventures with foreign manufacturing companies and the international distribution of the latter's outputs;
- provision to smaller businesses of complete export management packages, including market research, finance, documentation, delivery and insurance;
- operations on foreign exchange and commodity futures markets;
- countertrade.

Use of a *sogo shosha* provides the exporter with a ready-made distribution system, accompanied by advice on market trends and customer requirements. They deal with all aspects of import documentation, warehousing and internal transport, and are trusted by the Japanese buying public (thus enhancing the imported product's image in the local market). The nine biggest *sogo shoshas* handle no less than one-fifth of all Japanese domestic wholesale trade. Unfortunately, they are only interested in high-volume deals, and because they are so large and general will not provide a tailor-made marketing service for specific imported products. Other problems with selling via a *sogo shosha* are first that the supplier loses all control over product presentation and customer care, and secondly that the profit margins available to the exporting firm are lower. Also they might not have the specialist knowledge or even interest to promote a particular product effectively. Hence smaller and more specialized exporters may prefer the services of a *senmon shosha*, of which there are over 10,000. *Senmon shoshas* are better perhaps for specialized products that require expert knowledge of particular niche markets. However they have less financial resources than the *sogo shoshas*.

About 199 European international trading companies have offices in Japan, usually concerned with the importation of specialized products, especially capital equipment. They understand European as well as Japanese business methods and have intimate knowledge of Japanese distribution systems.

Other wholesale facilities

Apart from *sogo* and *senmon shoshas*, Japan has an extensive wholesale system, with very many establishments (15 per cent of which are located in Tokyo). There are nearly twice the number of wholesalers per 1,000 head of population than in the United States or

Western Europe, and on average they serve many more retailers. Half of all the country's wholesalers employ less than four workers. Ties between wholesaler, manufacturer and retailer are close and intricate. It follows that introducing a new product to the Japanese market can involve lengthy negotiations with a number of intermediaries in various parts of the country. The enormous size of the wholesale system provides the exporter with a wide choice of options, as there will be dozens if not hundreds of wholesalers competent to handle the product. Equally the use of wholesalers necessarily adds a further mark-up to the final selling price of items.

Retailing

The country has over 1 million retail outlets, ranging from large supermarkets and department stores to a multitude of one-person businesses. Japanese retailers expect prompt delivery, substantial assistance from suppliers in promoting the goods, and the option to return slow-moving items without permission. The latter practice emerged from the tradition of Japanese retail outlets being small and unable to keep unsold stock for long periods. Retailers carry few inventories as a result of the general lack of storage and warehousing facilities in the country. Warehouse rents are very high, so that most storage is done by wholesalers. The cost and difficulty of storage has led to demands for frequent delivery of small orders and hence great emphasis on the need for reliable suppliers. Wholesalers typically provide retailers with long credit periods (normally 120 days), and offer numerous ad hoc rebates and special discounts for large orders, cash payment and for retailers' participation in sales promotions and displays.

Japanese consumers visit small retail outlets frequently and buy small quantities of goods (especially fresh food, which often is purchased on a daily basis). Small shops account for half the total number of retail outlets but only a tenth of aggregate sales. Larger units invariably use the latest point-of-sale information technology for administering their operations. Japan has 10 per cent more retail outlets than the United States, despite having only half the population.

The continuing existence of so many small retail outlets is encouraged by Japanese law, which requires that all plans for new stores above a certain floor space be subject to approval by specially convened committees comprising representatives of consumers, local small- and medium-sized stores and the local chamber of commerce. An important development has been the establishment of stores offering attractively priced goods imported from other places on the Pacific Rim (notably South Korea and Taiwan). Chain stores import centrally and in bulk; smaller retailers increasingly belong to joint purchasing arrangements.

These long and complicated distribution channels result in the prices of imports rising by three to five times their FOB level (see Chapter 3) prior to their reaching the end consumer. Larger retailers often apply a 100 per cent mark-up. Although the same distribution rules apply to local as well as foreign businesses, critics sometimes allege that the system unfairly discriminates against imports by hoisting their selling prices way above the cost of manufacture. Obviously, the shorter the chain of distribution the better from the exporter's perspective.

OCEANIA

The name 'Oceania' is used here to describe the collection of countries comprising Australia, New Zealand and the Pacific islands of Melanesia, Micronesia and Polynesia. Oceania countries have experienced lower rates of growth than places on the Pacific Rim, but represent stable and well-developed markets. Business practices in most of Oceania are Anglo-American in nature. Oceania covers a vast geographical area, and distribution problems make direct marketing an attractive proposition for many categories of product. Direct shipment to customers from (say) Europe or North America might be prohibitively expensive and it is common for bulk shipments to be made to storage points at strategic locations followed by local posting of individual items. Direct marketing is particularly appropriate for countries with a single-language press (which is usually English). Printing and mailing can be undertaken within the Pacific Rim (Singapore and Malaysia, for example, have extensive facilities for these activities) and postage rates are low.

Australia

Australia comprises six states and one territory, each with its own government. The country was founded by European immigrants, and customer behaviour closely parallels European norms. New South Wales has a population of about 6 million. The Northern Territory in contrast has barely 160,000 people (of whom 73,300 live in Darwin, the capital) despite its enormous size. Queensland has a population of 3 million, South Australia has 1.5 million people, Victoria 4.4 million and Western Australia (which covers an area larger than all of Western Europe) 1.6 million. Not surprisingly for a country so large, air transport is a critically important means for transporting goods. Railways and main roads link all of Australia's major cities, and there are extensive urban road and rail services. Two consequences for business of Australia's immense size are the need to appoint different agents in different regions (or an agent with nationwide representation) and the advisability of shipping exports to several Australian ports, rather than to a single port followed by time-consuming and expensive transportation across the continent.

Most of the Australian population live on the east and south-east coasts of the country. Sixty per cent of Australians have British ancestry, although since the early 1970s about half of all new immigrants have come from Asia. Australians increasingly think of themselves as belonging to an 'Asian' country. The majority of Australians are Protestants, although there is a substantial Catholic minority and all other major religions are represented in the country. Australia has vast natural resources and a diverse industrial base. Per capita GDP is comparable to that of Western European countries and is the second highest in Asia after Japan. Aboriginal rights are currently a major factor in Australian politics: the indigenous population has a far lower standard of living than the rest.

Australia is the world's largest exporter of wool, beef, coal and a number of important minerals. Three-quarters of the working population are engaged in services, which contribute 60 per cent of the country's Gross Domestic Product. Real GDP grew steadily during the 1980s, averaging just under 3 per cent per annum (higher in the later years of the decade). However, the economy then contracted between 1991 and 1995, while unemployment and foreign debt rose. A general problem with doing business in Australia is the country's tendency to experience large swings in its economic fortunes, as evidenced by big changes in inflation and rates of economic growth.

Tariffs currently average 10 to 15 per cent, the highest of the world's developed countries, but low compared to most places on the Pacific Rim. Non-tariff barriers exist in relation to technical standards, testing requirements, labelling and certification. Prior to the conclusion of the Uruguay Round of the GATT negotiations, Australia imposed quotas against textiles, clothing and footwear, motor vehicles and any items from specified developing countries. These are now being phased out.

Australia's largest trading partner is Japan, which takes 24 per cent of the country's exports and supplies 18 per cent of its imports. The United States is the other country with which Australia conducts most of its import/export trade. Otherwise the European Union provides about 20 per cent of Australia's imports and takes around 12 per cent of the country's exports. New Zealand and China are increasingly important for Australia's foreign trade. Japanese businesses have made extensive investments in Australia, and now own many Australian firms. Like the United States, Australia is turning towards the Pacific Rim and is benefiting from the fast growth of economies in the Pacific area, notably through the sale of raw materials to industrialized areas on the Pacific Rim. The country entered a free trade agreement with New Zealand in 1992 and in 1993 put forward a plan for a regional Common Market of 15 Pacific states, including China, the United States, Japan, the 'four dragons' and the ASEAN countries.

New Zealand

New Zealand lies 1,930 kilometres from the south-east of Australia and comprises two main islands: North Island, which contains the country's capital (Wellington, population 331,100) plus the largest city, Auckland (952,600), and South Island, which contains one-third of New Zealand's 3.4 million population. The country also controls four Associated Territories in the South Pacific, including the Cook Islands. Eighty per cent of New Zealand's population are of European origin, 12 per cent are Maoris, 4 per cent are Pacific Islanders.

Most of New Zealand's foreign trade is with Australia, with which a free trade agreement came into operation in 1995. Australia takes about 20 per cent of all New Zealand's exports, and provides a fifth of the country's imports. Other major trading partners are Japan, the United States and the EU. Main imports into New Zealand are motor vehicles, plastic products, machinery and mineral fuels. Although New Zealand is an important *exporter* of agricultural products, agriculture employs less than 10 per cent of the country's labour force and contributes just 9 per cent to its GNP.

The New Zealand economy declined in the 1970s and early 1980s as traditional industries (especially textiles and agricultural equipment) faltered. This forced the New Zealand government to overhaul the country's extensive state sector, abolish domestic subsidies and generally liberalize internal trade. It appears that the measures were successful, and by the 1990s the rate of growth of GDP exceeded 3 per cent annually. Prospects for New Zealand are seemingly bright: there is evidence of significant export-led growth (notably through increased sales to China, Taiwan and South Korea), inflation has been virtually eliminated, and revenues from tourism have reached unprecedented levels. The country has much to gain from the Uruguay Round of the GATT negotiations as it is an efficient producer and exporter of a wide range of food products.

The Pacific Islands

These comprise nine independent political units, four self-governing colonies of other countries and eight dependencies of these countries. They range from large islands that are rich in natural resources (notably Fiji and Papua New Guinea) to tiny coral atolls with a sparse population. Most of the countries with their own government only became polit-ically independent within the past 40 years. The peoples of the area belong to three cultural groups: *Melanesian* (which includes most inhabitants of the Solomon Islands, Fiji, Papua New Guinea and Vanuatu), *Micronesian* (see below) and *Polynesian*. Population growth is rapid in all areas, placing great strains on economic and social infrastructures. Christianity (and localized versions of it) is the dominant religion throughout the region. Business opportunities in the Pacific Islands arise from increasing urbanization of the population (there is much migration to towns in all areas), and from 'Westernization' accompanied by growing demand for basic consumer goods. All the Pacific Islands are heavily dependent on imports. Foreign exchange is short, as most Islands' exports comprise basic commodities (coffee, sugar, etc) that frequently experience large price falls and changes in foreign demand. The region receives large amounts of foreign aid, typi-cally for infrastructure development. This generates significant demand for imports, but is liable to sudden withdrawal on political grounds, bearing in mind the overall instabil-ity of the area. There is huge potential for the development of tourism and associated industries. Also the Pacific Islands are benefiting enormously from the rapid economic growth currently occurring around the Pacific Rim, where raw materials from the Pacific Islands are used for shipping and transit purposes.

Living standards vary enormously from country to country. For example, Fiji (pop-ulation 775,000) has a per capita GDP nearly four times higher than the average for the poorer Islands (notably Tuvalu, Kiribati and the Solomons). Life expectancy in Fiji is about 70 years; in Papua New Guinea and some other areas it is just over 50. Essential characteristics of the region are as follows:

- **Cultural diversity**. Each island has its own unique features and history. Note that three-quarters of the Pacific Islanders live in rural areas with strong local cultural influences.
- **Political instability in some areas**. This includes ethnic conflict between indigenous peoples and the descendants of other ethnic groups brought in by Western powers during the period of colonial rule. In the 1980s violence flared in Fiji, Papua New Guinea, New Caledonia and Vanuatu.

- **Vast distances separating small centres of population**. The people of a single political entity can be spread over thousands of kilometres.
- **Inland transportation in the larger islands leaves much to be desired**. Even in Papua New Guinea (population 4 million), for example, dense forests and lack of roads cause communities to be self-contained and relatively isolated.
- **Linguistic diversity**. Melanesia has 1,200 languages; Micronesia and Polynesia have about 50 each. English and French are the official languages of government, but local communities use their own language.

Micronesia

This comprises the Marshall Islands, Palau, the Mariana Islands, the Federated States of Micronesia, Kiribati (a collection of 33 islands scattered across 3.2 million square kilometres of the Pacific but with an aggregate population of less than 350,000), the island of Nauru (population 10,500) and various United States Trust Territories. Collectively they occupy 20,125,000 square kilometres, though only 2,160 square kilometres is land. There are about 600 individual islands, of which only 65 are populated. The peoples of Micronesia speak any one of nine local languages (excluding English and Japanese). The main ethnic groups are Polynesians, Malayans and Melanesians; most inhabitants are Christian. Micronesians are engaged predominantly in subsistence agriculture. The essential problem for the development of industry and tourism in the area is the vast distances between individual islands and hence the high costs of transportation. The area has much potential for tourism, although the distances between centres obviously present a problem. Sixty per cent of visiting tourists are from the United States, a quarter from Japan.

Melanesia

Papua New Guinea consists of 600 islands spread over nearly 465,000 square kilometres, beginning about 160 kilometres north of Australia. The largest island (New Guinea) shares a border with Indonesia. Most of the 4 million population are Christian. Not surprisingly in such a geographically fragmented country, several hundred languages and dialects are spoken, with English as the language of government and Pidgin English as the main common tongue.

Most Papuans are engaged in subsistence agriculture, although industry and trade are developing rapidly in consequence of the discovery of valuable mineral deposits (including gold and copper) in certain islands. This economic expansion is creating new demands for both industrial and consumer goods. Australia supplies half the country's imports, followed by Japan, the United States and Singapore. Half the population is under 20 years of age. The population is widely dispersed across the country. Only 5 per cent of the country's surface area can be cultivated, the remainder consisting of rainforest and mountains. Agriculture contributes 20 per cent of GDP and employs 80 per cent of the workforce. The country exports oil and minerals and is forecast to become the world's second largest gold producer by 2010. Unfortunately the terrain is rugged and generally inaccessible, increasing the cost of resource extraction. Air transport is critically important for the transportation both of goods and of passengers. There are airports in all 20 of the country's main urban areas plus about 100 airstrips elsewhere.

Although Papua New Guinea has abundant natural resources, it does not possess the skilled labour necessary to exploit them. Hence most significant enterprises are foreign owned, a fact that sometimes leads to political disruption. The country is generally unstable, with occasional insurrections and regular fighting.

The Solomon Islands lie to the east of Papua New Guinea. Each island is very small (the largest is only 193 kilometres long) and has a population overwhelmingly dependent on subsistence agriculture. Wood products and tourism are the only significant industries. Most Solomon Islanders are Christian.

Vanuatu is a double chain of 80 islands stretching for about 900 kilometres to the southeast of the Solomons. French and English are widely spoken, plus Pidgin English. Most Vanuatuans are engaged in agriculture and fishing, although there is some light industry, and tourism is rapidly expanding. The bulk of the country's foreign trade is with France, Japan and Australia.

Fiji comprises 322 islands (105 of which are uninhabited) in the South Pacific about 3,000 kilometres west of Australia. Ninety per cent of Fiji's foreign earnings derive from tourism and the export of sugar. Most of the country's trade is with Australia, New Zealand, Japan and the United States. Fiji has many light industries (notably textiles, wood products and boat building). However, there is much ethnic strife within Fiji (in the past Fijian business has been dominated by the country's 50 per cent Asian population) and the state is politically unstable.

Polynesia

Polynesia is sparsely populated and extends westwards from American Samoa and the Cook Islands (administered by New Zealand) to the largely uninhabited British possession of the Pitcairns. The largest administrative unit in the area is French Polynesia, centred on Tahiti. French Polynesia is an integral part of the French Republic, governed by a French appointee. The territory covers 4,000 square kilometres, but has a population of less than a quarter of a million. It comprises 130 islands, notably the Windward and Leeward Islands, which contain Tahiti. Eighty per cent of French Polynesians are Christians: 55 per cent Protestant and 25 per cent Roman Catholic. Most inhabitants are engaged in agriculture. There is much potential for the development of tourism.

Western Samoa can also be included in the Polynesian group. This comprises nine islands, the largest of which covers 1,610 square kilometres. Most Western Samoans are engaged in subsistence agriculture, although the country's government is anxious to develop light industry and tourism. The country's main trading partners are New Zealand, Japan, Singapore and Fiji.

7

Third World countries

MARKETING IN THE THIRD WORLD

Another group of countries worthy of special attention is the 'Third World' of the poorest of the economically underdeveloped countries. Although the Third World is not a trading bloc as previously described, these countries do possess certain common characteristics with significant implications for international marketing and, in particular, the transnational standardization of campaigns.

What is the Third World?

The first problem is to define the meaning of the term 'Third World'. Initially it was used to distinguish the rest of the world from the 'First World' (Europe) and the 'New World' of North America. Today, however, it is generally used to describe those underdeveloped economies with the severest economic problems. The difference between 'underdeveloped' and 'developing' countries is itself important.

Less developed countries

According to the United Nations categorization, less developed countries are those that have a quarter to a third of their population engaged in agriculture, but which also possess a well-established industrial sector. Examples of developing countries on these criteria are Brazil, Algeria, Colombia, Turkey and Uruguay. There exist substantial industrial and consumer markets in these countries, with some sections of the population enjoying a high income and exhibiting all the characteristics of consumers in the more prosperous regions of the world. Developing countries can themselves be classified into two categories: richer and poorer. The former includes the oil-rich and newly industrialized countries plus some of the (relatively) wealthier Caribbean states. Poorer developing countries tend to be those with economies that depend on the export of a limited number of raw materials, causing them to be constantly short of the foreign exchange needed to import the capital equipment needed for diversification.

Underdeveloped countries

These range from countries possessing domestic industries that produce significant outputs of industrial and consumer goods, to subsistence economies with hardly any industries. Countries in the former category have an urban middle class, a national education system and an essentially literate population. Examples of such countries are Bolivia, Botswana, Jordan, Yemen and Senegal. Average incomes are low but rising, and there is a growing demand for consumer goods.

Subsistence economies, conversely, have populations that are predominantly engaged in agriculture, consuming most of their own production and exchanging any surplus for other goods. Literacy is low and unemployment in urban areas extremely high. Examples of subsistence economies are Afghanistan, Chad, Ethiopia, Nepal and Upper Volta.

The problems involved

Underdeveloped countries are trapped in a cycle of poverty (see Figure 7.1). They do not have industries capable of producing large amounts of goods, hence they have low living standards, low levels of exports, shortages of foreign exchange for purchasing imported industrial equipment, lack of consumer purchasing power, and (as a result) the absence of incentives for firms to invest in new industries. Extremely low per capita GDP is perhaps the dominant feature of what will subsequently be referred to as Third World countries. Further common characteristics are:

- basically agrarian economy, often with an industrial sector that operates quite independently of the economy as a whole;
- low to moderate rates of economic growth;
- rapid rates of increase in population;
- poor industrial infrastructure, widespread poverty, low life expectancy and high infant mortality;
- high unemployment combined with skills shortage and low rates of industrial productivity;
- low population density;
- remoteness of settlements.

Linguistic diversity is another factor in the make-up of many of the world's poorest states. Isolated regions may speak their own language, or perhaps an obscure dialect of the national language.

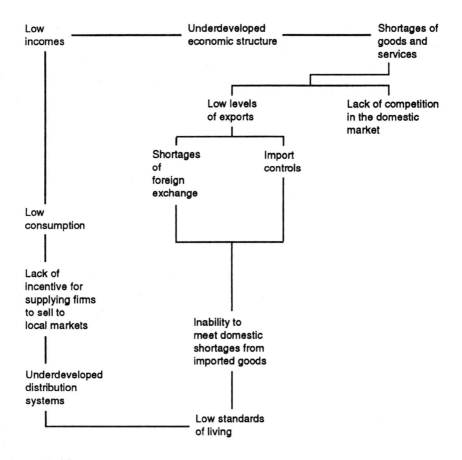

Figure 7.1 Problems of Third World countries

SELLING TO THE THIRD WORLD

Exporters to Third World countries want to supply goods that provide customers with maximum satisfaction and fully meet their requirements. However, customer purchases are severely constrained by low incomes, so that only a small range of low-cost items are purchased and customers are not able to demonstrate their preferences for product characteristics, styles, shapes, sizes and other selling points. In other words, consumers generate insufficient market information to enable suppliers to apply the marketing concept (see Chapter 1) in these countries. Underlying preferences are not revealed, and market research intended to uncover them is difficult to complete.

Many problems confront foreign businesses wishing to sell their products in Third World countries, as follows:

- End consumers will often be illiterate, and live in villages possessing minimal civic services (electricity, telecommunications, etc).
- Reliable marketing data are sparse because governments do not regard the establishment of national statistical services intended to collect and collate information useful for market analysis as a major national priority, being faced with pressing problems in other fields.
- Although there are widespread shortages of goods and hence a seller's market for many categories of items, demand is not matched by customers' ability to pay. How then should a company price its output in an extremely poor country?
- The enormity of the disparities in income, education and lifestyle found in the urban areas of Third World countries creates many difficulties for firms wishing to penetrate the several market segments they contain.
- Distribution channels are long and transport and warehousing systems frequently inadequate. An important consequence of long distribution channels is that exporters have to relinquish all control over final selling prices. Intermediaries' mark-ups fluctuate according to supply and demand and can be extremely high. Locally owned and controlled distribution enterprises run according to modern management methods are a single-generation phenomenon in many Third World countries. Hence, there are management skills shortages resulting in little delegation of authority and a handful of people taking all significant company decisions.

Distribution

Consumers in Third World countries tend to be geographically scattered and immobile, and to purchase in small units. Average household size is considerably larger than in developed countries, so that shopping trips involve purchases for many different family members.

The systems for distributing goods differ radically between richer and poorer areas. Urban dwellers have access to supermarkets and department stores; rural communities rely on small-scale general stores. Rural retailing is mainly non-specialist, with outlets supplying whatever goods are demanded and can be paid for by the local community at a particular moment in time. Specialized retailers are found only in towns with a large number of middle-class families. Towns have food markets with numerous individual market stalls alongside single-person permanent establishments. A number of Western companies have opted for personal selling as the primary means for marketing their products in the poorer Third World countries. Wages are low; individual sales people are often quite willing to travel by public transport (or even by bicycle) rather than requiring expensive company vehicles, and there is little scope for Western-style direct marketing.

Retailers in Third World countries are themselves served by import agents, national wholesalers, local wholesalers in towns and in rural areas, travelling sales vans and local food produce markets. These long chains of distribution result in part from the need to supply goods to large numbers of consumers dispersed over a wide geographical area. Wholesalers sell to retailers frequently and in small units. Import agents and larger wholesalers tend to be located around seaports and airports. Further characteristics of Third World retailing include the following:

- Extensive competition among small retailers but comparatively little competition among producing firms, owing to shortages of the capital and skilled labour needed to set up manufacturing businesses (whereas single-person outlets can be established at will). Also the governments of Third World countries sometimes directly control the activities of local manufacturing firms (via licensing, import regulations, etc) and restrict the local operations of foreign companies.
- High wastage of goods in storage due to inadequate facilities. Standards of local handling may be lower than in more economically developed countries.
- Transport is often poor and hence a limiting influence on the market areas of retail outlets, since the latter are dependent on customers who reside within a reasonable travelling distance. The worse the local transport system, the fewer the number of customers' shopping trips and the more difficult are deliveries made to customers from the retail outlet.
- The costs and difficulties created by the absence of economic infrastructures have meant there has been little incentive for distribution firms to develop large-scale retail marketing systems.

WHY SELL TO THE THIRD WORLD?

In view of these problems, why should exporters be interested in selling to the Third World? A number of reasons may be advanced:

- Firms prepared to seize the initiative and adopt long-term perspectives on Third World operations may well find that they face little local competition and (importantly) are able to tie up distribution systems in ways that would be unthinkable in developed countries.
- Many Third World countries export raw materials in exchange for imports of industrial equipment and finished goods. Demand for imports is growing and secure.
- Governments of Third World countries invariably express a desire to increase their rates of economic growth, as evidenced by large-scale public investment programmes (frequently financed by foreign aid from the rest of the world). This generates numerous opportunities for the export to these countries of industrial and agricultural equipment and other capital goods. Note that the release of foreign exchange to pay for imports is more likely the more closely the technology of the imported products complements the objectives of the government's economic development programmes as a whole.
- All Third World countries have at least one urban area with a small but prosperous middle class. The number of middle-income families in these countries is increasing annually.

- The modest stage of economic development of the Third World generates a large market for specific types of product in poor countries across the globe.
- Customers are generally less demanding than in developed countries, and might expect very little in the way of product promotion or development.

A problem that does arise, however, is that consumers are frequently unaware of the alternative products available and hence might be unable to evaluate the value for money of the item concerned. This could make consumers unwilling to purchase products the quality of which they cannot appraise.

Modifying the marketing mix

It may be appropriate to adapt a product or its manner of promotion (or both) to make it appeal to poorer and less literate consumers. Items might be simplified, instructions for use presented via pictures and symbols rather than words. Prices can be reduced through lowering the level of the quality of non-essential input components. Long geographical distances of customers from product repair and maintenance facilities can sometimes be dealt with by making products more robust and reliable, and by including spare parts for do-it-yourself repairs as an integral part of the product. Note the tendency of poorer Third World consumers to purchase non-food items less frequently than elsewhere.

Shopping (rather than advertising) is the primary source of information about goods in Third World states, with consumers typically seeking advice from peers prior to buying expensive consumer durables. Accordingly, conventional advertising activities can often be relegated to a subsidiary role. It is interesting to observe how advertising and other promotional methods in Third World countries typically comprise a mixture of primitive and basic techniques with the most up-to-date promotional devices. Thus local retailers might be using the most elemental 'hard-fact' information to advertise items, while customers are simultaneously receiving highly sophisticated advertising messages via radio or satellite TV. Overall, however, advertising is far more informative in poorer countries than elsewhere.

LATIN AMERICA

A quiet revolution has occurred in Latin America. During the 1970s and 1980s the area was characterized by strict state control over business, nationalized industries, trade barriers and currency inconvertibility, and the regular expropriation of foreign firms. All this has changed, however, and today there are wide-ranging privatization programmes, open markets, liberal trade policies, convertible currencies and extensive direct foreign investment. The region is far more politically stable under the democratic governments installed in the late 1980s than it ever was when ruled by military dictatorships; inflation rates are falling in many countries, and job prospects and economic growth rates are on the increase. Problems confronting the region include:

- Low per capita income, despite recent advances.
- Huge national debt, which result in large capital transfers out of the region and require deflationary government economic policies to reduce fiscal deficits.
- Unstable industrial relations in some countries.
- Political risk, not least because economic growth has yet to benefit large numbers of people. Expectations of improved living standards have risen in all sections of society, but the uneven distribution of income and wealth in Latin America means that mass poverty persists even while economies are expanding.

Positive features of the Latin America scene are that most of the region's major debtor countries have reached agreements with lenders to reduce and reschedule national debts, thus giving Central and South American governments room to manoeuvre when liberalizing and expanding their economies, and that protectionism is being abandoned throughout the area. Foreign investment is rising rapidly and substantially.

The International Monetary Fund predicts an average annual growth rate of about 3 per cent for Latin America, and it is not impossible that Latin America could take off and become the 'new Pacific Rim'. It is important to note that a large proportion of Latin America's middle and upper income groups (which account for a large proportion of total wealth) are concentrated in a handful of cities, creating geographically small local markets possessing tremendous purchasing power – ideal targets for high-priced consumer products.

South America

Argentina

Argentina benefits from rich natural resources, a highly literate population, an export-oriented agricultural sector, and a diversified industrial base. However, when President Carlos Menem took office in 1989, the country had piled up huge external debts, inflation had reached 200 per cent per month, and output was plummeting. To combat the economic crisis, the government embarked on a path of trade liberalization, deregulation, and privatization. In 1991, it implemented radical monetary reforms that pegged the peso to the US dollar and limited the growth in the monetary base by law to the growth in reserves. Inflation fell sharply in subsequent years, and in 2002 actually became negative. In 1995, the Mexican peso crisis produced capital flight, the loss of banking system deposits, and a severe but short-lived recession; a series of reforms to bolster the domestic banking system followed. Real GDP growth recovered strongly, reaching 8 per cent in 1997.

In 1998, international financial turmoil caused by Russia's problems and increasing investor anxiety over Brazil produced the highest domestic interest rates in more than three years, halving the growth rate of the economy. Conditions worsened in 1999 with

GDP falling by 3 per cent. President Fernando De La Rua, who took office in December 1999, sponsored tax increases and spending cuts to reduce the deficit, which had ballooned to 2.5 per cent of GDP in 1999. Growth in 2000 was a disappointing 0.8 per cent, as both domestic and foreign investors remained sceptical of the government's ability to pay debts and maintain its fixed exchange rate with the US dollar. One bright spot at the start of 2001 was the IMF's offer of $13.7 billion in support. During 2002, the banking system suffered a serious crisis, with the peso devaluing dramatically against the dollar, resulting in street riots and a collapse of financial confidence.

Argentina's population is more literate than in neighbouring countries, and the country's wealth is distributed more evenly. The country has abundant natural resources and a solid manufacturing base, the latter accounting for around 25 per cent of GDP and employing a fifth of the workforce. The liberalization of Argentine business occurred via a 'big bang' in October 1991, which removed thousands of regulations, including business start-up restrictions, the abilities of professionals such as accountants, lawyers, stockbrokers, etc, to charge fixed and predetermined rates of commission, state production quotas for a wide range of agricultural products, and numerous bureaucratic foreign trade procedures. A wide-ranging privatization programme was also initiated. Expansion of trade with Brazil is a major government priority. The MERCOSUR trade group of Brazil, Argentina, Paraguay and Uruguay agreed to become a customs union from 1 January 1995. A plan for a free trade area between the EU and MERCOSUR is under negotiation.

Bolivia

Bolivia has in practice three different economies operating within the same country. About 10 per cent of the population enjoy living standards at least equal to those of the Western European middle class, and a further 40 per cent are comfortably off and live in urban areas. The remainder are extremely poor, existing at subsistence level either in towns or in remote rural districts. Despite the country's abundant mineral deposits (which include gold, silver, tungsten, natural gas, lead and tin), Bolivia has Latin America's second lowest per capita income. Agricultural productivity has fallen, and there are poor internal communications. Oil fields are being developed by foreign investors. Mining and manufacturing activities are expanding; inflation and unemployment are going down. Agriculture contributes about 22 per cent to the country's GDP and employs half the workforce. Timber is an important industry: 60 per cent of Bolivia is covered by forests.

A problem for exporters is arranging overland transport to this (landlocked) country. There are Bolivian freezone areas on the coasts of Peru, Chile, Paraguay, Brazil, Argentina and Uruguay. Thereafter road journeys can be difficult and protracted.

Brazil

Brazil is self-sufficient in food and has vast mineral reserves and a well-developed manufacturing sector (which accounts for about 27 per cent of GDP). It is a huge country covering nearly half the South American continent. The population is young, with more than 35 per cent of all Brazilians being under 15 years of age. Around 85 per cent of the population are literate. The distribution of wealth in Brazil is extremely uneven: the top 20 per cent of the population receive nearly 70 per cent of national income, the bottom 20 per cent earn less than 3 per cent. This means that some Brazilians are very affluent indeed, and that many live in great poverty. In general, the wealthiest parts of Brazil are concentrated in the south of the country, in the provinces of Rio Grande do Sul, Parana, and Minais Gerais. Income levels and lifestyles here are the same as those in Europe or the United States, whereas in northern provinces such as Amazonas and Bahia the standard of living is nearer to that of India.

Brazil has numerous small firms and a diverse range of industries, especially machinery, textiles and clothing, food processing (Brazil is the world's second largest exporter of agricultural products), electronics and information technology. Agriculture accounts for 10 per cent of GDP and about 35 per cent of total exports.

Chile

Chile was among the first Latin American countries to introduce free market economic reform (including an extensive privatization programme) in the 1980s and to open up its markets to greater volumes of foreign imports. This resulted in economic growth, but the benefits of growth accrued mostly to the better-off section of the population; poorer groups have yet to be affected. The Chilean economy is peculiar in that the country's constitution has in the past required that a minimum proportion of national output be devoted to military spending (this being the price demanded by army generals when the country become a democracy). Hence Chile spends far more on armaments than its neighbours, at the expense of social programmes. Manufacturing is the country's most important economic activity, contributing 21 per cent to GDP and employing 6 per cent of the labour force. It is concentrated around Santiago and dominated by small enterprises. The Chilean government is keen to increase the country's involvement in foreign markets, especially in NAFTA and the Pacific Rim.

The poorer South American countries

Colombia, Ecuador, Peru and Paraguay rely predominantly on the exploitation of natural resources. All have initiated privatization schemes, but economic growth has been sluggish.

Peru is politically unstable, with regular insurgency and guerrilla fighting. The country's economy contracted by 23 per cent in the late 1980s, but stabilized from 1992 onwards. Inflation fell during this period, although living standards shrank dramatically. Drought and a cholera epidemic in 1991 created further problems. The Peruvian government has announced its intention to lift exchange controls, reduce import tariffs, encourage foreign investment and privatize state-owned industries (including oil).

Colombia is poised for muted growth in the next several years, marking continued recovery from the severe 1999 recession when GDP fell by about 4 per cent. President

Pastrana's well-respected economic team is working to keep the economy on track, maintaining low interest rates, for example. In accordance with its IMF loan agreement, the administration is also taking steps to improve the public sector's fiscal health. However, many challenges to improved prosperity remain. Unemployment was stuck at a record 20 per cent in 2000, contributing to the extreme inequality in income distribution. Two of Colombia's leading exports, oil and coffee, face an uncertain future; new exploration is needed to offset declining oil production, while coffee harvests and prices are depressed. The lack of public security is a key concern for investors, making progress in the government's peace negotiations with insurgent groups an important driver of economic performance. Colombia is looking for continued support from the international community to boost economic and peace prospects.

Despite the country's bad international reputation as a centre for drug smuggling and terrorism, its economy has prospered. This has enabled the Colombian government to initiate major programmes intended to eliminate illiteracy in Colombia's urban areas, provide basic education to 95 per cent of all rural dwellers, and generally promote infrastructure development (notably through road, port and railway improvements, water supply and sewage projects, and health care investments). It remains the case, however, that living standards are extremely low by international standards: barely a quarter of the rural population have access to safe water and only 10 per cent have adequate sewage facilities. Secondary schooling has been experienced by barely half the population.

A third of the population of **Ecuador** are native Indians, whose increasing demands for autonomous territories could result in political instability. One in three of the population is engaged in subsistence farming. Ecuador has substantial oil resources and rich agricultural areas. Because the country exports primary products such as oil, bananas and shrimp, fluctuations in world market prices can have a substantial domestic impact. Ecuador joined the World Trade Organization in 1996, but has failed to comply with many of its accession commitments. In recent years, growth has been uneven due to ill-conceived fiscal stabilization measures. The aftermath of El Niño and the depressed oil market of 1997–98 drove Ecuador's economy into a free-fall in 1999. The beginning of 1999 saw the banking sector collapse, which helped precipitate an unprecedented default on external loans later that year. Continued economic instability drove a 70 per cent depreciation of the currency throughout 1999, which eventually forced a desperate government to 'dollarize' the currency regime in 2000. The move stabilized the currency, but did not enable the government to stay in power. The new president, Gustavo Noboa, has yet to complete negotiations for a long-sought IMF accord. He will find it difficult to push through the reforms necessary to make 'dollarization' work in the long run.

Paraguay is a largely agricultural country. Agriculture contributes about 27 per cent of GDP, with agricultural products accounting for 90 per cent of the country's exports and the agricultural sector employing nearly half of its labour. The nation is poor, unemployment is high, and foreign debts substantial. Access to Paraguay is via the River Paraguay to the Port of Asunción (1,500 kilometres from the sea) or overland on paved roads from Brazil or Argentina.

Unlike its neighbours, **Uruguay** has experienced modest growth in its population. The country is predominantly agricultural, relying heavily on beef and wool production.

Accordingly the Uruguayan government is keen to develop light industry. There is no heavy industry in this country. Uruguay's economic progress has been sluggish, although tourism has expanded significantly. Agriculture accounts for 80 per cent of export earnings, although traditional exports have been hit by protectionism and tough competition from the European Union.

Venezuela depends on taxes on oil extraction for 75 per cent of export income, around 40–45 per cent of government revenues, and this contributes 22 per cent of GDP. Inflation is rampant, but economic growth is progressing. About 45 per cent of the country's GDP derives from the oil and other industries, just 5 per cent from agriculture. Nevertheless, Venezuela is an important exporter of farm products. Income and wealth are distributed extremely unequally in this country: the average earnings of the top 10 per cent of households are about 15 times higher than the average for the poorest 10 per cent (see Crawley, 1993). There has been much rioting and civil unrest in recent years.

Central America

Apart from Mexico, the countries of Central America are generally poorer than the average for all Latin America. In the past the region has been politically unstable, although the situation has improved over recent years.

Costa Rica's economy is growing faster than any other in the area, although population increase is absorbing much of the additional output. Ninety-five per cent of Costa Ricans are literate. Inflation is high, but the country's prospects are very sound in consequence of its expanding industrial base and free trade agreement with Mexico. Sixty per cent of the country's export earnings comprise agricultural products (bananas account for a quarter of Costa Rica's exports), most of the remainder being industrial goods (notably chemicals, textiles and plastics). Most of the country's previously state-owned industries are now in private hands.

Cuba, one of the few Communist countries remaining in the world and the only one in the Caribbean, has not even begun to recover from the loss of its (heavily subsidized) trade with the former Soviet Union. Today's CIS requires market price transactions conducted in convertible currency. Unemployment is known to be high and living standards falling. There is stringent food rationing and limitations on the consumption of a variety of non-food items. A quarter of the country's tractors and a third of all buses have been withdrawn from use because of an oil shortage. The true extent of decline is hard to assess, however, because of the lack of reliable statistics on this country.

The **Dominican Republic** is a poor country with a stagnant economy. It has under-developed industrial, transport and communications infrastructures, high inflation and much unemployment.

El Salvador is politically unstable and has a weak economy that depends heavily on the export of a handful of agricultural commodities. The principal export is 'mild' coffee, which accounts for 60 per cent of export earnings. There has been a partial privatization of the coffee trade. Other major crops are cotton, sugar cane, maize, beans and rice.

Guatemala is another politically unstable country, the economy of which, nevertheless, has grown significantly in the 1990s. The agricultural sector accounts for about a quarter of GDP, two-thirds of exports, and half of the labour force. Coffee, sugar and bananas are the main products. Former President Arzu (1996–2000) worked to implement a programme of economic liberalization and political modernization. The 1996 signing of the peace accords, which ended 36 years of civil war, removed a major obstacle to foreign investment. In 1998, Hurricane Mitch caused relatively little damage to Guatemala compared to its neighbours. Ongoing challenges include increasing government revenues, negotiating further assistance from international donors, and increasing the efficiency and openness of both government and private financial operations. Despite low international prices for Guatemala's main commodities, the economy grew by 3 per cent in 2000 and by 4 per cent in 2001. Guatemala, along with Honduras and El Salvador, recently concluded a free trade agreement with Mexico and has moved to protect international property rights. However, the Portillo administration has undertaken a review of privatizations under the previous administration, thereby creating some uncertainty among investors.

Honduras's economy has also been disrupted by warfare, although military rule officially ended in 1990. The country's involvement with fighting in Nicaragua drained it of foreign exchange, forcing drastic curbs on imports, which continue to the present day. The economy is dominated by agriculture, which accounts for 30 per cent of GDP, 55 per cent of the workforce and 65 per cent of all exports. Manufacturing is undertaken mainly in small firms and, while it employs 13 per cent of all Honduran workers, is generally underdeveloped. However, small-scale manufacturing is growing and now accounts for 30 per cent of all manufacturing employment. Economic growth has been mediocre. Honduras relies heavily on foreign aid, but has been able to recover rapidly from the effects of Hurricane Mitch, and is expected to achieve respectable economic growth during the early part of the 21st century.

Civil war caused **Nicaragua**'s GDP to contract annually from 1986 to 1992, with only moderate growth thereafter. The country has no reserves of foreign exchange and imports are severely restricted. Inflation is under better control than in the past, currently running at 11 per cent rather than the several hundred per cent it reached in the past. Relative peace and the introduction of a market economy have not generated the economic benefits promised by the government. The country is expected to benefit from the Heavily Indebted Poor Countries Initiative, which the World Bank introduced in 2001 to reduce the foreign debt burden for poor countries.

Panama's GDP plunged by 16 per cent in 1987 and took several years to recover. However, manufacturing has expanded significantly and the country is re-establishing itself as an important international banking centre. Panama's economy is based primarily on a well-developed services sector that accounts for 75 per cent of GDP. Services include the Panama Canal, banking, the Colon Free Zone, insurance, container ports, flagship registry, and tourism. A slump in Colon Free Zone and agricultural exports, high oil prices, and the withdrawal of US military forces held back economic growth in 2000. The government plans public works programmes, tax reforms, and new regional trade agreements in order to stimulate growth. Agriculture's share of GDP has fallen to about 10 per cent. Panama is politically unstable, yet inflation is low by Central American standards and there is considerable foreign investment.

THE INDIAN SUBCONTINENT

Southern Asia, comprising India, Bangladesh, Pakistan and Sri Lanka, is one of the poorest areas in the world. It has a huge population but extremely low per capita incomes, slow rates of economic growth, and generally lacklustre economic performance. There is less investment than in Pacific Rim countries and heavy reliance on agricultural products. All four countries are short of foreign exchange and depend substantially on remittances from their citizens who work abroad. Special problems attached to doing business in the Indian subcontinent include:

- Extensive bureaucracy, rules and regulations affecting business operations.
- Monopoly control over key distribution systems in certain areas exercised by a handful of firms.
- Very high tariffs and stringent controls over imports, aggravated by regular foreign exchange crises. Imports of certain consumer goods are forbidden; some industrial equipment cannot be imported without a declaration that it cannot be supplied by a local firm.
- Inefficient industrial infrastructure.
- Currencies are not generally easily convertible.
- Much business has to be conducted with inefficient public sector enterprises.
- Governments offer little genuine protection to the owners of intellectual property.

Bangladesh

Bangladesh is flat, low-lying and criss-crossed by a large number of rivers, making it highly vulnerable to the cyclones, storms and floods that regularly afflict the country. A third of the entire country is under water during the annual monsoon. Eighty per cent of the population depend on the land and 85 per cent live in rural areas. About 87 per cent of Bangladeshis are Muslims, 12 per cent are Hindus, the remainder are mostly Christians and Buddhists. Bangladesh's inhabitants depend substantially on foreign aid, which provides half the country's foreign exchange and contributes 10 per cent of Gross National Product. Other problems facing Bangladesh include:

- A high rate of population increase, exacerbated by the influx in the early 1990s of around a quarter of a million Muslim refugees from Burma (Myanmar).
- Political instability.
- Very high wage costs for such a poor country (above those of Sri Lanka, where per capita GDP is nearly three times higher.) Also the country is unlikely to attract significant amounts of foreign investment in competition with other poor Asian countries,

such as Vietnam. Per capita real income has been essentially static, the average increase in GDP of about 2.5 per cent per year being matched by a corresponding expansion in the population.
- The fact that few of the country's firms are able to compete in international markets. Bangladesh's largest industries are in garments (a third of which go to the European Union) and jute, although the latter is in recession.

On the positive side, the rate of economic growth is rising, as is the level of exports (particularly of textiles and garments). Several important economic development projects are progressing.

India

India comprises 23 states plus several smaller territories. The larger states have populations bigger than those of the majority of the world's countries. Most states differ from each other in terms of culture, language and political orientation. The diversity of India is manifested in ethnic divisions (ranging from the Aryan peoples of the north to the Dravidians of the south), agricultural fertility (and hence rural incomes) and adult literacy, which is below 50 per cent in certain regions. Eighty per cent of the population live in villages. There are about 120 million affluent Indians, with living standards at least comparable with those of Western Europe, and around 400 million people officially classified as unable to afford the basic necessities of life.

It is important to remember that, despite the extent of poverty within India, the country is not intrinsically poor. It is self-sufficient in agriculture in aggregate terms, has extensive natural resources, good communications, a commercial infrastructure and an extensive manufacturing base. India is the twelfth ranking industrial country in the world. The main problems are high rates of population growth, low rates of industrial and agricultural productivity, ethnic violence, high foreign debt (the servicing of which absorbs 25 per cent of annual earnings of foreign exchange), high inflation, and a desperately uneven distribution of wealth and income. Economic growth is around 2.5 per cent annually, about the same as the rate of increase of population, so that real per capita GDP is virtually static. India has 120 million Muslims, 25 million Christians, and 20 million Buddhists and Sikhs. Otherwise most Indians follow the Hindu religion. Hindus themselves segment into four major castes plus the Harijans (untouchables). There are sub-castes within each caste.

Two-thirds of the country's population is engaged in agriculture, although some industries are well developed. Heavy industry (especially iron, steel and transport equipment) has expanded greatly over the past 20 years. Trade liberalization is proceeding and is unlikely to be reversed. However, most categories of imports still require licences, possession of which (together with shipping documents) allows foreign exchange to be obtained from authorized banks. The middle class is growing rapidly, and the demand for consumer durables (according to the Indian national statistical services) continues to expand, especially among rural dwellers. The attractions of doing business in India are its vast number of consumers (so that even a modest improvement in living standards can lead to greatly increased sales), and its continuing status as a democratic state, this having enabled it to avoid some of the bloody revolutions, coups d'état and civil disturbances of other countries in the region. The major drawback of doing business in India is the crippling level of bureaucracy.

Pakistan

Pakistan is the richest of the four countries with a per capita GDP about 20 per cent higher than in India. Ninety-five per cent of the population are Muslims, and the Islamic religion is highly influential in all aspects of life. Nearly half the population are under 15 years of age and only 2.5 per cent over 65. Sixty per cent of all Pakistanis are illiterate (compared with 52 per cent in India). Half the country's workforce is employed in agriculture. Manufacturing accounts for 11.5 per cent of all employees, 17 per cent of GDP and nearly three-quarters of all exports. Attempts to modernize the country's industrial infrastructure by an extensive privatization programme have proved problematic: the nationalized businesses were in such a poor state that buyers were reluctant to go ahead, and the country's industries are therefore moribund. Import licences are necessary for most categories of goods, and import regulations are generally complicated. However, there are few exchange controls and external trade is being liberalized.

Sri Lanka

Sri Lanka has extensive natural resources, good internal communications and a well-educated population. Drought is a significant problem in this country, but is being tackled via a number of major irrigation and power generation programmes. The main threat facing Sri Lanka is the seemingly endemic conflict between the country's Buddhist Sinhalese (who account for 74 per cent of the population) and Hindu Tamils (who comprise about 18 per cent). Muslims, Christians, ethnic Malays and Eurasians also live in this country. Superimposed on religious and ethnic divisions are factional political rivalries that frequently erupt into fighting. Racial violence has frightened away foreign visitors, disrupting the country's potentially lucrative tourist industry.

In 1977, Colombo abandoned statist economic policies and its import substitution trade policy for market-oriented policies and export-oriented trade. Sri Lanka's most dynamic sectors now are food processing, textiles and apparel, food and beverages, telecommunications, and insurance and banking. By 1996 plantation crops made up only 20 per cent of exports (compared with 93 per cent in 1970), while textiles and garments accounted for 63 per cent. GDP grew at an annual average rate of 5.5 per cent throughout the 1990s until a drought and a deteriorating security situation lowered growth to 3.8 per cent in 1996. The economy rebounded in 1997–98 with growth of 6.4 per cent and 4.7 per cent – but slowed to 4.3 per cent in 1999. Growth increased to 5.6 per cent in 2000, with tourism and exports leading the way. But a resurgence of the civil war between the Sinhalese and the minority Tamils and a possible slowdown in tourism dampened the country's economy in 2001. For the next round of reforms, the Central Bank of Sri Lanka recommends that Colombo expand market mechanisms in nonplantation agriculture, dismantle the government's monopoly on wheat imports, and promote more competition in the financial sector.

AFRICA

African contains a collection of heterogeneous economies, including some that are quite well off (oil-rich Libya, for instance) and others, like Ethiopia, which rank among the poorest countries in the world. The continent is politically disunited, although the Organization of African Unity (OAU) encourages intra-African trade and there is some economic cooperation among many African states. Lower tariffs between African countries seem inevitable, possibly in conjunction with the erection of common tariffs against the rest of the world. Arabic-speaking North African states are discussed later in the chapter.

A huge problem facing Africa south of the Sahara is that, in aggregate, population increases are negating the consequences of economic growth (which averaged about 3 per cent per annum in the 1990s), essentially because of the uneven distribution of income within the continent (meaning that the extra people are predominantly destitute poor without the means or possibilities to obtain the income needed to purchase significant amounts of goods). To the extent that expanding populations do create fresh market opportunities, these will occur in consequence of the present low level of urbanization of Africa compared with most of the world's other regions.

According to World Bank figures, the population of major African cities is growing at two to three times the (high) rate of national population increase, placing enormous pressure on local welfare services. South African cities are expanding particularly rapidly in consequence of all their districts being opened up to Black residents (under apartheid Black people were forcibly prevented from migrating to cities), and the attractions of city dwelling compared with rural conditions. If present trends continue, then the populations of many African cities will grow fourfold over the next 20 years, creating numerous opportunities for infrastructure development, the provision of equipment for improving urban life, and the sale of goods to urban dwellers as urbanization accelerates towards international norms.

Another depressing statistic relating to sub-Saharan Africa, excluding South Africa, is the decline in the share of industry in the region's Gross Domestic Product (matched by a corresponding increase in the share of agriculture), accompanied by acute poverty. Foreign aid has risen, but there is little direct foreign investment (less than US$20 billion per annum for the whole of Africa in the mid-1990s). Trade between these countries and the outside world is about the same today as in the early 1980s. UN figures suggest that more than half of all sub-Saharan African countries except South Africa depend on just one or two commodities for more than 70 per cent of their export income, making them extremely vulnerable to downturns in external demand.

Several African countries depend totally on foreign aid; many more are heavily reliant on aid payments. Aid donors, however, are increasingly reluctant to transfer resources to undemocratic countries in view of the political instability (and hence regular civil wars, insurrections, guerrilla fighting and subsequent waste of the aid money donated) that the absence of democracy frequently involves. At the time of writing it is unclear whether aid-dependent African states will accept more democratic forms of government and, if not, whether the flow of aid will be diminished. Prospects for business in these countries will be extremely bleak in the latter situation. Democratization, conversely, might cause governments seriously to tackle corruption, allocate national resources more fairly, and open their economies to foreign trade.

Exporters to Africa are confronted by a maze of regulations, which are subject to regular and unanticipated alteration. Hence supplying firms need to monitor import and foreign currency regulations on a continuous basis (controls and prohibitions can be introduced with less than 24 hours' notice) and to take great care where African sales are concerned. Special problems connected with doing business in Africa include:

- Extensive trade barriers, including measures to protect local industries, to correct balance of payments deficits and to improve the incomes of particular interest groups. As well as tariffs and quotas there are occasional bans on all forms of 'non-essential' goods to certain countries for prescribed periods (normally in consequence of balance of payments crises). Eighty per cent of all products imported to Africa south of the Sahara excluding South Africa are subject to non-tariff import barriers of some kind, notably discretionary licensing and restrictive foreign exchange controls.
- Large fluctuations in currency exchange rates.
- Prohibitions on hard currency leaving specific countries for anything up to several years at a time.
- The need to obtain a licence for the import of many items to poorer African countries.
- Absence of proper links between urban centres and rural areas, resulting in the fragmentation of markets and hence the absence of distribution economies of scale.
- Statutory requirements for pre- and post-shipment inspections for quantity and price comparison for many categories of item, especially where transfer pricing is involved. Importers are only allowed the foreign exchange needed to pay for consignments if the requirements are satisfied.

The interior

Africa has 13 landlocked countries. Overland transport routes are often substandard and airlinks can be poor. This greatly increases the cost of exporting to these countries. Major road systems linking landlocked countries with West and North African ports are planned but have yet to be constructed. The Trans-African Highway Programme, when completed, will run north to south from Tunisia to Botswana, and west to east from Senegal to Kenya. Direct routes between Mombasa, Lagos, Cairo and Dakar are intended. Exporting to a landlocked territory presents a number of difficulties, as follows:

- Consignments can be held up for long periods at two or three points in the transport system. Goods have to be warehoused during the delays at considerable expense.
- Because the interior of Africa is huge and the number of coastal ports limited, serious port congestion sometimes occurs. The sea journey from Western Europe to (say) Dar es Salaam or Mombasa in East Africa normally takes less than four weeks (depending on the number of calls at other ports en route), but it can take up to a further five months for a cargo to reach its final inland destination.
- Export documentation needs to be completed and dispatched long in advance of the transportation of the consignment. Translations of documents may be required as shipments cross national borders. Missing documents or even slight errors within them can cause long hold-ups. Note that communications between African towns might be poor even though communications between those same towns and cities in Europe, Japan or North America may be excellent.
- Sufficient funds of the correct local currencies have to be instantly available in order to meet ad hoc forwarding and off-loading charges, border transfer fees, etc, at national frontiers.
- Shortlanded cargo (ie deficiencies in the delivered quantity compared to the amount stated on transport documents) can be a major problem. Shortlanding results from many factors, including pilferage, lost and split consignments caused by port congestion, inadequate facilities for loading and unloading railway wagons, damage incurred during road journeys on unlit and unsurfaced highways, and frequent shifts of the same consignment between road, rail and water transport.

Such difficulties normally make it essential to engage a specialist freight forwarder with well-established facilities in the territories concerned. This increases the cost of exporting to such regions, but the use of a forwarder without proper experience of inland African trade can lead to financial disaster.

Important African countries

Angola is a rich country both in terms of its mineral resources (which include large amounts of oil and diamonds) and its fertile agricultural land, yet the overwhelming majority of Angolans are poor – due essentially to 30 years of intermittent warfare (civil and with outside states), lack of economic infrastructure and drought. Famine has affected 1 in 10 of Angola's 10.6 million population in recent years. Peace with South Africa enabled formal demobilization to begin, but disputes between internal factions have led to continued internal fighting. In particular, the oil-rich province of Cabinda is seeking independence from the rest of the country. Nevertheless, Angola has great potential and a significant manufacturing sector. Foreign investment is encouraged (via special tax reliefs, exemption from import duties and guarantees on the repatriation of profits) and the country is receiving large amounts of foreign assistance. Real GDP has expanded by an average 7 per cent per annum in recent years, though growth is retarded by shortages of skilled workers, many of whom prefer to work abroad. Licences are required for all imports into the country.

Ghana is another country rich in natural resources but possessing extremely low per capita GDP. Most Ghanaians are engaged in agriculture, and the country is self-sufficient in food. Otherwise the mining of gold, diamonds and other minerals is the main employer of labour. In the early 1990s Ghana embarked upon a Structural Adjustment Programme organized and supervised by the World Bank and the IMF and requiring the country to liberalize its internal and external trade, privatize state-owned industries and reduce budget deficits. The immediate consequences were higher prices and unemployment and reduced living standards. However, growth rates increased, and there is much new investment. Whether the Structural Adjustment Programme will succeed in the long run has yet to be determined.

Ghana is ethnically diverse. Akans make up about 44 per cent of the population. Several other tribal groups have significant minority representations. Ghanaians are noted for their interest in religions, which exert great influence on all aspects of local life.

Kenya is home to 40 ethnic and tribal groups ranging from Somalis in the north to the Masai cattle herders of the south. The dominant tribe is the Kikuyu, who inhabit the central highland and in the past have dominated business and politics. The tribal and cultural diversity can be a major problem for firms wishing to do business in Kenya. Most Kenyans are employed in agriculture, which accounts for about 25 per cent of the country's Gross Domestic Product. Textiles and clothing, tourism and the manufacture of machinery and transport vehicles are the other main industries.

Kenya has the third largest economy in sub-Saharan Africa (after South Africa and Nigeria) and has the best developed manufacturing sector in East Africa, although it employs less than 10 per cent of the country's workforce. Trade with South Africa increased by 1,000 per cent in 1992 (albeit from a low base) following the lifting of UN sanctions and there is much potential for the long-term development of strong trading links between the two countries. Growth has averaged 5 per cent per annum in recent years and a Structural Adjustment Programme (see above) is under way. Unfortunately the rate of increase of Kenya's population is the ninth highest in the world, negating many of the potential benefits of economic expansion. Further problems facing the Kenyan government include high unemployment and inflation, drought and civil unrest (including both tribal and religious conflicts). The last has had an adverse effect on tourism, the number of arrivals not having expanded as envisaged in the country's national plan.

Mozambique has been devastated by civil war and is totally dependent on foreign aid. The World Bank categorizes Mozambique as one of the world's poorest countries. Railway and communication systems were destroyed in the war, and there is regular famine. The country is rich in natural resources, but lacks governmental, economic and business structures. It is home to numerous tribal groups, though the Makua-Lomwe dominate in the north and the Thonga in the south. A significant number of Asians also live in the country. Many Thongans work in South African mines, and the remittance of their wages back to Mozambique is a major source of foreign exchange for the latter. Most of the population are engaged in agriculture and live along the coast and in the country's fertile river valleys. Some light industry has survived, and there is great potential for developing heavy industry and mining once the political situation has been settled. According to the World Bank, at least half of all Mozambiquans are undernourished.

Nigeria has many tribes and over 250 local languages and dialects, although Hausa, Yoruba and Ibo dominate. English is the official language. The great majority of Nigerians living in the north and west of the country are Muslims. Christians form a majority in the south. There are in addition many local religions. Nigeria's civil war of 1967–70 related to ethnic divisions, which continue to cause problems (voters tend to elect officials on ethnic tribal rather than political grounds).

Nigeria has oil, natural gas and other natural resources. However, the country's industrial sector is underdeveloped and the shortage of foreign exchange is endemic. Numerous coups d'état have occurred in Nigeria, which in general is politically unstable. Economic growth has been mediocre, although manufacturing (which contributes about 8 per cent to GDP) has expanded as the demand for import substitute goods has risen (the country not having the foreign exchange to pay for certain imports). Also there are vehicle assembly and iron and steel industries. Nigeria possesses Africa's second largest economy after South Africa. Trade with Nigeria is difficult and subject to much delay and bureaucracy: in common with other West African states, corruption is rife and little can be achieved without offering substantial bribes to officials and others.

Tanzania's economy has been in decline since the early 1970s and today depends almost entirely on agriculture (much of it subsistence farming). Inflation and unemployment are extremely high, internal road and rail communications poor, and there is much illiteracy. The World Bank estimates that Tanzania's economy will have to grow by 6 per cent per annum for 12 years simply for the country's standard of living to approach the regional average. Nevertheless, the country has gold and diamond mining industries and there is much potential for tourism once Tanzania's basic economic and social problems have been resolved. Tanzania is ethnically diverse and has over 120 tribes, a number of which are extensions of the Xhoas peoples of Southern Africa. The two largest tribes are the Sukuma and Nyamwezi. All imports require a Foreign Export Allocation Allowance Licence, without which the National Bank of Tanzania will not allow payment for the goods. In 1993 the government of Zanzibar established a number of 'free economic zones' on the territory. Tanzania's entire economy used to be subject to central planning and control, but at the time of writing is being opened up to private enterprise.

Zimbabwe has a well-developed industrialized economy by regional standards in Africa, as well as a strong agricultural sector. Mining of chromium, copper and tungsten are important activities. The country's economy has grown steadily and presents numerous opportunities for the sale of industrial equipment and other capital goods. Manufacturing (which accounts for 30 per cent of GDP) expanded in part because of import substitution programmes initiated during the period of UN sanctions against the former white minority-ruled state of Rhodesia. Zimbabwe has a young population (45 per cent of all residents are under 15 years of age and less than 3 per cent over 65), only two-thirds of which are literate. Alas, the country (like Tanzania) has a major AIDS problem with (according to World Health Organization) up to a third of the population carrying the HIV virus, concentrated among newly born infants and young adults. Zimbabwe ranks as the fifth country in the world in terms of AIDS cases per 100,000 inhabitants. This epidemic is predicted to slow the population growth rate and to place great strains on the country's medical and social welfare services. Zimbabwe's prospects are closely tied in with those of South Africa, with which it does much trade and upon which it depends for imports of manufactured goods and for access to seaports.

South Africa

The Republic of South Africa dominates business in the southern part of the continent. Founded on mining, the South African economy has diverse industries, abundant natural resources and is self-sufficient in food. South Africa is the world's largest producer and exporter of gold and diamonds and possesses extensive deposits of platinum, chromium, manganese and other valuable ores. Nevertheless, manufacturing is the biggest sector of the economy, contributing 30 per cent of the country's GDP. Machinery and transport comprise the major component of manufactured output (18 per cent of the total), followed by agriculture and food processing (13 per cent). Most South African exports (predominantly gold, minerals and base metals) go to Italy, Japan, the United States, the United Kingdom and Germany in that order. Germany provides about 20 per cent of the country's imports; the United Kingdom and Japan supply about 11 per cent each, the United States about 16 per cent, and Italy 5 per cent. The main import markets are for machinery, transport and other equipment, chemicals and oil. South Africa has a population of about 41 million, of which over 70 per cent are Black. Overall the population is extremely young: 38 per cent are under 15 years of age, just 4 per cent are over 65. There are nine main languages, Xhosa, Zulu and Sesotho being the most widely spoken. Afrikaans and English are the languages of government. Thirty per cent of the population is illiterate.

Paradoxically, trade sanctions against South Africa's former apartheid regime actually strengthened its manufacturing sector: new home-based defence industries were established, coal-to-oil conversion plants set up and heavy engineering sectors developed. By the time UN sanctions were lifted (in 1992/93) the country had become an important exporter of armaments in its own right. Sanctions did reduce foreign investment, however, and the expansion of indigenous state-funded industries meant extensive government spending financed by foreign loans. Interest rates and inflation rose during the 1980s, the South African currency weakened and the government was forced to seek a massive rescheduling of the country's external debt. Fearful of the country's potential for political instability in consequence of the continuation of White minority rule, foreign lenders withheld further funding in the absence of political reform, and many multinational companies sold up and moved out. Confronted with these realities the Republic's government negotiated peace settlements in Angola, and the African National Congress (ANC) abolished the apartheid system, and held multi-racial elections in 1994.

The future of South Africa

Abandonment of apartheid has led to the establishment of numerous trading links with other parts of the continent. South African trade with the rest of Africa south of the Sahara rose by 40 per cent in 1989, and around 20 per cent annually in the 1990s. Another potential benefit is the scope for reduced military spending both by South Africa itself and its neighbours. There should in principle be a big increase in intra-African trade and greater mobility of resources throughout the southern part of the continent. Much depends on whether foreign investors return to the country. There is a great deal to attract foreign firms (especially those intending to use South Africa as a base for trading throughout the southern part of the continent). As Black income levels rise, consumer markets are potentially huge. Further prospects for increased international trade arise from fresh links with Egypt, Kenya and the CIS. Nevertheless, many uncertainties surround the viability of South Africa as a nation state, including:

- Tribal conflict, including the possibility of protracted civil war between Inkatha and the ANC.
- Potential disruptions arising from the desires of certain White minorities to establish their own White 'homelands' in the Transvaal and/or the Orange Free State.
- The future of the four Black 'homelands' artificially created by the former apartheid regime. These lands occupy 13 per cent of the existing Republic's surface area.
- Extremely high unemployment among Black workers, in conjunction with escalating violence and social unrest.

Note, moreover, that Botswana, Lesotho, Swaziland and Mozambique have in the past received revenues from South Africa, either directly in the form of aid, or indirectly via remittances from migrants working in the Republic. This assistance might cease as the new South Africa addresses its own (pressing) economic problems, with far-reaching political consequences.

THE MIDDLE EAST

This region includes all the Arab countries plus Iran. The Arab world comprises around 150 million Arabic-speaking people in 20 countries, linked by a common heritage, culture and language but with extreme differences in political orientation. Living standards vary enormously, ranging from affluence in the oil-rich Gulf states to dire poverty elsewhere.

European colonization of the region began in the early 1800s. Britain and France effectively controlled most of the Arab world until the mid-1900s, which witnessed the establishment of the state of Israel – an event with political repercussions extending to the present day. The other major 20th-century event affecting Arab countries was of course the oil price increases of the 1970s and early 1980s, which increased enormously the spending power of certain Middle Eastern countries (Alnasrari, 1991). Conventionally, two criteria are used to differentiate Arab countries: politically radical versus politically conservative and oil-rich countries as opposed to those without substantial oil reserves.

Within some of the oil-rich countries there is rapid growth in non-oil sectors brought about by extensive government investment, continuing growth in import demand, and a rapid increase in the education levels of consumers, with consequent demands for sophisticated and high-quality products (Goldschmidt, 1991). Suppliers from all over the world compete within these markets (especially firms based in the Pacific Rim) and local consumers are spoiled for choice. A number of oil-rich Arab countries (notably Saudi Arabia and the Gulf states) derive around 90 per cent of government revenues from oil and have high per capita incomes but a limited industrial base. Other states with oil resources have encouraged industrial diversification, usually within a framework of rigid state control (Iraq, Libya and Algeria fall within this group). The major Arab countries without extensive oil reserves (Egypt, Jordan, Syria, Morocco, Sudan and Tunisia) depend on industry and agriculture. *All* Arab countries import significant volumes of industrial and transport equipment and technical services.

The political situation of many Arab countries is highly unstable and liable to sudden and dramatic change. Political risk in the Middle East frequently involves religious factors, since the opposition to the government of several Middle Eastern countries has a fundamentalist religious base. Note, however, that it may well be that a multitude of secular opposition groups are using the various Islamic factions as convenient vehicles for resisting the status quo. Other risks include the possibilities of a long-term decline in the price of oil and a deterioration in relations between local nationals and the large numbers of foreign workers in many Middle Eastern countries. A factor encouraging political uncertainty is perhaps the absence of democratic government (in the Western sense) throughout the region. Note that the United States depends on the Middle East for nearly half of its oil imports, giving the former a big incentive to intervene to promote political stability in the area.

The role of Islam

The dominant factor unifying the Arab world is perhaps the Islamic religion, which began in the sixth century AD and profoundly affects all aspects of life (including business) in Arab countries. Islam brought together tribal groups that had been at war for centuries and facilitated Arab expansion into Europe (notably Spain) and central Asia (Turkey, Persia and so on). Islam is the primary driving force behind contemporary Arab culture and society, affecting all aspects of behaviour, attitudes, beliefs and morals, and the adoption by Arab countries of Western products, technologies and consumption patterns in certain areas has to be viewed against the background of Islamic religious norms. Islamic law forbids a variety of products in some Muslim countries: anything related to pork (including pig-related toys and puppets), games that include cards, dummies with human faces, items in the shape of the Christian cross, books with titles that could have a sexual connotation. Representations of the human figure are not permitted (which explains the absence of sculpture and painting in the Arab artistic tradition, which focuses on ornamentation, music and poetry). Laws relating to these matters are enforced by the religious police, who are empowered to ban the sale of unacceptable items and/or confiscate stocks of products.

Care is needed over the depiction of women. Some Islamic fundamentalists assert emphatically that the role of woman is fully prescribed by religious teachings, ie to look after husbands and families and to have little or no involvement in business or wider social affairs. Other Moslems adopt an entirely different view and the issue is hotly debated within Islamic circles. Exporters to Arab countries need to tread warily in these respects, and it is generally difficult for women managers to do business in certain Arab countries.

The Arabic language

The Arab world is generally proud of its ancient language, and although English is widely used for international business, correspondence in Arabic is greatly appreciated. Arabic is a subtle and richly contextual language capable of describing highly complex concepts and emotions (Mansfield, 1981). This fact has been put forward as an explanation for the perceptions sometimes held by Western business people that Arab business people lean towards excessive rhetoric, exaggeration and over-assertion when discussing commercial issues. Arab peoples have a long and varied history as international traders. Arab business people are renowned for being shrewd and competent negotiators. Note, moreover, that the traditional Arab virtues of hospitality, honour and good manners are as important in business as in any other walk of life in Arab countries.

Doing business in the Arab Middle East

A major advantage to doing business in the Arab Middle East is the region's stable and homogeneous culture compared to many other areas of the world. Cultural traits within one Arab country are likely to be replicated in others, so that promotional messages appropriate for one Arab country will probably be suitable elsewhere. Note also that lifestyles in several Arab countries are being influenced by Western media (satellite television, for instance) and products, and by tourism. Many influential Arab families have their children educated in the West. Key factors of the Arab regional market are as follows:

- Tariff rates are generally low and access to markets is easy. Trading systems are well developed, and there is a big demand for imported consumer durables.
- There is widespread government involvement in industry and trade. State authorities collect all oil revenues in oil-rich countries and spend them as they think fit, eg on development projects or the import of specific categories of product. Governments are big employers of labour and major purchasers of industrial goods, and might control imports and/or the availability of foreign exchange. Foreign participation in joint ventures with local businesses might also be subject to regulation.
- Privately owned distribution channels are mostly controlled by family firms rather than joint stock enterprises. Chains of distribution are long. A consequence of family

control of businesses is lack of delegation of decision-making in many firms. The people in charge decide everything of significance, including many matters that would be regarded as technically routine in the West: sourcing, letters of credit, specification of payment terms (CIF, FOB, etc) and so on. This can result in the intense 'personalization' of business relations. 'Falling out' with the wrong person can lead to disaster.

- Population growth rates are high. Younger people are beginning to exhibit consumption patterns dissimilar to those of their parents.
- Business services (advertising and market research agencies for example) are underdeveloped and frequently foreign-owned. There is a paucity of market research data and intense shortages of trained marketing services staff.
- The oil-rich Arab countries have large (predominantly male) immigrant populations, comprising professionally qualified Westerners plus industrial labourers from poorer Middle East and Asian stages. These immigrant groups represent substantial markets in their own right. Note the extensive social security, health and public education systems established in oil-rich Middle Eastern states, which (as long as oil revenues continue) result in increases in population, leading to additional aggregate buying power.
- A 'Western' image can be a powerful selling point in the oil-rich Arab countries, so that little or no product or promotional modification might be required.
- The Arab market is spread over an extensive geographical area. This can lead to insufficient 'critical mass' for penetrating particular areas, ie there is not enough concentration of marketing effort and resources in the development of selected market opportunities.
- Numerous export opportunities have arisen from the rebuilding of Kuwait. The other major importer in the Middle East has been Iran (a non-Arab country), which in the early 1990s embarked on a major programme of national infrastructure development. Overall, however, growth rates in the Middle East have been low (owing mainly to depressed oil prices in the 1980s), and the richer Arab countries have chosen to invest predominantly in non-Arab countries. Future growth is expected in the fields of retailing and retail technology, business services, and the local production of quality consumer goods.

Important Middle Eastern countries

Algeria is an oil-dependent country and as such extremely vulnerable to events in the international oil market. The decline in oil prices during the mid-1980s prompted Algeria's government to initiate a series of major economic reforms, which, in consequence of the country's weak and inefficient pre-existing industrial structure, led to mass unemployment (especially among young people). Also the currency was devalued to about half its initial value, making imported consumer goods extremely expensive. Living standards fell, Islamic fundamentalists challenged the government and great political instability ensued.

Most of the country consists of the Sahara Desert, with the majority of the population living near the coast. Trade with Algeria is difficult. There are shortages of foreign exchange and rigorous import controls apply to most categories of goods. About a quarter of the Algerian workforce is engaged in agriculture, which contributes about 12 per cent of GDP (marginally more than manufacturing, which employs around 14 per cent of the working population).

In **Egypt**, 9 out of 10 people live in the fertile Nile Valley and Delta; the rest of the country is mostly desert. Agriculture contributes 20 per cent of the country's GDP, but is generally inadequate and food imports (which account for 65 per cent of total food consumption) are rising. Manufacturing and mining are the other main economic activities, though both are inefficient by international standards.

Egypt's role in the Gulf War was rewarded by its allies through their cutting the country's foreign debt by a third (previously Egypt's total external debt exceeded the value of a full year's Gross National Product) and by advancing several billions of dollars' worth of loans. In return the Egyptian currency was made convertible and internal and external trade liberalized. The International Monetary Fund is also making funds available, provided the country reorganizes and denationalizes certain public sector companies. This has proven difficult in practice because of a shortage of buyers and lack of an adequate capital market within the country.

Public sector imports are regulated by annually budgeted foreign exchange allocations. Only government-authorized private companies and trading organizations may import goods, and licences are required. All private sector imports must be financed under letters of credit. Foreign exchange for imports has to be obtained from an authorized bank, and a special currency rate of exchange may apply. Problems confronting the Egyptian government include a high population growth rate, high unemployment, increasing dependence on imported food and the increasing number of Egyptians who work in other Middle Eastern countries. The latter trend has contributed to Egypt's foreign exchange revenues as workers remit their earnings to the home country but makes Egypt vulnerable to downturns in these foreign economies. Islamic fundamentalism has the potential to destabilize the country politically, especially if the economy deteriorates.

Iran represents a large and expanding market (population 61 million), with by far the highest level of GDP in the region. Iran's economy is a mixture of central planning, state ownership of oil and other large enterprises, village agriculture, and small-scale private trading and service ventures. President Khatami has continued to follow the market reform plans of former President Rafsanjani and has indicated that he will pursue diversification of Iran's oil-reliant economy, although he has made little progress towards that goal. The strong oil market in 1996 helped ease financial pressures on Iran and allowed for Tehran's timely debt service payments. Iran's financial situation tightened in 1997 and deteriorated further in 1998 because of lower oil prices. The subsequent zoom in oil prices in 1999–2000 afforded Iran fiscal breathing room but does not solve its structural economic problems, including the encouragement of foreign investment. Iran is being targeted by exporters in many countries, with French, South Korean and Swedish businesses having increased their market share substantially in recent years. Countertrade is frequently necessary in consequence of the country's acute shortage of foreign exchange.

All imports must be authorized by the Ministry of Commerce, which decides whether specific import licences are required and which may impose registration fees and the deposit with an Iranian bank of a certain proportion of the value of a consignment. The Iranian government is intent on developing:

- the country's construction industry;
- gas and offshore oilfields;
- the petrochemical industry;
- agriculture;
- the manufacture of machine tools.

It is also building rail networks to link southern Iran with the Muslim states of the former Soviet Union. The aim is to reduce Iran's overdependence on the oil industry and to earn foreign exchange (of which there is a severe shortage). Development is being hampered by the need to import large quantities of food. A number of new food processing plants are scheduled for construction, although food production in general is frequently interrupted by natural disasters (earthquakes, flooding, etc).

Of those employed, about 39 per cent are involved in agriculture, 12 per cent in manufacturing and the same in construction. Mining employs just 6 per cent of the workforce but contributes 13 per cent of Iran's GDP. Iran has large Kurdish and Azeri ethnic minorities in its northern provinces. Also there are several Islamic fundamentalist and other opposition groups within the country and there is much violent civil unrest.

Nearly all of **Israel**'s foreign trade is with the European Union, NAFTA and Japan. The country has diverse manufacturing industries including electronics, general engineering, aircraft, chemicals, textiles and food processing. Tourism is an important source of foreign exchange and is expanding. Israel faces a number of major economic problems, including:

- how to pay for the resettlement of the target of 1 million Jewish immigrants from the former Soviet Union;
- high unemployment;
- heavy dependence on economic assistance from the United States, without which tax rates would have to increase dramatically.

Jordan's economy suffered badly during and after the Gulf War. Transit trade with Iraq (a major source of export income) has deteriorated, and large numbers of Jordanians working in Kuwait and other Gulf states were sent home, causing both a fall in foreign exchange remittances and a rise in Jordanian unemployment. Jordan is a small country with inadequate supplies of water and other natural resources such as oil. The Persian Gulf crisis, which began in August 1990, aggravated Jordan's already serious economic problems, forcing the government to stop most debt payments and suspend rescheduling negotiations. Aid from Gulf Arab states, worker remittances, and trade revenues contracted. Refugees flooded the country, producing serious balance-of-payments problems, stunting GDP growth, and straining government resources.

The economy rebounded in 1992, largely due to the influx of capital repatriated by workers returning from the Gulf. After averaging 9 per cent in 1992–95, GDP growth averaged only 1.5 per cent during 1996–99. In an attempt to spur growth, King Abdallah has undertaken limited economic reform, including partial privatization of some state-owned enterprises and Jordan's entry in January 2000 into the World Trade Organization. Debt, poverty, and unemployment are fundamental ongoing economic problems. Other problems facing Jordan include potential for political instability arising from widespread poverty and challenges mounted by various Islamic fundamentalist factions, water shortages and heavy dependence on imported oil and other energy.

Kuwait possesses between 15 and 20 per cent of the world's known reserves of oil, although Kuwaiti oil production has declined steadily over the past 20 years. Oil revenues have been used in part to diversify the country's manufacturing base, which now contributes 30 per cent of GDP. Investment has focused on light engineering, paper, cement and fishing. More than half of Kuwait's 1.7 million population are under the age of 14. Note that 400,000 Palestinians and Jordanians were expelled from the country following the Gulf War. The country's immigrant workforce is now mainly Asian. There are around 700,000 native Kuwaitis.

Morocco embarked on a major programme of economic liberalization in the late 1980s (after it ran out of foreign exchange reserves). The need for import licences has been abolished and tariff rates have tumbled (currently averaging 12 per cent). GDP is growing at about 4.5 per cent annually; budget deficits have been cut and the balance of payments has improved dramatically. Problems facing the Moroccan government include a high rate population increase, extremely high unemployment, an unskilled labour force and widespread illiteracy. Most Moroccan workers are engaged in agriculture. The country has no indigenous oil but does possess substantial deposits of other minerals. Tourism is a major industry, contributing much to Morocco's foreign exchange earnings. Manufacturing contributes 20 per cent of GDP, with significant food processing, textiles, clothing and machinery and transport sectors.

Saudi Arabia has a fertile plain along the Gulf coast, while the rest of the country is predominantly semi-arid desert scattered with oases. Irrigation is a major issue in this country (which has a minute annual rainfall) and much government expenditure is devoted to irrigation projects. Saudi Arabia has a rapidly expanding population. Ninety per cent of the country's exports and two-thirds of GNP are attributable to oil, of which Saudi Arabia is the world's third-largest producer. The country is largely self-sufficient in agriculture, and has a number of light manufacturing and services industries, although manufacturing only contributes about 8 per cent of Gross Domestic Product. Overall economic growth has been satisfactory, the problem being that much of its benefits are absorbed by the fast-growing population. Oil reserves are vast, thus securing the country's long-term economic (though not political) future. Threats to Saudi Arabia include possible political disruption (the country is an absolute monarchy with minimal democratic processes) and long-term reductions in the price of oil. Another problem is Saudi Arabia's heavy dependence on foreign labour: about 4.5 million foreigners live and work in the country.

At least one-third of all **Syrians** are engaged in agriculture, which accounts for 30 per cent of GDP. Irrigation and the availability of water is a major problem in this country. The construction by Turkey of dams on the Euphrates is a major source of potential conflict between the two countries. Syria's government is nominally committed to the liberalization of the country's economy, including convertibility of the currency and the privatization of enterprises, although neither of these have actually been achieved. There is little manufacturing industry and the country is heavily dependent on the sale of oil. Syria's backing for the US-led coalition in the Gulf War led to substantial aid from the West and the Gulf states. Peace with Israel would greatly improve Syria's economy, both in terms of increased possibilities for trade and the resulting potential for reducing the country's extensive expenditure on armaments.

Part III

Organizing for international markets

8

International marketing research

THE FUNCTION OF MARKETING RESEARCH

Application of the international marketing concept necessitates the precise determination of consumer demands and characteristics in order to satisfy consumer requirements. International marketing research is the vehicle through which the firm gathers and processes relevant information on foreign markets and operations. Its purpose is to help the firm improve the quality of its marketing decisions, apply the correct marketing mix and adopt the correct marketing strategies in each of the countries in which it does business. As a management tool, international marketing research can help the firm to reduce its exposure to risk, avoid errors, identify opportunities and match the firm's capabilities with foreign openings. It requires procedures for collecting, storing, classifying, interpreting and reproducing relevant information. A distinction might be made between international marketing *intelligence*, ie information about the overall market environment gathered on an ongoing basis, and *functional research* concerning particular aspects of the firm's marketing activities (see Figure 8.1). In practice the division between the two is frequently blurred.

International marketing research is necessary in order to decide which foreign markets to enter and the best mode of entry (exporting, licensing, joint ventures, etc) to each country. Other specific questions that international research might address are:

- which advertising messages to transmit, the prices to charge, which distribution channels to use and whether to modify existing products;
- where to position a company's product in each national market;
- the advertising media to be used in each country;
- whether to standardize or customize advertisements.

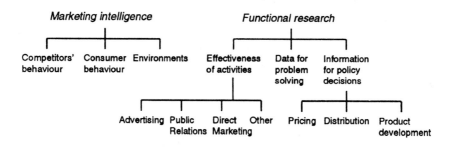

Figure 8.1 Marketing research requirements

Failure to undertake international marketing research might result in higher selling and distribution costs, lost opportunities and the company entering the wrong markets.

in practice...

Marketing research in Germany

During 2001, market researchers in Germany reported that response rates were seriously down. The problem was most widespread among IT and telecom professionals: these people reported getting up to 12 'cold calls' per day from market researchers, and consequently were refusing to participate in the research. Such professionals will often respond by saying that it is not company policy to participate in research: this has the further advantage of preventing the researchers from asking who else in the company might be able to help.

In many cases, companies really do have a policy against participating in research. This comes about as a result of pressure from two directions: firstly, that responding to research can represent a considerable investment of time on the part of the respondent, especially if calls are coming in as frequently as 12 per day. Secondly, some sales people still use the cover of market research as a way of lulling the respondent into a false sense of security. This practice is called 'sugging' (selling under the guise of market research) and is regarded as unethical – but still goes on.

For researchers, the problem has become a major one. Some commercial market research companies have adopted a policy of paying respondents for their time. Others have tried to access data through pan-European sources, but this has proved extremely difficult since EU data protection law varies from one member state to the next, making it almost impossible to find a comprehensive source for everything.

Data protection law in Germany is strict. In one case, Resource (Marketing Research) Ltd was asked to conduct a customer satisfaction survey on behalf of a large German IT provider. The German company was unable (under German law) to give the market research company a list of its customers, so the company had to cold-call IT customers at random to find the German company's customers. Such operations are wasteful, and irritating for those people who are not customers of the client company.

The future appears to lie in Web-based marketing research, not just for Germany but also throughout Europe. Some observers believe that, within five years, the majority of research within the EU will be conducted with people who have 'opted-in', and agreed to act as respondents for all and any research. Whether this option will be available for the rest of the world is doubtful – so much of the world is not Internet-enabled, or has doubtful connections at best. Whatever the long-term position, though, market researchers are certainly having a difficult time at present.

INFORMATION NEEDS

Information is needed on the environmental conditions prevailing within relevant countries, on variables affecting specific marketing decisions (choice of advertising media, pricing, selection of distribution channel, etc) and on trends in various markets (tastes and fashions, demographic change, and so on). Further issues for which research might be necessary are shown in Figure 8.2. Desk research involving secondary data (where applicable) is appropriate for some of these requirements; field research within the market may be needed for the rest. Collecting marketing information on numerous foreign countries is a potentially colossal task that could totally dominate the firm's marketing efforts, crowding out other important activities.

In industrialized Western countries, most information emanates from the central statistical offices of national governments, and thus relates to the situations pertaining within national boundaries. Additionally, the administrative organizations of international trade groups such as the EU and the Latin American Free Trade Association publish information on regional trends and comparisons of statistics on member states.

The first step is to gather information of a general nature on each foreign market that might be a candidate for entry. The range of available data is very broad (see Table 8.1), and needs to be categorized in an appropriate manner.

THE MARKETING INFORMATION SYSTEM

Marketing intelligence and functional research combine to create the firm's international marketing information system (Figure 8.3), which covers market analysis, competitor analysis and the assessment of risks and potential returns. Examples of the types of information that an effective international marketing information system will generate include:

- trends in sales in various countries, especially market failures;
- changes in the composition of the buying public;
- sales by product, region, customer type and selling method;
- average order size and customer spend;
- profitabilies of various products and market segments;
- feedback from customers obtained through sales call reports, questionnaires and market surveys;
- promotional costs and consequences.

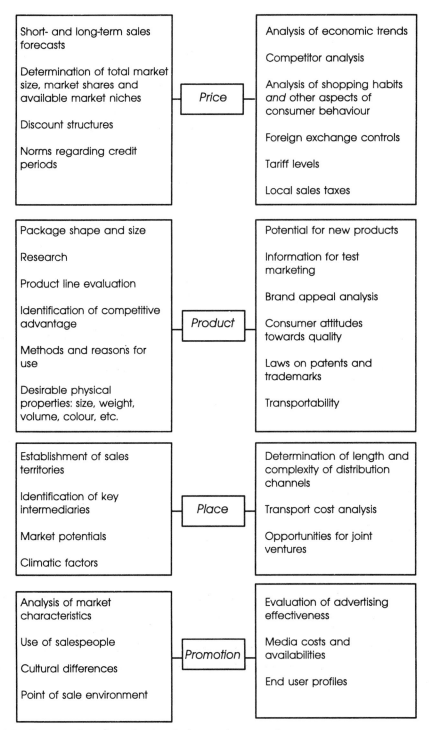

Figure 8.2 International marketing information requirements

Table 8.1   Types of data

Geographical parameters	Total population
• Total GDP	• Proportion of population within each age range and income group
• GDP per capita	• Ratio of urban to rural dwellers
• Economic trends	• Occupational breakdown of working population
• Balance of payments position: future foreign exchange problems	• Population growth rate
• Tariff and non-tariff barriers	• Lifestyle analysis
• Exchange controls	• Consumer tastes
• Structure of imports by value and product	• Average family size
• Rates of growth of imports	• Average age of dwellings by region
• Growth rates of market sectors, especially those that represent attractive markets	• Religious groupings
• Political stability	• Languages
• Government controls and attitudes towards business	• Literacy rates
• Consumer expenditure by volume and product category	• Schooling and length of time spent in education
• Rate of investment in fixed capital and industrial equipment	• Health care availability
• Wage rates by gender and occupational category	• Mortality rates
• Number of doctors per 1,000 population	• Per capita expenditure on medical products
• Legal constraints on business, and internal restrictions on trade	• Debt collecting facilities
• Quality of, and ease of entry to, distribution channels	• Advertising costs
• Competitors' prices	• Transport infrastructure

A marketing information system is a set of activities that are carried out on a regular, ongoing basis. For example, a firm might monitor the local news media on a daily basis for information that might be relevant. Information about competitive activity, about potential political changes, and about the economy will be available from these sources. Regular analysis of sales invoices might also generate useful information about trends in the market.

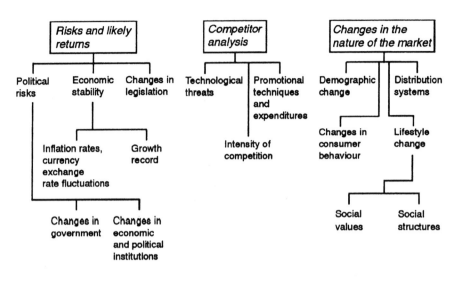

Figure 8.3 The international marketing information system

Sources of information

Secondary information for in-house research is available from:

- Publications of national statistical offices. All countries have state statistical services that collect data, conduct surveys and publish the results. This information is often available on CD ROM, but for some countries the information is likely to have been produced for political rather than economic reasons, so may not be reliable.
- Directories and data books issued by private publishing companies (Euromonitor's *International Marketing Data and Statistics*, for example).
- Databases held by database hosts such as DIALOG or FT PROFILE.
- Statistics gathered by international organizations, notably the OECD, United Nations, European Commission and the International Monetary Fund. In recent years, the United States's CIA has found a new role in publishing background information on every country in the world – a far cry from its Cold War spying activities.
- Chambers of commerce and trade associations, either in the home country or in the target market.
- Market research reports published by market research companies. Again, these may be available from companies in the home country or in the overseas market.
- Trade and technical magazines. For some countries, these may not be readily available, or may be published in a foreign language. The latter case points up the importance of language skills for would-be international marketers.

The quality of secondary information can vary enormously from country to country. Generally it is the case that the lower the per capita GDP within a country, the more diffi-

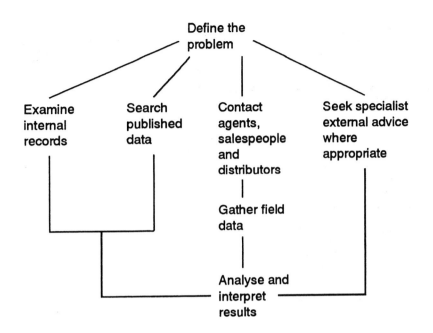

Figure 8.4 Gathering information

cult it is to research. Secondary data is harder to find and less reliable the poorer the country. The procedure for gathering information is illustrated in Figure 8.4.

HS numbers

Trade information on products is classified in most countries under Harmonized Commodity Description and Coding System (HS) numbers, which must be quoted in customs documentation when items are exported or imported. National customs offices will advise firms of the appropriate HS number for their product. Published tables that convert local classifications into HS numbers exist for countries that use different systems. A special easy-to-use version of the HS system is used within the EU and is known as TARIC.

Primary research

All the problems of domestic primary marketing research are replicated at the international level, and are more severe. Specification of research objectives is complex, and the execution of the research is difficult. The research design has to be modified in each country according to local cultural, economic, social and institutional factors. Questionnaires have to be translated or completely fresh ones devised; new sampling

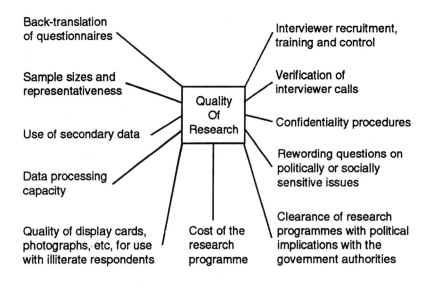

Figure 8.5 Checklist for completing international marketing research

frames (eg electoral registers, telephone books, etc) must be defined. Data collection procedures will vary from area to area. All these matters (and others – see Figure 8.5) impinge on the quality of the outputs from an international marketing research exercise. Further special problems relating to the design of international marketing research activities include the following:

- Since information relating to several countries (each possibly possessing a unique marketing environment) has to be gathered, a decision is needed regarding whether the research is to be managed at the head office or local level. The problem with centralization is that head office is forced to rely heavily on secondary data when evaluating issues, and could miss important factors. If, on the other hand, research is subcontracted to local research companies (which themselves might be subsidiaries of international research groups), then extra costs are incurred and the commissioning firm could lose effective control over the process.
- It is more difficult to establish an appropriate unit of analysis at the multi-country level than for domestic research. For example, it may be necessary to examine the same market segment across several countries, an entire regional grouping of countries, specific sectors within particular countries, etc, depending on corporate objectives and product category.
- Qualitative data collection and analysis techniques are subject to cultural bias on the part of the foreign researchers implementing them.

- Survey methods have to be varied according to literacy and education levels, consumer responsiveness to being asked questions and the communications media available in various countries (Malhotra, 1988).
- Field experiments are difficult to replicate in different countries in consequence of the influence of cultural factors.
- Researchers are likely to be ignorant of foreign marketing environments, institutions and media, resulting in their not knowing where to begin their investigations.
- Lack of familiarity with foreign data sources and the inability to assess the reliability of the information they supply may lead to bad decisions.
- Coordination and control problems may arise from the need to conduct research across national frontiers, especially when there are different research objectives in different countries.
- It may be necessary to rely on anecdotal evidence in order to assess the market situations of certain countries.
- The financial costs of collecting primary data in countries that have no marketing research infrastructure are very high.
- It is difficult to compare research results from one country with those of others. Customization of questionnaires, etc to suit local conditions is obviously desirable, since otherwise the information collected might be deficient, but may mean that the results from various countries are not comparable because of differences in:
  - meaning and interpretation of data categories;
  - accuracy and precision of measurement;
  - coverage;
  - reliability of information (Malhotra, 1991).
- Attitudes might be expressed in different ways in different countries.
- Biases can arise from interactions between researchers and the people they are investigating. In some cultures there is a strong tendency for respondents to acquiesce to what they perceive questioners to be looking for. Elsewhere there is great reluctance to answer questions in general or on particular topics. Asian respondents in particular (notably in China and Japan) are notorious for agreeing with any proposition implicit in market research questions – regardless of their actual opinions – in order not to distress or offend the party conducting the research. In other parts of the world there are observed tendencies for respondents to exaggerate, to voice extreme opinions or even to lie about certain subjects.

Interpretation of research results

There are two contrasting approaches to the interpretation of research results. The first asserts that consumer attitudes and behaviour are unique to the particular culture within which they arise. Each country is said to have specific values and modes of expression that are best understood in their own terms (rather than by comparison with the norms of other societies). Therefore research methods must be adapted to fit the unique circumstances of each country and (importantly) no attempt should be made to compare data and results from different countries or to infer that conclusions drawn in one country will be valid elsewhere. Research should focus on the identification and measurement of variables specifically relevant to the country concerned.

The alternative view is that universal commonalities exist among consumers in different countries. Hence it should be possible to develop standardized procedures for measuring and analysing these common characteristics. The precision, reliability and accuracy of information will of course differ from state to state, but the same concepts and research methodologies are valid in all countries. According to this school of thought the role of research is to investigate universal behavioural tendencies, attitudes, etc, and to devise culture-free ways of evaluating them. Researchers may legitimately adopt international perspectives (as opposed to studying behaviour within a particular system) and use the same criteria to compare behaviour in disparate countries. The advantage of taking this view is that cross-border comparisons are more likely to be valid when the same research programme has been used in both cases.

International marketing research is perhaps more interested in identifying cross-cultural similarities than in analysing national differences, since this enables firms to transfer products and strategies for marketing them across national frontiers. Note, however, that different research methods might be applied to the investigation of commonalities in different markets.

Analysis of competitors

Considering the high costs of international marketing research and the uncertainties involved, it is not surprising that some companies choose not to commit extensive resources to this activity, relying instead on close observation of the activities of local competing businesses. Note, moreover, that bad decisions resulting from the analysis and interpretation of faulty research data will actually reduce company profitability. Competitor analysis can be highly cost-effective, and needs to encompass the following:

- Details of the strengths and weaknesses of competitors' products and how these compare with the outputs of the firm in question. This information is available from competitors' brochures, leaflets and other promotional literature and/or through purchasing their products. To evaluate competing brands the firm could ask a sample of its own customers to comment on the quality of competitors' outputs.
- Why competitors choose to operate in particular markets. The absence of competition in a particular market could indicate an inhospitable environment, possibly including negative government attitudes towards foreign companies.
- How competitors are organized: their distribution systems, whether they have departments for brands or for functions, nature of subsidiaries, etc. Lists of distributors are usually given out freely in response to customer enquiries. Also competitors' advertisements often specify where and how their products may be purchased.
- Competitors' terms of sale, credit periods, levels of after-sales service and so on.
- The financial performance of competing firms. It is easier to obtain this information for limited companies (which must publish their accounts) than for other types of

business. Trade magazines frequently publish market surveys with analyses of the major businesses in particular markets. Such articles present estimates of the total extent of markets, the market share of various firms, competitors' histories, profitabilities, selling and distribution methods and advertising style.

- The themes and concepts used in competitors' promotional materials. This requires the collation of a folio of each competitor's advertisements.
- Competitors' product development strategies. Introductions by competitors of new products or product features, or competitors' acquisitions of other businesses in order to obtain their brands. Also the market sectors covered by competitors, their packaging, distribution arrangements, sales promotions and public relations events.
- Prices and pricing history of competitors' brands, particularly the environmental changes that caused alterations in pricing strategies.
- The timing and seasonality of competitors' campaigns, and the implications of these timings for how competitors perceive their target audiences. Competitors' rotations of radio or television stations, magazines, etc.

The drawback of observing competitors is, of course, that competitive advantage is unlikely to come from following what competitors do. Deviating from what the competitors do might equally be disastrous, and means that market research needs to be undertaken – which of course takes the company back to step one.

Market analysis

Market surveys might cover such matters as:

- demographics, such as the age structure of the population, religious groupings, the number of households and average household size, social conditions, regional distribution of the population and its rate of expansion;
- market size and structure;
- macroeconomic influences, eg inflation and unemployment rates, trends in Gross Domestic Product, business confidence indicators, and so forth;
- consumer characteristics in terms of cultural attitudes (marriage and divorce rates, for example), educational levels, living standards, average income and income distribution;
- spending patterns in relation to percentages of consumer purchases made in supermarkets, hypermarkets, independent retailers, department stores, and so forth.

THE RESEARCH PROGRAMME

The starting point of an international marketing research exercise is the precise definition of its objectives, followed by an estimate of how much it will cost. The feasibility of the intended research needs to be assessed. Specific terms of reference for the programme will then be drafted, possibly relating to the identification of such factors as:

- the tastes, lifestyles and spending patterns of customers in target foreign markets;
- the nature of local distribution channels, especially the number and calibre of retail outlets;
- the average local income and the distribution of wealth, living standards, housing, education, etc;
- the local business practices in foreign markets;
- the availability of manufacturing, packaging or labelling facilities in other countries;
- the analysis of competitors' activities (see above);
- the sizes of various market sectors, their buoyancy and growth prospects.

Thereafter the process is as shown in Figure 8.6. Formulating an effective research programme is a difficult task, requiring skill, effort and persistence. It involves the identification of relevant issues, the extent and availability of the necessary information and the costs and characteristics of key databases, hard copy and other data sources.

MARKETING RESEARCH IN THE THIRD WORLD

Although it is extremely difficult to conduct marketing research in Third World countries, research is perhaps the most reliable way to determine the essential characteristics of consumer environments and behaviour in these countries. However, the question arises as to whether the research methods commonly used in industrially advanced economics are realistically applicable to Third World markets, since data collection problems are so severe that the preferences and opinions of only a small part of the population can be obtained. Specific problems encountered when seeking to undertake research into Third World markets include:

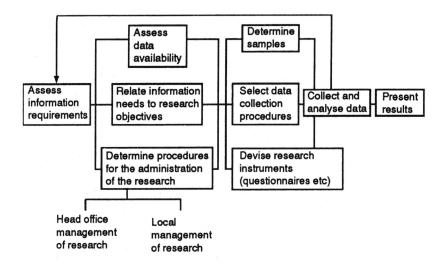

Figure 8.6 The process of international marketing research

- Lack of published information (government statistics, data books, market surveys, etc) on market characteristics. Most Third World governments have rather more pressing problems to deal with than collecting business statistics.
- Absence of local research companies able to gather accurate information. The small average size of enterprise common in Third World countries means there are few local businesses with the resources necessary to buy significant amounts of marketing research.
- The lack of a common language with some countries.
- Inability to identify the nature and size of dwelling units. In some Third World countries people live in tents or other temporary accommodation, and in India many people live on the streets of the cities. Also, census figures on numbers of individuals in each household are likely to be inaccurate.
- Data collection difficulties due to poor mail and telecommunications systems, low literacy rates (inhibiting the use of questionnaires) and unwillingness of consumers in some areas to answer questions.
- Absence of a pool of trained and experienced marketing research interviewers.
- Inadequate sampling frames, ie the inability to identify meaningful samples of consumers upon which to generalize. It may be that there is no electoral register. High birth rates and population shifts from villages to towns can quickly make census data obsolete. Sampling bias is likely to be extremely high in such circumstances.

in practice...

Mysore Breweries

K P Balasubramaniam had an MBA and a bottling business he inherited from his father. Originally, the firm bottled Coke, but Balasubramaniam decided that working for foreigners was not the way forward for an Indian firm – so he gave the soft drinks business to one of the firm's partners and obtained a brewing licence from the Karnataka government. The new brewery, Mysore Breweries Limited, began by importing brewing technology (and brands) from Carlsberg in Denmark. This quickly proved to be problematic – market research showed that Indians did not like the flavour of the Danish beer, so Balasubramaniam developed several brands that have flavours designed for Indian taste buds.

India, as a country, has a mixed attitude to alcoholic drink. In many states, alcohol is banned altogether, and in most states it is regarded as something that is tolerated rather than embraced. Alcohol consumption is often severely constrained by law, and is carried out very discreetly. However, in states such as Andhra Pradesh, Goa and Punjab, alcohol is accepted.

At first, MBL did not do well – until Balasubramaniam hit on the idea of developing specific beers aimed at specific states. Research showed that foreign beers were not well regarded, and that drinkers would welcome the chance to buy Indian-made beer. As a result of this, the brewery's 'Knockout' brand, a strong beer developed for Andhra Pradesh, was sold as a mass-market beer to undercut United Breweries' premium beers. 'Knockout' was an instant success, and was rapidly followed by Cobra, which is the leading Indian export beer, widely sold in curry houses throughout the United Kingdom. In a market dominated by foreign imports and foreign partnerships, MBL has managed to make its Indian roots into its strength. The company has steadfastly refused to enter into foreign partnerships, and looks set to topple United Breweries from its position of dominance in the Indian beer market.

ORGANIZING RESEARCH

Firms may conduct foreign research themselves, or use specialist market research businesses for this work. The latter undertake a wide range of investigational duties, including consumer sampling, test marketing, interpreting foreign statistics, estimating competitors' market shares, determining the costs and benefits of various distribution options, and so on. A commissioning company can choose either a market research firm based in its own home country, or a foreign research company located in the local foreign market concerned.

Home-based research firms

A home-based research company could do the work itself – sending out its own staff to visit local markets as and when necessary – or might subcontract to foreign researchers, or place the assignment with its own branch or subsidiary in the foreign country. The advantages of using a domestic firm include the following:

- One-stop shopping: a large research company should be capable of supplying all the client's research needs.
- The research firm will possess wide-ranging experience of similar assignments already completed for other businesses. Hence the client benefits indirectly from other companies' research efforts.
- When choosing a research firm the client can conveniently invite proposals from several domestic research firms, compare their costs, personally discuss its requirements with each candidate and examine examples of past assignments completed for other clients.
- The commissioning company can quickly evaluate the quality of the research firm's work.

A domestic research firm might claim that it is fully competent to operate in all foreign markets. However, this need not be the case. And if the company simply subcontracts to locally based foreign research firms, the client not only loses control over the work, but also its brief to the domestic research company may not be comprehensively and accurately transmitted to the latter's contact abroad. Also there is no easy way to establish whether the local subcontractor is performing satisfactorily.

in practice...

Braun

Braun, the German personal appliance manufacturer, has a centralized market research department employing multilingual researchers each with several years of international experience. The firm itself is organized into product divisions, and each researcher has responsibilities corresponding to the work of each division. Within product divisions there are various subsidiary businesses, the four largest of which have their own market research departments that conduct local research and feed information to the company's centralized market research office, which takes major decisions on the basis of this stream of data. Two-way communications between head office and subsidiary researchers provide for the cross-checking of translations, provision of specialist help and advice on particular issues, local control over subcontract research agencies and general co-ordination of all the company's market research activities.

Local researchers

The problems with using a resident foreign research company are:

- the expensive and time-consuming need to visit the firm;
- the fact that (normally) the laws of the other country will apply if the client has to sue the research company for incompetence and/or failing to complete the project;
- the difficulty of appraising the research firm's performance.

However, local representatives are closer (culturally as well as geographically) to local consumers and should be better able to assess local consumer attitudes and tastes.

in practice...

Unilever

Unilever is a good example of a company that uses a decentralized approach to market research. The firm has numerous local products tailor-made for particular national markets that are researched locally. For genuinely international brands a 'lead country' approach is adopted, ie a country considered to contain large numbers of consumers likely to be attracted to the brand is selected for intensive market research, followed by research into the key marketing variables relevant to the proposed new product conducted by decentralized units across several different countries. The decentralized research cross-checks the results obtained in the lead country and looks for possible local factors that might impede the introduction of the item to the local market.

9

Market screening techniques

CHOOSING MARKETS

Choosing which market to enter is a key strategic decision. In some cases this will mean choosing a country or group of countries, in other cases it will mean choosing a market segment that crosses national (and even cultural) boundaries. Having considered the world situation and carried out some appropriate research, the firm's next move is to select an appropriate market, the appropriateness to be decided in the light of the firm's overall strategic vision.

Firms contemplating international marketing campaigns need to determine the regional economic groupings, individual countries and specific market segments in which they intend doing business. In principle, every country in the world is a candidate for market entry. It is necessary, therefore, to reduce the list of possibilities to manageable dimensions.

Marketing opportunities in foreign countries usually exist but are difficult to locate. Searching for export markets is akin to exploring for geological mineral deposits: direct observation may be impossible, but the probability of their presence can be assessed from the characteristics of environments where they might be found. Two approaches to the location of suitable countries and/or market segments within countries are: either to define the characteristics of the target consumers and then examine countries in order to determine which countries contain sufficient numbers of that customer type to make entry worthwhile or, alternatively, determine the markets in which it will be easiest to sell the company's product (eg because a significant proportion of the population speaks a certain language, or since local business methods are essentially similar to those found at home) and adapt the firm's output and advertising messages to make them suitable for those markets.

Adoption of either of these approaches does not necessarily rule out the other and plain common sense may enable the firm immediately to select suitable countries and target consumer types. Normally, however, a significant amount of research is required.

Thus a logical, disciplined and structured approach to market selection must be applied. Clearly it is important to eliminate as quickly as possible all markets offering little chance of success (in view of the high cost of conducting research), but it is also essential not to be too hasty and improperly knock out candidate countries with genuine potential.

Some of today's poorer countries will be tomorrow's most dynamic markets, and the speed of transition is increasing. For example, Turkey and Brazil doubled their per capita GDPs over 20-year periods in the 1950s and 1960s. South Korea and China achieved this feat in 10 years (the former from 1966, the latter from 1978), and current growth rates in the Far East and the Pacific Rim will reduce the necessary period still further. The key unifying characteristics of countries that have achieved the highest rate of economic growth appear to be:

- rapid growth of technological developments, often through imitating the products and methods of more advanced states;
- the existence of a sufficient number of skilled workers able to operate new technologies;
- low wage costs compared to rival countries;
- competitive business environments;
- involvement in international trade.

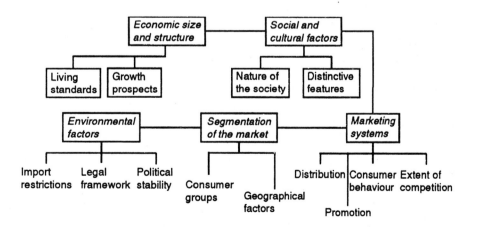

Figure 9.1 Categorization of information for market screening

IDENTIFYING APPROPRIATE MARKETS

Identifying appropriate markets involves screening countries against a series of factors. Some factors will be more relevant to some companies than will others, but the key areas of interest are as follows (see Figure 9.1):

- **Market size**. In general, the bigger a country's population the better, since, other things being equal, more potential customers can be approached. Note, however, that a large part of the population might not be remotely interested in buying a particular type of product or may not have the money to do so. Other important considerations are the age structure of the population and its rate of expansion. High population growth is a double-edged sword from the exporter's point of view: it creates more consumers but may at the same time reduce average living standards and per capita GDP. It is a fact that the poorest countries have the highest rates of population expansion. Further indicators of market size include:
  - levels of domestic production and imports to the market of the item in question;
  - number of firms serving the market;
  - level of exports of the product from the foreign country (if this is high it might suggest limited demand for the item within the market);
  - rate of increase of the local price of the product relative to the local rate of inflation (a large differential implies a heavy demand for the item).
- **Structure of the population**. Different age groups have disparate needs, incomes, perspectives and buying habits, so that the age structure of the population could be crucial for products that appeal to particular age categories. The geographical area over which the population is distributed might also be important. The lower the population density per square kilometre, the more difficult and expensive it is to distribute goods.
- **Economic development**. It may be possible to identify countries at the same level of economic development and with consumers who exhibit the same patterns of demand. For countries at a similar level of economic development as the country of the exporting firm it may be appropriate to find the variables with which demand for the company's product is most closely correlated within the domestic market, and then look for these variables in other countries. The degree of organization of the population may be a relevant factor. City dwellers tend to be better educated than people who live in remote rural areas. They are easier to reach and more likely to respond positively to conventional advertising messages. Communications, transport and warehousing systems are more advanced. Urbanites are usually more cosmopolitan in outlook than their rural compatriates. Note, moreover, that illiteracy rates are high in many countries with large numbers of rural dwellers. How a particular market will progress might be predicted from a careful analysis of how other countries with a similar economic background but at a more advanced stage of industrialization have themselves progressed.
- **Income and wealth**. These might be measured by Gross Domestic Product in total and per head of population (noting the great disparities of income and wealth that

exist within many countries), private consumption spending, and ownership rates of motor cars and consumer durables. If most people have an income near the national average their purchasing habits are likely to be the same. Typically, however, very many people are far below the average, indicating large differences in living standards, with a few consumers being extremely rich and the majority poor. In effect there are two economies coexisting within a single country, and marketing to each requires its own special approach. An even distribution of income and wealth is desirable for marketing consumer durables and other middle-income products; uneven distribution might help sales of extremely expensive, superluxury items. Another relevant factor is the country's rate of inflation, which determines real (as opposed to nominal) changes in standards of living.

- **Business environment**. Local religious or cultural norms may influence the consumption of certain items. National laws could demand special guarantees, after-sales service, safety standards and so on not required in the exporter's country.

    The importance of tariffs as a decision variable will depend not only on their levels but also on the extent of local production of the item, since local producers do not have to increase their selling price to cover the tariff. A firm might not be able to afford specialist staff with linguistic capabilities, and therefore choose markets with well-established intermediaries and within which it is normally possible to conduct business in a familiar language. Here the company will be looking for markets within which exist well-developed and easily available ancillary business services: advertising agencies, public relations consultancies, market research firms, etc.

- **Storage and transport facilities**. The climatic conditions that prevail in certain countries may make them unsuitable for particular products. Road and railway systems might be inadequate for effective distribution of the exported goods.

- **Political considerations**. Political instability causes loss in business confidence since exporters fear they will not be paid. Foreign governments could impose maximum prices. There are risks of ideological disputes between the governments of exporters' and importers' countries.

- **Local competition**. Foreign markets already served by many suppliers are, of course, difficult to enter. Note also that existing local firms often enjoy easy access to local capital markets and may control local distribution channels. Competitive intensity is more important the simpler the product and hence the greater the difficulty of differentiating a particular brand from those of competing businesses.

Firms often approach countries with which the firm's home country has a psychological proximity. For example, UK firms frequently target the United States because of a perception that the cultures are similar. This can lead to problems: the United States is a long way away, and is not as culturally close as might at first appear. The European Union is much closer physically, and in the vast majority of cases has cultures similar enough for cultural differences to have very little negative impact on sales. Likewise, Spanish firms often target Latin America, and French firms target former colonies in the Pacific, Africa and the Caribbean.

Field work

Field work is expensive but sometimes essential, especially where it is difficult to measure a market's size and characteristics from published data and where consumer attitudes and behaviour cannot otherwise be assessed. No field trip can cover every aspect of factors relevant to possible entry; rather, a successful field trip will encompass a sample of contacts that are truly representative of local customers, businesses and institutions. Follow-up enquiries via post, telephone and fax should then be possible. The overall process of market screening is illustrated in Figure 9.2.

Market attractiveness indexes

Some firms compute indexes of market potential from weighted averages of whichever of the above-mentioned variables they consider most appropriate to marketing their products. Hence countries are ranked according to the number of points they score on key variables relevant to the market entry decision, with scores being given for factors such as GDP in aggregate and per head of population, rates of ownership of consumer durables, particular socio-demographic variables (life expectancy, consumer educational levels, consumer buying habits and so on, according to their expected influence on sales of the product). Stages in the implementation of a points system for comparing potential markets are as follows:

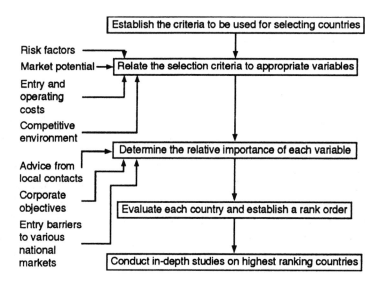

Figure 9.2 The process of market screening

1. Based on the firm's overall corporate strategy and a pragmatic assessment of its resources, strengths and weaknesses, management lists the criteria to be used in the analysis: eg tariff levels applying to the product in question in each country, transport costs, size of the market, ease of promotion within the country (advertising restrictions, etc), competitive intensity, risk factors, distribution facilities and so on.
2. Weights are assigned to the perceived importance of each variable depending on the nature of the product and the firm's particular circumstances.
3. All countries and/or markets that seemingly offer profit potential are listed. Published data are collected plus any other conveniently available information on candidate countries under the selected criteria.
4. Countries are categorized into three groups: probables, possibles and 'no hopers'. The last are discarded.
5. The research effort applied to probable entry countries is intensified. Further general information on possibles is collected and, if appropriate, certain possibles are promoted to the probable category. The remainder are dropped.
6. Points are allocated to each variable for each remaining country. Outside advice is taken where appropriate.

The main problems are deciding the weights to attach to each variable (especially total population and GDP) and the high sensitivity of the results to changes in weights. Comparability exercises are complex, subjective and sometimes based on unreliable data, so the results need to be treated with extreme caution. The major justification for completing a market comparability analysis is perhaps the discipline it imposes on the managers involved, requiring them to think carefully about their intended actions and to adopt a logical and systematic approach to the problem.

Problems with market screening

Many of the practical problems associated with international marketing research apply also to market screening, including:

- The high financial cost of gathering information on many foreign countries.
- The vast number of potentially relevant variables and the difficulty of deciding which ones are critical.
- The extent and frequency of dramatic changes in foreign market conditions.
- The fact that the initial screening process needs to rely on whatever published information about candidate countries happens to be available in the exporter's home country. Data for certain countries are unreliable, the base years of statistical series will differ, and many gaps in data are likely. Population age categorizations might not be the same, especially for 'young' people, who might be defined as between 15 and 24 years of age, 14 and 18, 13 and 20, etc.

It is important that the results of the exercise do not lead a company to spread its resources too thinly over numerous foreign markets. Administrative duties multiply as the special needs of each new market have to be dealt with, and increasing amounts of (expensive) marketing research are required. At the same time, part of the purpose of international marketing is to spread risk across a range of markets, which means that the overall risk reduces as more markets are entered.

MARKET SEGMENTATION

Some foreign consumers will be more interested in buying the firm's product than others, so it is necessary to discover the type of person most likely to purchase the firm's output in terms of such variables as consumer age, sex, income, family size, living standards, lifestyle, buying habits, attitudes and geographical location.

Market segmentation means breaking down the total market into self-contained and relatively homogeneous subgroups of consumers, each possessing its own special requirements and characteristics. This enables the company to modify its output, advertising messages and promotional methods to correspond to the needs of particular segments. Accurate segmentation allows the firm to pinpoint selling opportunities and to tailor its marketing activities to satisfy consumer needs.

Data on consumers' ages, sex, income levels, occupations, educational backgrounds, marital status and social class can be extremely useful in identifying the whereabouts of potential markets. Each time a fresh variable is added to the analysis the narrower the target market becomes. This results in a more precise specification of the customer type being sought, hence enabling the firm to identify an assortment of promotional methods that cater for this segment (Baalbaki and Malhotra, 1993). A problem arises in that the market definition may become so narrow that a large number of genuine prospects are excluded, so that messages are not drafted to appeal to these consumer groups. The objective, therefore, is to subdivide the market accurately without precluding bona fide opportunities.

in practice...

House of Darts

House of Darts is a UK manufacturer of dart-related products (dartboards, flights, wallets, clocks, pens and pencils, mugs, etc) that sells more than 95 per cent of its output abroad. Precise targeting of niche markets (which extend to 81 counties) has been crucial to the firm's international marketing success. Various types of soft-tip darts (with plastic points for throwing at plastic honeycomb-structured dartboards) are sold in numerous countries, the product being differentiated by colour, design of dart flights (national flags, faces of celebrities, pictures of animals, insignia of football teams and so on) and equipment size. The game of darts is regarded as a 'pub game' in some countries, as a family game in others, or as a competitive sport elsewhere. Depending on the region involved, darts may be seen as a game for young children, for young adults, or for older people. This affects the sort of retail outlet most effective for carrying House of Darts products. The firm's promotional literature is translated into seven languages and mailed twice annually to 8,000 customers throughout the world.

Lifestyle (psychographic) segmentation

Segmentation according to economic or demographic variables assumes that most of the consumers within the economic or demographic category concerned behave in a similar manner. In fact, consumer attitudes, perspectives and purchasing behaviour can differ remarkably within market groups possessing nearly identical demographic characteristics. For example, two households may be located in the same area and have equal incomes, yet exhibit enormous differences in their consumption patterns according to their lifestyle, attitudes and aspirations.

Hence the incorporation into the analysis of a psychosocial dimension to reflect consumer lifestyles, personality types, interests, leisure activities, perspectives and opinions is likely to sharpen the firm's targeting. The term 'psychographics' refers to the systematic study of consumer lifestyles, attitudes, interests, opinions and prejudices as they affect purchasing behaviour. Psychographics seeks to sketch profiles of particular consumer groups and hence identify demands for certain products from key variables that characterize consumer types. For instance, an outdoor type who enjoys sport, fast cars, action-packed television programmes, etc, may be attracted by products with rugged images that correspond to these conceptions. This kind of analysis distinguishes between consumers in terms of their activities, interests and opinions, particularly their use of leisure, stance on ethical and social issues, and attitudes towards themselves and the environment in which they exist. Psychographics can be a useful supplement to demographic analysis, allowing the firm to segment a market more precisely.

Importance of lifestyle

Lifestyle is the consequence of many interacting variables: income, upbringing, experiences, relationships with others, cultural influences, and so forth. It involves a pattern of living habits, leisure pursuits, types of entertainment purchased, degree of involvement with the community and so on. 'Vicarious participation' in a certain desired way of life (eg healthy, sophisticated, outdoor, 'man-about-town', etc) is sometimes possible via consuming goods mentally associated with the lifestyle to which the individual aspires. Lifestyles have been analysed and classified into a number of categories. The aim is to identify in consumers certain common characteristics, such as:

- whether they are motivated by materialistic or non-materialistic drives;
- the extent to which their main concern is merely to exist and survive rather than engage in luxury and/or conspicuous consumption;
- whether their outlook is 'conservative and traditional' or whether they are 'innovative and adventurous';

- the degree of logic and rationality they apply to purchasing decisions;
- whether they are 'inner directed' (ie concerned with personal growth, individual freedom and human relations) or 'outer directed' materialists who gain greater satisfaction from physical consumption of goods;
- attitudes towards home, family, security and the propriety of the status quo.

For each of these decisions a number of subcategories may be discerned (eg ambitious achievers, the near-destitute struggling poor, the materialistic young, etc) within various countries. In the international context, lifestyle analysis has become extremely important in recent years, particularly in Third World countries, where an emerging middle class seeks to adopt the lifestyle of Western countries. This necessarily means acquiring Western products and adopting Western customs. For example, it is by no means unusual to see Christmas trees, complete with artificial snow and robins, in tropical countries where such imagery has no natural place. The influence of Hollywood and the international TV industry has had a marked effect on Third World lifestyle aspirations, with consequent opportunities for opening up new markets.

Problems with psychographic segmentation

Criticisms of the psychographic approach include allegations of superficiality, inconsistency of proposed categorizations over time, and failure to relate the assumed existence of particular groupings to casual factors. The analysis rests on the assumption that consumers have stable values, beliefs and attitudes that are not subject to sudden and unpredictable change. Casual observation of human behaviour suggests that this is not always true. Other problems include the following:

- The psychosocial categorizations used in psychographics are highly subjective and open to numerous interpretations. What exactly is meant by terms such as 'sophisticated', 'reflective', 'persuadable', 'redefined', etc?
- Psychographic analysis for products that are used by a wide range of types of consumers is a waste of money.
- Implementation of campaigns resulting from segmentation exercises requires the existence of highly specialized media vehicles (newspapers, magazines, radio stations, etc) capable of carrying specially devised messages to narrowly defined target groups.

Feasibility of market segments

To be a feasible candidate for market entry a segment must be genuinely homogeneous and capable of precise definition, large enough to justify a substantial promotional effort, and not present major logistical difficulties. Note that a market segment within a single country may be insignificant of itself, but when aggregated across several countries might contain a large number of potential consumers. Improved transport and communications and the liberalization of movements of capital and labour within regional groupings mean moreover that specific market segments are today covering more and more consumers than ever before. People may live under different political, religious and cultural regimes but nevertheless have very similar lifestyles, thus having the same consumer needs and responding to common promotional themes and messages. Hopefully the buying characteristics of consumers within a particular market segment in one country will mirror those of people in the same market segment elsewhere.

10

Entering international markets

THE DECISION-TAKING PROCESS

Decisions concerning the mode of a firm's entry to particular foreign markets are among the most crucially important that its management will ever have to take. Once an entry method has been selected, its implementation has significant implications for a wide range of international marketing concerns. Selling prices, for example, need to reflect the extent of intermediaries' mark-ups; the size of a business's sales force may depend on whether it deals with wholesalers or sells direct to retailers; contracts with agents and distributors can lock the supplying firm into long-term commitments from which it is difficult (and perhaps extremely expensive) to withdraw. Indeed, a company's entire international marketing programme might be substantially determined by how it chooses to enter foreign countries. Thus, time and effort must be devoted to the decision-taking process, and extensive market research may be required.

The firm needs to consider carefully all the available options, the costs, possible loss of control (over product presentation to final customers for instance) and the risks involved. Moreover, the market entry methods chosen have to relate to the company's overall strategy, goals and the time periods in which it wishes its objectives to be achieved. To some extent, the choice of entry method is constrained by the level of resources available to the firm, although many other factors need to be taken into account as well as financial, human and other resource requirements. The options for entering foreign markets are:

- exporting;
- use of agents and/or distributors;
- joint ventures with foreign firms;

- licensing and franchising;
- management contracts;
- contract manufacturing;
- establishment of foreign branches and/or subsidiaries (including direct foreign investment in manufacturing plant);
- direct marketing via the Internet.

Each of these has a particular mix of cost, risk and ease of control (see Bartlett and Ghousal, 1989, and Brooke, 1992, for further information on this point). Operation of foreign subsidiaries, for example, typically involves a high start-up cost and substantial losses if foreign establishments fail, but there is total control over all promotional activities and the distribution of goods. Indirect exporting carries little risk but the firm cannot determine its final selling prices in foreign markets, how the product is presented to end-users, customer care, and so on. Market entry options are outlined in Figure 10.1.

Criteria for selecting an option

These should relate to the firm's overall corporate strategy and the extent, depth and geographical coverage of its foreign operations (Kwon and Konopa, 1993). Does the company want long-term involvement with international markets, or opportunistic export sales? Specific criteria are:

- the business's financial resources and hence its capacity to purchase or set up foreign establishments;
- physical and technical characteristics of the product (simple products are easy to manufacture abroad);
- availability of marketing and general business services in target foreign markets;
- ease of communication with intermediaries (agents, consortium buyers, etc) in specific countries;
- local constraints on the foreign ownership of businesses and/or licensing arrangements;
- the degree of market penetration desired (deep penetration normally requires a permanent presence within the country concerned);
- the firm's experience and expertise in selling and operating abroad;
- size of the margins taken by intermediaries in particular countries;
- tariff levels, quotas and other non-tariff barriers within a market;
- availability of trained and competent personnel for staffing foreign subsidiaries;
- political stability of the foreign countries the firm wishes to enter and other risk factors;
- how quickly the firm wishes to commence operations in the market (outright purchase of a fully operational local business is usually the speediest method);
- volatility of, and competitive intensity in, the countries concerned;
- the ease with which intellectual property can be protected (this is particularly important for licensing and joint ventures).

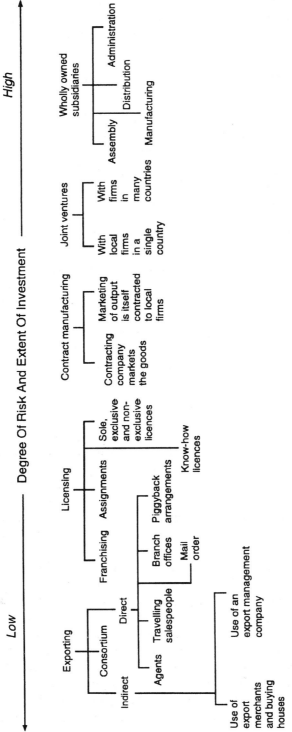

Figure 10.1 Market entry options

Large firms with substantial foreign operations typically find they need to adopt a variety of methods for doing business in various national markets: exporting to some; manufacturing, licensing or operating joint ventures elsewhere.

AGENTS AND DISTRIBUTORS

The difference between an agent and a distributor is that whereas the latter actually *purchases* a supplying firm's products (assuming thereby full responsibility for their condition, sale and any bad debts), agents put their clients in touch with third parties but then 'drop out' of resulting contracts, so that the agreements are between the agent's client and third parties, without the agent being further involved. An agent will find foreign customers for a company's products, but if the goods are defective, damaged or delivered late it is the client and not the agent who is responsible. Agents usually operate on a commission basis and may be either *brokers*, who simply bring together buyers and sellers without ever taking physical possession of the goods, or *factors*, who do hold stocks of the goods (eg in showrooms and/or warehouses) until customers are found and who sometimes sell under their own name and decide on final selling prices. A *del credere* agent is one who, in return for a higher commission, indemnifies the supplying firm against the customers' bad debts.

Factors (or distribution agents as they are sometimes called) are normally preferred when the product might be required at short notice, sells better in showroom surroundings, and is normally sold after customer examination and in small quantities. Clearly the distinction between an agency agreement and a distribution agreement can become blurred, especially if the agent is acting as a factor. Distributors typically demand exclusivity. Exclusivity clauses in a distribution agreement can create legal difficulties, because exclusive trading arrangements are not generally permitted under the competition laws of most industrialized countries. Even if no exclusivity arrangement is specified, a distributor will almost certainly insist on receiving more favourable terms than other purchasers, again causing legal problems. In the European Union, geographically exclusive distribution agreements are exempt from competition law provided: there exist alternative sources of supply of that type of product in the area covered; and customers in the distributor's territory are free to obtain the goods from at least one other source apart from the exclusive distributor. This latter source could be a distributor in an adjacent territory, or direct supply from the supplier's own premises. Also, at least one of the parties must have a turnover of less than €100 million per annum.

The comparative advantages of having agents rather than distributors, selection criteria and the key elements to be incorporated into contracts, are set out in Tables 10.1 and 10.2. Agents' commission rates require tight contractual specification, specifically in relation to whether the principal will pay commission on orders received from the agent's territory that did not pass directly through the agent but which might be indirectly attributable to the agent's work (repeat orders, for example). Also, contracts must specify when exactly commission is payable: on receipt of an order, on delivery of the goods or on final settlement of the resulting invoice. Is commission still payable if an order is cancelled at a late stage or if the customer's firm goes bankrupt? How frequently will accrued commission be handed over – monthly, quarterly, semi-annually or when?

In some countries, notably France, the conditions under which agents are employed are subject to national employment law, which means that firing an agent is far from simple, especially if the arrangement has been continuing for some time.

When choosing an agent or a distributor, the criteria shown in Figure 10.2 should be taken into account.

When drawing up a contract for a distributor or agent, the following factors should be included:

- the parties to the agreement;
- the products and the territories to be covered;
- whether the contract is exclusive (only one client) or not;
- the duration of the contract;
- provision for settling disputes;
- responsibility for marketing activities (for example, advertising and PR);
- probationary period;
- targets or minimum sales levels required to retain the agreement;
- confidentiality agreements;
- termination clauses for both parties;
- meanings of key words and phrases, preferably in all the languages concerned;
- the jurisdiction under which disputes will be settled, in other words which country's law will the contract be interpreted under;
- any restrictions on competition between agents of the same company.

Table 10.1   Advantages and disadvantages of using agents

Advantages	Disadvantages
• Operations are subject to direct control by the client	• Agents require considerable support from the client company
• Agents are usually very familiar with the local market	• Agents may not be as familiar with the client firm
• Agents will have appropriate contacts for arranging after-sales service, etc	• Agents act independently, so may set up deals with firms with whom they have an arrangement
• Less financial risk – no sales, no costs	• Unless sales happen very quickly and easily, agents will concentrate more effort on other clients
• Agents may also act for other firms, so may be able to create synergies	• Agents often act for more than one firm, so may have conflicts of interest
• No long-term commitment on the part of the client means that it is easy to withdraw from the arrangement	• Less commitment to the client may reduce incentive to sell

Table 10.2 Advantages and disadvantages of using distributors

Advantages	Disadvantages
• Credit risk is reduced	• Distributors might go out of business
• Distributor assumes full responsibility for sales	• Control is less than would be the case with directly employed sales people
• Less supervision is needed than with agents	• Distributors have more of a stake in the business than agents, and might therefore demand more of a say in how things are done
• Local image for the product	• Distributors may distort the brand values
• Distributors cover warehousing costs	• Warehousing might be cheaper if arranged in bulk for several distributors
• Close relationship means that market information is more readily available	• Distributors can easily defect to the competition, taking sensitive information with them

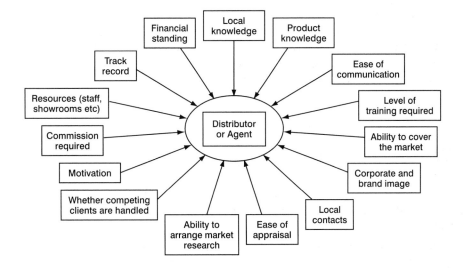

Figure 10.2 Choosing an agent or distributor

For agents, the contract will also include commission rates, disclosure agreements, responsibility for credit control, and restrictions on what the agent can and cannot commit the client to. For distributors, the contract should include agreement on discount rates, responsibility for after-sales service, liability for defective or damaged goods, and responsibility for promotional literature.

in practice...

Church and Company

Church and Company of Northampton is a quality men's footwear producer that uses foreign agents to handle virtually all the firm's export marketing. Each agent controls the distribution of Church footwear in a particular geographical area, conducts due diligence on potential retail outlets, assesses the suitability of outlets for the promotion of traditional hand-cut shoes, monitors other brands carried by suitable retailers and undertakes research into the local market. The justification for engaging agents as the primary exporting medium is that local tastes for various types of shoe and the most appropriate ways of marketing them vary significantly from country to country, the only common element being the high standards of craftwork embodied in the product. In southern Germany, for example, there is great demand for lighter and softer leather footwear, whereas in some other regions the solid 'classic' style of heavier shoe is extremely popular. And local preferences are liable to change at short notice, as is the case with any fashion item. Thus, each agent needs an intimate knowledge of the local market for top-quality clothing and footwear. Church will not interfere with an agent or override their decisions unless exceptional problems arise. Contacts with agents are maintained through visits:

- by Church managers to the country concerned;
- by foreign agents to the Church factory or London showroom; and
- through meetings at international footwear exhibitions.

Fax and telephone communications occur on a daily basis.

in practice...

Benetton SpA

Italian clothing manufacture Benetton SpA makes extensive use of agents to distribute its products. Agents spend one week at company headquarters twice a year in order to examine the next season's collection and to collect samples of items for presentation to retail outlets in the agent's (exclusive) territory over the next month. Orders from outlets are dispatched to headquarters on a daily basis, with the items then being dispatched to customers from central Benetton-owned warehouses. Agents receive a 4 per cent commission but do not actually handle the goods. Payments by customers go direct to Benetton HQ. Outlets themselves consist of franchised shops bearing the Benetton name, specialist knitwear stores, dedicated Benetton boutiques located in quality department stores and a handful of Benetton-owned shops. Subcontractors undertake 80 per cent of physical production; the remainder is by Benetton-owned factories throughout the world.

Agents select the locations for new Benetton shops, find potential franchisees, and train and assist franchisees to set up their outlets. Many agents are themselves storeowners and are thus able to train franchisees within their own stores. Also, an agent can be a franchisee operating one or more Benetton-named outlets that act as an example of correct display and business methods for other Benetton shops. An important role of an agent is to monitor trends in youth culture and buying habits in their area, typically by having young assistants visit bars, discotheques, etc, to observe young people's dress and behaviour 'in the field'.

Agency law

Although agency law differs between different countries, some general principles apply to the law of agency in all countries, namely that:

- An agent cannot take delivery of the principal's goods at an agreed price and resell them for a higher amount without the principal's knowledge and permission.
- Agents must maintain strict confidentiality regarding their principal's affairs and must pass on all relevant information.
- The principal is liable for damages to third parties for wrongs committed by an agent 'in the course of his or her authority', eg if the agent fraudulently misrepresents the principal's firm.

Thereafter, however, agency law differs markedly between countries, especially in relation to agents' rights on termination of their contract. The European Union situation has been largely reconciled by a directive on agency effective in all EU member states since 1994. Under the directive, an agent whose agreement is terminated is entitled to:

- full payment for any deal resulting from their work (even if it was concluded *after* the end of the agency);
- a lump sum of up to one year's past average commission;
- compensation (where appropriate) for damages to the agent's commercial reputation caused by an unwarranted termination.

Outside Western Europe, some countries regard agents as basically employees of client organizations, others see agents as self-contained and independent businesses. It is essential to ascertain the legal position of agency agreements in each country in which a firm is considering doing business.

Support and motivation of agents and distributors

Exporters support and motivate their agents and distributors through a variety of devices, including the following:

- significant local advertising and brand awareness development by the supplying firm;
- participation in local exhibitions and trade fairs, perhaps in cooperation with the local intermediary;
- regular field visits and telephone calls to the agent or distributor;
- establishment of regional offices to coordinate communications with the firm's agents or distributors in a particular area;
- regular meetings of agents and distributors arranged by and paid for by the supplying company in the latter's country;
- competitions with cash prizes, free holidays, etc, for intermediaries with the highest sales;
- provision of technical training to intermediaries;
- suggestion schemes to gather feedback from agents and distributors;
- circulation of briefings about the supplying firm's current activities, changes in personnel, new product developments, marketing plans, etc.

LICENSING AND FRANCHISING

Industrial or commercial expertise may be sold in foreign countries via patent licensing, know-how licensing (see below), franchising or through the provision of technical expertise under a 'management contract'.

Licensing

Firms that possess patented inventions, registered trade marks or specialist know-how that can be kept confidential may decide to license foreign firms to make and market their products. Licensing will only work if it is possible to protect patents, etc legally and comprehensively in licensees' countries. The advantages and drawbacks of licensing are listed in Table 10.3, and the key elements that need to be included in a licence agreement in Table 10.4. Licensing is especially appropriate where:

- it is not feasible to set up in a particular country, but where legal protection of intellectual property is required;
- the cost of transporting goods to the local market would be prohibitive; 'home-grown' product images will improve sales;
- the licensee will have to purchase input components or materials from the licensor;
- the licensor is already exporting directly to more markets than it can conveniently handle.

Table 10.3 The advantages and drawbacks of licensing

Advantages	Disadvantages
• No capital investments for the licensor	• May be difficult to verify sales figures
• Can be undertaken by small firms	• Lower revenue to the licensor
• Immediate access to local expertise	• Licensee acquires know-how and may set up in competition
• No tariff or transport costs	• Quality levels might not be maintained
• Materials and components might be sold to the licensee	• Complex contractual arrangements may be necessary
• Licensor usually receives an initial lump sum payment	• Many possibilities for conflicts and misunderstandings
• Risk of failure shared with licensee	• Licensee might not fully exploit the local market
• Allows entry to markets otherwise closed to exporters	• Licensee's firm could become insolvent and cease production
• Provides income to help offset research and technical development expenditure	• Licensee might be less competent than at first expected
• No export know-how required	
• Licensee does not have to invest in research and technical development	

Table 10.4 The licence contract – key elements

• Fees and royalties	• Minimum production levels
• Geographical area covered by the agreement	• Termination and renewal arrangements
• Permissible selling prices	• Ownership of new inventions resulting from the licensor's work
• Quality control arrangements	• Licensee's capacity to become involved with competing products
• Frequency of payments	• Licensee's capacity to subcontract
• Confidentiality requirements	• Support services to be given by the licensor (eg training)
• Procedures for settling disputes and which country's law shall apply to the agreement	

Lee Cooper

UK jeans and casual wear manufacturer Lee Cooper began licensing its trade mark in the early 1970s. The first licence was issued to a single firm in New Zealand; by 1990 the company had entered into 25 licence agreements in 20 countries worldwide. Responsibility for Lee Cooper's licensing operations rests with a subsidiary specially set up for the purpose and which seeks out new licensing opportunities. The latter have arisen where local demand is insufficient to justify a full-blown export operation, where there are substantial tariff and/or non-tariff barriers to market entry, or where advertising, local distribution and customer care are difficult. Licensing has also been used to gain experience of local conditions prior to a major assault on the market. Lee Cooper regards licensing as an essential ingredient of its desire to establish a genuinely international brand. Note how blue jeans have become more than a product; they have become a universal symbol of the Western lifestyle throughout the world.

Potain SA

Potain SA is a French company manufacturing cranes for use in the construction industry. Initially a large exporter of its output, the company moved towards foreign manufacture, either in a Potain subsidiary or through granting licences to foreign firms. The company's licensing policy is to use licensing as a means for entering remote or 'difficult' markets subject to extensive controls in imported goods. Licensees produce the heaviest and bulkiest parts of a crane, while Potain or one of its subsidiaries supplies the more technically sophisticated parts, which the licensee then puts together. Potain provides extensive technical support and technology transfer to its licensees, thus creating the possibility that some of them might eventually turn into competitors. Hence the company is not willing to license its latest technology, insists on a minimum five-year licensing contract, and ensures that a certain proportion of the components in cranes manufactured by the licensee are always supplied from France. Additionally, the firm specifies minimum quality levels for items produced under licence and will not grant exclusivity to any licensee outside the latter's own country.

Source: Adapted from Stacey (1993)

Types of licence

The main categories of licence are as follows:

- 'Assignments' whereby the licensor hands over *all* its intellectual property rights in relation to a particular patent, trade mark, design or whatever to a licensee. The latter may then use these rights as it wishes.
- 'Sole' licences, under which the licensor retains rights but agrees not to extend licences to anyone other than a single licensee during the period of the agreement.
- 'Exclusive' licences, which require licensors not to use their patents, trade marks, etc, for their own businesses while licensing contracts are in force, leaving these rights entirely to licensees for a pre-specified period (see Christou, 1990). Non-exclusive licences allow licensors to distribute licences to several licensees simultaneously.
- 'Know-how' licences covering confidential but non-patented (and perhaps non-patentable) technical knowledge.

Franchising

With a franchise agreement a foreign firm adopts the franchisor's entire business format in the local market – its name, trade marks, business methods, layout of premises, etc. Additionally the franchisor provides (in return for a royalty and lump sum fee) a variety of supplementary management services: training, technical advice, stock control systems, perhaps even financial loans. Hence the franchisor retains complete control over how the product is marketed, but the franchisee carries all the risks of failure. International franchising allows companies to expand rapidly from a limited capital base (Abell, 1991). It combines the technical experience of the franchisor with the intimate local knowledge of the franchisee. The question of import duties does not arise unless the foreign franchisor supplies input materials. Indeed, the governments of many host countries welcome franchising as it facilitates inward technology transfer, creates local employment and stimulates the development of new small businesses.

Franchisees are self-employed, not employees of the parent company, and rarely possess rights against a parent organization in the event of either the entire system or just an individual outlet collapsing. Also they are usually tied to supplies from the parent organization at supply prices determined by the latter (which buys raw materials in bulk at big discounts). Franchise contracts typically contain detailed rules concerning product presentation, layout of premises, etc, plus arrangements concerning exclusivity, the franchisee's ability to engage in other business activities and eventually to compete with the franchisor, the duration of contracts and what happens when they expire (eg whether higher royalties may then be demanded).

Holiday Inns

Holiday Inns is an international chain of hotels, 9 out of 10 of which are franchised. International franchising facilitates the establishment of an internationally consistent image and standardization of services and quality management systems, yet allows a centralized reservation system. Note that franchising enabled the creation of an international hotel network at a speed impossible were the parent company to have set up its own establishments in each country in which it decided to operate. Marketing and advertising is centrally administered. The reservation system links by satellite many thousands of terminals in airline reservation offices, travel agents and other travel outlets.

Management contracts

Here a firm in one country provides a team of expert managers to an enterprise in another for a fixed period under contract. Typically the team will install a new system, train local personnel and then hand over the entire system to local control. (The latter procedure is referred to as a *turnkey* arrangement.) Otherwise the contract might cover an ad hoc project or technical services agreement. A management contract could be used to supplement a separate licensing, joint venture or contract manufacturing arrangement and may be tied in with an agreement whereby the client will take subsequent supplies or equipment from the contracting firm. Equally a firm might provide management expertise to one of its major suppliers. Here the management team will be drawn from one of the parties to the agreement, which might result in that firm's managerial resources becoming overstretched.

Advantages to the supplying firm are that few overheads are involved, that returns to the firm providing the management expertise are predetermined and that there is little risk of expropriation. Problems include the potential for disagreements between the foreign management team and local managers over what constitute the best working methods and that local employees might be untrainable. Also the arrangement may be more expensive for the client than simply bringing in outside consultants on an ad hoc basis, and the contractor might not be genuine in its commitment to training local personnel.

Turnkey contracts enable clients to have a new system installed to a predetermined specification, new technologies can be acquired quickly, and there is a lower risk of failure for the client firm. However, the contractor might be slow in 'turning the key' (ie training up local workers to the level necessary to take over the plant) and the client becomes totally dependent on the contractor's goodwill.

BRANCHES AND SUBSIDIARIES

The difference between a branch and a subsidiary is that whereas a branch is a direct extension of the parent firm into a foreign country (so that the parent is legally responsible for all the branch's debts and activities), a subsidiary is seen in law as a separate business from the firm that owns it. A subsidiary is responsible for its own debts and (unlike a branch) is subject to exactly the same taxes, auditing, registration and accounting regulations as any other local business.

Whatever its form, a local establishment can recruit staff who are expert in the nuances of the local market, are fluent in the local language, but nevertheless are subject to the parent firm's direct and immediate control. Other reasons for wanting to set up a permanent local presence might include communication difficulties with local intermediaries, lack of commitment on the part of the commission agents, costly margins taken by independent distributors, and escalating administrative costs as foreign markets develop. Also, local competitors' activities may be observed at first hand.

Branches

Branches are easy to set up and to dismantle, but complicated tax situations can arise because some countries (for example Spain and the United States) relate the amount of tax payable by branches to the worldwide profits of their parent companies. Normally branches are concerned with the transport and storage of goods, marketing, the provision of after-sales service and liaison with local banks, advertising agencies, suppliers and distributors, and so on. Local assembly and/or manufacture is normally undertaken by other means. In most (but not all) countries the existence of a foreign branch has to be registered with local governmental authorities. Usually the registration procedure is straightforward, comprising the deposit of a simple form plus translated documents attesting the whereabouts and solvency of the parent organization.

A branch and its parent are regarded as part and parcel of the same legal entity, so that the profits/losses of the branch are treated as those of the parent firm and are shown as such in the latter's accounts. The essential characteristics of branches in comparison with those of subsidiaries are listed in Table 10.5. Major factors to be considered when selecting the precise location of a branch or subsidiary within a country include nearness to consumers and/or centres of commercial activity, availability of government investment grants and subsidies, proximity to neighbouring markets, transport facilities and, for manufacturing subsidiaries, access to local sources of materials and input components. Other criteria might include labour and other operating costs, the availability of high-calibre employees and the whereabouts of competitors.

Marketing subsidiaries

A marketing subsidiary in the local market can monitor trends on a continuous basis, provide after-sales service, liaise with local advertising and research agencies, arrange for

Table 10.5 Branches and subsidiaries

Branch	Subsidiary
• Parent liable for all debts	• Usually incorporated as a limited company
• Does not require its own capital or directors	• Taxed as if it were a separate local business
• Special tax rules apply, depending on the country concerned	• Can raise capital in its own name
• No company formation or winding-up procedures are needed	• Maintains its own accounts independently of parent enterprise
• Accounts are incorporated into those of the parent enterprise	• Can apply for government regional development and R&D grants
• Losses can be offset against parent company's profits	• Accounts must be independently audited
• Branch employees can (but need not) be regarded as employees of the parent organization	• No need to disclose the accounts of the parent
• Assets can be transferred from the parent to the branch without incurring tax liability	• Carries a local identity
• Often there are low rates of tax on repatriation of profits	• Internal reorganizations can occur without having to report this to the foreign authorities
• Branch profits may be taxed in the head office country even though they have not been repatriated	• Shares in the company can be sold to outsiders

warehousing, transport and distribution, collect debts, and possibly sell the product in neighbouring countries. If the supplying firm has a significant number of travelling sales people it is convenient for them to have a home base in the local market. Also the need for agents and foreign intermediaries might be removed. Often the stimulus for setting up a marketing subsidiary is lacklustre performance in a region compared with competing firms that do have a local presence. Note that the establishment of a marketing subsidiary will release marketing resources at head office that might be put to better use.

in practice...

BMW

A good example of a firm using marketing subsidiaries for foreign sales is the German motor manufacturer BMW, which sells about half its output outside Germany. The company had found that its previous distribution system – based on wholesalers, import agents and direct sales to large retailers – was expensive and unwieldy. Also, wholesalers were beginning to sell vehicles to the general public in competition with BMW-authorized retail dealers. Hence the company established a wholly owned marketing subsidiary in each country in which it sold vehicles. The role of the marketing subsidiary is to import BMW vehicles, distribute them to authorized local dealers and generally coordinate marketing and promotional activities in the country concerned. Former wholesalers and import agents can still import BMWs and resell them, but no longer receive the 15 per cent commission previously paid to these firms.

INTERNATIONAL MARKETING THROUGH THE INTERNET

E-commerce has probably been the biggest revolution in international trade in the past 20 years, outranking even the trade agreements and tariff barrier reductions that have done so much to free up trade. The Internet operates through the World Wide Web, a conglomerate of privately owned computers, which link together to create a communications and information resource outside the control of governments and which has virtually no regulation. This lack of regulation has led to a burgeoning of Web sites, with everything on them from political comment through to advertising slogans, but at the same time it has led to a proliferation of racist sites, pornography, and sites that would be considered libellous if there were any way of controlling what is said on them. Part of the reason for the lack of control of the Internet is that it transcends national borders.

The evidence is that e-commerce has been most successful in business-to-business markets. Buyers are able to obtain product information and tenders from firms in any part of the world: in this sense, the Internet acts like a permanent international trade fair, which can be visited 24 hours a day from any time zone.

The Internet has been less successful in consumer markets. Even some very big players like Amazon.com have failed to show a profit, although other firms who have used the Internet as an adjunct to a bricks-and-mortar business have been rather more successful. Such clicks-and-mortar companies find that people will often use the Internet to gather information about products, then contact the firm either by telephone or by calling into the premises in order to make the final purchase. The main exception seems to be travel, with airlines such as easyJet and air-ticket brokers reporting strong take-up rates on Internet purchasing. Having said that, most of these firms offer discounts for Internet bookings: a cynical person might ask why they need to do this if booking over the Internet is so much easier and better than booking in person.

Figure 10.3 shows some of the steps on the road to online success. Some steps are more important than others, depending on what the firm is trying to achieve and what the market conditions are.

There are a number of techniques available to companies to promote/generate traffic to their homepage, many of which are offline (for example TV ads, newspaper ads, and billboards). Online techniques are shown in Table 10.6.

Traffic sustaining is about ensuring that customers return to the site, and spend longer on there than they do on other sites. A homepage should provide users with an experience that cannot easily be replicated by traditional media. On top of this it should also provide the users with added value so they have a reason to return in the future. The main traffic-sustaining factors are as follows:

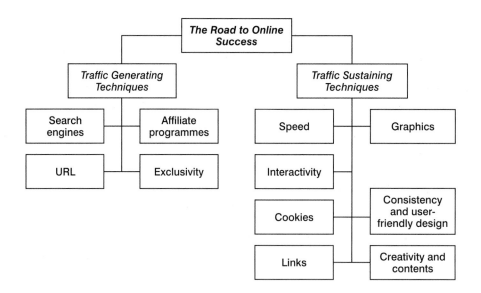

Figure 10.3 The road to online success

Table 10.6 Online traffic generating techniques

Technique	Explanation
Search engine	To submit the company's URL to various search engines is probably the single most important step a company can take in order to promote its homepage (Sellers, 1997). There are several search engines/portals on the Internet and it is not possible to optimize the company's position on all of them since the search engines/portals use different techniques in order to rank a site. It is therefore best to focus on a small number of search engines/portals since this will produce the best result in the end
Affiliate programmes	Under an affiliate programme the company pays its Web site partners a commission for every customer they send to the home page. Affiliate programmes are effective, but are relatively little known and are under-used: what makes affiliate programmes so effective is that companies only pay for results and not for exposure. Hence both partners are therefore interested in helping each other to get the most out of the deal. (Bove-Nielsen and Ørsted, 2000)
URL	Having an URL that is easy to remember, short, relates to the company and can be written in English, also helps to generate traffic to a homepage
Exclusive offers	An exclusive offer is something customers will not be able to find anywhere else. This could (for example) be up-to-the-minute-pricing, online ordering discounts, product specials or even downloadable screensavers with company logo, etc

- **Speed**. Web site visitors will not wait around too long for the page to download.
- **Graphics**. The customer needs to be able to see what the company has to offer, but at the same time the graphics should not be too detailed, as this increases the download time.
- **Interactivity**. Being able to complete the transaction online is an obvious aid to sales, but even allowing the customer to explore the product information is an aid to retention.
- **Consistency and user-friendly design**. A site map is helpful, and a consistent design ensures a feeling of familiarity when using or revisiting a site. If search buttons and help buttons are used frequently, this is a sign of a poorly designed site.
- **Cookies**. A cookie is a small program stored on the visitor's computer that collects information about the visitor's use of the site. This makes it possible for companies to personalize the site to the individual user (using the right language, for example). There is a possibility that the European Union will ban the use of cookies, because some users regard them as an invasion of privacy, but a possible compromise is that cookies will only be placed with the express permission of the visitor.
- **Creativity and contents**. A creative, interesting-looking site will encourage more visits and especially more repeat visits than a dull, factual site. Obviously this should not be done at the expense of speed or readability.
- **Links**. The number of links to and from a home page is positively correlated with hit rates (Dholakia and Rego, 1998). However, when a company exchanges links with another company there is a downside, because it gives the visitors an opportunity to leave the home page.

The Internet is undoubtedly developing fast (in fact, on a daily basis). This means that circumstances and situations will change. From an international marketing perspective, however, it is undoubtedly the case that the borderless market provided by the Internet will be an important factor in the globalization of business.

FOREIGN MANUFACTURING

High tariffs, quotas, heavy transportation costs and national 'local content' rules may cause a company to consider manufacturing items locally in a foreign market rather than shipping them from abroad. Two options are available: manufacture in an establishment owned wholly or partly by the firm in question, or 'contract manufacture' whereby the firm places orders with local businesses for the production of goods, which it then sells locally or exports. Local manufacture can be dovetailed to the needs of local distribution arrangements and numerous cost savings may be obtained. A 'home-grown' image is attached to the goods, and delivery and customer service mechanisms should improve.

Contract manufacturing

Contract manufacturing has a number of advantages over direct foreign investment, although it can only occur if firms with the skills and capacity to undertake contracts operate within the area concerned. The advantages include:

- not having to invest large sums of money in capital equipment;
- easy withdrawal from high-risk markets;
- avoidance of involvement in industrial relations with local workforces.

Resort to contract manufacture may result from domestic production facilities being overloaded, through no suitable licensees being available in a difficult-to-enter market or in consequence of government-imposed barriers and prohibitions on other forms of entry. It is particularly suitable for companies with high-level marketing skills and facilities but no experience of physical production.

Problems with contract manufacture include the difficulties of monitoring and maintaining quality levels, of protecting any intellectual property embodied within the manufactured item and of preventing the foreign firm setting up in competition (perhaps covertly) once it has acquired expertise in making the product. Note, moreover, that the local firm may require substantial technical back-up, possibly extending to the training of its employees.

Direct foreign investment (DFI)

Firms invest directly in foreign countries to obtain:

- the benefits of lower production costs;
- local technical expertise; and
- local foreign government investment grants.

Complete ownership of a foreign subsidiary means there is no scope for arguments with partner firms, there is total and immediate control over operations, and subsidiary operations can be fitted into the parent company's overall corporate strategy. Also, local restrictions on imports are circumvented, the local delivery of output might be greatly improved and better aftersales service provided. The close link between local production and local marketing might enable more rapid product modification in response to changing local demand. The major problem with DFI is, of course, that it requires substantial capital investment that cannot be sacrificed easily, whereas cancellation of a contract manufacture agreement is (subject to the details of the contract) cheap and straightforward. Apart from the local availability of manufacturing resources (labour, materials, etc), the decision whether to invest in foreign manufacturing capacity will normally depend on such factors as the political stability of the country being considered, the extent of government investment grants and subsidiaries, legal matters such as the ease of patent protection, wage and other costs, restrictions on the repatriation of profits and taxation.

BMW in South Carolina

Prior to the early 1990s the German motor manufacturer BMW had never manufactured motor vehicles outside Germany except in a very small assembly plant in South Africa. Confronted with ferocious competition in world markets from Japanese (and other) motor manufacturers that located their production sites within foreign markets (hence avoiding import duties and attracting substantial investment grants from national governments) the firm decided in 1992 to set up its first ever significant foreign manufacturing plant on a greenfield site in South Carolina in the United States. This would establish BMW as a 'local' producer within NAFTA (see Chapter 5) and provide a springboard for exports from the United States to places on the Pacific Rim. BMW feared high external tariffs against foreign motor vehicles resulting from the formation of NAFTA, and the company had recently experienced a sharp decline in its US sales (a major problem considering that the United States is the world's largest car market). Other factors influencing the decision to begin manufacturing abroad included:

- The need to protect foreign markets against the appreciation of the Deutschmark. Note in particular that the exchange rates of several large EU countries frequently nosedived against the DM, meaning that BMW had to increase local selling prices by a significant amount in order to maintain its Germany currency revenue. A US supply point enabled such markets to be serviced from a country not necessarily affected by internal EU exchange rate fluctuations.
- Low labour costs in South Carolina compared to Germany.
- Some 150 million dollars' worth of tax relief offered by South Carolina's state government.
- The availability of low-cost inputs from Mexico.
- Forecast expansion in the US luxury car market.
- Undercapacity in BMW's German production units.
- The example of the Japanese companies Honda, Nissan, Mazda and Toyota, all of which have US manufacturing operations. Collectively these companies account for 30 per cent of the North American market.

In fact, BMW has made substantial inroads into the US market as a result of this investment, to the point where Ford's Lincoln Mercury subsidiary has had to make major investments in promotion to counteract the BMW success. Having local manufacturing capacity has enabled the firm to respond much more quickly to market fluctuations, and to badge itself as 'Made in the United States', a major selling point for patriotic Americans.

Screwdriver establishments

A domestically produced item can be labelled has having been 'made in' the country concerned. But what is a 'domestically manufactured' product? Japanese companies operating in Britain, for example, are sometimes accused of establishing 'screwdriver' establishments intended merely to assemble imported components and then pass the resulting product off as 'Made in the United Kingdom' (hence qualifying for tariff-free access to any EU country). Problems of determining a finished item's country of origin include: definition of what constitutes the 'last stage' in the production cycle (arguably this should be prior to final assembly) and measurement of the 'local content' of products. Should this occur through counting the number of imported elements (and if so at what level of detail), or by assessment of monetary values? In the latter case should cost value or market value apply? Currently the EU requires cars manufactured by Japanese firms in the United Kingdom to have at least 65 per cent local content. So contentious are these issues that the European Commission has set up a Committee on Origin to assess where the majority of value added took place in respect of disputed items.

Acquisitions versus new business start-ups

The advantages of buying a local business outright – rather than incorporating an entirely new company – include the avoidance of start-up delays and expenses, immediate possession of a functioning administrative structure, and possibly the acquisition of an existing distribution system with staff, transport vehicles, etc. On the other hand, the acquired business will have to be integrated into the purchaser's current organizational system, and implementing changes in the purchased firm's management methods may prove difficult. Further potential pitfalls associated with foreign acquisitions are that:

- Control difficulties created by having to manage a large and diverse organization could arise.
- Market conditions might suddenly change following a costly acquisition.
- Key employees in the acquired business might resign.
- New competitors may emerge (attracted perhaps by the publicity surrounding the initial takeover).
- Certain staff in the acquired business might not be worth employing, hence involving the acquiring company in dismissals and consequent employee compensation claims.

Trends in DFI

The first post-Second World War wave of direct foreign investment or DFI was from the United States into Western Europe between 1946 and the mid-1960s. Reasons for this upsurge in international investment probably included the formation of the European Economic Community (and hence the establishment of common external tariffs against imported goods); higher tariffs in non-EEC Western European states; and the advantages to firms of being able to control foreign operations directly, cut out intermediaries, coordinate activity on an international basis, use internal resources to finance operations, and procure/manufacture their own inputs and move them around subsidiaries in foreign countries. (These advantages are known as 'internalization' factors.) Another reason for US direct investment in Western Europe during the post-Second World War years appears to have been the difficulty of protecting the intellectual property embodied in licensing agreements, with numerous patent violations taking place within this period.

US companies then began to invest in developed markets outside Western Europe, and in the developing countries of Latin America and the Far East. Growth rates were high in all these regions, and international business cycles were (conveniently) out of synchronization in various parts of the world: when the United States was in recession at least one of the other regions would be experiencing a boom. In the 1980s large-scale Western European direct foreign investment began in the United States, with European firms buying up US companies at a bargain price – as a result of the low-profitability levels of US industry in the previous decade. European businesses also started to invest heavily in the Pacific Rim. The 1990s saw further DFI by US and Western European companies, plus a big upswing in Japanese, Korean and other Asian countries' investments in Europe (including Eastern Europe), China and the United States, as well as in Asia itself. DFI seems likely to continue at a high level, moreover, in consequence of the opening-up of new markets and the general increase in world trade, the ongoing liberalization of economies (including the removal of exchange controls) throughout the globe, and the establishment of numerous common markets and other regional trading blocs with common tariffs.

Further specific motives for investing directly in foreign countries might involve communication difficulties with local representatives, lack of commitment on the part of commission agents, costly margins taken by independent distributors, and escalating administrative costs connected with organizing foreign operations from a company's home base. A permanent local investment enables the investing enterprise to do business just as any other local firm, which might be necessary or desirable in order to exercise close control over local marketing, or where a regional identity is necessary to create a credible image for the company.

'Local' images can be extremely valuable for foreign businesses. Customers and dealers might be attracted to a local firm they come to regard as being fully committed to a permanent presence in the country concerned. Local competitors may be considerably more sensitive to and react more vigorously against the actions of foreign rivals than against domestic businesses, and host country governments might turn a blind eye to low-price strategies intended to dominate local markets if the firm involved is perceived as a domestic enterprise. Other reasons for commencing foreign production include:

- the need to engage in local assembly or part-manufacture;
- desires to minimize worldwide tax burdens;
- acquisition of know-how and technical skills only available locally;
- wanting to spread the risk of downturns in particular markets;
- especially favourable economic conditions in certain countries: bouyant markets, rising consumer incomes, easy access to finance, low interest rates, etc;
- local content requirements;
- a desire to protect supplies of new materials and components only available from foreign countries;

- undercapacity at home;
- faster access to the local market;
- lower operating costs;
- availability of investment grants from foreign governments;
- problems with licensees and the need to protect intellectual property;
- high transport costs associated with exporting.

Investment strategies

These may be product driven, market driven, or technology driven. Product-driven strategies arise when a firm's welfare depends critically on the properties, capabilities or composition of a specific product. For example, an international oil company cannot survive unless it continually explores for fresh reserves of crude oil and arranges for its processing and distribution. Hence it needs to invest in oil refineries, pipeline networks and so on in order to serve chosen markets. Many natural resource-related industries pursue product-driven investment strategies, as do pharmaceutical companies, ceramics manufacturers and other businesses that are locked into a specific type of product. Market-driven strategies relate to the quest for new markets, served by foreign-owned local manufacturing plants and distribution systems. This type of DFI typically arises when a firm's existing markets cannot absorb its potential output. Technology-driven strategies are found among enterprises that rely on the application of state-of-the-art technologies for their competitive advantage. Such firms invest in order to undercut the prices of foreign local competitors using out-of-date production methods, or to introduce completely new products to foreign markets.

Diversification

Diversification strategies may involve the supply of completely new products, entering fresh market segments (possibly using modified versions of existing brands), or imitating the products of other firms (subject of course to patent restrictions). Note how the last practice can itself generate the inspiration and know-how necessary to develop completely new items. The need to diversify could arise from loss of traditional products or markets, overdependence on a handful of customers, increased competition, or large seasonal variations in demand. Further reasons for diversification might be the existence of spare capacity within the firm that can be utilized through the supply of fresh products; successful research and technical development activities resulting in new products and applications; or attempts to strengthen a hold on a market by controlling diverse activities connected with it, eg a paper manufacturer diversifying into carton making, wallpaper production, gift wrapping manufacture, etc. This is an example of 'concentric' diversification involving a common technological base and market outlets. Similar marketing methods will (normally) apply to the firm's diverse outputs.

Advantages and disadvantages of diversification

In principle, diversification should lead to a recession-proof company, with a slump in one market being offset by expansions elsewhere. Lucrative opportunities can be exploited as they emerge so that the firm's profit-earning potential is extended, while profits earned in certain areas of a diversified company can be used to reinforce activities elsewhere. Unfortunately, diversification could result in the firm locking up large amounts of capital in particular technologies or administrative or distribution systems from which it cannot subsequently withdraw. Extensive diversification necessarily turns a company into a conglomerate of unrelated businesses, possibly with a complicated and unwieldy administrative structure that is difficult to manage. Invariably it requires significant changes to the firm's current organizational structure. 'Pure' diversification, ie that which extends the firm's activities to unrelated and unfamiliar products, is especially problematic and expensive, requiring the rapid acquisition of know-how and the deployment of large amounts of resources. New production and marketing methods have to be learned, and fresh relationships with third parties (input suppliers, agents, specialist consultancies, etc) established.

JOINT VENTURES

A joint venture (JV) is a collaborative arrangement between unrelated parties that exchange or combine various resources while remaining separate and independent legal entities. It is an example of a 'strategic alliance', which is a wider concept that embraces knowledge-sharing arrangements, mutual licensing, measures to control and utilize excess capacity, etc. Usually JVs are formed to undertake a specific project that has to be completed within a set period. They could involve each partner taking an equity stake in the venture (eg through setting up a joint subsidiary with its own share capital), or rely on contractual agreements between the partners (see Lewis, 1990; Lorange and Roos, 1992).

However they are constituted, JVs are increasingly popular as a means for entering foreign markets. They are flexible, can be quickly entered into and abandoned, enable the sharing of costs, yet often are just as effective a means for acquiring market expertise as are more direct forms of foreign investment. Moreover, they can be used to establish bridgeheads in a foreign market prior to major marketing efforts by individual participants. Problems with JVs include the possibility of disagreements over organization and control, methods of operation and the long-term goals of the operation, eg whether earnings should be reinvested in the venture or returned to participants. Other disputes might arise concerning pricing policy, the confidentiality of information exchanged between members, and about how underperformance by any one of the participants is to be dealt with (Haigh, 1992). For instance, should equal compensation be payable to each of the parties if the project is abandoned? The essential advantages and disadvantages of joint ventures are listed in Table 10.7.

Table 10.7 Advantages and disadvantages of joint ventures

Advantages	Disadvantages
• Higher returns than with licensing/franchising • Shared knowledge and resources • Can include partners from many countries • Possibly better relations with national governments in consequence of having a local partner • Substantial control over production and marketing • Direct feedback on local conditions • Instant access to local expertise • Firms can gain instant access to partner's distribution systems • Shared risk of failure • Develops a critical mass very quickly • Ideal for partners with near-identical products • May be available in countries where outright takeovers of local firms by foreigners is not allowed • Less costly than acquisitions • Firms can expand into several foreign markets simultaneously for low capital cost • Shared cost of administration • May avoid the need to purchase local premises and hire new employees	• Potential for arguments and disagreements • A partner firm might not pull its weight • Need to share intellectual property • Difficult to integrate into an overall corporate strategy • Partners are not free to act as they wish • Corporate objectives of partners may conflict • Transfer pricing problems as goods pass between partners • The importance of the venture to each partner might change over time • Problems of coordination and control • Profits have to be shared with partners • Possible differences in management culture among participating firms • Dissolution may require protracted negotiation • Possible lack of overall leadership and hence non-completion of critically important tasks • Completion of a JV project might overburden a company's staff • Partners may become locked into long-term investments from which it is difficult to withdraw • Possible arguments over which partner is responsible for budget overspends and how these should be financed

in practice...

Mikma

Mikma is a large and long-established Russian manufacturer of electrical household appliances and is located in the suburbs of Moscow. Manufacturing capacity began to exceed domestic demand in the early 1970s, prompting the enterprise to seek export opportunities, initially through the Soviet Union's Foreign Trade Organization, which handled all aspects of the firm's export transactions. As Russia's economy liberalized, however, Mikma was increasingly called upon to act on its own initiative in international trade. An important catalyst was the receipt of a large order to produce electric razors for a West German customer. In order to explore further possibilities in the West German market, Mikma contacted a major German manufacturer, which licensed the Russian firm to produce its razors and market them anywhere in the world, provided they would not compete with the German company's own output. This prevented Mikma from entering the most lucrative international markets, but (importantly) it enabled the firm to acquire valuable experience of foreign sales, to learn about Western expectations regarding product quality and to explore the preferences of Western consumers. Next the firm linked up with the Swiss company TRNH AG in a deal whereby the latter marketed a variety of Mikma's products in Western Europe. The arrangement was highly successful, leading the US company Nypro Inc to approach both TRNH and Mikma with a view to marketing Mikma's output in the United States and other countries outside Europe. Certain products were shipped to Nypro in kit form for subsequent assembly. Nypro supplied technical help and capital equipment to the enterprise.

Source: Adapted from Reuvid and Bennett (1993)

in practice...

Pepsi

Pepsi-Cola's entry to the Indian market in the early 1980s involved far more than purely commercial activities. Local soft drinks companies lobbied the Indian government to prevent Pepsi operating in the country, and a number of Indian politicians were opposed to multinational corporations on ideological grounds. To cope with these problems Pepsi formed a consortium with a number of influential Indian businesses that had powerful voices in government circles and then put to the Indian authorities a package whereby market entry would be accompanied by:

- a countertrade deal whereby payment for imported Pepsi concentrate would be in the form of agricultural products that Pepsi would then sell in other countries;
- establishment of production and distribution units in high-unemployment rural areas; and
- technology transfer in relation to bottling, packaging, water treatment and food processing.

Matters to be determined prior to the establishment of a venture include:

- its objectives;
- legal rules regarding ownership (limits on foreign shareholdings for example);
- composition of the management team;
- responsibilities for financing, liaising with other firms, use of facilities, quality control, administration of the venture's employees and the purchase of equipment and supplies;
- legal form and capital structure;
- reporting procedures and control systems;
- how policies are to be determined, and which partner is to take which decisions;
- the nature and extent of the information necessary to undertake the project and who will collect and analyse the data (note that information gathering can be extremely time-consuming and expensive);

- priority activities;
- who is to be responsible for troubleshooting;
- responsibilities for training employees involved in the venture;
- expected rates of return on investment.

The contract establishing a joint venture needs to encompass such matters as:

- financial contributions;
- management structure;
- division of profits and losses;
- what proportion of profits (if any) is to be ploughed back into the venture;
- geographical coverage of the venture's activities;
- ownership of resulting intellectual property;
- methods for establishing transfer prices;
- confidentiality of information provided by each partner;
- procedures for resolving disagreements;
- partners' abilities to transfer their shares in the venture to third parties;
- exit provisions, ie how an unsuccessful joint venture will be wound up.

Note that the control of a JV need not correlate exactly with the division of profits. The latter might be split equally, while one of the partners has a majority of votes in or directorship of the venture.

Selecting joint venture partners

Partners should have proven knowledge, expertise and experience of local business conditions and practices. A prospective partner should be able to conduct or commission local market research and possess extensive contacts with local banks, businesses and providers of specialist services. The firm should be easy to contact and should provide precise and regular feedback on local market conditions. Obviously the partner needs to have resources (staff, technical facilities, management systems, etc) sufficient to undertake the collaboration. Further selection criteria are the firm's track record, how long it has existed and its general business reputation; and how readily the quality of the potential partner's work can be appraised.

The ideal joint venture materializes when participants can pool complementary skills. For example, one partner might supply the technological know-how, another raise the necessary finance and a third provide local marketing expertise and facilities. Risks are spread among the partners, yet a local image is applied to operations in the country of each participating firm.

Banks, chambers of commerce and trade associations, and government export service departments (Britain's Department of Trade and Industry, for example) can be extremely helpful in suggesting possible partners. Western European firms, moreover, can use a European Union scheme (the Business Corporation Network) to find partner firms. A critically important step in the selection process is the exercise of 'due diligence' in relation to an intended collaborator. This means verifying the other business's value and activities and will normally involve an assessment of its creditworthiness (probably undertaken by an international credit reference agency), inspection of its accounts and the evaluation of its technical and managerial competence. Further considerations are the prospective partner's quality assurance procedures, and the compatibility of its working methods with the searching business's own procedures: partners should share the same managerial culture and outlook on issues and events.

HUMAN RESOURCE ASPECTS

Visits to customers by sales people 'in the field' establish a social relationship between the firm and its customers, enable the local market testing of products, and can be used to resolve amicably customer complaints and other problems. Sending representatives to foreign destinations is expensive, but still far cheaper than establishing a permanent presence in other countries, especially when the total value of orders is likely to be small.

Sales people based in the home country are more likely to be used when order values are high, and when there is no intention of creating a long-term relationship with buyers in the foreign market. For example, major civil engineering projects or defence contracts are almost always going to be handled by sales people who travel out to the foreign buyers: contracting to build a suspension bridge is unlikely to be a weekly occurrence, and therefore the civil engineering firm concerned would be hardly likely to set up a sales force in the target country to handle the deal. On the other hand, factoring motor components would require a local sales force, who would almost certainly be recruited from nationals of the target country.

Management of an export sales force

Export sales people must have all the qualities expected of a first-class domestic sales person, namely:

- the ability to identify and understand consumer needs;
- the ability to formulate solutions for customers based on the firm's product range;
- the capacity to conduct marketing research during visits (including the examination and assessment of competitors' activities) and to brief agents and distributors.

Thereafter the character of an export sales person's duties differs considerably from that of someone concerned purely with domestic sales in several important respects:

- The export sales person (ESP) has to be an order-maker rather than order-taker. A high level of responsibility has to be assumed. ESPs negotiate with customers and have to take significant decisions; they represent the top management of the exporting company and cannot be seen to be constantly referring back to head office for instructions (otherwise there is little point in sending an ESP in the first instance – the deal could just as well be concluded by correspondence). It follows that the ESP needs to be highly knowledgeable about the technical aspects of the product. Note that ESPs normally deal with very senior managers in client organizations. Hence they need to be able to weigh up situations, assess risk, evaluate options on the basis of limited information and take on-the-spot decisions without consultative support.

- As well as possessing linguistic skills, an ESP needs to have the patience necessary to cope with long periods spent travelling (and all the problems and frustrations attached thereto: lost luggage, incorrect hotel reservations, etc), a cool temperament and the ability to cope with stress.
- ESPs have to be able quickly to acclimatize to local cultures, customs and business practices. A flight from (say) the Middle East to Scandinavia takes but a few hours, yet the differences in approach to business in the two locations are worlds apart. Business cultures differ across a wide range of matters: punctuality, mode of dress for and conduct during business meetings, whether the use of handshakes and calling people by their first names are appropriate, conventions concerning the discussion of business over lunch, the role of humour during conversations, and many other details.
- An ESP's work regularly takes the person into unfamiliar environments within which they must operate alone and without supervision. Hence, they must be a mature, stable and dependable individual who genuinely likes foreign travel and can be relied upon not to waste time in remote foreign locations.
- A neutral stance on political and social issues is required. The ESP needs to be diplomatic, sensitive to local cultures, and adopt a genuinely international perspective – temporarily forgetting that they are a national of a particular state. Prejudices have to be forgotten, and people and organizations accepted as they are, without challenging their behaviour or attitudes.

The problems involved

Special problems confronting the ESP are that:

- The (foreign) company that the person represents may not be known to the potential customers that they visit, and customers might not have the facilities or inclination to complete credit checks.
- It is necessary to produce some concrete and visible evidence of the supplying firm's ability to deliver on time, at an appropriate level of quality, and to provide prompt and efficient after-sales service. Foreign buyers frequently assume that problems can be sorted out more quickly and easily with local businesses than with an enterprise in another country.
- The ESP has to be able to answer on-the-spot queries regarding (for example) technical servicing, transport arrangements and schedules, penalty clauses, contract details, and so on.

Social isolation is another potential problem. Personal relationships with colleagues and customers during an assignment will usually be of a strictly formal business nature, leading perhaps to loneliness, boredom and the collapse of personal motivation. Unfortunately, personal friendships in foreign countries are difficult to establish because the individual will not be in one place for a period long enough to build up such relationships outside work. During a field trip the ESP is constantly on duty, meaning perhaps that they are working 14 hours per day for five days a week, with long journeys, checking in and out of hotels, etc, at weekends. Business might have to be conducted in the evenings, reports to head office have to be written, plans for the next leg of the trip drafted, and so on. The ESP's job can be physically as well as mentally exhausting.

Recruitment, deployment and control

A firm can adopt any one of the following options for organizing its foreign selling operations:

- Use of a team of sales people based at company headquarters who travel to foreign countries.
- Employment of sales people who live and work abroad but report directly to and are controlled by head office. The individuals involved may be recruited in the head office country or in the countries in which they operate.
- Establishment of foreign branches or subsidiaries that assume responsibility for managing the local sales force (including recruitment, training, deployment and compensation).
- Close liaison with sales people employed by local distributors and agents.

The second option will reduce sales people's travelling time and expenses, but may not be suitable for a technically complicated product. In the latter case it might be better to have home-based people who travel out to any customer in any location. Large companies taking large orders have advantages here, since small firms dealing in low quantities must pay their sales staff similar wages to bigger firms whose staff sell larger amounts. The second option also has the advantage that individuals become familiar with business customs and cultures in the areas they cover and with local transport arrangements (an important consideration in remote regions – knowledge of road networks, railway systems and timetables, etc, can greatly improve an export sales person's efficiency in the field). The language factor can be crucial: no internationally travelling export sales person can possibly be fluent in the language of *every* country that they will be called upon to visit. Yet the ability to speak the client's language is extremely desirable as it greatly improves the flow of communications, avoids misunderstandings (interpreters are fluent in the relevant languages but may not be familiar with the meaning of technical terms relevant to the industry concerned), and enables the sales person to grasp the essential character of the customer's requirements.

Locally recruited staff will be fluent in the language of the country concerned and should be fully conversant with local business practices. Note, moreover, that as business education is increasingly common throughout the world, there is today a much higher probability of being able to recruit local staff familiar with the management practices standard in most economically advanced countries. Typically the parent company will seek to recruit local people already trained and experienced in the rudiments of selling, since a foreign company is unlikely to possess the knowledge or facilities for training recruits in the nuances of local selling norms, legislation or sales techniques particularly relevant for consumers in a certain country. However, the recruiting firm may wish to supplement recruits' previous training via the provision of company-specific courses, information on selling methods that have succeeded for the product in other markets, courses on the technical aspects of the product, and so on. Senior local sales staff might participate in seminars attended by colleagues from several different countries.

Unfortunately for the foreign company, the locally recruited staff who experience these supplementary training activities and who then develop high-level business contacts in consequence of working for the firm (especially if it is a well-known international company) will become targets for the recruiting activities of local rival businesses and may well be headhunted and poached by them. Hence it becomes necessary to pay local recruits premium wages, perhaps thereby removing a part of the financial benefit of using local sales people for marketing the product.

Selling through a permanent foreign establishment

A strong argument for having some form of permanent presence is that, quite often, potential customers are not convinced by a simple visit from a foreign export sales person that the exporting company is genuinely committed to staying in the market. Costs are incurred in accepting fresh suppliers and customers may feel that a new foreign supply channel might disappear overnight. Also, a local base is appropriate for servicing a highly competitive market wherein local firms constantly communicate with customers and provide high-profile customer care programmes that can only be properly administered from a permanent local base. Note that a local sales force is particularly valuable in countries where there are extensive restrictions on the advertising of the product in question and/or a shortage of media in which to advertise. Also, low local wage levels might make the employment of a substantial sales force extremely attractive when compared to the cost of other means for promoting a product.

Use of expatriate staff

Setting up and running a foreign presence is likely at some stage or other to involve the use of expatriate staff who work in the foreign branch or subsidiary for a substantial period. It seems, however, that the number of expatriate staff employed by international businesses is declining (Boyacigiller, 1991), essentially because of their high cost (as much as four times the base salary of a person of equivalent qualifications working in the home country), limited effectiveness in consequence of cultural, linguistic and legal factors, and the difficulty of recruiting people of the right calibre who are willing to work abroad for long periods. Failure of expatriates to settle into foreign environments is common. Frequently cited reasons for an early return to the home country include:

- Children not making progress at school.
- Concerns for family safety.
- A spouse not adjusting to local physical and cultural environments (see McEnery and Desharnais, 1990, for a discussion of this problem). Many executives possessing qualifications suitable for expatriate assignments will themselves have professionally qualified spouses who have their own career aspirations and who will object to moving to a foreign country. It may be necessary for the employing company to find a foreign local job for the expatriate's spouse as well as for the expatriate.

Another problem is that the use of expatriates in senior positions within the foreign subsidiary necessarily blocks promotion opportunities for locally recruited staff, the most able of whom will thus not remain with the firm for very long. Note, moreover, that whereas nationals of European Union countries are free to work anywhere in the EU for as long as they wish, outside the Union (or for non-EU nationals wishing to work in the EU) a work permit is necessary and this can be extremely difficult to obtain in certain countries. Sometimes an expatriate is only allowed to stay in a country long enough to train a local person to take over his or her position.

Nevertheless, the use of expatriates might be unavoidable for firms selling recently developed highly technical products unfamiliar to the local market. Indeed, there could even be a prestige image attached to having a product presented by a foreigner. Effective utilization of expatriate staff requires the following:

- careful determination of the remuneration package, taking account of all the extra costs involved (removal, school fees for children, etc) and the need to induce good quality people to live and work in an unfamiliar foreign country;
- a plan for reabsorbing the former expatriate to head office on completion of the period abroad (Moynihan, 1993);
- dovetailing the foreign assignment into the expatriate's overall career development programme;
- precise specification of the expatriate's objectives and expected performance standards while abroad;
- prior training in the business methods and culture of the country to be visited, given perhaps by people who have recently returned from the country concerned.

Hitachi Data Systems

Japanese computer mainframe supplier Hitachi Data Systems operates in more than 30 countries worldwide, across a variety of industry sectors. The company is organized on a regional basis and is a large employer of foreign and expatriate workers. Hitachi's policy on the remuneration of locally recruited employees is to pay the local market rate in the country concerned, regardless of skill level. Hence there is no company-wide job evaluation scheme, although staff appraisal is administered centrally and benchmarked against key competencies deemed appropriate for various levels of employee. The firm has decided to pay all its employees a wage in the upper quartile of the range of wage rates available for a particular type of work in the local area. This market-driven approach to wages is alleged to give the company the flexibility it needs to respond quickly to change in local labour markets, while still being able to attract high-calibre workers. Trends in local wage rates are carefully monitored to ensure that Hitachi's own pay levels are competitive. The flexible approach also applies to the management of expatriates. In some cases an individual is kept on the payroll of the Hitachi unit operating in their own country; in others the person is treated as just another local employee in the host country. The main determinants of which option is selected are: the period of the foreign assignment; and the wage necessary to induce the best people to work abroad.

Note that foreign postings typically enhance a manager's long-term career prospects, so that a high salary is not necessarily the primary reason for completing a foreign assignment.

Nat West

NatWest is another company heavily involved in the management of expatriate staff. This UK-based banking group has over 100,000 employees, nearly a fifth of whom work in subsidiaries overseas. Foreign staff are recruited locally, although the bank typically has about 200 people on transfer from the United Kingdom to other countries at any one time. Also there are considerable numbers of 'inpatriates' from other countries temporarily working for NatWest in the United Kingdom. The bank's policy on expatriate and inpatriate employment is to have people complete ad hoc (rather than very long-term) assignments abroad, while maintaining their home country standard of living. Hence the individual's basic wage and conditions of employment remain constant, and are supplemented by special allowances if the cost of living is higher in the foreign country than at home. Expatriates are encouraged to rent their home country property while they are abroad (rather than selling it and buying a house in the host country) and receive extra payments for travel home and for boarding school fees. The bank operates an international graduate recruitment programme using its subsidiaries in various countries. Recruits are trained to work in their home country, although foreign secondments are an important element of the scheme. The aim of the programme is to recruit high-calibre, well-motivated and multilingual people and to encourage international perspective throughout the group.

Profile of the international marketing manager

The international marketing manager must be able to organize their firm's entry to new foreign markets, to negotiate international deals and to implement licensing, franchising, agency, distribution and joint venture agreements. They need:

- to possess a working knowledge of business methods, cultures, organization and policies in various countries and of best practice in foreign firms;
- to be aware of the nature and patterns of international trade and competent in the techniques of international trading;
- to be sensitive to the needs of the changing international business environment and be able quickly and easily to transfer their knowledge and skills between firms and operational cultures.

The individual must be geographically mobile, capable of adapting to the culture and business methods of any country, and able to communicate effectively and exercise inter-personal management skills in multicultural situations. Also the person needs to be:

- knowledgeable about international markets;
- willing and able to cope with rapid technical, organizational and environmental change;
- capable of working with fellow managers of different nationalities and of contributing to multinational project teams;
- able to handle a lifestyle that involves much foreign travel;
- capable of adopting a broad perspective on complex business deals and have the breadth of knowledge to be able to negotiate effectively with foreign clients and supplying organizations;
- knowledgeable about international distribution arrangements and the problems and opportunities involved;
- competent to discuss with line managers and functional specialists issues and policies relating to company finance, marketing and market entry, establishment and control of foreign operations, etc.

Once a foreign operation is well established, it is likely that local national managers, rather than expatriates from the company's home country, will be employed. This will cut costs, provide for long-term continuity in administration, and create a career ladder for locally recruited staff. However, there could be a loss of head office control, and relations between head office and its subsidiary will become more formal.

The next stage of development occurs when the nationality of the manager of any part of a company's activities becomes a matter of indifference: the manager might be recruited and trained in any country. A problem here is harmonizing the salary structure for people doing similar work in different countries. A common approach in this instance is to pay wage rates appropriate for each host country, although this makes it difficult to attract high-calibre managers to assignments in low-wage states. If specific managers are paid higher remunerations than the norm in the latter countries, then big discrepancies may arise between the salary levels of managers within particular units, leading perhaps to bitter resentments and demotivated staff.

THE PROCESS OF INTERNATIONALIZATION

Distribution channels

A channel of distribution is a series of intermediaries that handle, store and/or assume ownership of goods as they pass from producer to end-consumer. Channels of distribution for international marketing can be very long, as there are channels both within and between countries. The terms 'channel design' or 'channel management' are used to describe the process of evaluating channel options and selecting particular intermediaries and thereafter monitoring their work. Decisions regarding distribution channels are critically important; they affect pricing and product quality policies, the volume of clerical work undertaken and the extent of potential bad debt. Choice of a distribution system obviously depends on the nature of the produce (direct mail is not suitable for bulky and/or high-value items), and on the following factors:

- **Duration of the total order cycle**. For each of the available options the firm needs to compute the average period likely to elapse between the receipt of an order and the actual delivery of the goods. Estimation of these lead times requires breaking the order cycle down into subdivisions for order processing, documentation, warehousing, packaging, loading/unloading and intermediate handling, and final delivery.
- **Effects of non-availability in local markets**. Occasional stock-outs in foreign warehouses or retail outlets may be acceptable provided stock replenishments are quickly available. Warehousing is extremely expensive, so it is necessary to balance cost against the possible bad image that the odd stock-out may create for the firm.
- **Frequency and size of customer orders**. Management must examine carefully the pattern of local demand for the type of product involved, and analyse the extent and periodicity of sales fluctuations, market growth trends, geographical dispersion of purchasers, etc.
- **Distribution costs**. These have to be evaluated with respect to transport costs, warehousing expenses, clerical workload, levels of intermediaries' mark-ups within the system, the interest loss attributable to having capital tied up in the volume of stock necessitated by each distribution option, order processing, and packaging and breakage expenditures.

- **Degree of control over the system**. Certain types of distributor assume control over product pricing, advertising and presentation. How reliable are such distributors in these matters? Might they price the goods at an inappropriate level? Technically complex goods and/or those requiring specialist after-sales service are perhaps less suitable than others for distribution through numerous intermediaries.
- **Spread of the market**. The method selected should provide adequate geographical coverage of the market.
- **The share of the target market**. How much share does each alternative command, and what is the effectiveness of the various options for penetrating the market?
- **After-sales service**. This covers the extent and character of the after-sales service (if any) that the firm will be expected to provide.
- **Promotional costs**. These include advertising, merchandising and related expenditures.
- **Image**. This covers whether the distribution channel considered enhances or detracts from the image of the product.

in practice...

BICC-VERO

BICC-VERO Electronics Ltd has opted for a fully centralized international distribution system, subject to tight head office control. The company supplies circuit boards for computers, electronics cabinets, aluminium and plastic housings for circuitry, and similar products. It has subsidiaries in the United States, Germany, France, Italy, Sweden and Austria. Originally, each subsidiary held its own stocks of finished products and determined its own inventory levels. If there was no subsidiary in a particular country, then a stockholding distributor would be appointed. Not all the firm's products were made available in all countries in consequence of differences in market demand.

A number of factors caused BICC to change its approach to distribution: there was an increasing tendency for the firm's larger customers to insist on the same product being instantly available throughout the world (in order to service all their international operations); a general liberalization of import controls on the company's outputs occurred in the late 1980s; and an important new product, the IMRAK cabinet, was introduced, which had to be stacked in component parts and assembled on-site to customer order – as opposed to being built and stocked as self-contained units to be purchased off-the-shelf. There were over 100,000 possible configurations of the standard unit, so a central stock of components was required to ensure that a sufficient variety of parts was always available. It made little sense to have separate and duplicate stocks of low-value easily transported components in several countries. The French town of Metz was chosen as the location for the central warehouse because of its nearness to key markets. Piece parts are manufactured in Britain and shipped to France. Metz has excellent air, rail and motorway links with the rest of the world, and any subsidiary or distributor is guaranteed delivery within a very short period.

Choice of intermediary

In selecting a particular intermediary the exporter needs to examine each candidate firm's knowledge of the product and local markets, experience and expertise, required margin, credit rating, customer care facilities and ability to promote the exporter's products in an effective and attractive manner. Specific desirable characteristics of an intermediary are:

- a solid financial base;
- a well-established corporate image in the local market;
- a good track record of selling similar items;
- wide geographical coverage;
- a large sales force;
- substantial warehousing facilities and a willingness to place large orders;
- procedures for prompt settling of suppliers' invoices.

Collaborative international marketing arrangements

Exporting businesses can form joint ventures to market their collective output in foreign countries. This spreads costs and means that ancillary services too expensive for a single firm can be arranged. The consortium might export under a separate corporate identity, negotiate bulk rates for transporting joint consignments, conduct international marketing research, draft uniform terms for contracts of sale, and arrange for the collection of debts.

Small firms sometimes enter into 'piggyback' deals with large companies that already operate in certain foreign markets and are willing to act on behalf of other businesses that wish to export to those markets. This enables larger companies to fully use their sales representatives, premises, office equipment, etc, in the countries concerned. The 'carrier' will purchase the goods outright or act as a commission agent, and may or may not sell the 'rider's' product under the carrier's own brand name, depending on the form of the agreement. Sometimes the carrier will insist that the rider's products be similar to its own in view of the need to deal with technical queries and after-sales service 'in the field'. Piggybacking has the following advantages:

- 'Riders' can export conveniently without having to establish their own distribution systems. They can observe carefully how the 'carrier' handles the goods and hence learn from the carrier's experience – perhaps to the point of eventually being able to take over their own export transactions.
- Carriers broaden their product range without having to manufacture extra products.
- Economies of scale in bulk distribution become available.
- The carrier's overall business image may be enhanced through being seen to carry additional products.

The rider obtains access to all the export facilities and resources of the carrier, while the latter sells items that might fill a gap in its own product line. Problems that might arise include:

- lack of commitment on the part of the carrier;
- riders failing to supply the carrier on a continuous basis;
- loss of lucrative sales opportunities in regions not covered by the carrier.

in practice...

Imperial Chemical Industries

Imperial Chemical Industries' 'Tradeway' system handles the work of 300 UK companies (mostly small businesses) that sell to ICI's 150 overseas markets. The system operates as a conventional agency, using ICI's extensive network of offices and sales organizations in foreign countries, although the company will only offer its services for the marketing of chemical products that complement its own product range. Riders benefit from ICI's massive experience of foreign trade and its well-established facilities. ICI gains through its foreign sales offices being able to supply a wider range of terms, plus the agency commission.

Other well-known examples of piggybacking are the Singer Sewing Company, which carries other companies' sewing threads, fabrics and other sewing accessories closely related to its own, and the General Electric Company, which distributes a wide range of electrical goods produced by other businesses across the world.

in practice...

Penguin Books as distribution agent

Penguin Books has an international distribution network that it makes available to small publishing firms. The latter retain copyright ownership and editorial control, while Penguin publishes, distributes and handles the sales and international customer service requirement of the books involved. In effect, Penguin acts as a distribution agent for other publishers, thus exploiting to the full the foreign representation systems and international marketing expertise that it has built up over several decades.

Sister companies

A further option is to seek a 'sister company' in a foreign market. Sister companies are foreign firms offering similar products that are of similar size and structure to the one looking for a partner. They not only act as a foreign agent but also advise on local conditions, translate documents, and generally provide support and comfort when things go wrong. The other firm offers reciprocal facilities to the foreign business. There are regular meetings and exchanges of information, and possible exchanges of staff for short periods. Ideally the sister company should be engaged in complementary rather than competitive lines of work and face the same sorts of problem. Piggyback and sister company arrangements might be better than the appointment of foreign agents in that:

- the small exporter's product might 'plug a gap' in the partner's own product range, saving the partner the cost and inconvenience of having to develop and introduce a similar product;
- the partner is likely to be dealing only with its own and the other firm's products, whereas export and import agents typically handle a wide range of (sometimes competing) product lines;
- great expertise and attention may be devoted to the exporter's specific problems.

Collaborative international marketing arrangements involving many member firms are common in certain countries (Japan for example) and industry sectors. Such partnerships can enable the group to develop the 'critical mass' needed to penetrate a foreign market, to tender for large orders, to share technical and financial resources and to operate in a wider range of countries than otherwise would be the case.

Establishing permanent facilities in other countries

Communication difficulties with ad hoc representatives, lack of commitment on the part of commission agents, costly margins taken by independent distributors and escalating administrative costs may cause a firm seriously to consider the option of setting up subsidiary businesses in foreign countries – each with its own employees, premises, warehouses, delivery vehicles, and so on. A permanent local presence enables the company to operate as if it were a local firm. Companies establish foreign subsidiaries in order to:

- spread the risk of downturns in particular markets;
- reduce production costs (eg because of cheaper raw materials or labour);
- obtain investment grants from foreign governments;
- acquire know-how and technical skills only available locally;
- minimize their worldwide tax burdens;
- engage in local assembly or part-manufacture;
- project a local identity.

A permanent local presence is particularly useful in situations where there are long channels of distribution, where the product is technically complex and requires extensive after-sales support, or where large-scale ongoing advertising and/or sales promotions are necessary.

in practice...

Penguin Books as internationalized company

Penguin Books (a subsidiary of Pearson PLC since 1970) is a good example of a firm that internationalized its operations gradually over time. In the late 1930s and 1940s the company began exporting to the United States, Canada and Australia, followed by the setting-up of simple sales representation systems with basic marketing facilities coordinated and controlled from London. As sales and market share increased in these countries, local subsidiary companies were formed to take over the role of local agents and to organize distribution in the national market direct. These middle-aged businesses carried stock and imported from the rest of the group. Operations were systematically extended to other (predominantly English-speaking) countries such as India and South Africa. In the larger and more secure markets (Australia, for instance), full-scale publishing companies were created working in partnership with the parent organization rather than as subsidiaries, although directors of Penguin UK typically occupied a number of seats on the boards of the local publishing companies. More recently Penguin has operated across southern Asia and continental Europe, offering sales facilities only. Penguin's strategic objective in the internationalization sphere is to offset less successful activities in one market against growth in another. Economic recession in a particular country hits book sales in that country extremely hard, but Penguin is able to overcome this problem by spreading the risk across a wide number of markets, not all of which will be in recession at any one time.

THE GLOBAL COMPANY

The next stage in the internationalization of a firm's horizons and activities is for it to become a genuinely global business. A global company is one that *owns* production, distribution and other units in foreign countries and plans the utilization of its resources on a global scale. It invests internationally in the acquisition of raw materials and subsidiaries supplying input components and sells through its permanent establishments abroad. 'International' businesses have a home country and do business in foreign countries. Global corporations conversely are not reliant on a single home base. They need not be large corporations; rather they are firms of any size that recognize the benefits of operating on the global level. Global corporations can reduce their sourcing and distribution costs compared to national businesses, can avoid tariffs, quotas and other trade barriers faced by exporters, and are able periodically to shift operations from high-cost to low-cost countries. The focus of the business has shifted from contract supply arrangements with local businesses towards direct investment in physical plant.

Global corporations can penetrate markets throughout the world from supply points in several different countries, supplemented perhaps by exports from the parent firm plus ad hoc licensing and contract manufacture agreements. Their managements plan, organize and control company operations on a worldwide scale, with national markets being regarded as little more than segments of a broader regional customer base. Further characteristics of global corporation activity are that:

- Operations are located wherever is appropriate to enable goods to be sold in the company's most important markets.
- Technologies are developed in whichever countries have the necessary skills, research infrastructure and facilities.
- Finished goods, raw materials, component parts, know-how and managerial personnel are freely exchanged between operating units.

Every global corporation has its headquarters in some country or other and has a majority of shareholders from a particular country. The norms and cultures of the headquarters country are bound to pervade the entire organization. Yet the adoption of a world view by headquarters executives is essential for successful international operations. Practical manifestations of a global perspective could include:

- everyone concerned with management regarding foreign operations as of at least the same level of importance as domestic selling;
- allocation of top jobs to foreign nationals;
- genuine attempts to integrate activities on a worldwide basis;
- rewarding successful foreign subsidiaries more highly than domestic country units in appropriate circumstances;
- joint strategic decision-making by headquarters staff and managers of subsidiary units.

Integration of the marketing function at the global level means that product and branding decisions are taken having regard to the facilities and opportunities available in various countries, including the costs of storage and transport, trade restrictions, availability of ancillary services and so on. This creates many possibilities for economies of scale in marketing operations and the spreading of costs over multiple markets.

For and against the global company

The case in favour of the global corporation emphasizes its role as an agent of change and progress, helping to create a worldwide economic order based on rationality, efficiency, and the optimal use of resources. Host countries acquire plant and equipment that otherwise would not be available, accompanied by the skills and know-how necessary for its operation. Local recruitment of junior managers creates a pool of managerial talent in the local community that can transfer its abilities across a wide range of industries. Prices are lower in consequence of economies of scale; domestic employment is stimulated. The latest technologies, management techniques and business methods are diffused internationally. Note, however, that the proposition that global corporations allocate resources across the globe in an optimal manner rests on the proposition that the world's resources are best utilized through the interplay of unfettered market forces. The problem is that open and competitive markets exist in some parts of the world, but not in others, so that distortions in free market mechanisms will arise in some areas – generating side-effects that upset the entire worldwide resource allocation process.

Global corporations have been accused of 'economic imperialism', of not respecting human rights, supporting repressive governments and paying bribes to secure political influence. Further allegations are that global corporations have:

- not accepted responsibility for unsafe products;
- supplied products that are inappropriate to local needs;
- promoted goods that waste valuable resources in poorer countries;
- engaged in misleading and deceitful advertising in Third World countries;
- undermined ancient cultures and traditions through the use of ubiquitous advertising and marketing methods.

In the 1960s and '70s many national governments sought to control global corporation activities, for example by having host country civil servants on subsidiary boards, special taxes, exchange controls, requirements that local subsidiaries employ a quota of locally recruited employees or enter joint venture agreements with local businesses, local content requirements, and so on. Nowadays, however, countries are generally loath to impose restrictions on global corporations for fear of losing valuable foreign investment. Other reasons for the contemporary widespread acceptance of global corporations by national governments include:

- The emergence of large home-grown international businesses in a number of under-developed states.
- A wider dispersion of the home countries in which global corporations are based. Japanese, Korean and other Asian global corporations have brought different approaches to host country relations compared to firms from Western Europe and (especially) the United States.
- Increasingly ferocious international competition among global corporations, which made them keen to establish good relations with host country governments.
- Development of better negotiating skills by host government representatives. Ministers and senior civil servants became adept at securing the best possible deals when bargaining with global corporation managements.
- Greater cultural sensitivity on the part of global corporation managers resulting from their longer experience of doing business abroad.
- An increase in the number of small firms operating on the global scale.

11

Export methods and procedures

DECIDING TO EXPORT

Export means producing a product in one country and selling it in another. Exporting is not limited to physical products: the United Kingdom has major export markets in banking, insurance and education that are often serviced without any UK national ever leaving the country and with no more physical product than some documents and contracts actually crossing borders.

Governments are usually in favour of exporting and encourage it because it improves the balance of payments position, and (in effect) transfers unemployment to other countries. Most governments are therefore more than happy to provide help for exporters, either in the form of subsidies (which may not always be legal) or in the form of advice and practical help. For example, governments will often help exporters to exhibit at international trade fairs, and will provide expert local advice from economic attachés at the embassy in the foreign country. In most cases, however, exporting means shipping physical products, and this chapter concentrates mainly on this type of export.

The export of a consignment of goods to a foreign country involves transportation, insurance of the cargo and/or of payment for the goods extensive documentation, packaging and labelling, and organizing payment. Pre-shipment inspection and foreign technical standards also require attention.

TRANSPORT

Transport is a critical element of the wider subject of 'logistics', ie the analysis of the cost, efficiency and feasibility of the various models of transport and temporary storage needed to shift goods to their destinations – safely and with minimum pilferage and other materials loss – at the right time. Products have to be available for purchase where and when they are required. Key characteristics of the main methods for transporting goods between countries are shown in Table 11.1.

In selecting a means of transport the exporter needs to balance cost against speed and dependability. Specific factors influencing this choice include the urgency with which customers require the goods, the nature of the product (weight, dimensions, perishability, ease of handling), and customer preferences regarding the reliabilities of arrival dates. The value of the goods might also be important, since the risk of pilferage has to be considered if a consignment is of high value and insurance costs on high-value consignments are greater the longer the goods are at risk.

Other relevant considerations are convenience of collection by customers, intermediate handling and storing charges, special packaging costs, spoilage rates, documentation expenses, and the interest on capital forgone through having money tied up as goods in transit for various journey times.

Table 11.1   International transport methods

Road	Rail	Sea	Air
Door-to-door collection and delivery of loads	Suitable for bulky loads and transport over long distances	Cheap but slow	Very fast
Minimal intermediate handling	Transhipment necessary	Transhipment necessary	Not suitable for bulky loads
Slow over long distances	Fast over long distances	Need to book space well in advance of shipment	Few airports in remote areas
Can go to remote rural areas	Set timetables	Port congestion may delay unloading of cargoes	Not affected by geographical obstructions (mountains, rivers, etc)
Not affected by public transport strikes	Increasing number of high-speed services to continental Europe via Eurotunnel	Significant documentation needed	Subject to weather delays
Heavy traffic congestion on some routes		Flexible (there is usually a choice of ships going to the required destination)	Delays occur through labour disputes at airports
Subject to weather delays		Higher insurance costs than for air transport	Diversions sometimes necessary
Limited size of load			
Lorries may have to return empty			

Sea transport

Sea freight includes scheduled services (referred to as 'liner' services) that sail according to a strict timetable and other vessels, sometimes referred to as 'tramp' ships, that depart only when they have a full cargo. Liner services charge uniform rates applicable to all shipping companies. Tramp rates vary between vessels. Sea freight charges are quoted on a unit weight/volume basis, so the firm pays a certain rate for either so many kilograms weight or a corresponding number of cubic metres. Supplementary charges may also be specified, eg for additional fuel or extra unloading costs owing to port congestion.

Shipping companies have agents who advertise the space available on vessels and book cargo to fill it, taking a commission from ship owners. Usually an agent will arrange for loading. Booking space for a consignment involves completing the shipping company's (or agent's) booking form and standard shipping note (SSN). The latter advises the shipping company on what is to happen to the goods on arrival at the foreign port, ie who will pick them up, who will pay unloading charges, whether the consignment is to be placed in a warehouse within the docks, etc. An SSN also acts as a request to the destination port authorities to receive and handle the shipment. Accordingly, the port authorities must sign a copy of the SSN and return this to the exporter as proof of delivery. All the major shipping companies offer 'less than full container load' (LCL) groupage services.

The bill of lading

This is the contract between the exporter and the shipping company. It also functions as a receipt for the goods, specifying whether they were loaded in a satisfactory or damaged condition, and a document of title, meaning that the consignee named on the bill of lading has the legal right to claim the consignment.

A clean bill of lading refers to goods received on board in apparently good condition and with no shortages. A short-form bill of lading is one that does not show the shipping company's terms and conditions of carriage on the back. The customer can transfer the right to collect the goods by endorsing the bill accordingly. Hence, a bill of lading is a 'quasi-negotiable' document of title.

The normal bill of lading is a 'shipped bill' that attests that the goods are on board. A 'received' bill states that the goods are at the port of shipment, but not necessarily on board the vessel. Received bills are *not* documents of title. A 'through' (transhipment) bill of lading is used when sea transport forms only part of a journey and it is more convenient to prepare a single contract document than separate documents for each carrier. A 'stale' bill of lading is one that arrives at the customer's premises after the goods have arrived at the port of destination. In the absence of a bill of lading the customer can only obtain possession of the goods by giving the shipping company a bank letter of indemnity, which protects the shipping company against subsequent claims.

For small loads and/or short journeys the shipping company might issue a 'data freight receipt' (DFR sometimes called a sea waybill) rather than a bill of lading per se. DFRs are the sea transport equivalent of air waybills (see below) in that they act merely as receipts for goods and as evidence of contracts of carriage and do not relate to the ownership of goods.

Legal status of the bill of lading

Bills of lading are said to be documents of 'possessory' title but not 'proprietary' title, meaning that:

- Since a bill of lading represents the goods while they are in transit, the transfer of a bill of lading effectively transfers possession of the goods and therefore the obligation to pay for them when they are received (but not at the moment of the handing over of the bill of lading).
- Only the holder of the bill of lading may collect the goods. If, however, the bill of lading is lost, destroyed or not available for some other bona fide reason, or if perishable goods arrive before the buyer receives the bill of lading, then the carrier may lawfully release the goods on receipt of a letter of indemnity from the party picking up the consignment. Suppose that the latter is not in fact the rightful owner of the goods and that the true owner of the goods subsequently appears with a bill of lading. In this case the carrier has committed the unlawful act of 'conversion' and may be sued for damages by the rightful owner. The carrier in turn recovers the loss from the bank that issued the letter of indemnity.
- Possession always passes the moment a bill of lading is transferred, but *ownership* only passes when the parties intend it to pass, as evidenced by the sales contract.

As receipts, bills of lading provide only prima facie evidence that a certain quantity was received on board, that packaging marks were in order and that the goods were apparently in good condition. Nevertheless it is up to the carrier to prove that the items stated were not in fact put on board or were not loaded in a certain condition. The ship's master need only attest to the receipt of goods in *seemingly* good condition, and is not expected to investigate their inner qualities.

Charter parties

A contract under which an *entire ship* is hired to a user is called a charter party (CP). There are two forms: *non-demise* CPs, whereby the ship owner provides the vessel and crew, and *demise* CPs, which furnish the vessel only. A 'voyage CP' is for a specific journey(s); a 'time CP' contracts the ship for a stated period.

Airfreight

In the past, airfreight has been restricted to the transport of high-value low-bulk consignments. Increasingly, however, new and inexpensive aircraft are available, capable of carrying larger and heavier loads. Indeed, it is now cheaper to send certain goods by air than by any other method. Moreover, speedy delivery means less stockholding, faster settlement of invoices and hence better use of working capital. Certain intermediate warehousing costs may also be avoided since goods can go straight from the airport to customers' premises.

Airfreight is especially useful, therefore, for goods where demand is seasonal or highly variable, as it becomes possible to meet new orders immediately without having to store goods in local warehouses. (The cost of warehousing may average as much as one-third the value of the stored items.) Space can be booked direct with an airline or via a cargo agent. The latter helps consignors to arrange shipments and documentation, and will organize goods collection services if required. Airfreight rates are quoted by weight and volume, with the customer paying according to whichever is the higher value.

The international airlines fix their prices through the International Air Transport Association (IATA), although competition does exist via a variety of special discounts offered to customers. Price fixing does not apply to consignments big enough to justify chartering an entire aircraft. Rates for this vary widely, depending on:

- the type of aircraft chartered;
- the urgency of the trip; and
- the time of year the aircraft is required.

However, a chartered aircraft is not necessarily cheaper than schedule freight services, since the charterer may have to pay for the entire round trip if the chartered plane needs to return empty.

The air waybill

This is a consignment note issued by the airline. It is not a document of title. However, provided the goods are addressed to the person (customer, agent, distributor) named on the air waybill and that person settles any outstanding freight or airport charges, the goods will be handed over on landing if the consignee has the order number and offers proof of identification.

Road and rail

Road and rail transport (sometimes in conjunction with ro-ro ferries – see below) over long distances are frequently combined via the use of standardized detachable interchangeable 'swap body' containers, ie self-contained trailers on their own wheels that can be exchanged between cabs as opposed to 'flat' trailers on to which containers have to be loaded. The entire swap body can be uncoupled from a cab, rolled on to a road train for long-haul rail transport, and rolled off and attached to another cab at its final destination. Most national railway companies belong to an international system for re-routing empty containers following their unloading at the point of destination. Goods are transported under an 'international consignment note', which lays down internationally agreed standard conditions of carriage.

For relatively short international journeys, straightforward road haulage avoids the need for transhipment of goods (ie having to unload and reload consignments between different modes of transport), thus reducing handling costs and pilferage losses. Final delivery by road is convenient for customers and flexible (routes and destinations can be altered quickly and at will). The problem, of course, is the possible absence of loads for return journeys. Road hauliers need to make the fullest use of vehicles, especially the cabs ('tractors') of articulated lorries, and will incorporate the costs of any time a vehicle is not earning money into quoted delivery charges. An international transport agreement, known as the TIR (Transports Internationaux Routiers) convention, has for many years enabled road hauliers to seal their vehicles in the exporter's country, travel across national frontiers without interference, and have all documentation processed at the final delivery point.

A road haulier's receipt for accepting a consignment is called a CMR (Convention de Marchandises par Route) note. This records the contract of carriage, but does not provide evidence of ownership of the shipment. The CMR lays down standard international contractual conditions for road transport, covering liability for loss or damage to goods and the maximum value of insurance claims against the haulier.

Cabotage

Cabotage means the carriage of cross-directional loads on journeys within a country's national frontiers. Many countries restrict road and air carriers' abilities to engage in cabotage so that, for example, a foreign road haulier will be allowed to deliver an export consignment to a certain city, but not then pick up a load for delivery to another city in the same country. Restrictions on road (but not air) cabotage within European Union countries have been abolished.

GIT liability insurance

Exporters sometimes suppose, erroneously, that road hauliers assume full liability for losses to goods in their care via hauliers' own goods in transit (GIT) liability insurance. In fact the standard conditions of carriage offered by hauliers impose upper limits on the compensation payable in the event of damage or loss to consignments, leaving a large shortfall for valuable cargoes. For example, the UK Road Haulage Association's standard contract limits compensation to £1,300 per tonne, so that if a cargo weighing 5 tonnes and worth £25,000 is lost, only £6,500 is payable. Similar conditions apply in other countries under the CMR (see above). Exporters can only obtain full cover on their cargoes by taking out their own cargo insurance policy (see below).

Ro-ro ferries

Roll-on roll-off (ro-ro) ferries carry complete vehicles or the trailers of articulated lorries (ie ones that comprise two separate parts: cab and trailer, connected by a bar or some other linking device). Ro-ro facilities exist along the entire European and North American coastlines and in all the major ports in the major trading countries of Asia Pacific.

Ro-ro is cheap because goods handling is reduced to the absolute minimum (no lifting gear is required and marshalling is easy) and because (multi-million pound) vessels can turn around extremely quickly. However, the effective payload of the trailer of an articu-lated lorry transported in this manner is substantially lower than (say) a rail or conven-tional sea container in consequence of the extra weight of the wheels and frame of the vehicle and the additional space these occupy.

Freight forwarders

External assistance with international transport and associated documentation is avail-able from freight forwarders and integrated carriers (see below). Freight forwarders are businesses that specialize in the international movement of goods and that advise clients on packaging and labelling, warehousing, and which modes of transport are most suit-able for carrying a client firm's output, taking account of its size, weight, characteristics and the urgency of the delivery. A forwarder will assume full responsibility for documen-tation and insurance, book air freight or ferry space for consignments, arrange for the collection of goods from sea ports, railway stations or container depots in other countries, and organize final road delivery. Forwarders take their profits from fees charged to client companies, from commissions taken from the airlines, shipping companies, etc, with which they book space, and from bulk discounts given by carriers and commercial ware-houses in recognition of forwarders' groupage (consolidation) services.

Groupage is the process whereby a forwarder collects at one of its depots numerous small shipments bound for the same destination and consolidates them into a single large consignment. Substantial discounts are available for the bulk transportation of consolida-tion consignments, part of which the forwarder will pass back to small business clients in the form of lower freight prices. Moreover, a forwarder can often avoid the losses result-ing from lorries and containers having to return from particular destinations empty, since forwarders continuously liaise with each other and swap counter-directional loads. The problem with groupage is that a specific consignment may be stored at the forwarder's collection depot for several days awaiting a consolidation into which it conveniently fits.

Integrated carriers

For certain consignments speed is vital, especially where customers operate just-in-time production systems or where the benefits of faster delivery greatly outweigh the addi-tional cost. Integrated carriers offer immediate door-to-door collection and delivery services but without any need for groupage. They use scheduled services that run regardless of loading, so that goods are guaranteed to be delivered within a specific time.

DOCUMENTING A CONSIGNMENT

A large number of documents are needed to export goods, and can account for about 5 per cent of the cost of a consignment (significantly more if documents contain errors that lead to hold-ups in delivery and payment). The extent of export documentation is attributable to the very many bodies and intermediaries requiring information about shipments: carriers, customs and docks authorities, banks, and managers of container depots, agents, warehousing firms, and so on. Mistakes in documents cost money. Differences in goods descriptions, discrepancies in order and consignment numbers, uncompleted boxes on customs forms, absence of instructions for disposal of shipments on completion of their journeys and so on may cause long delays and serious financial losses. Goods arriving at sea ports or rail or air terminals without proper identification will be placed in local warehouses that charge storage fees to the parties eventually collecting them. And late delivery to consumers creates bad customer relations and leads to eventual loss of orders. The process of documenting an export consignment is outlined in Figure 11.1. Some of the names of the necessary documents are self-explanatory. Others are explained below or elsewhere in the text.

On receipt of an enquiry the exporter needs to check the feasibility of its fulfilment in terms of export licences, etc. Note that for a DDP (delivery duty paid) or CIF (cost insurance and freight) contract the obligation to obtain the licence is on the seller; otherwise the obligation is subject to agreement. The exporter may have to issue a pro forma invoice, ie one specifying full details of costs and delivery, even though the customer has yet to place an order. This might be necessary for the customer to obtain an import licence. Also, the customs authorities of certain countries demand a certificate of origin attesting the country from which the item came and that it has not passed through certain other countries.

Another possible requirement is for a 'consular invoice', which is an attestation by a representative of the importer's country who is based in the exporter's country to the effect that the goods specified in the pro forma reasonably correspond to the price stated. The purpose of consular invoices is to prevent transfer pricing and hence the avoidance of import duties through invoicing at artificially low levels. Typically the attesting person is an employee of the embassy or consulate of the country concerned. They will make an assessment based on published market data, local trade practice, trade magazines, price lists of other firms, invoices for similar items issued by alternative suppliers, and possibly an expert independent opinion in appropriate cases (eg for high-value consignments where fraud is suspected). Fees are payable for each attestation. Within the European Union, documentation has been standardized in order to minimize the delays at borders, and to encourage the free flow of goods between member states.

Electronic data interchange

Computerized facsimile document transmission systems are increasingly used for the interchange of export/import documentation. For the individual exporter, a computerized documentation system ensures that invoices and air waybill numbers coincide, that identical goods descriptions apply to all documents, that booking sheets relate to the proper loads, etc. All the information for documenting a consignment to a known customer or of a particular product type is quickly assembled, payments cycles are shortened, and errors (and hence clerical costs) reduced. The fully integrated electronic mail

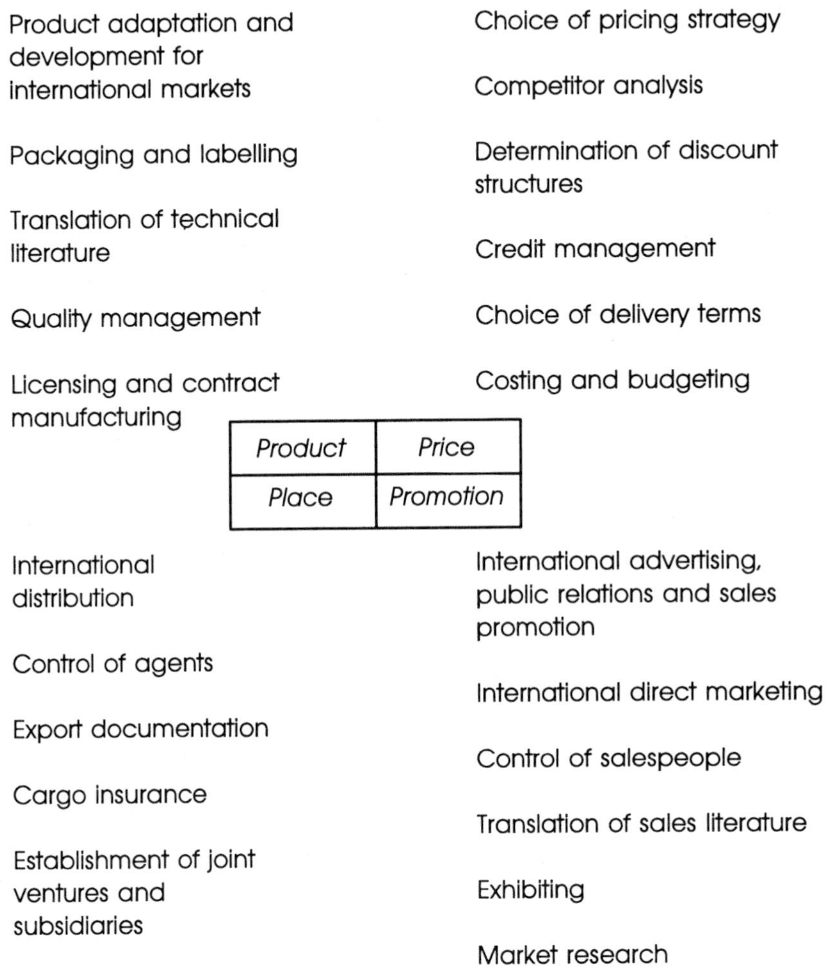

Product adaptation and development for international markets

Packaging and labelling

Translation of technical literature

Quality management

Licensing and contract manufacturing

Choice of pricing strategy

Competitor analysis

Determination of discount structures

Credit management

Choice of delivery terms

Costing and budgeting

Product	Price
Place	Promotion

International distribution

Control of agents

Export documentation

Cargo insurance

Establishment of joint ventures and subsidiaries

International advertising, public relations and sales promotion

International direct marketing

Control of salespeople

Translation of sales literature

Exhibiting

Market research

Figure 11.1 Documenting an export consignment

exchange of documents between exporters, customers, public authorities, banks, carriers, agents and distributors, customs, dock and harbour authorities, etc, is called electronic data interchange (EDI). A major advantage of EDI is its avoidance of the need to rekey information into different computers at various stages in the chain of distribution. Hence there is no chance of errors (which cause transport delays and hold-ups in payment) creeping into documents through frequent rekeying. The main problem, of course, is the incompatibility of computer hardware and systems, making it difficult for computers in different countries to interconnect.

Pre-shipment inspection

Customers may insist that the goods they purchase conform to a certain quality standard (ISO 9000, for example) and/or rigid design specifications, and reserve the right to reject consignments not meeting the stated requirements. To save the cost of shipping goods to their final destination only to have them turned away on design/quality grounds, exporters might arrange for the pre-shipment inspection (PSI) of the goods at the supplying firm's home country premises. Another reason for PSI is to enable the governments of importing countries to ensure that import consignments are genuine and not merely a device for transferring hard currency out of the country (eg by importing crates marked 'machinery' but in fact only containing boxes of sand, and remitting a hard currency payment to a foreign country to the value of the nonexistent machinery). This form of PSI is most common in economically underdeveloped countries, and is usually carried out by an organization, Société Générale de Surveillance SA, specially constituted for this purpose. The document confirming that all is in order is known as a 'clean report of findings'. Physical standards PSIs might be undertaken in accredited test centres in the exporter's country, or in situ at the exporter's premises by a representative of the importing firm.

The contract of sale

This is perhaps the most important document of all and needs to incorporate details of the price of the goods, parties to the sale, delivery terms (CIF, DDP, etc), the latest dispatch date, the mode of transport to be used and the method of payment. It should also specify which country's laws are to apply to the contract, details of letter of credit arrangements (where applicable), and all the documents required by the buyer prior to payment. Further clauses that might be included are:

- A price escalation clause entitling the supplier to increase the selling price by any unforeseen additional production or transport costs incurred between the dates of quotation and delivery.
- A penalty clause for late delivery.
- An arbitration clause specifying that a certain international body shall resolve any disagreement arising from the contract.
- A *force majeure* clause defining each party's rights and duties following the occurrence of events beyond their control, eg that the contract ceases to be binding if there are dock strikes, political disturbances in either country, sudden imposition of foreign exchange controls, etc.
- A reservation (retention) of title clause (see below). These are sometimes referred to as Romalpa clauses, after the name of a famous test case that established their legitimacy.

Reservation of title (RT) clauses

With a 'a simple' RT clause the supplier delivers the goods to the purchaser but retains legal ownership of them until payment has been made. 'Extended' RT clauses come in two varieties: first, the buyer is regarded as an agent of the supplier and, if the goods are sold to a third party, the money received is viewed as being 'held in trust' on the supplier's behalf. Thus, should the first buyer become insolvent before paying the supplier, the latter has a claim on that firm's assets even to the point of being able to reclaim the goods in question from a third (or subsequent) party to whom they were resold. Secondly, the clause may state that if the goods supplied are used as inputs (eg all raw materials) to other goods, the original supplier retains a financial interest in the final goods that result, unless the final goods possess a different 'commercial identity' from the original goods' input. For example, a supplier of leather to a handbag manufacturer was held not to have title to handbags sold to the public by the manufacturer, despite the existence of an extended RT clause.

CARGO INSURANCE

Cargo insurance typically costs about 1 per cent of the value of consignments, which are normally insured for CIF shipment plus 10 per cent (to cover incidental expenses attached to the loss). Four basic principles apply to all forms of insurance: indemnity, insurable interest, good faith and proximate cause, although some of these are amended for contracts involving foreign trade. In Britain, the law concerning export cargo insurance is largely contained in the 1906 Marine Insurance Act.

The principle of 'indemnity' is that the insured cannot profit by a loss, eg by insuring goods for more than they are worth. For marine insurance, however, the law accepts that the market value of a cargo may fluctuate in value during transit, so it is possible to pre-specify the sum payable if the cargo is lost, even if this exceeds the cargo's actual value at the moment of loss. Insurable 'interest' in ordinary insurance means that the insured must own the goods, and that they can only be insured once. This is not the case for marine insurance, because anybody who stands to benefit from a cargo's safe and punctual arrival (firms awaiting vital raw materials for example) may insure it. 'Good faith' is the requirement that all material facts be disclosed to the insurer. 'Proximate cause' is the principle that the cause of the loss has to be first- and not second-hand; eg a cargo might be destroyed by a fire that itself is the result of a dockside riot, in which case the question arises as to whether riots are covered by the policy.

Average

In cargo insurance the word 'average' means 'loss'. Particular average is a partial loss caused accidentally. General average is a partial loss deliberately incurred, eg if an aircraft is in danger of crashing and the captain decides to jettison cargo to lighten the load. With general average, the loss is intended to benefit everyone, hence all parties are expected to contribute proportionately towards the cost, even if certain consignments have not been touched. Compensation for general average is available through standard cargo insurance policies.

Most policies are 'with particular average', meaning that partial losses accidentally caused are fully covered. Otherwise the policy is 'free from particular average', so that claims for accidental partial losses will not be met. Prior to 1974, each country applied its own formula to the computation of general average. Since then, however, most policies adhere to the 'York-Antwerp Rules', drafted by the International Law Association. Otherwise, general average is calculated according to the law of the country of the port of destination.

Types of cover

Cargoes may be insured for journeys by sea, land and air. The term 'marine insurance' is used to cover not only the insurance of goods at sea but also losses on land that are incidental to a sea voyage. Thus a marine insurance policy can cover the transportation of a cargo from the warehouse of the seller to the warehouse of the foreign buyer, subject to agreement. The standard form of policy used for marine insurance is the 'Lloyd's Marine Policy' (after Lloyd's of London, the world's principal insurance organization), which contains one of three sets of clauses, known as Institute Cargo Clauses A, B and C, which specify the cover the policy affords. Clause A provides the 'all risks' cover; B and C cover particular risks, with C giving cover only against major catastrophes. All three cover general average (see above) plus 'transit cover' against pre-shipment and post-shipment risks between a named inland source of supply and a named inland final destination. However, none of the three afford cover in respect of war damage or strikes: separate clauses must be inserted to insure against these risks. It is not possible to insure unlawful cargoes, or against damage resulting from the 'inherent vice' of the goods (eg innate propensity towards spontaneous combustion).

'Open cover' is available for exporters who continuously dispatch goods to foreign destinations. Here, a single policy applies to all consignments, which are declared to the insurance company on a monthly or quarterly basis. Payment occurs as goods are shipped, not in advance. A 'floating policy' covers a number of pre-specified shipments, for which a lump sum advance premium is payable. 'One-off' policies are known as *facultative* policies, and may be 'voyage' policies (whereby the cargo is insured from one specific place to another) or 'time' policies, ie the policy expires after a definite period. Note how the INCOTERMS (see Chapter 13) require that if goods are sold CIF, then the *seller* must take out the insurance, which can have Institute Cargo Clause A, B or C. For a C&F (cost and freight) contract neither party need take out insurance, and the goods travel at the risk of the buyer.

Policies frequently specify 'franchises and excesses'. A *franchise* in this context is any percentage loss beneath which the underwriter will not pay compensation; eg if the loss is less than (say) 5 per cent of the value of the goods, the exporting firm must bear this itself. An *excess* is an amount deducted from the compensation payable, eg if the exporter is liable for the first £250 of the total loss.

Shortlanding certificates

If a carrier (shipping company, road haulier, etc) discharges a consignment of lower quantity than stated on the transportation document (a bill of lading for example), then the carrier or its agent should issue a certificate confirming the shortlanding. This certificate is necessary in order to lodge an insurance claim in respect of the missing cargo. Carriers are (not surprisingly) reluctant to issue shortlanded certificates, as by so doing they imply acceptance of liability for the loss. Hence they will insist on first conducting their own investigation (eg to establish whether the missing units were accidentally discharged at a previous destination). Some carriers will offer ex gratia payments of (say) 50 per cent of the shortfall, in order to avoid having to deal with a claim from the customer's insurer. Import duty is, of course, not payable on the proportion of the cargo shortlanded.

Air transport

Insurance can be effected either through the use of the standard marine insurance policy, suitable endorsed, so that the standard Lloyd's policy is the relevant insurance document, or through ad hoc cover offered (at a price) by individual (though not all) airlines.

CUSTOMS DECLARATIONS

All exports except for parcel post and certain samples must be declared to the exporter's national customs authority on the appropriate document, quoting the relevant HS number. For parcel post the declaration is embodied in the document completed by the exporter when contracting its national postal service to deliver the parcel. Note how a 'parcel' might actually be a large and quite heavy consignment. In Britain, for example, a parcel can be up to 4 metres long and weigh up to 100 kilograms. In most countries the declarations may be made either on a shipment-by-shipment basis (completing a separate form for each assignment) or on a time basis through obtaining a customs registration number and declaring all shipments occurring during a month on a single date at the end of the month.

It is the importer's responsibility to tell the customs authorities of the country of importation that the goods are being imported and to present the correct information. Goods will be held up in customs until the duty on them has been paid (either by the importer or the exporter as determined by the contract of sale), unless they are going to a bonded warehouse or freezone (see below). 'Entry forms' must be completed informing customs of the quantity, type, value and destination of the consignment. Customs officers have the right to inspect goods and accompanying documents and, if they inspect, the cost of resulting damage to packing cases, etc has to be borne by the importer. Entry forms may be lodged a few days prior to importation in order to speed up processing. Otherwise they must normally be deposited within 14 days of arrival, or the imported goods will be sent to a special warehouse and storage charges will be imposed.

Customs entry may involve the production of a 'carnet', ie a document that enables the firm to move goods temporarily between different countries without having to pay any tax or customs duties. Carnets are used extensively for shifting exhibition materials, samples to be shown to customers, demonstration equipment and other working materials. Note, however, that they have not been necessary within the EU since the completion of the Single Market at the end of 1992.

Chambers of commerce that belong to the International Chamber of Commerce are allowed to issue to businesses 'ATA' (*admission temporaire*) carnets valid for most countries. The exporter has to deposit with the chamber of commerce the value of the highest customs duty that would otherwise be payable on the goods, this being returned when the items come back to the home country. If the terms of the carnet are violated, the chamber of commerce pays the deposit over to the customs authorities of the relevant country. UK exporters can take advantage of the (chargeable) ATA carnet indemnity scheme established by the London Chamber of Commerce and a number of Lloyd's underwriters. Under the scheme the exporter does not have to turn over any cash in order to provide the security deposit; rather a charge is registered against the assets of the exporting firm. If anything does go wrong the chamber must settle up with the appropriate customs authorities *before* attempting to recover the outstanding amount from the exporter. Note the usefulness of carnets for the movement of (substantial) consignments sent on what in effect is a sale or return basis following inspection by the potential customer.

Customs planning

National customs administrations operate disparate practices in relation to a number of matters, including:

- their interpretation of the HS number to which items should be ascribed;
- whether duty payable on goods released from bonded warehouses is charged at the currency exchange rate prevailing at the moment of release or at the moment of entry to the warehouse;
- whether (as in the United States) the authorities reserve the right to charge *ad valorem* tariffs on the basis of local market selling prices rather than on the importer's buying price.

It is essential that the importing firm minimizes the amount of duty it is obliged to pay on imported items, so careful 'customs planning' is necessary to optimize the importer's position. This can be achieved by delaying payment of duties until the last permissible moment, by applying that description of the imported goods that classifies them in the lowest possible tariff category, and possibly by importing products as sub-assemblies rather than as finished items. Customs planning is particularly important (and complicated) for firms whose products include imported raw materials and/or components since the range of potential reliefs, scope for redefining the character of goods, possibilities of altering the route by which items enter a country (which can greatly affect their liability for duty), methods of valuing imported goods for tax purposes, and so on increase gently.

Release of dutiable imports

Dutiable imports can be brought into a country and stored in a 'bonded warehouse' free of import duty whereby duty has to be paid only when they are released. While in a bonded warehouse, the goods can be repackaged, manipulated and further processed. If the goods are re-exported, then no duty at all is payable. Bonded warehouses are supervised by the customs authorities of the country in question. A 'freeport' serves the same function as a bonded warehouse but comprises a designated wider area at a seaport where goods can be stored and worked on free of duty. Inland 'freezones' are the same but usually located near airports. Other names for freezones are 'export processing zones' and 'investment promotion zones'. Today there are several hundred freeports/zones throughout the world, accounting for anything up to 10 per cent of world trade.

Freezones vary in relation to the extent of tax relief afforded to the firms operating within them. In several Pacific Rim countries freezones offer total exemption from *all* forms of taxation (not just customs duties), and have minimal health and safety regulations. Significant investment incentives (cash grants, generous depreciation allowances, etc) might be available. An interesting comparison is between countries that establish freezones within or immediately alongside currently *prosperous* areas (as happens in the Pacific Rim) and those that locate freezones in economically depressed regions in order to create local jobs. The latter approach has been used in Western Europe (notably in Britain), but does not appear to have met with much success.

Advocates of freezones argue that they remove the bureaucratic paperwork attached to customs and other export/import procedures, concentrate export processing services and facilities (insurance, packaging and labelling, pre-shipment inspection and certification, etc) in a small area and create local employment. Critics of the system allege, conversely, that they serve merely to divert to certain locations activities that would have occurred anyhow and deprive governments of tax revenue. Freezone warehousing is especially valuable where the imported goods are subject to a quota restriction, since the exporter can be sure that consignments will not be refused entry to the country on arrival if a quota threshold happens to have been exceeded. The items can be stored duty free until the next quota period.

CREDIT INSURANCE

Insurance against foreign customer default is available from private insurers and in very many countries from government-backed export insurance organizations. Policies may be comprehensive or specific. Comprehensive policies offer guarantees against all short-term credit risks. Specific policies cover particular risks on long-term credit for projects involving major capital goods. Comprehensive cover applies to transactions involving up to six months' credit and will indemnify losses incurred through insolvency of or failure to pay by the foreign customer, the latter's refusal to accept goods already dispatched and extra handling or transport charges owing to the necessary diversion of a consignment from its planned route, if these cannot be recovered from the buyer. Export credit insurers will not offer full indemnity to exporting firms, which must normally bear up to 10 to 15 per cent of the loss. Full indemnity might encourage firms to exercise insufficient care in choosing potential customers.

Because national governments wish to promote their countries' exports they might unfairly subsidize the cost of export credit insurance offered by the state-backed insurer in order to give their domestic firms a competitive edge in international markets. To prevent this, 22 of the world's leading industrialized countries concluded in 1978 a 'Consensus Arrangement' aimed at limiting state subsidy of export insurance. Minimum interest rates and maximum repayment periods were specified in order to avoid 'interest rate wars' between countries as national governments increasingly contributed to firm's export insurance costs.

FINANCE OF FOREIGN TRADE

Payment by cheque (or direct debit, telegraphic transfer of funds, or any other method that relies entirely on the buyer's eventual willingness to settle the debt after the goods have been forwarded) is known as open account settlement of international transactions. It is risky, but inevitable in many situations. Customers' cheques will usually be drawn on customers' own local bank, thus creating delays in payment as cheques are returned to source for clearance. Delays can be minimized, however, using the bankers' SWIFT (Society for Worldwide Interbank Financial Telecommunications) system, which is a computerized means of speeding up international payments. SWIFT is based in Belgium and jointly owned by the large European and North American banks. Payments other than by open account typically involve the preparation by the seller of a bill of exchange.

Bills of exchange

A bill of exchange is a document, drafted by the seller of goods, instructing the buyer to pay the seller an amount of money either on receipt of the bill or (more commonly) on a specified date in the future (eg in three months' time). A bill that requires payment immediately or within three days of acceptance is called a sight bill or draft; one that is to be settled in the future is referred to as a term, usance or tenor bill. The seller is the 'drawer' of the bill, the buyer the 'drawee', the seller's bank the 'remitting' bank and the importer's bank the 'collecting' bank.

If a customer defaults on a bill of exchange the first step towards recovery through local courts is to have the bill protested. This means getting a notary public (ie a local person legally qualified to attest and certify documents) to ask the customer for payment or reasons for non-payment. The latter are put into a formal deed of protest, which is then placed before a local court as evidence of dishonour.

Documentary collections

With a documentary collection the exporter makes out a bill of exchange and gives it to its own bank, together with various documents (eg the insurance certificate, invoice, transit documents) required by the customer prior to taking delivery. The exporter's bank now sends the bill to the customer. If the bill is a sight bill, the customer settles it at once. If it is a term bill, the customer accepts it by signing the bill (to acknowledge existence of the debt) and the bill is returned to the exporter's bank, which now becomes responsible for collecting the money. All the documents that provide title to the goods are handled by the exporter's bank, which will only release them to the customer at the time of payment. The process of documentary collection is summarized in Figure 11.2. Technically, all bills of exchange remain drafts until they are formally accepted, though nowadays the word bill is generally used for all circumstances.

Acceptance credits

Once accepted, the bill becomes a 'negotiable instrument', ie it can be sold to another party. Hence one possible way of dealing with an accepted bill is for the exporting firm to sell it to its own bank at a discount. The bank then collects the money when the bill matures. Thus the bank assumes the risk of non-payment. This is sometimes called an acceptance credit transaction. It is an example of 'without recourse financing', ie if the customer eventually defaults, the bank cannot go back to the exporter and demand compensation.

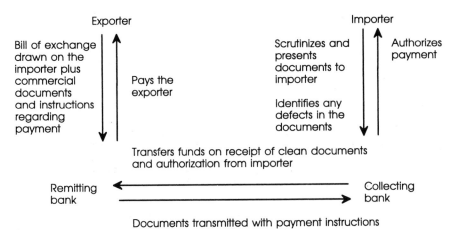

Figure 11.2 Documentary collection

Alternatively the exporter could keep the bill until it falls due for payment and itself collect the money, or borrow money from its bank using the accepted bill as security. In the latter case the bank might want a guarantee that the bill will definitely be settled, eg by requiring the importer's bank to promise to honour the bill if the importer defaults. The term 'avalised bill of exchange' is applied to a bill that carries such an undertaking. If the bill is not avalised and the buyer defaults, then the bank will still expect the exporting company to repay the loan. This is an example of 'with recourse' financing. The International Chamber of Commerce publishes a set of guidelines – *Uniform Rules for Collection* – for the use of bills of exchange, which can be legally binding if a contract so stipulates.

Documentary letters of credit

Such a letter is an undertaking issued by the customer's bank to pay a stated sum of money to the exporter, providing certain pre-specified conditions are met. These conditions normally relate to the receipt by the importer's bank of a number of properly completed documents (including documents of title) relating to the transaction, notably the transport document (bill of lading, air waybill or whatever), the invoice, the insurance certificate and (where appropriate) dangerous goods notices, packing lists, pre-inspection certificates, bank indemnities, and so on. A bill of exchange might also be included in the bundle.

The process of letter of credit settlement is outlined in Figure 11.3. First, the foreign customer approaches its bank (called the 'issuing' or opening bank) and asks it to open a letter of credit in the exporter's favour. The letter of credit will specify when payment is to be made (eg on presentation of documents or at a later date) and which documents must be submitted prior to the paying bank releasing the money. On issuing the letter of credit the

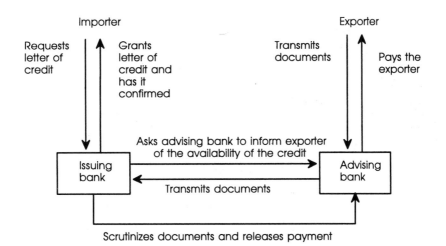

Figure 11.3   Documentary letter of credit

bank assumes liability for the debt. Sometimes the exporter specified in the letter of credit is referred to as the 'beneficiary', while the importer is called the 'account party'.

Next, the exporter or its bank (known as the 'advising' bank) is informed that the credit has been opened and of the exact conditions to be met prior to releasing the money. (Other titles for the advising bank are negotiating bank, accepting bank or paying bank.) The goods are now sent off and the documents forwarded to the bank that is to pay the money. A bill of exchange may or may not be included in the documents, depending on the precise terms of the credit. On receipt of the documents the paying bank checks them and, if they are in order, releases payment. Alternatively, if payment is to be through a bill of exchange, the bank accepts and returns this on behalf of the customer. In the latter case it is the bank and not the customer that honours the bill of exchange when it matures. Finally the customer's bank passes the documents to the customer, provided the latter has paid in to the bank the amount due or has negotiated an overdraft.

A 'confirmed' letter of credit is one the settlement of which has been guaranteed by a bank in the exporter's own country. The exporter is paid by its local confirming bank, which then collects the money from the foreign bank issuing the credit. The confirming bank has no claim on the exporter if the credit is not honoured. Currently, nearly all letters of credit are irrevocable, meaning that the customer cannot arbitrarily cancel them. The International Chamber of Commerce has published a set of model rules for the use of letters of credit. These are binding on all parties if the credit bears an endorsement stating that it is 'Subject to ICC Uniform Customs and Practice for Documentary Credits'.

Performance guarantees

The converse to a letter of credit from the buyer's point of view is the need to be assured that the supplier has the technical and financial resources to deliver the goods on time. Thus the exporter may be required to provide a 'bid bond' issued by the exporter's bank at the time the exporter tenders for a large contract. The bid bond (typically representing 2 to 3 per cent of the contract value) is forfeit if the contract is awarded to the bidding firm, which then decides not to accept it.

Rejection of documents

The 'doctrine of strict compliance' applies to the documents involved in a letter of credit transaction, meaning that buyers or their appointed representatives (including banks) are legally entitled to reject any document that is defective even if the goods are perfectly sound and have been delivered strictly according to contract. Note that the right to reject documents is quite separate from any right to reject goods. The former does not imply the latter. If a bank is handling the import transaction it will scrutinize the documents and if there is any discrepancy will refer the matter to the buyer for instructions. The purchaser may formally waive the defect or insist the offending document(s) be represented. Title to the goods does not pass from seller to buyer until the documents have been accepted.

Examples of reasons for rejection include bills of lading with incorrect dates of shipment, unsigned documents, misspelt company names and addresses, and contradictions in the descriptions of goods. Importers and their banks normally wish not to have to part with their money until the last possible moment, so they will not remit payment unless the documents are exactly correct. Delays tie up working capital, the cost of which must be added to the bank's fees and administrative costs attached to letter of credit settlement. In practice, a large percentage of letters of credit are not settled by paying banks on first presentation because of errors in documentation (up to 30 per cent according to some estimates).

Other types of documentary credit

Back-to-back (counter) credits involve two separate letters of credit. The first is in favour of the exporting company, which now instructs its own bank to issue a second letter of credit in favour of one of the exporter's own suppliers (eg to provide raw materials necessary to produce the goods). A *deferred payment* credit is a letter of credit specially designed to give importers extra time to pay. The deferment period may terminate on a predetermined date regardless of when the goods are dispatched, or be due for settlement a certain number of days after delivery. A *red clause* credit authorizes the importer's bank to pay the exporter before presentation of documents. Other names for red clause credits are 'packing credits' and 'anticipatory credits'. *Revolving* credits are letters of credit used to cover a number of consignments when the exporter wishes to avoid opening a series of individual credits. Revolving credits apply to a number of different consignments within an agreed limit. Hence the credit amount is automatically renewed without formal amendment.

A *standby credit* is a letter of credit with an extended period for payment. Under the arrangement the importer's bank stands ready to honour the credit if the exporter can prove that the importing firm has failed to meet its obligations. The purpose of a standby letter of credit is to allow the participating business to trade on an open account basis, so that the credit is never actually used except in the event of default by the buyer. Standby credits are non-performance documents used only when the importer does not perform a contracted duty. The standard documentary letters of credit referred to in the text, conversely, are performance documents, ie payment occurs given the presentation to a bank of satisfactory documents, proving export of the goods. In other words, a standby credit comes into play if something does not happen rather than when something does. *Transferable credits* are letters used by intermediaries in the export trade that enable the intermediary to transfer part of the money released under the credit direct to the intermediary's supplier(s).

FACTORING AND FORFAITING

Factoring

Factoring means the sale (at a discount) to an outsider of debts owed to a business. The factor takes over the administration of the client company's invoices, collects the money and (importantly) assumes the risk of customer default. 'Invoicing discounting' is a similar technique. Here the exporting company receives a cash payment (effectively a loan) from the invoice discounter against the value of the invoices issued to customers, but retains responsibility for debt collection and for an agreed proportion of bad debts.

The problem with factoring and invoice discounting is the cost. The exporter might only receive 75 to 80 per cent of the face value of invoices. Also, the client company is usually expected to sign a 12-month agreement with the factor or discounter so that it becomes locked into using factoring/discounting services. Another possible difficulty is a deterioration in customer relations. The factor will collect debts either under its own name – which might irritate the client's customers – or under the client's own letterhead. In the latter case, however, it will still pursue long-outstanding debts vigorously – in the client's name – regardless of possible damaging effects on customer relations.

Credit factors are, however, expert in the laws and techniques of international debt collection. Usually they operate through international networks of factors, providing reciprocal services for fellow members. These networks enable factors in various countries to communicate with end-customers in the latter's own language and to apply collection procedures appropriate to the country concerned. The client receives an 'up-front' cash payment and incurs minimal administrative debt-collecting costs.

Forfaiting

This is an increasingly common method for financing the sale of capital goods that customers are not obliged to finish paying for until a long time in the future. The exporting company drafts not one but a series of bills of exchange – each with a different time to maturity – for acceptance by the purchaser. The first bill – representing the customer's first instalment – may be payable three months after beginning the project, the second bill (for the second instalment) may be due six months after that, the third a few months later, and so on. Following their acceptance, these bills may then be discounted en bloc by the exporter, today, at the exporter's bank in exchange for a cash payment.

Advantages of forfaiting are that it is financing without recourse (although the exporter's bank may insist that the bills of exchange be avalised) and that since bills of exchange are sold to the bank at today's known rate of discount the exporter pays what is in effect a fixed rate of interest on the money raised. The amount available to the exporter is known with certainty and there are no risks of currency exchange rate depreciation, so that forward planning is facilitated.

Problems are the loss in revenue resulting from discounting the bills, bankers' administrative fees, and the need to persuade customers to accept bills of exchange issued for work that will not be completed or goods that will not be supplied until a long time in the future.

APPENDIX – THE EXPORT PLAN

As soon as the firm has decided to take exporting seriously, it needs to prepare an export plan (see Figure 11.4), the purpose of which is threefold:

- to compel management to examine the merits of exporting critically, objectively and systematically;
- to generate commitment to exporting among those who will be involved in implementing the process;
- to establish priorities and to relate exporting to the firm's overall corporate plan.

The plan itself should be in report format, with the following headings:

1. **Reasons for exporting**. Where the idea of exporting came from. What the business hopes to achieve from exporting. How exporting will benefit the firm and how it relates to the business's overall strategies.
2. **Markets to be entered**. Rationale for the choice. Threats and barriers to entry and how they will be overcome. Profiles of potential customers. Market research already undertaken. Which market segments offer the best chances of success. Customer ordering systems. Pricing strategies to be adopted. Tariff levels and local sales taxes in each market.
3. **Competitive situation in target markets**. Extent and nature of local competition. Critical success factors within target markets. Likelihood of fresh competitors entering target markets. Sources of competitive advantage for the exporting firm. Analysis of competitors' marketing strategies.

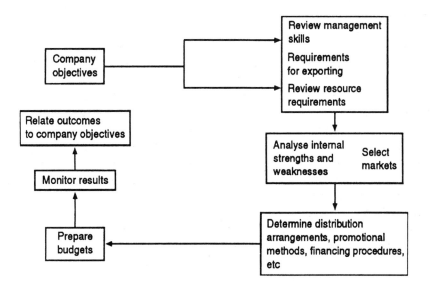

Figure 11.4 An export plan

4. **The product(s) to be offered**. Review of the firm's product range and, where necessary, details of how it will redesign products to make them appeal to wider international markets. Analysis of current product standard legislation relating to the firm's sales in the foreign countries concerned and how it will amend production processes to ensure the company's goods comply with legal requirements. Unique selling points. Comparison with the products of competitors. Who will buy the product and why. Aftersales and customer care facilities and requirements.

5. **Research methods**. The information-gathering system that is to be used to collect new data on foreign developments affecting the business. (Sources may include trade directories, online services provided by chambers of commerce or trade associations, government-funded research schemes, etc.)

6. **Promotional methods**. Identification of the market segments in selected foreign countries most likely to buy the firm's products and assessment of the best ways of reaching these potential customers. How existing sales literature will be redrafted to make it suitable for use in other countries.

7. **Export formalities**. Listing of all the export licences, etc the company will have to obtain, dangerous goods certificates, special taxes, registrations with foreign governmental bodies, etc. Specification of who is to be responsible for export documentation and for ensuring that all legal requirements are met.

8. **Organization**. Proposed structure of the export department. Who will be in charge. Extent of administrative support. Relations between export managers and other departments.

9. **Human resource requirements**. Itemization of the management skills required for successful entry to foreign markets. (These may include language skills, export documentation and administration, trading in foreign currencies, familiarity with European advertising media, etc.) Listing of the training necessary for the business's staff to become expert in each of these areas. Extent to which it will be necessary to engage outside consultants.

10. **Transport and distribution**. The options, procedures and costs of transporting goods to foreign destinations. Availability of alternative distribution channels. Special distribution problems (breakages, perishability of output, need for expensive packaging, possibility of contamination) and how they will be overcome. Measures to prevent pilfering. Warehousing requirements. Location of possible centres for warehousing goods in foreign countries. Identification of foreign locations suitable for the establishment of local administrative offices, manufacturing, packaging and labelling facilities, etc. The regional investment incentives available in these areas.

11. **Objectives and budgets**. Estimates of export start-up costs. How financing requirements will be met. Allocation of overheads to the export function. Cash-flow forecasts. Key objectives, sales targets and breakeven points. Timetables for achieving objectives.

12. **Contingency plans**. Details of what will happen if foreign distribution is disrupted. Alternatives available. Possible effects of bad weather, dock strikes, etc. Proposed consignment and payments insurances and their costs.

12

International and global products

THE NATURE OF INTERNATIONAL PRODUCT POLICY

A company's international product policy derives from its objectives, resources and market opportunities. Objectives are relevant because they determine the firm's attitudes towards risk (and most product development involves a high degree of risk), its expected returns on investments in new products for international markets, and the nature and extent of the markets and market niches in which it wishes to do business. Resources determine the firm's capacity to engage in technical research, to advertise and otherwise to promote and distribute new items. Market opportunities arise from shortcomings in local competitors' outputs in foreign countries and from changes in consumer demand and/or circumstances (rapidly increasing living standards, for example).

The existence of global segments has led to an increased interest in developing global products. The economies of scale are such that companies can develop a product that appeals to a very tiny proportion of the population of any given country, but has a very large market globally. This means that smaller segments can be targeted without losing scale advantages. Thinking global also means that components can be sourced from a wide variety of countries, with accompanying economies.

International product policy concerns the determination of the mix of products and product characteristics that best satisfy the needs of consumers in the firm's markets in various parts of the world. Hence it requires decisions on:

- Global product lines (ie groups of products related by common characteristics and/or sold to the same category of customer). Product lines might be extended in order to satisfy the requirements of specific foreign markets or niches within them, or rationalized in order to produce a small range of items with genuinely global appeal.

- Whether to use a standardized product for all international markets or adapt products to satisfy the particular needs of each country or market segment.
- Maintenance of existing products, ie making sure they continue to satisfy consumer requirements and are being marketed properly.
- Branding for international markets.
- Identification of new product opportunities and the development of new products.
- Packaging and labelling.
- Product testing.

In taking decisions on these matters the firm needs to pay attention to the product life-cycles of the items it supplies to various markets (see appendix to this chapter) and the overall portfolio of products that it offers for sale.

PRODUCT POSITIONING

Positioning means finding out what customers think about the firm's products in relation to competing products, with a view either to modifying the product (plus associated advertising and other publicity) in order to make it fit in with these prescriptions, or to changing the product's position in consumer's minds. Positions depend on the nature of the product, competing products and on how consumers see themselves (the lifestyles to which they aspire, role models, etc). Suppose, for example, that competing models of a certain type of product are rated by customers according to just two variables: reliability and price. Let there be six competing models, A to F. A survey of consumer opinion might indicate that their market positions are as shown in Figure 12.1, which is an example of a 'perceptual map'. The size of each circle indicates that model's market share. Model A is the market leader. It is expensive but reasonably reliable. B and C are small followers, serving niche markets in the high-price, high-reliability zone. F is cheap but unreliable; E is about average on both counts, and so on.

Examination of a perceptual map can reveal gaps in existing market provision. Clearly it is essential to select the correct variables for the axes of the diagram. Examples of possible variables are after-sales service, convenience in use, speed of operation, attractiveness of packaging, etc. Note that a product's position in consumers' minds can be shifted through modifying its characteristics, and through advertising and public relations and other promotional activities. Deciding on the variables to include in the analysis might require significant research, which normally would be undertaken by a market research company.

Where to position

Companies normally wish to position their brands so as to make them appeal to a pre-determined consumer group. This might require a promotional campaign to alter the ways in which an item is perceived by the target group. A great deal depends on the

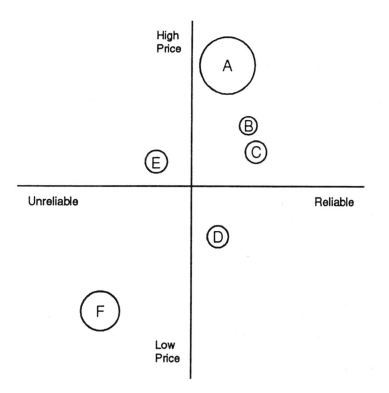

Figure 12.1 A perceptual map

decision where to try to position a particular brand relative to competitors' outputs, including the target market groups to be contacted, the creative strategy that will underlie the campaign, and the cost of the firm's promotional effort.

Positioning in one country is hard enough; having to position in several disparate countries is *much* more difficult. The basic question is whether to conduct extensive research into consumer perspectives on the product in just one country and use the results for positioning in all other national markets (assuming that the motives underlying consumer purchasing decisions about the product are essentially similar in all the national markets being considered), or to repeat the exercise (expensively) in each market and attempt different positions for the product in each country. A number of factors should influence the decision whether to go for a single position or different positions in various countries, as follows:

- The extent to which a product's selling points are perceived similarly in different countries. Items close together on a perceptual map are seen by customers as being similar (even if by objective standards they are not) and hence might be expected to compete against each other more directly than with other brands.

- Whether the item fulfils the same consumer needs in each market.
- The degree of direct and immediate substitutability between the advertised output and locally supplied brands (if this is high, the appropriate position for the product should be self-evident).
- Special advantages the advertised brand has to offer.
- Whether the brand name and/or product features need to be altered for use in different markets.
- The scope of the product's appeal: whether it sells to a broad cross-section of consumers (in relation to their age, sex, income level, lifestyle, etc) or only within small market niches.

A product is anything a firm has to sell, whether this be a physical good or a service. Products are defined in terms of their characteristics and the customer satisfaction they provide. Consumer perceptions of an item's need-fulfilling properties can vary substantially from country to country, so that a product's position in the market may differ from state to state. A luxury in one of the world's regions might be regarded as a necessity elsewhere. Items can fulfil a purely functional and utilitarian role in one market, yet be seen as fashion goods in others.

TIME-BASED COMPETITION

New products not only need to possess novel and attractive features in order to succeed in today's highly competitive world; they must also be introduced quickly. The term 'time-based competition' is used to describe product policies that focus on the rapid development of new models. In other words, firms might prefer to produce new products faster rather than make them better or more cheaply (Stalk, 1990). The rationale for this is as follows:

- Many consumers are willing to pay premium prices for recently developed items.
- Computer-controlled robotic techniques of manufacture (referred to as 'flexible manufacturing') mean that firms can produce small batches of items customized to meet the requirements of specific groups of customers. They do not need to rely on economies of scale from mass production in order to obtain competitive advantage. Hence frequent introduction to a market of small outputs of alterations of a core product may be appropriate.
- Speeding up the production process generally leads to savings in inventory and working capital.
- Accelerating the pace of innovation can generate fresh ideas and thinking that lead to important new inventions.
- Firms can behave opportunistically, exploiting lucrative market segments as they appear.
- Parallel sequencing of product development and production activities is often possible.

- Research and technical development is extremely expensive. The shorter the period the firm is spending money on this the better. Sometimes an item is 'good enough' even though further technical research on it would be beneficial. Also there is a tendency in certain companies to overload their product research and development departments with too many disparate projects.
- Product life cycles are shortening for the majority of product categories, with many product offerings now being judged as much on fashion as on any other purchasing criterion.

Problems with time-based competition are that the costs of rapid new product development could be extremely high and that the administrative procedures necessary for time-based competition might be complicated and/or overstretch the organization's resources.

in practice...

Philips

Philips, the giant Dutch electronics company, has operated internationally for decades. A relatively recent development, however, has been a dramatic reduction in the duration of the life cycle of many of its products. Consumer electronics items had an average life expectancy of nearly two years in 1980, just over one year by 1991, and less than three months by 2001. Shortening product lifecycles were accompanied by an intensification of international competition and falling prices for consumer electronics items worldwide.

Clearly, measures were needed to reduce the time taken by Philips to bring new models to the market. Part of the problem is that Philips' core business, the manufacture of light bulbs, is not noted for innovation. This meant that the corporate culture was not easily adapted to becoming innovative. Accordingly the company entered into a range of strategic alliances and joint ventures intended to develop new technologies, penetrate fresh market segments quickly, and share the costs of rapid new production introduction. Examples of ventures undertaken in the early 1990s include partnerships with SGS-Thomson in the field of silicon technology, the American Whittle Communications Company (interactive video), Grundig of Germany and JVC of Malaysia (CCRs), and Sony of Japan (digital audio equipment). Philips' UK subsidiary, Mullard, has been at the cutting edge of defence technology for several decades now. The moral of the story is that innovation can be bought in, provided the management are aware of its own shortcomings and act accordingly.

STANDARDIZATION VERSUS MODIFICATION OF PRODUCTS

The essential strategy choice confronting the international business is between selling the product it happens already to supply, and making products that are adapted to particular foreign markets. As with any segmentation question, there is a trade off: the greater the modification, the greater the costs and therefore the higher the premium that has to be paid by customers. In some cases this makes very little difference: for example, McDonald's hamburgers are produced locally in every country the firm operates in, so adapting the product for India (where the cow is sacred) merely meant using mutton instead of beef in the burgers. A bigger problem for McDonald's lay in adapting the fries for vegetarians: previously they were fried in beef fat, which gave them a distinctive flavour. McDonald's had to develop an artificial flavouring for vegetable oil in order to retain the 'beefy' flavour of the fries.

Modification of products

The aim of product modification is usually to increase worldwide sales of the firm's core products via:

- the satisfaction of different customer needs in various national markets;
- retention of existing customers through keeping the product up to date;
- matching the product attributes offered by competing firms; or
- improving product features across the board.

Complementary products might be introduced to stimulate sales of existing lines, eg by improving the usefulness of currently produced items (gardening tools or DIY power accessories, for example). (Branded foodstuffs are frequently sold in complementary product lines so that a new variety can be conveniently 'slotted in' to the line currently on offer.) Entirely new products may be devised to replace existing outputs and/or to reach completely new markets abroad.

Some of the main factors likely to encourage the modification of products for foreign markets are listed in Table 12.1 Cultural differences and variations in local tastes are obviously important, as are local educational and literacy levels (a 'simple to use' version of a high-tech product might be developed if local customers would have difficulty in understanding the original model).

The need for extensive product modification is a common impetus for firms to establish local manufacturing or assembly facilities in foreign countries, as it could well be cheaper to set up a new establishment to produce what is essentially a new product near to end-consumers rather than make major changes to existing production lines and procedures at home. The development of numerous product ranges and modifications necessarily causes the firm's organization to become complicated, so that sophisticated management control procedures have to be applied.

Standardized products

Several difficulties confront the firm that decides to modify substantially its product range and/or develop new products for foreign markets, notably that:

- The company may possess insufficient experience and technical know-how of different products and how to market them.

Table 12.1 Factors encouraging product modification for foreign markets

Physical factors:

- Climate
- Living conditions
- Compatibility with locally produced items
- Transport situation
- The uses to which the item might be put in different markets
- Literacy and technical skills of users
- Consumer care facilities

Market factors

- National consumer taste
- Nature and extent of competition
- Desirability of foreign images for products
- Preferred package size
- Consumer buying habits
- Income levels (poor countries might need low-quality products)

Legal factors

- Technical standards
- Patent laws
- Packaging requirements
- Local content rules
- Health and safety regulations
- Consumer protection laws
- High tariffs that encourage potential local manufacture

- Technical research and development efforts become fragmented as increasing amounts of resources are devoted to issues pertaining to the special requirements of particular national markets.
- Extra promotional costs are involved.
- There is duplication of effort within the business.

Supplying a single unmodified product leads to reduced stockholding costs (because demand in any market can be met from a single inventory of the same item), facilitates the development of technical expertise in a narrow area, and allows the interchangeability of spare parts and input components between supply points in various locations. Not surprisingly, therefore, most international businesses wish to alter their core products as little as possible. If modification is obviously necessary (manifest perhaps in low sales in certain countries of an item that is highly successful in other parts of the world), the situation might be remedied through minor alterations: packaging, size or colour, length of warranty, carrying facilities, etc. It is the case, moreover, that few items in practice are amenable to a genuinely global approach in view of the market, legal and physical factors precipitating product modification in various countries. Even a product such as Coca-Cola has had to be differentiated in certain markets. Often, therefore, partial modification occurs, with changes being implemented until the cost becomes prohibitive.

Pegasus and Saari

The UK business software group Pegasus teamed up with the French firm Saari to develop standardized stock control, invoicing and accounting packages for use in any European company. Accounting methods vary from country to country, but there exists a substantial set of core techniques common to all systems that make standardized international accounting software products feasible. The aim was to produce an international core package that, at the touch of a button, could be adapted to suit the accounting requirements of any specific country. Costs were shared 50/50, with project headquarters being based in Paris because of that city's close proximity to key continental European countries. Problems with standardization included:

- variations in national legal requirements regarding the information to be included in business accounts;
- different conventions regarding the location on documents of payment dates, debit and credit entries, etc;
- differences in the accounting jargon used in various countries;
- technical programming difficulties arising from the fact that file headings had to accommodate words of different length as the package moved from one language to another.

To market the standardized pan-European package the partnership established links with software houses in Germany, Italy, the Netherlands and Scandinavia, hence providing direct access to a quarter of a million potential end-consumers and 5,000 dealers. Note that the accounting profession is much larger in the UK than on the European continent and that UK-inspired accountancy-related documentation was already widely used in many continental countries.

The undifferentiated product

Supplying a single undifferentiated product intended to satisfy customer needs in a wide range of countries has a number of apparent benefits: economies of scale in production, concentration of technical research into a limited area, standardization of marketing and distribution methods, fewer staff training requirements, and so on. Accordingly, firms do sometimes grasp the nettle and attempt to create universal products (hopefully) suitable for all markets in all parts of the world. Maximum standardization is suitable where:

- there exists a large market across several countries and where cultural differences do not necessitate adaptation;
- the product has a strong brand image;
- consumers in new markets are likely to respond well to intensive advertising of the item;
- the fundamental need that the product aims to satisfy is basically the same in all national and market segments;
- after-sales service is easily standardized.

National images might be a factor encouraging the use of a single unmodified product. Japanese goods, for instance, are generally regarded as reliable, high quality and technically excellent: positive images that will help an overtly Japanese item to sell in any market. French perfumes are another example. If the product is not to be altered the question arises as to whether the ways in which it is promoted need to be changed.

NEW PRODUCT DEVELOPMENT FOR INTERNATIONAL MARKETS

Any product offer that *consumers* regard as an addition to their available choice can be regarded as a 'new' product. Thus a new product could be an original invention, a modification of an existing item, the firm's own version of a product already supplied by a competitor, or merely a change in how an item is packaged and presented (Walsh, 1992). Inventing and bringing to the market a completely new product can be enormously expensive, and the risk of failure is high (the majority of new inventions with a commercial application are financially unsuccessful). Hence there is a strong incentive for firms to develop current product offerings, introduce complementary products, diversify product lines and duplicate competitors' best-selling items rather than invest in basic technical research leading to completely new product concepts. The process of product development is shown in Figure 12.2, which begins with idea generation. Possibilities for new products derive from a variety of sources: Figure 12.3 gives some examples. New product development can rely on the special skills, competence and experience of the existing business, or involve joint venturing or the acquisition of other enterprises

In considering the feasibility of an idea it is necessary to define the *concept* of the intended new item: what it will do, the benefits it will provide to customers, its market

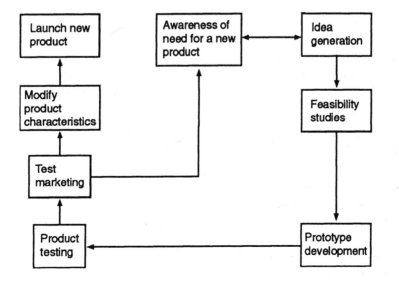

Figure 12.2   The process of new product development

Technical research	Market research	Suggestions of agents, distributors or salespeople
Employee suggestions	Ideas generated by involvement with joint ventures	
Difficulties encountered in selling existing products in various foreign markets		Monitoring and analysing new patents registered by other firms and by individual inventors
	Examples set by competitors	
Customer complaints or suggestions	Acquisition of other firms	Unplanned discoveries

Figure 12.3 Impetus for new products

position, and how it will differ from current or possible future products offered by competing businesses. Cost and technical features are then considered and market research initiated. Typically the firm is confronted with a number of options for new product development, so a process for screening competing ideas needs to be implemented. The process of screening of proposals for new products is outlined in Figure 12.4.

International Distillers

International Distillers and Vintners is the world's largest drinks company, measured in terms of wines and spirits turnover. It has no centralized new brand development system. Rather, all senior managers are expected to come up with ideas and, for those that are accepted, thereafter to 'champion' them through to their launch. This policy was adopted because of:

- the fast-changing nature of the wines and spirits market;
- the need constantly to introduce large numbers of new brands in order to maintain market share; and
- the comparative ease with which proposed new brands could be test marketed.

The firm possesses a chain of off-licences and numerous public houses and restaurants, so that test marketing can be carried out quickly and inexpensively. A number of spectacular successes have emerged from the implementation of this policy, notably Bailey's Irish Cream (the world's largest-selling premium liqueur), Malibu and Le Piat d'Or. The problems with the policy are the large number of new product ideas that have to be evaluated, the extent of test marketing that has to be undertaken, and the amount of senior management time absorbed in thinking up and championing new products.

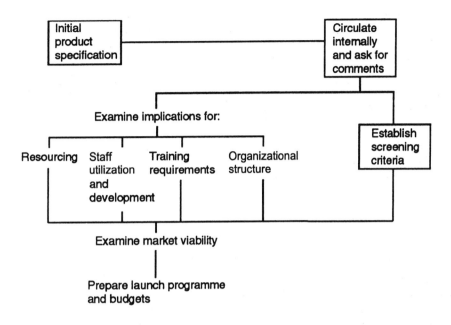

Figure 12.4 Screening of proposed new products

The screening process

Initial screening normally involves the circulation to all interested parties within the organization of details of the proposal (bearing in mind the need for confidentiality) together with a request for comments. Then screening criteria need to be established and the organizational implications of proceeding with the new product examined (resources, departmental structure, training requirements, etc). Normally the work will be undertaken by a committee comprising representatives of various functions (production, marketing and so on) and, importantly, people with first-hand experience of having seen the new product development process all the way through. Screening criteria will probably relate to expected rates of return over certain time periods, the extent to which the new product will utilize existing or easily acquired resources, availability of the requisite technical skills and know-how, financing requirements, and marketing viability factors (price, distribution, etc). Also the supply of the intended new product must fit in with the organization's overall goals and long-term strategies. Further matters requiring consideration in the screening process are shown in Figure 12.5

Location of new product development activities

Responsibility for new product development (NPD) might be centralized in the home country or, for businesses with foreign subsidiaries, decentralized to centres abroad.

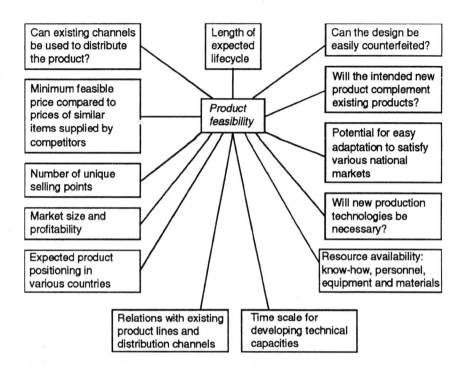

Figure 12.5 Screening criteria

Many new ideas can emerge from decentralized NPD arrangements, as the employees of foreign establishments may hold completely different perspectives on the activities of the parent firm. Specific advantages to using foreign centres for NPD are that:

- Local subsidiaries are perhaps more likely to recognize the specific needs and preferences of consumers in local markets.
- Using a diversity of foreign NPD operations might lead to greater creativity than may emerge from a single centralized source.
- The staff engaged in foreign local product research might be cheaper to employ than in the head office country.
- Local technical research and development frequently attracts substantial cash grants and other incentives from host country governments.
- Subsidiaries in industrially developed countries should be able to monitor the latest technical developments occurring within these countries.

In principle, local subsidiaries should be better able to relate to local market requirements, but may lack the resources and technical expertise necessary for successful NPD work. Also the concentration of new product research and technical development in a central unit might create economies of scale within the firm's research function (eg by avoiding duplication of effort, the need to recruit foreign researchers and other set-up costs), faster communication between research personnel and senior head office management, and (importantly) tighter control over security and the protection of intellectual property. The latter is a major problem in certain Asia Pacific countries, especially the Philippines, Taiwan and Malaysia.

International test marketing

Prior to committing itself to marketing a new consumer product on a global scale, a company will usually select a limited number of areas in different parts of the world where it can test its entire marketing programme. The justifications for international test marketing are that it supposedly lowers the risk of subsequent failure, establishes or refutes the validity of the basic concept of the new product, and provides a basis for forecasting future sales. Hence, for each group of countries in which the item is to be sold the company needs to identify towns, cities or rural locations that possess characteristics as near as possible to the averages for the region as a whole. In Western Europe, for example, Belgium is frequently used for test marketing because its population age profile, average household size and structure of consumption of various categories of goods are very close to pan-European norms. The general process of international test marketing is outlined in Figure 12.6.

Test marketing is difficult within a firm's home country; on a global scale the problems become considerable. The major difficulty is of course that successful outcomes to market testing in one country might say very little about an item's prospects elsewhere. Note the necessity for physical product testing in *each* target market in view of national differences in environmental conditions, how the product will be used, wear-out rates, the length of

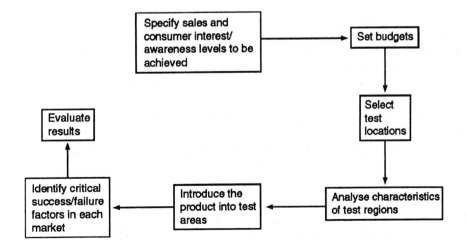

Figure 12.6 International test marketing

the chain of distribution, and legal requirements for safety testing and certification in various states. Further problems arise in relation to:

- correctly interpreting the responses of customers in different countries;
- the multiplicity of factors potentially affecting global sales;
- inadequate knowledge about the effects of competitors' actions in other countries.

Also, the presentation of the product (advertising and other promotional messages, package size, etc) might have to vary from country to country in view of legal and cultural differences, hence making it extremely difficult to compare test results from various regions. International test marketing is expensive (much duplication of effort is involved), and arguably makes little difference to the risk of failure in view of the complexities and enormous number of factors potentially involved. It delays the introduction of a product into new markets and gives competitors extensive information on what is going on. Mental speculation about likely outcomes is, some would argue, just as reliable a guide to future prospects as is a costly test marketing programme.

PACKAGING

Packaging is critically important in international marketing, for two reasons. First, the degree of physical protection needed to protect items is often greater for exported goods than for domestic sales. Long sea or road journeys might be necessary, with much intermediate handling and sharp changes in climatic conditions. Secondly, packaging is a key element of brand development in various foreign markets. A distinctive package helps the consumer instantly recognize a brand, and conveys messages about the item's ability to satisfy the customer's requirements.

Normally an exporter will want the minimum packaging to ensure that goods reach customers in a reasonable condition. Factors affecting choice of a package include the cost of packaging materials, the amount of intermediate handling the goods will receive, the value of the item, whether an expensive package is necessary to enhance the image of the product, and breakage and spillage costs (sometimes it pays to spend less on packaging and accept that more items will be lost or broken in transit). The mode of transport is also relevant. Seafreight, for example, usually requires heavier packaging than freight shifted by other methods.

It is not a good idea to state the contents of packages on outside covers as this encourages stealing. Rather, each package should simply bear a unique consignment number, the address of the consignee, plus an indication of how many packages are contained in the shipment (eg 2/4 indicates the second package of four). For high-value consignments it may be appropriate to use a false name for the recipient. Otherwise a potential thief might know that the addressee regularly imports expensive items and might be inclined to steal anything addressed to that customer. There are internationally accepted symbols to indicate hazardous goods and/or special handling requirements. Savings might be available through transporting in bulk and packing locally, especially if a special pack is needed for the local market.

Insurance claims for damage to goods in transit will fail if it turns out that the goods were inadequately packaged. Losses can occur through pilferage, bad handling, shock (caused, for example, by a ship rolling in heavy seas or the shunting of railway wagons), or atmospheric changes. A problem relating to insurance claims is that shock damage may not be immediately apparent. Outside containers may remain intact even though their contents have been broken, so that it is difficult to establish precisely when the damage happened. Goods sent by air normally need less packing than goods shifted by surface transport.

National differences in packaging requirements

It is important to establish at an early stage the packing requirements for deliveries to specific countries as there might be special regulations concerning such matters as the materials used (prohibitions on flammable packaging or wood that does not carry a declaration that it is free of disease and insects for example). Straw is forbidden as a means of packing imports in many countries (on long sea journeys straw can become damp and infested with disease and vermin), or is only accepted when accompanied by an approved disinfection certificate. Markings in addition to the normal shipping marks may also be needed. Most countries have a national authority to help exporters in these respects. In Britain, the function is undertaken by the Research Association for the Paper and Board Printing and Packaging Industries (known as PIRA) and by the British Standards Institution (BSI). PIRA will provide information on the properties of packaging materials and whether they conform to recognized standards. BSI is able to advise on climatic conditions likely to be encountered worldwide with indications of the packing protection necessary. Advice on export packaging is also available from freight forwarders and specialist export packing firms, and from cargo insurance companies. Requirements for the packaging of dangerous goods are, of course, extremely stringent and the supplying firm must ensure they are satisfied prior to shipment. Otherwise the goods might be stopped in transit and the exporter might be liable to heavy penalties. Modifications to packaging for various countries may be necessary in consequence of national differences in:

- the mechanical equipment used to handle goods in various countries;
- customers' goods inwards reception facilities (eg whether they are prepared to break bulk at the doorstep);
- likely storage periods in destination ports and inland warehouses;
- the quality of local warehousing facilities;
- consumer income levels – low incomes imply lower usage rates of many products than in richer regions and hence smaller purchase amounts;
- shopping habits – if consumers shop (say) fortnightly rather than twice weekly they will buy larger packages.

Also there might be special rules on the disposal or compulsory recycling of packaging materials. Germany, for example, has laws that require retailers, manufacturers and distributors to accept back all returned packaging, including crates, cardboard boxes, plastic containers and drums.

A *packing list* (also known as a 'weight list' or 'packing specification') is a statement of the goods supplied in a particular consignment, indicating which packages contain which goods and full details of the size, marking and weight of each package.

CUSTOMER CARE

Customer care is far more than after-sales service, although the latter is an essential part of the company's total customer service effort. Satisfied customers repeat their purchases and introduce new consumers to the firm. Note, moreover, that it is much cheaper to obtain a repeat order than an order from a completely new customer, since no additional advertising or other selling effort is involved. A procedure for creating satisfaction among foreign customers is essential. Hence, a comprehensive audit of all the company's existing customer care activities is required in order to ensure that they are suitable for customers in foreign markets. The audit should examine:

- the availability of spare parts and servicing facilities;
- the length of product guarantees compared to those offered by competitors;
- the clarity of translated instruction manuals;
- the availability of post-purchase advice on use of the product;
- efforts to maintain contact with existing foreign customers, via mailshots, newsletters, etc, in order to inform them of new models, product improvements and so on;
- the accuracy and appearance of translated documents sent to the customer (invoices, for example);
- the ease with which foreign customers can place orders;
- the extent to which customers are consulted prior to modifying products;
- the extent to which information is given about ingredients, product uses, etc;
- the courtesy of company representatives;
- the availability of emergency help to customers;
- the convenience to customers of the systems through which they pay for their purchases.

Guarantees

Guarantees (warranties) are an increasingly important tool in international marketing. They attest the supplying firm's commitment to quality and customer service, promote the product, and help assuage consumers' doubts about a foreign business's commitment to provide maintenance facilities, spare parts, etc. The basic policy issue connected with the provision of guarantees to foreign customers is whether the after-sales service will be arranged by the supplying firm's local agent or undertaken by third parties that the firm contracts direct. The arguments for having an agent provide after-sales service are that:

- Agents are near to end-consumers and can communicate with them in language they understand.
- The agent has an incentive to ensure that goods are delivered in first-class condition.
- The agent becomes 'locked into' dealing with the exporting business.

However, the investment necessary to provide sound after-sales service can be extensive and agents who furnish these services must be trained, will require more extensive communications with the supplying business than otherwise would be the case, and need guaranteed continuity of supplies of spare parts. And the agency contract stipulating who precisely shall be responsible (and financially liable) for the service will necessarily be complicated. However it is done, it is essential that the extent and quality of after-sales service provided to foreign customers be carefully monitored to ensure that standards are being maintained.

Another important question is whether the supplier should apply the same warranty conditions in all countries, or vary the terms from country to country. Application of identical conditions is suitable for firms with global products sold internationally (especially if cross-border serving might be required) and where buyer needs and use patterns are essentially similar in all countries. Note, however, that standardization of warranty conditions does *not* offer economies of scale, as typically occurs with the standardization of products or promotional messages. Also there is no point in offering universal guarantees if the firm cannot arrange worldwide servicing. Arguments for varying warranty conditions are that:

- It enables the firm to respond to variations in the warranties offered by competing companies, without imposing extra costs elsewhere.
- There are few cost advantages to standardization.
- Differing climatic and other use conditions can make it inappropriate to offer long guarantees in certain markets.
- It may be difficult for a firm supplying an item from several production units in various countries to maintain a uniform level of quality of output.
- Legal requirements on warranties vary from one country to another.

TRADE MARKS AND BRANDING

A 'trade mark' can be any word, symbol or collection of words and/or symbols used to identify goods and to distinguish them from the outputs of other businesses. Brands take this concept further. A brand is a collection of attributes, beliefs and values that attach to a named product. For example, the Virgin brand has a set of values based around a no-nonsense, maverick set of products that question the established approach to doing things. This brand has values that extend across a range of products from airlines to record shops to financial services. Brand values also apply to products such as Marmite or Hovis that have only one product in the range.

Purpose of branding

Through giving a particular trade name or logo to a firm's product and then seeking through advertising and other promotional activities to associate attractive characteristics with the product, the firm enables its customers to recognize its output and – having once purchased and been satisfied with it – to avoid needing to re-evaluate its worth prior to repeating the purchase.

Customers may then continue choosing the firm's branded products that they already know and trust. Thus, having created a brand identity in a foreign market, subsequent advertising and other promotions can be directed towards establishing brand loyalty via the reinforcement of existing favourable images. People will immediately identify the branded item: the firm need not provide fresh information about it in each and every promotional campaign.

Brands do not always carry the same set of values in different countries. Stella Artois is positioned as a premium brand in the United Kingdom, but in its native Belgium (not France, as the UK advertising implies) it is regarded as a standard, mid-range beer.

Consequences of not branding

Neglecting to brand output in a sufficiently distinctive manner may mean that much of a firm's foreign advertising expenditure is wasted since its advertising messages might serve merely to promote the generic type of product to which its output belongs rather than its *specific* output, so that the firm is in effect advertising partly for the benefit of local competing businesses (Kapferer, 1992). Therefore the firm needs to *particularize* its product's unique characteristics and relate them to an attractive and clearly identifiable brand image. Once a brand has been brought to customers' attention, selling costs diminish because: advertising attracts custom to the firm's own brand rather than to that class of product generally and distributors and retailers are more willing to handle the goods on account of known demand for the firm's particular branded output.

A company that sells to foreign customers via a long chain of distributors, agents and retailers needs to ensure that its output retains its unique brand identity right up to the moment of sale to final consumers. Otherwise, mixing up or repacking of products by distributors or retailers may render the firm's goods indistinguishable from other brands – the final customer is denied the opportunity consciously to select the output of the business concerned.

Nature of branding

Brand images encapsulate whole collections of product attributes and special features. Consumers come to know what the brand represents and may thus satisfy their requirements without careful thought or research. Also they can avoid repurchasing unsatisfactory items. A firm selling several products in the same country must choose whether to allocate separate brand names to individual products or establish a generic 'family' brand covering all versions of its output.

The latter approach can be highly cost-effective, especially if the various products are closely related through associated usage (toiletries, for example) or a common channel of distribution, a common customer group or similarity of prices. This is because the entire product range may then be advertised under a single brand name, thus cutting the cost of advertising individual brands separately. Moreover, additions to product lines are introduced easily and inexpensively since no extra advertising or promotions need be incurred. The new product is simply incorporated into existing advertising literature – the firm does not have to establish a completely new individual brand image. Separate brands are essential, nevertheless, in order to appeal to different market segments.

Global brands

The question of product standardization has already been considered earlier; that of standardizing rather than customizing advertising campaigns is discussed in Chapter 14. Global branding means using the same brand name and promoting the same brand image in all countries in which the company does business (for example Coca-Cola). This contrasts with the practice of having a separate brand identity for the same product in each national market (for example Nescafé Gold Blend, which sells as Oro in Denmark and Taster's Choice in the United States). Some of the main advantages and disadvantages of global and national (local) brands are listed in Table 12.2.

It is still possible to have a global *brand* even if the product to which the brand name and image refers is itself differentiated, in order to accommodate specific national requirements. This might lead to economies of scale in advertising and other forms of promotion across national markets.

Whether it is appropriate to have a global brand depends in large part on the factors that determine the desirability of standardized worldwide advertising and some of the factors pertaining to product standardization (see above), particularly regarding international commonalities in distribution arrangements and facilities, pricing structures, lifestyles and cultural considerations, nature and strength of competitors' brand images in each foreign market, how consumers use the product in various countries, and national legal constraints on how the item may be promoted (media availability for example). The essential argument in favour of the global brand is the increasing homogeneity of lifestyles, consumer perspectives and retailing and other distribution systems throughout the world. Against this are the many critical differences in the marketing techniques applicable for economically developed and underdeveloped countries, and the continuation of significant cultural differences among consumers in various countries.

A global brand may or may not occupy the same position in each national market. In the former case it might be necessary to vary the mix of advertising, public relations, sales promotions, etc, in order to maintain the desired position in different countries. Positioning a brand in the same location in all markets has a number of practical advantages, as follows:

Table 12.2 Global brands versus national brands

Global brands

Advantages	Disadvantages
● Suitable for global products	● A single brand name and/or identity might not be appropriate for every country
● Facilitates worldwide advertising and promotion	● Several market niches might exist within a particular country
● Easier administration	● Lack of flexibility
● Can be advertised in similar media throughout the world	● Only suitable for simple products
● Extensive research can be undertaken on key variables that determine the global image of a global brand	● Might sell at different prices in different countries because of disparate tariff levels, sales taxes, and economic conditions

Local brands

Advantages	Disadvantages
● Local consumers can relate to the brand name and image	● High financial cost of legally protecting multiple brand names
● Marketing efforts can be concentrated into specific segments	● Higher advertising costs
● Flexible (ie can be amended to suit local circumstances)	● Complicated administration
● Suitable for companies operating in a limited number of markets	● Susceptible to local imitation
● Image can be tailored to local uses of the product	

● A similar price can be charged in each market, so that common price lists, catalogues and other price-sensitive promotional materials can be printed. Also the firm is not open to accusations of unfairly charging too high a price in certain markets.

● The firm can concentrate all its creative efforts on a handful of variables equally relevant to all markets.

● Similar demographic and lifestyle variables will be researched in each of the countries in which a product is sold.

Financial value of an international brand

Increasingly, brand values appear as intangible assets in company balance sheets and the amounts stated have significant implications for the borrowing powers of a business. Ultimately, the only way to value a brand is to sell it to the highest bidder on the open market. Unfortunately, there is typically no genuine competitive market when a brand comes up for sale: bilateral haggling between the brand owner and a single possible buyer normally applies. The vendor will probably begin the negotiations from a brand valuation based on the worth of the brand when used in the vendor's own business, which will depend on factors such as:

- an estimate of the difference between the retail price made possible by selling the firm's output under the existing brand name and the price for which it would have to be sold if unbranded;
- the long-term stability of demand (and hence of output and the use of productive capacity) created by consumer loyalty towards the brand;
- relations between the brand image and the firm's overall corporate image;
- the amount that has been spent on introducing and developing the brand (market research and advertising costs, agency fees, sales promotions, expenses, etc);
- the number of countries in which the brand can be used without significant adaptation.

Potential purchasers of an existing brand will be concerned with the following:

- consumer brand awareness and brand loyalty independent of the company owning the brand;
- the magnitude of the flow of income expected to be generated by the brand in comparison with the return to be had from investing in some other form of assets;
- fluctuations in annual sales and the expected life of the brand;
- the brand's ability to stand alone and create profits without having to rely on the sale of other goods, brands or services.

Selection of brand names

Brands intended for use in foreign markets need to have names that are internationally acceptable, distinct and easily recognizable, culture free, legally available and not subject to local restrictions. A brand name is far more than a device to identify the supplier of a product; it is part of the promotion mix and a means for arousing in consumers a set of emotions and mental images conducive to selling the item. Short, simple, easily read and easy to pronounce brand names are usually best for foreign markets. Such names should be memorable, and not readily confused with competing firms' outputs. Also they can be used in several markets simultaneously, for family branding, and may be supported within advertisements by a wide variety of pictorial illustrations. Admittedly, simple names (especially those that have been specifically made up to have a neutral meaning) are not necessarily relevant to the product, nor do they imply specific product attributes. However, they do avoid many potential problems, and certain desirable images can be associated with a simple brand name through skilful advertising.

Translation of a brand name can present a problem. A brand name that has no literal meaning but which sounds nice may not sound so nice in another language. Additional problems occur when the literal translations of words are technically correct and have no hidden meaning but the translated words rhyme with obscene foreign slang or with non-colloquial foreign words that are extremely inappropriate for promoting a product. There are many famous examples of this having occurred, and some TV presenters delight in finding brand names that do not readily translate. The Vauxhall Nova translates as 'no go' in Spanish, and Snickers means 'laugh behind someone's back' in the United Kingdom. Herculian carpeting became 'the carpeting with the big bottom' when used in Spain. There is a German product called 'Zit' which could not be used as a name in the United Kingdom for obvious reasons; the Spanish crisps 'Bum!' are also unlikely to find a UK market.

Protection of trade marks

In some countries the first user of a trade mark becomes its lawful owner. Elsewhere, formal registration with state authorities is required. Another important difference is between countries that require owners of registered trade marks to use them during specific time intervals (usually three to five years) or accept that other firms may appropriate them after the specified interval has elapsed. The term 'brand piracy' has been used to describe the practice of people other than the original brand name user registering the brand name of a company just about to enter a country in which formal registration is necessary, and then 'selling' the brand name back to the company concerned. 'Passing-off', ie making a slight change in the lettering of a brand name or a cosmetic alteration to the design of a logo in order to pretend that the item is the same as the original branded product is also termed brand piracy.

Failure to take legal action to protect a brand name can result in it falling into the public domain as a generic product title. Examples of brands that have suffered this fate include kerosene, celluloid, thermos, aspirin, and linoleum. All these began as brands, but may now be used by any manufacturer. This problem is especially severe when there is no generic term that adequately describes a broad type of product, resulting in the name of a well-known brand being commonly used as a proxy for the entire product category.

To avoid this happening it is necessary to use a proper noun for the brand name, immediately following the word describing the class of product (linoleum floor covering, for example). The problem for brand names that are simultaneously used in different countries, of course, is the possible non-translatability of the proper noun into other languages and/or its untranslated non-acceptability in foreign markets.

Because not all countries recognize the principle that the person or organization first using a brand name, logo, etc, has legal ownership of the intellectual property, it becomes necessary formally to register the firm's trade marks in every country in which it intends doing business. This process can be extremely expensive, adding up to 15 per cent to the costs of new product development in certain circumstances. Legal actions to protect trade marks are also very costly. Note that in some countries it may be necessary to register a brand name at frequent intervals, with any brand name not registered in the correct manner becoming available to any other business.

The EU Trade Mark Regulation 1993

Pan-EU trade mark protection can be acquired via the EU Trade Mark Regulation agreed in 1993 (but not actually implemented until 1996/97). This does not interfere with national trade marks already registered in each EU country, but instead creates a procedure enabling nationals of EU (and certain other) states to obtain from a central EU Trade Mark Office (EUTMO) an EU Trade Mark that enjoys identical legal protection in all EU countries. An EUTM can be obtained as an alternative to a national trade mark. For existing trade marks, the equivalent national trade mark will be suspended once an EUTM is registered, although national trade mark registration systems will continue to co-exist alongside the (voluntary) EUTM scheme. Applications for EU Trade Marks can be made through national patent offices or direct to the EUTMO in Alicante, Spain. Obviously the name must not already be in use within an EU state. It is up to aggrieved parties to petition the EUTMO for prohibition on the use of their trade marks by other firms. Appeals against the decisions of the EUTMO are heard first by a Board of Appeal and then by the European Court of Justice. Civil actions for damages resulting from an infringement of a registered EUTM are heard in the national courts of the country in which the violation allegedly occurred.

EUTMs have a (renewable) life of 10 years from the date of registration. Registration empowers an EUTM holder to prevent any other person or organization from using the same trade mark for similar goods or services or from imitating the trade mark, eg by changing a few letters in the name while retaining its essential character so as to 'pass off' products. Other firms are not permitted to exploit the commercial value of the trade mark, eg by mentioning it in the promotional literature of other businesses. EUTMs cease to have effect if they are not used for five years, or if the acts or omissions of the EUTM's owner allow it to become a generic product title. It is up to a third party to make a formal application to the EUTMO to have an EUTM revoked. The EUTM Regulation itself was preceded (and made possible) by a 1988 directive on the harmonization of trade mark legislation, which obliged countries to harmonize national rules regarding the rights conferred on registration of a trade mark and the tests applied when deciding whether a trade mark can be registered. There will of course be cases where firms will have to continue registering national rather than EU trade marks, for example if two businesses in different parts of the EU are independently using the same trade mark. Also national registration can be cheaper than using the EUTM scheme, especially if the firm operates predominantly within just one or two EU countries.

COUNTERFEITING

Counterfeiting (ie the imitation of a branded product with the intent to deceive or defraud) is big business in the international economy and is continuing to expand. Cosmetics, wristwatches, pharmaceuticals, chemicals, fashion clothing, books and computer software are particularly susceptible to copying. Low-quality copies of a company's product devalue the company's image (product guarantees on counterfeits are obviously worthless) and deprive it of income (Rice, 1992). Sometimes, however, the counterfeits themselves are of extremely high quality. It might even be the case that significant quantities of counterfeit goods find their way into a firm's 'official' distribution systems and recognized retail outlets, selling alongside the original version (Cordell and Wogtada, 1991). It is not surprising therefore that a number of multinational companies have on occasion compromised with counterfeiters by giving them bona fide contracts to manufacture their products. Note the high cost of hiring private security firms to track down counterfeits, compile dossiers, gather hard evidence, bring court actions and enforce judgments.

Certain less developed countries (particularly in Asia) have extremely lax laws where counterfeiting and the misuse of trade marks are concerned. Developing countries sometimes defend this on the grounds that it is unreasonable to expect them to establish highly expensive search and evaluation procedures for assessing the validity of applications for patents and trade marks. Also it can be argued that intellectual property protection creates monopoly situations, higher prices and less employment in the poorer countries of the world.

A number of international conventions and agreements have been concluded to provide residents of member countries with intellectual property protection in other states. One example is the Madrid Agreement of 1988, whereby the holder of a trade mark may register it with the World Intellectual Property Organization (WIPO) in Geneva in order to extend cover to about 30 countries worldwide. WIPO circulates the trade mark to all countries that have signed the Madrid Agreement, where it is processed according to local intellectual property laws. The applicant then receives a bundle of national trade mark registrations.

There is also the Paris Convention for the Protection of Industrial Property, signed by 90 countries. Members are obliged to recognize all intellectual property rights over patents, trade marks, etc, held by residents of other member countries. Hence each member country must afford the same degree of protection over intellectual property to nationals of other member states as it gives to its own citizens. Someone registering a trade mark in one country has up to six months' grace prior to having to register in another (12 months for patents), and the owner's rights over the intellectual property are automatically maintained during this period.

Moreover, patents registered in various countries need to be 'worked' – ie the patented product must actually be produced and/or sold – periodically. Patents that are not exploited for a certain period (this varies according to the law of the country concerned – two years is typical) may be subject to 'compulsory licensing', ie another firm can apply to a court for permission to utilize the patent under licence from the inventory. The court can compel the latter to issue a licence on terms that the court considers reasonable.

The Inter-American Convention of the United States and most Latin American countries provides protection essentially similar to that afforded by the Paris Convention. The European Patent Convention makes it possible to obtain patent protection throughout the European Union with a single application (made through the inventor's own national patent office). The 'exhaustion of rights' doctrine applies to all EU patents, no matter where they are registered. This means that a patent holder of a product patented in any one EU country cannot prohibit its sale in others, ie the patent holder has no right to prevent the export of the patented item to other EU countries.

The Uruguay Round of the GATT negotiations changed GATT rules to enable countries with industries that fall victim of significant counterfeiting to impose severe retaliatory measures against offending countries and patent and trade mark holders to have counterfeit goods confiscated and sold off.

APPENDIX – INTERNATIONAL PRODUCT LIFE CYCLES

Products are sometimes compared with people in that they are conceived and born, mature, decline and eventually die. Hence a product has a 'life cycle' comprising a series of stages. The *introductory phase* is characterized by high expenditures (for market research, test marketing, launch costs, etc) and possibly by financial losses. Early customers will be attracted by the novelty of the item. Typically these customers are younger, better educated and more affluent than the rest of the population. Technical problems are likely and, realizing this, many potential consumers will delay purchasing the product. No competition is experienced at this stage. Advertising is normally the most important element of the marketing mix during the introduction. The aim is to create product awareness and loyalty to the brand.

There should now follow a period of *growth*, during which conventional consumers begin to purchase the product. Competition appears, so advertisements should attempt both to reinforce customer loyalty and to broaden the product's appeal. Next, the product enters its *maturity* phase. Here the aim is to stabilize market share and make the product attractive (through improvements in design and presentation) to new market segments. Extra features might be added, quality improved and distribution systems widened. Most consumers have by now either tried the product or decided not to buy. Competition intensifies; appropriate strategies now include extra promotional activity, price cutting to improve market share and finding new uses for the product.

Eventually, the market is saturated and the product enters its phase of *decline*. Public tastes might have altered, or the product may now be technically obsolete. Sales and profits fall. The product's life should now be terminated, otherwise increasing amounts of time, effort and resources will be devoted to the maintenance of a failing product.

In normal circumstances, the sales of a product will vary over its life cycle as shown in Figure 12.7, although special factors might cause sales to move in other directions. Figure 12.8 gives examples of common deviations from the norm. In Figure 12.8, situation 1 might result from the entry to the market of an unsuccessful competitor who initially takes sales from the firm in question but loses them when customers find that the rival's product is inferior. Situation 2 could arise from the discovery of new uses or applications for the item or the addition to it of fresh characteristics, leading to sequential regeneration of sales. In situation 3 sales have reached a plateau and do not decline because of lack of competition. Situation 4 illustrates the 'leapfrog effect', so called because a new model is introduced to replace an existing version at periodic intervals. Note that products can sometimes be rejuvenated by quite minor changes in style. Life-cycle analysis (manifest in the detailed monitoring of trends in profitability and sales, changes in market share, consumer surveys to establish the proportion of first-time and repeat buyers, etc) is commonly used as a basis for marketing decisions, especially concerning new product development and product withdrawal. It forces a company's management to think hard about its products' future prospects and to assess the likely consequences of fresh competition. Strengths and weaknesses of products are identified, and external threats and opportunities exposed.

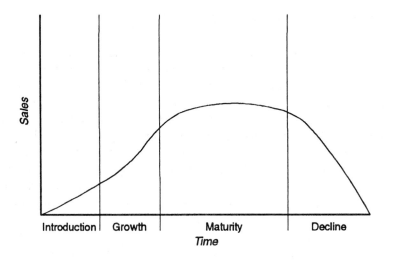

Figure 12.7   The normal product life cycle

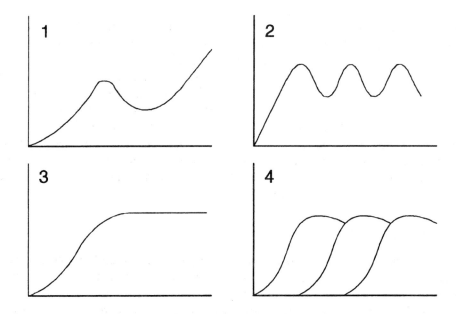

Figure 12.8   Possible life cycle patterns

Product life cycles and international marketing

The product life cycle hypothesis has direct parallels in international marketing (Wells, 1972). An item is introduced to a foreign country and at first has little or no serious competition. Then local suppliers imitate the product, so that several companies now sell the item. Hence product differentiation via the addition of new features, provision of service facilities, etc, becomes necessary in order to secure a competitive edge. Local competitors might even improve upon the product and begin to export their versions of it to the originating firm's own country. Competition intensifies, and price-cutting occurs until the product is no longer profitable to supply and is phased out. Note that foreign imitators might enjoy lower labour and other local production costs, and spend nothing on new product development. The exporter conversely has to pay transport costs plus import duties. Thus the exposing company is likely to establish its own local manufacturing facilities in order to be able to compete on price with local firms. Also it must quickly create a strong brand image and effective communications with agents and distributors 'in the field'. The above is offered as an explanation of direct foreign investment (DFI) in less-developed economies by firms from richer countries, ie that DFI has been the only way to compete against locally based low-cost imitating businesses.

Entry to new markets

Products may be in differing stages in their life cycle in various countries. An item that is nearing saturation in, say, the United States may be in its growth phase in Eastern Europe, and not even on the market in certain parts of the Third World.

If the same product is introduced sequentially to different markets of similar size and which exhibit closely similar patterns of consumer demand and behaviour, then the pattern illustrated in Figure 12.9 might be expected. To the extent that consumer and other national market characteristics differ, the shapes and durations of life cycles for various countries will diverge. Figure 12.10 shows one possible outcome. Note that the extension of a product's life via selling in a foreign market should *not* detract from the necessary task of developing new products. Only a limited amount of resources should be devoted to exporting obsolescent goods.

Product withdrawal

The argument for swift withdrawal of products nearing the end of their life cycle is three-fold: they create an out-of-date image for the supplying firm, they absorb resources that should really be devoted to new items, and they generate low rates of return. Reliance on such products, moreover, can divert attention away from the need to search for fresh products and markets. Companies engaged in international marketing, however, have options other than the simple withdrawal of a declining product, ie they can:

- Franchise foreign businesses to supply products in foreign markets as if they were the parent firm.

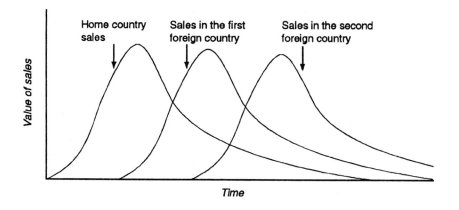

Figure 12.9 International product life cycle for a product introduced sequentially in different markets

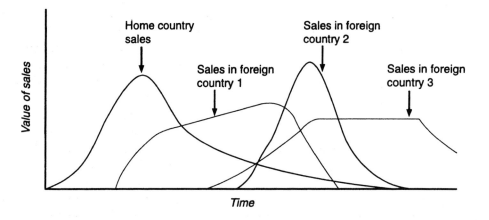

Figure 12.10 Product life cycle in countries with disparate market characteristics

- Issue licences to foreign manufacturers to produce items locally, with or without the licence extending to local distribution (this was the fate of a number of UK motor car models that went out of fashion in Britain).
- Shift the focus of international marketing activity to a market in which an item still has appeal.
- Maintain token production in a low-cost producing country, exporting the item from this country to the rest of the world. This might be useful in a situation where a brand has ceased to sell, but has an image inexorably intertwined with that of the supplying company.

Note that elimination is especially difficult when the item in question helps sell other products supplied by the firm.

Problems with the product life-cycle concept

Although it is a *conceptually* useful device, the PLC hypothesis has many problems. The length of life of a new product cannot be reliably predicted in advance, and many products cannot be characterized in life-cycle terms (basic foodstuffs or industrial materials, for instance). Importantly, variations in marketing effort will affect the duration of life-cycle phases and determine the timing of transitions from one stage to the next. Products do not face inevitable death within a predetermined period. Termination of a product's life is a management decision. Skilful marketing may extend a product's lifespan. Note, moreover, that management can never be sure of the phase in its life cycle in which a product happens to be at a particular time. How, for instance, could management know that a product is near the start and not the end of its growth phase, or that a fall in sales is a temporary event rather than the start of a product's decline.

The expected demise of a product can become a self-fulfilling reality; management may assume wrongly that sales are about to decline and consequently withdraw resources from the marketing of that product. Hence, in the absence of advertising, merchandising, promotional activity, etc, sales do fall and the product is withdrawn! Yet another problem is the enormous number of (sometimes random) factors that can influence the duration of phases, turning points and level of sales. Competitors' behaviour may be the primary determinant of the firm's sales, regardless of the age of the product.

In principle, the PLC curves demonstrated in Figure 12.9 might be generated by the consecutive introduction of a product to new markets, each fresh introduction occurring as saturation is achieved in the previous market. There is little evidence of this ever having taken place, however, which is not surprising considering that parallel exporting (see Chapter 13) is almost sure to occur in respect of successful products for which a significant demand exists in as yet untapped markets. Communication between markets is faster and more complete than ever before and only rarely is it nowadays the case that a product that is obsolescent in one country will be regarded as novel (or even acceptable) elsewhere. Another pertinent fact is that technological 'leapfrogging' is common for certain types of high-tech product, so that a new development can wipe out an item's usefulness long before its expected 'life' has expired.

13

International and global pricing approaches

FACTORS INFLUENCING PRICING

As readers who are already familiar with basic marketing theory will be aware, price is an important factor in the purchasing decision – but it is not necessarily paramount. Much depends on consumers' perceptions of the unique attributes of a product: its quality, reliability, image and need-fulfilling characteristics (Diamantopoulus, 1994). International pricing is a complex procedure: all the issues applicable to domestic price decisions might be relevant to foreign sales, and there are additional problems of lack of information, uncertain consumer responses and foreign exchange rate influences. In parallel with domestic marketing, the prices a company is able to charge in foreign markets depend on the total demand for the product in each country (which itself varies according to population, per capita income, tastes and fashions, seasonal factors and so on), the responsiveness of consumer demand to prices changes (so that if a small reduction in price leads to a large increase in sales, then a price cut will be economically worthwhile because extra sales will more than compensate for reduced unit revenue), expected behaviour of competitors, market response to promotional activity, and the unique selling points of the item concerned (it is difficult for a firm to increase the price of a product that consumers regard as homogeneous to a level above those charged by competitors, since customers will simply switch their expenditures elsewhere).

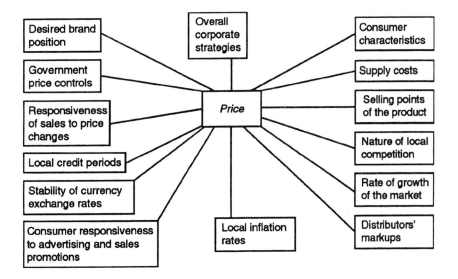

Figure 13.1 Influences on international pricing decisions

Influences on international pricing decisions are illustrated in Figure 13.1. Further factors affecting the selection of a price in a particular foreign market might include, firstly, the desired product position (note that an item regarded as a luxury in some countries may be considered a necessity in others, thus affecting the appropriate price), and secondly, the product's location in its life cycle in the market concerned (items can be in different phases of their life cycle in different countries). Product life cycle pricing is a cost-plus technique where the added profit margin is varied with respect to the maturity of the product. Following a product's initial introduction to the market, the price set may be high in order to recover development costs. The price is then systematically lowered so as to broaden the product's appeal and capture new markets. Then, the price might be increased to make attractive another similar product that the firm is introducing. Thereafter, the price could be drastically reduced to clear remaining stock.

INTERNATIONAL PRICING APPROACHES

Two general approaches to foreign pricing are available: cost-plus and strategic.

Cost-plus pricing

The firm's cost of production is of course a major factor affecting its pricing decisions. Firms must at least break even. But the volume of sales necessary to break even depends on the price per unit (high prices enable low-volume break even), while the number of units sold itself depends substantially on the unit price – since high sales are normally associated with lower prices. Thus firms must balance price and resulting sales against production costs. Unfortunately, unit production costs are themselves determined in part by the volume of sales because of fixed overheads. For instance, a factory rent of £100,000 spread over 100 units gives an overhead cost of £1,000 per unit; yet if 200 units are produced the unit overhead cost becomes £500 per item. This point is highly significant for firms exporting large amounts of their output because the volume of export sales achieved will help determine unit overheads and thus influence production costs (and hence selling prices) for domestic as well as foreign sales.

In practice, a firm might predetermine the length of a production run, add up all its anticipated costs – fixed and variable – and divide estimated total cost by planned output. Some percentage mark-up is then added to get a unit price. This approach is simple and computationally convenient, but it has drawbacks:

- Firms typically produce several different products. Allocations of overheads to the various items are necessarily arbitrary. Consequently, individual products may be over- or under-priced.
- Not all of a production run will necessarily be sold. Some units may have to be put into stock or scrapped, hence altering the unit production cost of the remaining items.
- The cost-plus method ignores consumer perceptions and therefore runs counter to marketing thinking. Apart from the possibility that consumers might be prepared to pay more for a product, there is also the point that consumers often use price as an indicator of quality. For example, when McDonald's opened in Moscow, the restaurant was perceived as an upmarket, expensive restaurant.

Still further problems attach to cost-plus approaches to international pricing in view of the difficulty of estimating all the extra costs (including overheads) associated with foreign sales (see Table 13.1) and the paucity of information on local competitors and market conditions and on the maximum price the local market will bear.

An international firm serving many foreign markets may experience great difficulty in relating its overheads to particular markets. For example, what proportion of senior management time should be assumed to be taken up by the firm's foreign operations? Should the business seek to cover *all* its costs including overheads ('full-cost' pricing) or merely the *variable* costs of foreign sales, regarding the latter as a bonus that contributes to total revenue but need not absorb overhead expenditures (these being fully recovered via the price charged on the domestic market)?

It is not uncommon for firms (unintentionally) to underprice their products in foreign markets, leading to unprofitable operations, retaliation by irate local competitors, possibly to an accusation of 'dumping' (see below) in a local commercial court, and the unpleasant task of having to raise prices from their established low but unrealistic level. It is far easier to get consumers to accept price *reductions* than the other way round!

Table 13.1   Possible extra costs of international sales

- Export packaging
- Cargo and payments insurance
- Foreign transport
- Freight forwarders' fees
- Wharfage charges
- Visits to foreign markets
- Translating and interpreting costs
- Forward currency exchange margins
- Customs duties
- Costs of credit
- Repacking charges subsequent to customs examination
- Miscellaneous bank charges

- Product modification costs
- Market research
- Foreign advertising and other promotional expenditures
- Relabelling costs
- Pre-shipment inspection costs
- Special discounts offered to gain market entry
- Agency fees
- Salespeoples' expenses and commissions
- Clearing agents' fees
- Insurance claims costs
- Documentation costs
- Greater risk of bad debts

in practice...

Amstrad

Amstrad Consumer Electronics PLC has an international reputation for supplying robust, reliable, 'no frills' yet high-quality merchandise. Prices are kept to the bare minimum in order to secure the mass sales needed to finance cheap but well-made products. Costs are minimized through using 'adequate' rather than state-of-the-art technology, the removal of superfluous accessories and facilities, not engaging in R&D and having a 'lean' administrative system. Components are manufactured in quantity in whichever country can produce them most cheaply to the required specification. The company's policy is to withdraw quickly from any line of product where sales are disappointing. Products are basic but attractively packaged and presented. Facilities and options that the majority of purchasers would never use are not included in the item. Nearly all production is subcontracted (typically to Far Eastern countries): the company owns just a single small factory in Hong Kong. Transport and distribution are also subcontracted. This lack of direct investment is plant and equipment enables Amstrad to abandon unprofitable products at little cost and without difficulty. Equally, new products can be introduced very rapidly.

Strategic pricing

Many companies begin their international marketing activities as *price-takers*, simply adopting the price levels and conventions of competing firms. As a price-taker the firm is able to maintain a stable market share, since by matching the price changes of competing businesses it prevents them from increasing their relative share of the total market (Walters, 1989). Note, however, that in meeting competitors' price cuts the firm might be compelled to operate on a low profit margin. A firm might be a price-taker at a different price in each of several different markets, the market price varying according to customers' perceptions of the need and level of quality of the product, income levels, number of firms involved, etc. Eventually, however, businesses might wish to apply to the foreign market one or other of the basic pricing strategies available for domestic trade, as discussed below.

Penetration pricing

With this strategy the firm combines a low price with aggressive advertising in order to gain a larger share of existing markets. The strategy is suitable where large outputs quickly lead to reductions in unit costs through economies of scale, but will not succeed if competitors can reduce their prices to correspondingly low levels. A danger is that prices might be set so low that they are not credible to consumers. There exist 'confidence levels' for prices below which consumers lose faith in a product's quality. Low prices can create in consumers' minds the perception that goods are shoddy, incomplete, have inadequate guarantees or offer poor after-sales service. This is a long-term strategy intended to build market share and lay a foundation for possible future price increases. It is expensive, and normally involves substantial expenditure on promoting the product. Further reasons for pricing at low levels in certain foreign markets might include:

- lower income levels of local consumers;
- intense local competition from rival companies;
- the reasonable assumption by some firms that since their research, product development and overhead costs are covered by home sales, then exporting represents a marginal activity intended merely to bring in as much additional revenue as possible – albeit at low selling prices;
- weak demand for the product in question in some markets.

in practice...

NEC Corporation

Japanese electronics supplier NEC Corporation has successfully implemented penetration pricing policies throughout the world. The procedure it adopts is to specify a desired rate of profit that is deducted from the price at which a new product is to be introduced, hence creating a target production cost that the firm's engineers are obliged to meet. Thus the product is designed at the outset to satisfy the cost constraint. Thereafter the company aims to reduce costs still further through long production runs of input components and the finished item. Great attention is devoted to the constant improvement of technical production processes. If fresh competition emerges or if market conditions alter while the product is being developed, the target cost might be reduced to an even lower level, placing enormous pressures on design and engineering staff.

The latter are expected to be cost conscious at all times and receive much training in this regard. Often, raw materials and input components are supplied from subsidiaries in the poorer countries of South-East Asia, where labour and other costs are extremely low. The company makes extensive use of robots and other forms of automated production.

Source: Adapted from Kobayashi (1991)

Skimming

With this strategy, attempts are made to 'skim the cream' from the top end of a market by charging high prices for luxury versions of established products. As the product penetrates the market, the price is steadily reduced until the product is available at all price levels. High-quality images are needed to justify the high prices charged, at least in the initial stages. Successful skimming requires significant numbers of high-income consumers prepared to pay top prices. If production costs are low the firm will earn exceptionally high profits.

With skimming, the firm trades off a low initial market share against a high margin. A foreign image can help a product sustain a premium price, provided the image involves special qualities or features not available in home-supplied competing goods. Eventually, as competitors enter the market and the initial novelty has worn off, the price must reduce. Problems with skimming are that:

- Maintenance of a high-quality product image typically requires energetic promotion, first-class after-sales service and a visible local presence, which may be difficult in a distant market.
- Having a small market share makes the firm vulnerable to aggressive local competition.
- If the item is sold cheaper at home or in another country, then parallel exporting is likely. This means that the product will be purchased from intermediaries in the cheaper country and re-exported.

Choosing a price for a product that is entirely new to a particular national market is especially difficult. There are few guidelines to help with making a decision, consumer loyalty does not exist, consumers have little perception of the item's characteristics and quality, and there are no alternatives against which the product may be compared. Problems are compounded when a product is technically sophisticated and requires extensive after-sales service and customer care. Most firms introducing new products in fact determine their prices by first establishing their costs, adding a mark-up and then modifying the outcome in the light of market conditions. The process for international pricing decision-making is outlined in Figure 13.2.

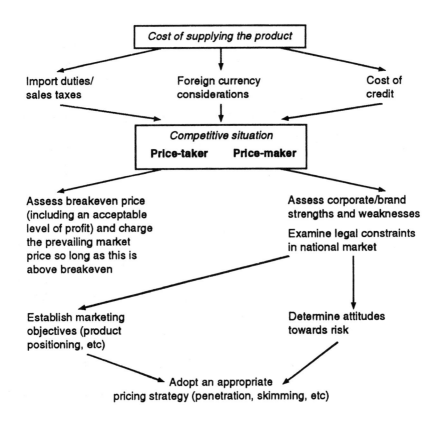

Figure 13.2   International pricing decisions

THE RESEARCH TASK

Key elements in the research programme for determining an appropriate price for selling to a foreign market are as follows:

● Compilation of a list of the retail prices of competing brands in the local market. Two problems are involved here: first the accurate identification of what local consumers perceive to be competing brands (such perceptions may differ radically from the supplying firm's initial assumptions about what represents a comparable competing item), and secondly the assessment of price differences for the same brands in various types of outlet and in main cities and provincial towns. Regional price differences can be enormous. Many firms ask their banks to arrange for the latter's foreign branches to conduct price checks in local markets, or for an embassy or consulate to undertake this task. If so it is important to ensure that a proper range of regional price variations have been recorded. The same applies to type of outlet, since often the same item is sold in supermarkets, department stores, via mail-order catalogues and via write-in newspaper advertisements, eg, at significantly different prices.

- Investigation of local distribution systems to establish typical mark-ups of various channels and categories of retail outlet. Deducting the normal mark-up from the local retail price provides a target figure at which the firm must supply the item to local intermediaries. It is also important to investigate the extent and nature of the discounts and credit terms being offered by local competitors.
- Determination of all import duties and local sales taxes and the circumstances in which they can be (lawfully) avoided.
- Sounding out the opinions of local contacts 'in the field' (agents, sister companies, retail store managers, etc) on the most appropriate price for the item.

INCOTERMS

Commercial documents such as invoices, letters of credit, contracts of sale, etc, need to specify a price and terms of trade that define precisely the duties and obligations of buyer and seller and, in particular, the exact moment at which ownership of (and hence responsibility for) goods passes from one party to the other. The various options have numerous legal implications, national commercial laws may conflict and arguments can arise concerning who is to pay for ancillary freight charges, consular fees, losses during transit, pilferage, and so on.

The International Chamber of Commerce (ICC) publishes a set of definitions of export delivery terms (INCOTERMS) for use in international trade. They are widely quoted and have a legal status in some countries. The definitions are updated periodically. Table 13.2 outlines the major INCOTERMS currently in use.

Note that DDP pricing is increasingly the norm in the European Union. Since the introduction of the euro in 12 member states, there is no reason to price in any other currency, and even in the non-euro states prices are often quoted in Euros. There is, of course, no problem with customs duties since there are no tariff barriers, but excise duties (on alcohol and tobacco in particular) still differ between member states and duty must be paid. Equally, *ex works* and other terms of delivery that impose extra work and inconvenience on customers are becoming unacceptable in many countries (not just in the EU). Customers will think twice about importing an item that is available from domestic suppliers if the process of importing incurs significant financial and other costs.

Unless INCOTERMS have been incorporated into the domestic law of the relevant country, they do not automatically apply if there is no reference to them in the contract of sale or transport documents. Thus, for example, use of the term 'CIF Sydney' does not guarantee that the INCOTERMS definition will be employed to resolve any dispute regarding the meaning of 'CIF', whereas appearance of the phrase 'CIF Sydney INCOTERMS' will indeed ensure that the appropriate INCOTERM shall apply. Many disputes have arisen over whether the use of an INCOTERM was or was not intended by the contracting parties.

Table 13.2   Main INCOTERMS currently in use

- **Ex works (EXW).** The goods are made available for the customer to collect from the exporter's (specified) premises in the firm's home country. Buyers take full responsibility for all transport and other risks and charges from the moment their consignments are collected.

- **Free on board (FOB).** The exporter (or freight forwarder, shipping company or other carrier) arranged for the consignment to be loaded on board a ship at a named port in the exporter's country. The buyer assumes responsibility for the goods the moment they pass over the ship's rail.

- **Free on rail (FOR)/Free on truck (FOT).** These are the FOB equivalents for rail and road transport.

- **Free carrier (FRC).** This is the same as FOB but applies where the mode of transport cannot be clearly defined, eg when goods are loaded on to a trailer or into a container for collection by another firm. The term may be used for any form of transport, including multimodal transport. Sellers fulfil their obligations when they hand over the goods – cleared for export – into the charge of the carrier at a specified place. A 'carrier' is any person or firm undertaking to perform or procure carriage of the goods by rail, road, sea, air, inland waterway, or by a combination of some or all of these modes. A 'container' is any equipment used to carry cargo in distinct units.

- **Free alongside ship (FAS).** The consignment is placed alongside a ship in a quay of a named port in the exporter's country and a port employee signs a declaration that this has been done. From that moment onwards the customer is liable for losses resulting from theft, natural deterioration, fire or other damage. The customer has to pay for loading the goods on to the ship.

- **Ex ship (EXS).** Goods are made available to the customer on board a ship at a named foreign port of destination. Normally, the customer is responsible for unloading the goods. If not, the term used is **Ex quay (EXQ).**

- **Cost and freight (C&F or CFR).** The exporter pays all the transport charges (excluding insurance, which is the customer's obligation) required to deliver goods by sea to a named destination. The customer assumes the risk of loss or damage to the goods from the moment they pass over the ship's rail at the port of embarkation. For C&F equivalents using modes of transport other than ships the term **OCP** might be used (or **DCP** if the goods travel in a container).

- **Delivered at frontier (DAF).** The customer takes responsibility for the consignment the moment it passes through a named frontier.

- **Cost, insurance and freight (CIF).** This is the same as C&F but includes the requirement that the exporter and not the customer insure the goods to their final destination. For methods of transport other than sea the term **CIP** might be used.

- **Carriage paid to (CPT).** This means that the exporter pays the freight charges to a named destination. However, the buyer assumes all risks of loss or damage to the goods from the moment the exporter has delivered them into the custody of the carrier. The term is especially useful for multimodal transport; if several carriers are involved the risks of damage or loss pass to the buyer at the time the goods are delivered to the first carrier.

- **Carriage and insurance paid to (CIP).** Here the seller has the same obligations as under CPT but must in addition arrange and pay for cargo insurance. Only the most basic insurance cover need be taken out.

- **Delivered duty paid (DDP).** The exporter assumes all the risks and expenses involved in delivering the goods to the customer's premises. (DDP used to be known as **Franco domicile** pricing).

FOREIGN EXCHANGE CONSIDERATIONS

Foreign exchange factors are critically important for pricing decisions, of course, since an appreciation in the currency of the country of the exporting firm means that the importer will have to pay more local currency to purchase the foreign currency necessary to settle an invoice of a given size. If the exporter quotes selling prices in the currency of the importing country (to make it as convenient as possible for residents of that country to purchase the item), then the exporting firm assumes the risk of a fall in the importing country's exchange rate reducing the exporter's return when the latter comes to convert accumulated foreign currency into domestic units. In the latter situation the exporting firm can sell to its bank, in advance, the foreign currency that its customers have been invoiced to pay. The bank will quote a fixed forward exchange rate for these transactions, which will apply to the conversions regardless of the actual spot exchange in force one month or three months (say) from today.

The bank will demand a reward for its services and therefore will quote an exchange rate for forward currency transactions that differs from the current spot exchange rate by an amount sufficient to cover the bank's exposure to risk and to make a profit. This obviously represents a (significant) cost to the exporter.

An exporting firm that invoices in local currency and that expects the spot exchange rate to move in its favour (so that it stands to raise more domestic currency when it eventually comes to convert than if converted today) may decide not to bother with forward cover. Another possibility available to exporters scheduled to receive foreign currency payments over a long period is to enter into an *option contract* with its bank whereby the exporter is given the right to sell to the bank foreign currency up to an agreed limit at a predetermined rate at any time within the next 12 months. If the spot exchange rate moves in one direction the exporter will exercise the option; if it moves in the other the option will not be taken up, thereby forfeiting the fee paid to the bank to purchase the option.

Other means for reducing currency risk are for firms to include renegotiation clauses in all sales contracts to enable them automatically to change the contract price in the event of significant exchange rate fluctuations, and the accumulation of (interest-earning) foreign currency balances in various countries to be exchanged for other currencies at appropriate moments or used to purchase local products for subsequent exporting to other markets. Note that such devices impose additional costs and inconveniences on exporting companies relative to locally based rivals.

Costs of currency fluctuations

Apart from the need to take out (expensive) forward cover, currency fluctuations create other problems for exporting firms, as follows:

- In normal circumstances increased costs lead a firm to raise its selling price, and vice versa. But regular price fluctuations (caused by changes in currency exchange rates) are entirely inappropriate for branded products for which the product price is a key factor in determining the brand's market position (see Chapter 12). Imported brands cannot compete effectively with locally produced outputs in these circumstances.

- Test marketing in foreign markets becomes almost impossible, since the price at which an item is test marketed might not be the price at which it will be sold following a large exchange rate fluctuation.
- Currency uncertainty makes it difficult to introduce new products to a foreign market due to the need to change their prices in line with exchange rate movements.

PRICE DISCRIMINATION AND PARALLEL EXPORTING

With price discrimination, different prices are charged in different markets for the same goods. There must be barriers – geographical distances, high transport costs or consumer ignorance – that prevent customers buying in one market and reselling at a profit elsewhere (see below). Prices for the same output exported to different countries may be expected to differ if only because of variations in national import duties, sales taxes, agency fees, distributors' margins and currency exchange rates (Weigand, 1991). In addition to these considerations it might be possible to charge high prices in high-income markets where the item has perhaps only recently been introduced and where it possesses a luxury image, and low prices in low-income countries where the product is at the end of its life cycle. Price discrimination recognizes that each market is to some extent unique regarding its composition, competitive characteristics and socio-economic features. Note, however, that the simplicity and administrative convenience of a uniform price structure are forgone.

Where price discrimination occurs it is possible (indeed likely) that 'unofficial' intermediaries will purchase the item in low-price areas and resell elsewhere at below the original exporting firm's recommended retail price. Such 'parallel exporting', as it is known, leads to an equalization of international product prices as it thwarts the exporting company's attempts to charge different prices in different countries. Note that parallel exporting may prevent an exporting firm acting as a price-taker in a high-price foreign market. Hence, local competitors will observe their prices being undercut via parallel exporters and may retaliate against the firm originally supplying the goods! Further problems created by the activities of parallel exporters include:

- Lower worldwide returns as a consequence of an exporting firm having to reduce its prices in lucrative markets.
- Possible damage to the company's corporate image caused by inadequacies in the intermediary's presentational and promotional techniques.
- It becomes difficult to engage distributors, who observe the item being sold by unofficial intermediaries with whom they have to compete.

Confronted with parallel exporting, there is little the supplying firm can do about it, as the practice is entirely legal and in keeping with the principles of free trade and open competition. Attempts at inhibiting the activities of parallel exporters (eg by refusing to trade with anyone who does business with a parallel exporting firm) would be unlawful in the great majority of countries in the world. Possible strategies for dealing with the problem are to purchase outright the business engaged in parallel export activity, or to engage them as authorized agents or distributors on high discounts. The problem of course is that new parallel exporters are likely to arise as soon as the existing ones have been dealt with.

PREDATORY PRICING

Predatory pricing is defined by the Organization for Economic Cooperation and Development (OECD) as the adoption by a firm of a price so low that competitors are forced to leave the market, thus enabling the predator to raise prices in the long run (OECD, 1989). According to the OECD, predation is commonest where the predator firm operates in many markets and/or where victims, potential competitors and national regulatory bodies do not have sufficient information to be able to prove that predation is taking place.

Predation in European Union countries can (but might not) be illegal under Article 86 of the Treaty of Rome, which prohibits large firms from abusing dominant positions through imposing 'unfair trading conditions' and outlaws the use of 'unreasonably low' prices in one market to protect markets elsewhere. However, the abuse (normally) would have to affect more than 5 per cent of the total market for the goods or services involved before it became actionable under EU competition law. Note, moreover, that a number of individual European countries have explicit laws that forbid the sale of products at less than their cost of production or purchase. 'Sale price' in this country is defined as invoice price *less* all rebates and special discounts. (Note how sales promotions can be caught by the latter provision.) Belgium prohibits retailers from selling to final consumers any product at a price below its cost plus overheads and 'normal' profit. In France, it is illegal to retail a product at any price that does not cover its purchase or production costs, taxes and cost of transportation (except for perishable, seasonal or obsolete goods, or when replacement items have fallen in price). Germany's 1986 Unfair Competition Act outlaws prices that are so far below cost that they are clearly designed to eliminate rivals through acts other than superior economic performance.

DUMPING

Dumping is defined by the World Trade Organization as any sale in an export market at a price below that charged in the supplying firm's own country (plus transport and foreign distribution costs), whatever the motivation (disposal of surplus stock, penetration of markets, etc) and is an 'unfair trading practice' under WTO regulations. Hence the governments of affected countries are allowed to impose special import taxes on offending products. Pricing at below full cost makes sound economic sense to the firm engaged in the practice if it has space capacity but is committed to long-term development of the market concerned (so that it needs to cover its short-term variable costs and make as much contribution to overheads as possible during a period of reconstruction), or is seeking to shift end-of-range stock.

Problems arise in assessing reasonable values for mark-ups attributable to transport, distribution and other costs involved in foreign selling, and from the common situation whereby firms supply a market with units of the same item produced by subsidiaries in several different countries, so that there is no single 'domestic' price for the purpose of comparison. WTO rules on dumping (which are embodied in Article 6 of the agreement) apply predominantly to predatory and/or persistent dumping intended to damage the local competition, rather than ad hoc attempts to dispose of surplus stock. Hence retaliation is only permitted if:

- sales occur at less than 'fair value';
- 'material injury' to domestic industry occurs; and
- the dumping is the 'principal cause' of injury to local firms producing 'like products' and not some other factor.

The customs authorities of individual countries decide whether an item has been 'dumped', although European Union countries apply a uniform calculation to the issue. Under EU rules the price considered is that that the exporting firm charges to non-related local distributors, *not* the price paid by final consumers. A non-related local distributor is one that is not tied to the supplying firm via an agency agreement or exclusive dealership. If all distributors are in fact 'related' to the supplying foreign firm, then the price charged to end-consumers is used. Anti-dumping taxes are sometimes known as 'countervailing duties', although the latter term is used more generally as a description of any import tariff intended to prevent foreign firms undercutting domestic suppliers.

in practice...

Dumping fax machines

In 1997, Philips of the Netherlands formally complained to the European Commission about the alleged dumping of personal fax machines in Europe by exporters in Japan and six other South-East Asian countries. Philip's case rested on two substantive allegations that 'underpriced' fax machines from the seven countries had increased their market share significantly in recent years, and that this increase in market share had exerted adverse effects on EU producers. Japanese manufacturers defended their behaviour on the grounds that, in reality, imports of personal fax machines into Europe from Japan had decreased rather than increased (in both unit and value terms) and that the prices of Japanese fax machines were generally higher than those of European manufacturers other than Philips. Also, leading EU fax producers such as Philips and the French company Sagem had recently expanded their outputs and sales.

This situation underlines the need for accurate and relevant information when adjudicating accusations of dumping. Another example of the importance of reliable information is the controversial US–Japanese semiconductor trade agreement signed in July 1996, which, it turned out, was based on erroneous Japanese market share data. Initially a sharp rise in the market share of foreign chip suppliers to Japan had been reported. It subsequently emerged that a small decline had in fact taken place. Market share information had been critical to the negotiations leading up to the agreement since the Japanese had argued that with the foreign market share of semiconductors standing at an all time high of 30.6 per cent there was no need for foreigners to demand easier access to the Japanese chip market. An agreement was eventually concluded, but the terms were much less stringent than if the correct data (prepared by the Japanese Ministry of International Trade and Industry) had been supplied. The US Semiconductor Industry Association (SIA) announced its suspicion about the mistake, which clearly benefited the Japanese. Accordingly the SIA demanded that Japan provide full reasons concerning the cause of the error, as the correct information could have exerted a heavy influence on the talks.

TRANSFER PRICING

Transfer pricing is the name given to the setting of the price levels at which a parent firm 'sells' its output to subsidiaries in other countries. Transfer prices need to be realistic in order that the profitability of various international operations may be assessed. Often, transfer prices are set at whatever levels minimize the firm's liabilities for import duties and company taxes. For example, a country may levy a high percentage tariff on a certain item, so that if a subsidiary 'imports' the item from its foreign parent at a very low nominal price only a small import duty is payable. Also, corporation tax is much lower in some countries than in others, so that it makes sense for the parent firm to reduce the book values of the profits made by its subsidiaries in high-tax countries (through charging high 'prices' for inputs 'purchased' from the parent), while artificially inflating the profits of subsidiaries in countries where business taxes are negligible. High transfer pricing ('over-invoicing') has been used by multinationals to extract hard currency from politically unstable countries, and could be used to circumvent national foreign exchange regulations intended to prevent hard currency leaving a country for anything other than bona fide import transactions. Also, high transfer prices result in the 'seller' accumulating money that might be invested more profitably in the seller's country than elsewhere.

National tax authorities obviously take a keen interest in transfer pricing practices. If, for example, a subsidiary sells its output to its parent at production cost, then it makes no profit and, prima facie, is not liable for tax! Governments adopt a variety of measures for dealing with this situation. The United States tax authorities, for example, require that a reasonable share of a US exporter's research and development expenditures be included in its export transfer prices, in order to ensure that income accumulates within the United States where it is subject to taxes. Also it can demand from exporters and importers detailed justification of large differences between firms' prices in various markets.

in practice...

Counting the cost

The returns to national tax authorities from investigations into global companies' transfer pricing methods can be immense. In 1995, the UK Inland Revenue reported that the ratio of the cost of gathering tax on transfer pricing against the value of the revenue generated was 240:1, compared with 75:1 on technical avoidance, 29:1 on tax investigation, 24:1 on tax fraud, and a mere 6:1 on employee tax. This obviously enhances the appeal to the tax authorities of transfer pricing work. In particular, the Inland Revenue is anxious to retain its right to examine transfer pricing transactions occurring in previous tax years, as the discovery of a single act of non-compliance by a large MNC in the past could generate (from the perspective of the tax authorities) a huge reward.

Setting aside tax and import duty considerations, considerable difficulties apply to the determination of a 'correct' transfer price. Possible criteria for setting the transfer price include:

- The price at which the item could be sold on the open market (this is known as 'arm's length' transfer pricing). This can overstate the contributions of the supplying unit (since market prices vary according to the proclivities of local supply and demand) and, of course, it is not suitable for items for which there is no open market (specialized input components, for example).
- Acquisition/production cost plus a profit mark-up. The problem here of course is deciding what constitutes an appropriate level of profit mark-up.
- Political negotiations between the units involved (a high or low transfer price can drastically affect the observed profitability of a subsidiary). Note the difficulties that arise if the 'buyer' happens to be the head office of the company.
- Senior management's perceptions of the value of the item to the firm's overall international operations.

Ignoring tax considerations, the solution normally adopted is that which (seemingly) maximizes profits for the company taken as a whole and which best facilitates the parent firm's control over subsidiary operations (Stroud and Masters, 1991). Arm's length pricing (see above) is the method generally preferred by national governments and is recommended in a Code of Practice on the subject drafted by the OECD (United Nations, 1983). Problems with setting a realistic transfer price are as follows:

- Disparate tax rates and investment subsidy levels in various countries.
- Executives in operating units deliberately manipulating the transfer price to enhance the book value of a subsidiary's profits.
- Differences in the accounting systems used by subsidiaries in different countries.

- Possible absence of competition in local markets at various stages in the supply chain. Thus a 'market price' in a low-competition area may be artificially high in consequence of the lack of local competition.
- If a price is set at too high a level, the 'selling' unit will be able to attain its profit targets easily (at the expense of the 'buyer') and this may lead to idleness and inefficiency in the selling subsidiary. Note that a subsidiary that charges a high transfer price will accumulate cash, which might be invested more profitably in the selling country than elsewhere.
- There might not be any other product directly comparable to the item in question, again making it difficult to establish a market price.

Special problems arise when goods are being transferred among the partners of a joint venture. Should the various members of the venture be regarded as 'subsidiaries' or as independent businesses required to pay a market price? These problems make it extremely difficult for national governments to control transfer pricing – yet another example of ways in which global corporations are able to circumvent elected national governments.

14

International advertising

THE NATURE OF INTERNATIONAL ADVERTISING

Successful international advertising requires careful attention to three major tasks: the production of advertisements suitable for international markets; the location and choice of the best media to carry messages; and (possibly) the selection and control of an advertising agency competent to undertake international work. This chapter focuses on the administration of a firm's international advertising effort, and on the creation of messages suitable for advertising abroad.

Demand for advertising

Certain common factors influence the levels of advertising expenditure that occur in all countries: company profitability, the extent of competition among businesses and (most importantly) the level of consumer spending. Thereafter, however, cultural and other national differences come to the fore, eg the means through which advertising is regulated (statutorily or by self-regulation), the severity of legal control and media availability (restrictions on television advertising broadcast time continue to apply in many places).

Moreover, advertising (and marketing generally) has benefited considerably from the removal of internal restrictions on business and the moves towards the market-orientated economic systems that have taken place throughout the world. Many state-owned newspapers, television companies and radio stations have been denationalized and broadcasting systems deregulated. Other factors encouraging the development of international advertising have been the widespread internationalization of big (and not so big) businesses and the huge increase in international competition resulting from various tariff-cutting measures (notably the General Agreement on Tariffs and Trade) that began in the 1960s and continue to the present day. Foreign entrants to domestic markets use aggressive high-quality advertising to introduce new brands and to increase their market share, forcing domestic companies to extend and improve their own advertising campaigns.

Computerization of printing technology has also increased the international demand for advertising. Print media are cheaper to produce than previously (hence reducing the space prices demanded by print media owners), and many newspapers and magazines now print simultaneously in several geographical locations. The latter is possible via telephone and/or satellite transmissions of pages from a single central control. Production of 'local' editions of newspapers and magazines enables their contents to be tailored to suit local requirements, creating many opportunities for advertisers to adapt their promotional messages to the needs of particular markets.

Objectives of international advertising

Precise specification of international advertising forces management to think clearly and to prioritize appropriate actions. Also, it becomes possible to assess the effectiveness of an international campaign. Major advertising objectives might include some of the following:

- **Increasing sales**. The fact that sales show an increase following a campaign is encouraging, but great care is needed to ensure that the observed rise is actually due to the extra advertising and not to some extraneous variable (collapse of a competitor, changes in taste and fashion, or a rise in consumers' incomes, for example). Another problem with interpreting the relation between advertising and sales in that the impact of the former on the latter is frequently delayed. A long period might elapse before the benefits of the campaign are realized, by which time several other influences might have intervened and caused observed sales levels to fall. In short, it is difficult and probably inappropriate to measure a communications medium against marketing objectives – communications media can only be measured against communication objectives.
- **Obtaining new customers**. Here it is necessary to establish the percentage of buyers who are purchasing the brand for the first time. This might not be easy and the services of a local market research company may be required.
- **Altering consumer behaviour**, eg increasing the proportion of customers who buy directly via mail order rather than through retail outlets.
- **Communicating brand values**. This is often a major function of international advertising, especially since brand values might differ from one market to the next.

Specific campaign objectives could involve the capture within a predetermined period of a certain market share, the creation of brand awareness and/or inducing consumers to switch brands, or persuading foreign distributors and other intermediaries to stock up with the advertised item. Further aims might be to:

- encourage consumers to increase the frequency of their purchases;
- induce customers to buy at different times of the year in order to even out seasonal fluctuations in demand;
- create the belief among consumers that a brand is the leader in its field;
- promote the environmentally friendly aspects of a product;
- defend an existing market, eg through maintaining brand loyalty via a creative strategy that focuses on reminding consumers of the key advantages of the brand;
- stimulate impulse purchases;
- improve the firm's corporate image among a particular target customer group;
- increase consumer awareness of the firm's products;
- generate a certain number of enquiries from specific customer types.

Rules for setting objectives

Objectives should be consistent. For example, that maximization of short-term returns usually implies the frequent switching of promotional expenditure from one market sector to others, and would not be consistent with the objective of attaining steady long-term growth of market share. Further rules for setting objectives are as follows:

- Objectives should follow a hierarchy, with the most general at the top and the most detailed and specific at the bottom.
- Each objective should be accompanied by statements of:
  - who is responsible for its attainment;
  - when the objective is to be achieved;
  - how the objective is to accomplished, including a specification of the resources necessary and where and how they will be acquired.
- Criteria for deciding whether an objective has been achieved should be predetermined.

Creative strategy

This concerns decisions about what needs to be communicated (images, messages, mental associations, themes, information, etc), how the communication will be effected, and what the communication is intended to achieve in terms of consumer behaviour in the country concerned. All these decisions have important implications for the choice of advertising medium, since certain media can better accommodate specific creative requirements (use of colour, written description, high definition, demonstration of the product, etc) than others. Creative strategy normally evolves from a statement of a basic selling idea, concocted by either the client firm or its advertising agency. This selling proposition will normally be little more than a couple of points outlining the essential theme upon which promotional messages are to be based. Each advertisement should have a *specific* creative goal, eg to explain how the advertised item meets consumer needs, or to position a product.

STANDARDIZATION VERSUS CUSTOMIZATION OF PROMOTIONAL MESSAGES

The basic issue in international advertising is whether to standardize advertising messages for common application in all countries, or to adapt them to meet the particular requirements of various markets or states. Standardization involves treating the world as one market, ignoring any apparent regional, cultural or national differences, and promoting the firm's output in exactly the same way in all states. Consumers with the same attitudes and buying habits are targeted in each country.

Single communications strategies rarely work for firms in the global arena. In fact, the few exceptions are so notable that they are used as examples time and again – Marlboro cigarettes, Coca-Cola, Levi jeans – and nearly all are from the United States. It is possible that the overwhelming influence of Hollywood in exporting US culture worldwide means that people in most countries are able to understand US cultural references (the Marlboro cowboy, for example) in a way that would not work for, say, the Brazilian gaucho or the Japanese samurai.

The case for standardization

Advantages of standardization are that it requires less marketing research than customization, is convenient and cheap to administer, and demands less creative effort (see Anholt, 1993, for further information on this topic). A single message can be devised for use throughout the world. Justifications for the standardized approach include the following:

- Lifestyles and consumer behaviour are increasingly homogeneous in developed countries. Also there are substantial similarities in the ways that people respond to the same advertising message regardless of where they live.
- There is a continuing urbanization of the world's population. Migration from rural areas to cities is greater today than ever before. City dwellers who follow the same working, shopping, travelling and living routines tend to adopt similar attitudes and lifestyles, regardless of the city or country in which they reside.
- Internationalization of the media (particularly television programmes and newspaper and magazine layout and contents) has led to the adoption of increasingly similar perspectives among people in all countries. Youth culture is remarkably homogeneous across countries. Young people tend to read the same sorts of magazines, watch comparable television programmes and wear the same type of clothes. As young people mature, they will carry these similarities in consumer patterns and attitudes into middle and later life.

Another important argument for standardization is that within every country there exist many consumers motivated by identical desires for quality, modernity and value for money in products. For evidence of this, one need only look at the huge successes achieved in Europe by Japanese companies committed to quality, standardization and the global approach. Further factors encouraging standardization include the following:

- New product introductions and turnovers are faster today than at any time in history. Customers are continuously exposed to unfamiliar and novel things, and do not regard as unusual or unacceptable fresh items or promotional messages quite different from those previously experienced.
- The industrial infrastructure of countries increasingly alike, and there are close similarities between national retailing systems. Supermarkets, hypermarkets and shopping precinct layouts are essentially the same in the urban regions of many states.
- Recently developed products normally adhere to internationally recognized technical specifications and thus possess the same characteristics wherever they are sold (eg DVD players, compact discs, microwave ovens, etc). It seems sensible, therefore, to promote these items in a standardized fashion.
- The risk of campaign failure is spread across several markets.
- Economies of scale could emerge from applying the same campaign everywhere. Campaign management can be centralized, and bulk purchase discounts on multi-vehicle advertising space and airtime obtained.
- The firm can adopt a uniform marketing mix (of advertising, PR, consumer research, etc) throughout the world.
- An international corporate image is created.

The standardized approach is often appropriate for advertising technically complex industrial products, as it ensures consistency in image and appeal and enables the targeting of technically minded consumers with very similar interests and educational background. Also the costs of customizing detailed and complicated advertising messages can be prohibitive for technically sophisticated products.

The case for customization

Customization may be essential in consequence of:

- cultural differences between countries and/or market segments within countries;
- language translation difficulties;
- differences in the educational background of target groups in various countries;
- non-availability of certain media (specialist magazines, for instance) in some regions;
- differences in national attitudes towards advertising;
- legal requirements in particular countries.

Alterations may take one or more of the following forms:

- **The use of different media**. For instance, listeners to commercial radio in one country may typically belong to a different socio-economic group from others.

- **Changes in symbols**, eg using a male rather than a female model as the dominant figure in an advertisement. This may be necessary if males are the primary purchasers of the product in some markets and females in others.
- **Changes in advertisement body copy**.
- **Changes in the fundamental selling proposition**. An example here is the presentation of a bicycle as a leisure item in one market, a fashion accessory in another, and a commuting vehicle elsewhere.

Arguments in favour of customization of messages are as follows:

- Consumers in many countries continue to be heavily influenced by national cultural and linguistic traditions.
- There are large variations in living standards between countries.
- Reliance on standardized campaigns arguably leads to promotional messages aimed at the lowest common denominator and hence to bland and uninspiring advertisements that – although they are *acceptable* everywhere – are not outstanding in any particular market. One approach to overcoming this problem is the creation of a substantial number of advertisements in a central organization, leaving local representatives to decide which to run in particular countries.
- The extent and nature of local competition varies from state to state. A certain type of campaign might provoke intense retaliation from competitors in one country but not in others. Competitors' advertisements may be of high quality in some markets but not elsewhere.
- Retailing structures, shopping habits and consumer buying motivations still vary between states for a number of types of product.

The main problem with customization is the extra costs of having to tailor campaigns for various market segments, including translation costs, higher agency fees for foreign work, and the cost of obtaining foreign currency to pay local media.

---

in practice...

Pepsi Cola

Pepsi-Cola is an essentially homogeneous product for which customized national marketing campaigns are typically required. In the United States (the company's base country) and certain other countries, a major thrust of Pepsi's advertising is direct comparison with Coca-Cola, the product's main rival. In many countries, however, comparative advertising is not allowed, so a variety of alternative promotional messages are utilized, eg Pepsi being drunk by women in swimsuits on a hot beach, by men (only) in some Middle Eastern countries, in bars as a supplement/alternative to alcoholic drinks (though not in Islamic countries), or at dances and other social functions. These advertisements are supported by music marketing campaigns based on currently well-known singers in the region concerned (different singers may be used in different countries, possibly singing the same song). Nevertheless, a common theme runs through all Pepsi's advertising messages, namely that Pepsi is youth, fun, the in-thing and the drink of the 'now'-generation.

Standardize or customize?

The degree to which the same message can be successfully applied transnationally depends on whether, in various countries, the product:

- is used in the *same* way;
- satisfies the same *consumer needs*;
- appeals to the *same consumer* type;
- can be sold at *similar* prices;
- is purchased in response to the *same consumer motives* (convenience, status, impulse buying, etc);
- can be advertised in the *same media*;
- is *perceived* by consumers in similar ways (eg technically complicated electrical equipment seen as performing exactly the same function regardless of the customer's location);
- is *evaluated* using similar criteria;
- has just one or two universally intelligible *selling points*;
- is purchased by consumers with *similar income levels*;
- is typically bought by the *same family members* (wives, husbands, parents, etc);
- is demanded in the *same package sizes and quantities*;
- is purchased with the *same frequency* (weekly, monthly, irregularly);
- appeals to similar *cultural traditions*.

Translation of messages

Accurate translation of advertising messages is (obviously) critical, and examples of absurdities arising from bad translation from English into other languages abound. Often, however, it is the implied *concept* underlying a translated message that causes the problem rather than the translated words themselves. Indeed, literal translations can be worse than useless, because the words transcribed may become totally incomprehensible – even ridiculous – when the *context* in which they are used is changed. Hence the translation needs to convert the *thoughts* and *ideas* behind sentences as well as the words themselves.

Translation is made easier if advertisements, sales letters, mail-drop leaflets and so on are drafted in simple English. It follows that colloquialisms, figures of speech, metaphors, technical terms and humorous expressions should always be avoided. The people who put together the initial copy should attempt to *think* in a multilingual way, assuming from the beginning that the material will be translated. Short and simple sentences are preferable to complex statements. The layouts into which copy is to be inserted should be large and open in order to accommodate the extra words sometimes created by translation.

THE INTERNATIONAL ADVERTISING AGENCY

The multinational agency

Confronted with the problems that international advertising involves, many businesses instinctively turn to an advertising agency for advice and practical assistance. Agencies employ or have instant access to expert copywriters, translators, photographers, sales promotion specialists, film-makers, package designers, media planners, market researchers, etc, skilled and experienced in the international field. Only the largest of big businesses can afford to carry such people in-house. Indeed, simply arranging and coordinating the services of these experts as external consultants and suppliers is itself a demanding task. Agencies may be 'full service', meaning that they cover the full spectrum of advertising duties, or specialist (sometimes referred to as à la carte), dealing only with certain aspects of the advertising business, eg media relations, creativity and production, industrial goods advertising, television commercials, or whatever.

Full-service agencies have branch offices throughout the world. They provide clients with 'one-stop shopping' in that they will supply *all* the client's advertising needs (creative design of advertisements, production of literature, media relations, etc) from a single source and allow the client to avoid paying profit margins to the several different links in the advertising chain (copywriters, photographers, printers and so on). Large agencies should already possess extensive stocks of research on foreign markets and buying habits within them. Other advantages enjoyed by large full-service multinational agencies include the facts that:

- Their volume of business means they can afford to pay high salaries to top-calibre staff in specific specialist areas (small companies could rarely justify such expenditure).
- The big multinational agencies frequently employ several people on each function (press releasing, copywriting, etc) so that cross-fertilization of ideas *within* functions can occur.
- They are able to provide simultaneous multi-market coverage and can coordinate campaigns in different markets.
- They possess the financial resources necessary to conduct extensive in-house research into markets, media effectiveness, advertising methods, etc.
- Large agencies have the capacity to design a multi-country campaign *centrally*, thus making for easy communication with and control by the client firm.
- There usually exists a common philosophy and standard working methods within all the subsidiaries of a multinational agency, so that the client firm knows precisely what it will get from the agency's subsidiary in any given country.

- Head office is able to monitor the quality of subsidiaries' work from a central control, hence enabling clients to avoid having independently to appraise the work of several agencies in different countries.
- Cross-fertilization of ideas among subsidiaries should occur (enhanced by regular exchanges of high-calibre creative staff), facilitated by the provision of specialist help and advice from head office.
- There is a central point for collating and analysing all the data on media costs, market conditions, socio-demographic trends, etc, gathered by subsidiaries in various countries.
- Subsidiaries can exchange proven top-quality artwork and TV footage, thus saving large amounts of money that can be passed back to the client.

Foreign local agencies

Despite the diverse and impressive activities of the large multinational agencies, the smaller local agency has survived – indeed prospered – in many countries. Small agencies, moreover, continue to attract significant volumes of work direct from clients in foreign states in addition to the assignments they undertake for local firms. The multinationals have been criticized for being bureaucratic, expensive and immersed in red tape and for having poor communications between offices in different countries, etc. Specific complaints have included the following:

- that the multinationals provide an uneven quality of service in their branches in various states, with high-calibre staff in some local offices and mediocre employees elsewhere;
- allegations of lacklustre performance, absence of fresh ideas, and the production of bland, dull, faceless and stereotypical copy;
- inadequate quality control arising from large agencies simultaneously having to process hundreds of campaigns;
- unwillingness of some large agencies to tailor their services to suit clients' needs, expecting the client company to adapt its campaigns to suit the conventions and organization of the agency;
- lack of attention to small/medium-sized clients from senior agency staff;
- inability to keep to copy production schedules, and requiring long lead times between clients commissioning an agency's services and the agency actually completing the work;
- lack of continuity of the agency personnel who work on a particular client's account caused by high staff turnover rates among the senior creative employees of large multinational agencies.

Advantages of using a local agency include:

- its ability to give a foreign firm a local image;
- potential for close and effective liaison between the agency and local distribution agents and/or other representatives;

- possibly a higher level of effort and commitment on the part of a local agency that needs to offer a better service in order to compete with larger and better known multinational rivals;
- flair and creativity that are sometimes absent in big international agencies.

The decision to use a local agency is easier perhaps for a client with just a single product that is to be advertised in a limited number of countries. Advertisers with multiple brands to be promoted in many countries, conversely, face several difficulties when using local agencies, including for example:

- the complexity of the arrangements that emerge;
- the administrative burden of the agency selection process that has to be undertaken many times;
- the need to communicate with a large number of agencies;
- problems of controlling and appraising the performances of numerous agencies.

Selection criteria

Advertising agencies are not noted for their modesty, and many will claim to possess expertise in all advertising specialisms in all countries in all circumstances at all times. The reality, however, is that each agency is likely to have greater experience and skill in certain fields and regions than elsewhere. It is essential, therefore, to examine carefully a candidate agency's past record, its list of clients, and to take up references.

Key criteria to consider when choosing an agency are the candidates' capacity to handle international programmes, their knowledge of and sensitivity towards cultural factors relevant in particular local markets, their experience of international work (including each agency's record of attracting clients from foreign states), their media evaluation and market research skills, and their creative approach and standards for international campaigns. Another factor relevant to the choice of an agency is the nature of the advertising to be undertaken. Corporate image advertising might be best completed by a single large multinational agency that operates throughout the world via its own subsidiaries. For niche marketing in specialist country sectors a local agency might be preferred. Another factor is type of product. The campaign for an item that is to be presented in a standardized format using the same advertising layouts and messages in all countries might be handled more conveniently by a single multinational agency. Specific questions to ask include the following:

- Does the agency possess an efficient translation service capable of identifying changes in the tone or meaning of an advertisement caused by translation?
- How intimate are the agency's contacts and relations with local media?
- How extensive are the agency's support services, such as advertisement pre-testing or access to mailing lists for direct-marketing exercises?

- In the case of a branch of a multinational agency, how do local staff compare with the agency's staff in the client's home country?
- Is the agency capable of devising an entirely new advertising campaign for the firm's product without having to 'import' ideas about the campaign from the advertisements the firm uses in its home country?
- What is the agency's track record regarding similar products in foreign markets?
- Does the agency offer adequate coverage of target market segments?

For large multinational agencies it is necessary to know:

- The income level and number of employees of each subsidiary in the countries where the client's products are to be advertised. This information is relevant considering the critical role of local subsidiaries in researching markets and implementing programmes.
- How subsidiaries communicate with head office.
- What other types of account are handled from each subsidiary's location.

For smaller agencies, the client should request examples of the discounts it has been able to obtain when purchasing space in local media and when hiring outside specialist services. It is also reasonable to ask for details of the research techniques it uses to collect data (examples of questionnaires designed by the local agency, for instance).

The agency proposal

Candidate agencies will submit proposals that normally include:

- a statement of the agency's perception of the problem that needs to be solved;
- how the agent will approach the job;
- a schedule of intended work;
- details of duties/research to be performed by the agent (and by the client); and
- materials and equipment to be supplied.

A proposed starting date will be specified, plus a price for the job and a schedule of payment. Review points during the campaign should also be suggested. The final choice should depend on the agency's experience, track record, cost, specialist knowledge, innovative and creative ability, and how easily its work can be appraised and controlled.

Organizing international advertising

A firm must decide whether to take all international decisions itself or rely instead on an advertising agency or on inputs provided by local distributors or other representatives. This choice needs to depend on the company's knowledge of advertising agency services in relation to its product, the reliability of advice given by local representatives, and whether local representatives demand active participation in the formulation of advertising strategies. Other criteria are:

- the firm's ability to coordinate diverse promotional activities and control foreign operations;
- whether its administrative system has the capacity to take on additional work;
- how easily it can monitor the consequences of international advertising campaigns;
- the volume of its international sales.

To evaluate the effectiveness of international advertising expenditure the firm must rely on feedback from local distributors (or other representatives) or hire the services of a marketing research agency. Two special difficulties arise: deciding evaluation criteria, given that national markets differ in many fundamental respects and the absence in many regions of research facilities for interviewing message recipients, assessing advertising recall, etc.

Ultimately, of course, the success of all advertising has to be measured against its ability to achieve communications objectives. If awareness has risen, or public perception of the brand has moved in the right direction, the campaign can be counted as a success.

REGULATION OF ADVERTISING

Each country has its own laws on advertising. In Europe, for instance, the use of superlatives is allowable in the United Kingdom, Belgium and Italy, but not in Germany or France (at least not on television). In the Netherlands, use of a superlative has to be backed up by factual evidence. Other practices that might or might not be illegal in particular areas of the world include:

- comparisons of an advertised item with competing products and/or mention of rival firms;
- advertising in foreign languages;
- use of pornography and sexual innuendo;
- advertising of 'health' foods, pharmaceuticals, war toys, alcohol and tobacco;
- use of children as models;
- the creative approaches that may be employed (for example, it is illegal in many countries to instil fear in consumers' minds in order to advertise products);
- the media permitted to carry advertisements and the amounts of advertising allowed in each.

Self-regulatory bodies representing advertisers, advertising agencies and media owners already exist in many countries. Most self-regulatory rules are based on the recommendations of the *International Code of Advertising Practice* issued by the International Chamber of Commerce (ICC). This is an international organization (based in Paris and having offices in 58 countries) formed to represent business interests throughout the world. Its aim is to standardize business practices and promote free international trade. In addition to its Code on Advertising (which first appeared in 1937 and is updated periodically), the Chamber publishes an *International Code on Sales Promotions Practice*, an *International Code on Direct Mail and Mail Order Sales Practice* and an *International Code on Direct Sales Practice*. These documents are intended to help harmonize advertising and direct marketing standards and to champion the cause of 'freedom of business speech and communication' in all countries.

The Code on Advertising is based on the principle that advertisements must be legal (within the legal parameters imposed by nation states), decent (according to prevailing national standards), honest and truthful. Advertising, the Code insists, should be socially responsible and not impair fair competition among businesses. Copy for advertisements must not deliberately mislead consumers regarding the characteristics of advertised products, eg their size, value, quality, ease of use, etc. (For a full explanation of the provisions of this and other Codes, of the cases for and against self-regulation (as opposed to statutory control) and of regulatory frameworks generally see Bennett, 1993b.)

INTERNATIONAL MEDIA PLANNING

International advertisers can purchase media space through advertising agencies, firms specializing in media buying (the so-called 'media independents'), directly from media owners and/or from 'media clubs' owned by advertising agencies. Agencies, independents and media clubs employ skilled and experienced media specialists whose sole job is to negotiate with media owners for the purchase of print space and airtime. Media buyers possess a comprehensive knowledge of available media vehicles (see the Note at the end of this chapter), their characteristics, prices, discount structures, and so on.

in practice...

Carlsberg

The Danish lager producer Carlsberg uses poster advertising extensively for international campaigns, since posters:

- offer a large display area, in colour, and provide language-free creative opportunities;
- can be utilized flexibly in order to support the differing sorts of sales outlets in various national markets;
- may be concentrated in those areas of town containing the largest numbers of potential Carlsberg drinkers;
- have a proven track record of cost-effectiveness for this type of product;
- can be used to supplement television advertising campaigns that, because of cultural and regulatory differences, vary from country to country.

Careful planning of media space purchases is essential for effective implementation of international advertising campaigns. Media planning is a complex and difficult activity requiring a detailed knowledge of international media costs, availabilities, discount possibilities, credit situations, vehicle reaches (see below), coverages, audience penetration, etc. It involves the determination of the best means for delivering, at the lowest available cost-per-thousand prospects, promotional messages to as wide an audience of target customers as possible and scheduling the appearance of advertisements so as to maximize consumer response and/or awareness. This necessitates matching carefully defined target market segments with media vehicles that possess audiences that closely parallel the characteristics of target consumer groups.

The media plan

Key elements in an international media plan include statements of campaign objectives, reach and frequency targets, a customer profile, media weightings (see below), an execution schedule and a budget. Specific issues that have to be addressed include:

- the total number of potential customers to be contacted in order to achieve particular sales/awareness targets in each national market;
- how frequently potential customers in each country must see advertisements before they get the message;
- the precise weeks/months in which advertisements should appear, the media to be used and the geographical areas to be covered;
- how many times a week/month the advertisements need to come out;
- the proportions of the advertising budget to be devoted to each medium and market.

Domestic and international media planning

Major differences between domestic and international media planning are that the latter requires longer lead times, involves high costs and is more complicated than for the home market. Specific international media planning problems include the following:

- Differing definitions of 'circulation', 'readership', etc, in different countries.
- Lack of accurate data on the extensive media overspill found in several states, eg French and Dutch publications sell extensively in Belgium, while there are small German-speaking communities in Belgium, Italy and elsewhere that purchase German newspapers and magazines, etc.
- Differing segmentations of newspaper and magazine markets in different countries – one example is the existence of large-circulation dedicated sports titles in some countries but not elsewhere.
- The enormous number of candidate media vehicles that have to be compared and considered when preparing a plan.
- Absence of reliable information on the number of 'pass alongs' for magazines and other publications in some countries.

Reach and frequency

The 'reach' of a media vehicle is that unduplicated proportion of a target audience exposed to an advertisement at least once during a specified time period, typically four weeks (giving rise to the 'four-week reach' figures quoted by magazines, television companies, etc). 'Frequency' is the average number of times within a pre-specified period (normally four weeks) that each potential customer is exposed to the *same* vehicle or advertisement. Hence, a frequency of two means that consumers on average see or hear the message twice during (say) four weeks.

A vehicle's 'gross rating points' (GRPs) are the result of multiplying its reach by the frequency with which an advertisement appears within the vehicle over a certain period. Hence it contains duplicated exposure, but indicates the 'critical mass' of a media effort. GRPs may be estimated for individual vehicles, for entire classes of media or for a total campaign. What constitutes an appropriate reach/frequency mix depends on the firm's overall marketing objectives, its product and marketing circumstances. High reach is necessary to build brand awareness or for repositioning a product in consumers' minds. A high level of frequency is appropriate when extensive brand awareness already exists. Frequency is useful, moreover, for raising consumers' realization that a campaign is under way.

New product introduction or entry to a fresh market normally requires media with high reach rather than intensive frequency, so that information about the product's availability is made known to the widest audience. High reach is also desirable if sales promotions are to accompany the advertising, in order to inform as many people as possible about special offers included in the campaign. Emphasis on frequency in a limited range of media might be appropriate in narrowly defined markets, or if the advertising firm wishes to avoid head-on confrontations with leading competitors (which a high reach campaign might provoke). Note, however, that in some situations competitors could be influenced the other way: high-frequency advertising could induce rivals to increase their own promotional efforts, whereas ad hoc single advertisements in high-reach vehicles might be ignored. Clearly, great discretion is needed when assessing competitors' likely reactions to a campaign.

Further factors affecting whether reach or frequency should be regarded as the dominant objective include the following:

- **The size and breadth of the area of the target market**. Attempts to capture a geographically small but carefully defined market segment typically require high-frequency advertising. Conversely, markets that are widely dispersed, geographically or demographically, demand high-reach vehicles.
- **The duration of the repurchase cycle**. Products that are frequently purchased require high-frequency advertising to remind consumers to buy. It is useful to know the proportion of customers that repeat their purchases over various time periods (one week, one month, two months, etc).
- **Specific characteristics of the product**. Consider baby products, for example. Consumers buy these regularly for a couple of years, but not at all thereafter (unless

another child arrives). Hence the advertiser's aim is to reach the largest possible proportion of each generation of new parents, eg by having a major high-reach campaign every 18 months. Another example is products the advertisements for which are seen by distributors (including retailers) as well as final consumers. High-reach media may capture the attention of both audiences.

Ideally, a campaign should have both a high frequency and an extensive reach, but constraints on advertising budgets necessarily create the need to trade off frequency against reach. Advertising space in vehicles that reach a large number of consumers (albeit on a single occasion) normally costs more than in vehicles with small audiences, hence reducing the funds available for repeating the advertisement.

Continuity

This means the timing of the appearances of an advertisement during a campaign. Choices are necessary between, on the one hand, a high number of appearances of the advertisement (using small layouts or short broadcast spots per advertisement in order to restrict costs), and, on the other, a small number of short but intensive bursts of more substantial advertising spread in some way over the campaign. The situation where there is no advertising during the periods intervening between big bursts is referred to as 'flighting'. 'Pulsing', conversely, means that the firm undertakes a heavy media effort once a year (say) with regular low-cost advertising between the major expenditures. Factors that should influence the timing of campaigns include:

- customer buying patterns in the country concerned (especially seasonal variations);
- peaks and troughs in competitors' advertising activities (indicating the overall pattern of demand for a product);
- budget constraints, particularly if these impose the need for flighting or pulsing rather than an even spread of advertising through the year;
- planned responses to competitors' predatory campaigns, eg if a competitive parity approach to advertising budgeting (see below) has been adopted;
- reliability of distribution arrangements, so that the availability of adequate supplies of the product can be guaranteed during periods of heavy advertising.

An evenly balanced schedule, with advertisements appearing at short, regular and predetermined intervals, is appropriate for reminder advertising for brands that need constantly to be kept before the consumer. It is also valuable in circumstances where vehicle reach increases steadily with subsequent repetitions of the advertisement. A major benefit of this kind of scheduling is that media vehicles will normally give large discounts on long-term contracts for the bulk purchase of space/time for regular periodic advertising.

Flighting, on the other hand, avoids the costs of advertising in periods likely to prove unproductive, although dangers exist that (substantial) expenditures might occur at the wrong times – with nothing in between. Also, consumers might forget the advertised product between flights! Pulsing is ideal when sharp fluctuations in sales patterns are evident, but is the most expensive of the options.

Weightings

The 'weighting' of a media plan means the balance of media types to be used in order to achieve advertising objectives. This should follow logically from the reach/frequency targets specified in the media plan. Thus, the maximization of reach will probably involve advertising in a wide range of media, whereas the maximization of frequency might require concentrating the firm's advertising into a single medium or vehicle. Factors affecting weighting decisions include the following:

- **The geographical spread of demand**. Large regional variations in sales may indicate the need to buy space in local media in certain areas in order to even out the pattern of demand.
- **Who takes purchasing decisions**. Decisions to buy children's products, for example, derive partly from parental choice and partly from pressure on parents exerted by children. How much should be spent on media seen by parents and how much on vehicles seen exclusively by children? A similar situation applies to consumer durables that require joint family purchasing decisions (motor cars, caravans and household furniture, for instance).
- **The physical characteristics of the product**. Items that benefit from appealing visual presentation (foodstuffs, for example) are heavily advertised in magazines because of the high-quality illustration possible using this medium. Television combines speech and movement and thus is ideal for *demonstrating* the use/consumption of a product. Daily newspapers are an excellent medium for exploiting opportunity markets (cold drinks in hot weather, motor antifreeze in cold periods, etc) where short lead times prior to the appearance of advertisements are required.
- **The product's purchase–repurchase cycle**. Fast-moving goods purchased every few days normally require media that communicate with consumers over the same duration.
- **The degree of attention the potential customer devotes to the medium**. Magazines are usually read more closely than daily newspapers. Radio is a 'background' medium to which listeners frequently pay little attention. If you want consumers to examine an advertisement in detail you need media with an atmosphere conducive to this.
- **Availability of distribution outlets in various markets**. There is little point in concentrating the advertising effort in media that serve markets/geographical areas where distribution is restricted or difficult, eg through advertising a product nationally when it is only available in a handful of major cities. Customers' annoyance at the non-availability of a heavily advertised item can greatly damage the image of a firm.

- **Push/pull considerations**. 'Push' strategies involve persuading distributors (particularly retail outlets) to stock up with the promoted item and hence to 'push' it onto customers. Accordingly there is much trade advertising, a heavy emphasis on explaining the product's appeal, and (importantly) the provision of information concerning special bulk discount and other incentive offers. 'Pull' strategies, conversely, seek to create demand among end-consumers, typically through television, popular newspaper and consumer magazine advertisements and/or sales promotions. Customers then 'pull' the product through the distribution system by demanding its availability in retail outlets. Different media weightings are appropriate for each strategy, although sometimes the differences between push and pull situations cannot be easily discerned, eg when advertisements aimed at final consumers are also seen by and influence distributors. Also the distinctions between 'trade' and 'consumer' publications may be unclear. In general, however, the better known to final consumers are the advertising company's existing brands, then the greater the chance that a pull strategy will succeed. Note the implications of the choice of a push or pull approach for campaign costs, since trade media rates are invariably lower than for end-consumer advertising (though consumer rates normally work out lower on a 'cost-per-thousand consumers exposed to the advertisement' basis).
- **Message content**. Advertisements intended to remind the consumer to buy the product require media that possess a high frequency of message repetition. Messages intended to influence the largest possible audience in the shortest time need different media types.
- **Likely responses of local competitors**. The use of certain media will inform local rivals about the firm's promotional efforts as they occur, inviting competitors to respond in appropriate ways. Other media (carefully targeted mail-drops for instance) are more discreet, and local businesses are not instantly aware of the advertising company's activities.

Assorted versus concentrated media

Using a wide range of media types within and across countries (ie the 'assorted' approach to media selection) has a number of advantages:

- It spreads the risk of certain media not performing as well as anticipated.
- There are 'carryover' effects on consumers, who see the product advertised in several places and might in consequence be persuaded to buy.
- Messages can be varied from one medium/vehicle to the next so as to make them appeal to different groups of consumers.
- A prospective customer who is not impressed by an advertisement in one medium may notice it elsewhere.
- Total reach will almost certainly be greater than occurs when using a single medium.

A concentration strategy, conversely, devotes the entire budget to just one type of medium. This allows the advertiser to direct maximum effort towards influencing a specific audience segment. Also it could enable the advertiser to dominate particular vehicles (to the detriment of competitors) for limited periods. Customers and distributors may be impressed at seeing so many advertisements for the product in the one medium, and large discounts could be available through bulk purchasing space/time in certain vehicles.

THE ADVERTISING BUDGET

There are two basic approaches to fixing the total international media budget. One is to ask 'how much do we need to spend?'; the other is to examine 'what can we afford?'

What do we need to spend?

Three methods are available here: the 'operational' approach (sometimes referred to as the 'objective and task' technique); the 'competitive parity' ('me-too') approach; and the 'responsibility accounting' method.

The competitive parity approach

This involves estimating and duplicating the amounts spent on advertising by major rivals. Unfortunately, monitoring the marketing expenditure of foreign-based competitors is far harder than monitoring home-country businesses – whose financial accounts (if they are limited companies) are open to public inspection and whose promotional activities are obvious the moment they occur. Use of the method assumes, of course, that competitors know what they are doing in relation to their advertising activities – which may not be the case. Also, competitors' overall marketing goals might be completely different from the aims of the firm in question.

The operational approach

An extensive and detailed investigation is conducted to establish all the tasks necessary to achieve pre-specified advertising goals (see above). The cost of each activity is estimated, costs are aggregated under various departmental headings and budgets are allocated accordingly. Problems attached to the application of this approach internationally are that:

- Objectives are typically less concrete for foreign than for domestic operations (on account of limited experience of local conditions and possibilities).
- It is not known a priori how much expenditure will be necessary to attain each objective.

- Targets set might not be realistic.
- Local market conditions may change unexpectedly, causing the need for a complete revision of advertising objectives.

The responsibility accounting approach

Individual managers are asked how much they need to spend in order to complete predetermined advertising tasks (reach a new market segment, persuade customers to accept a big price rise, etc). Resources are then distributed and the managers concerned assume personal responsibility for administering the resulting budgets. This method is harder to apply to international than to domestic advertising because:

- The people responsible for actually implementing advertising policies may be based abroad and hence difficult to inspect and appraise.
- A local representative's perception of the resources needed to achieve certain advertising targets may be quite different from those of someone in the advertising firm's home country.
- Delays in reporting information could make it difficult to establish whether advertising money is being well spent.

in practice...

Batchelor's Soups and Guinness

The two best documented instances of the relationship between advertising expenditures and sales are perhaps those of Batchelor's Soups and Guinness, both of which withdrew entirely from all forms of advertising for a significant period (Guinness in the late 1920s and Batchelor's in the 1950s). The consequence in each case was a significant upsurge in short-term profits (due to zero spending on promotion, while sales remained intact) followed by a steady decline in market share and eventual collapses in levels of sales, thus creating the need for extensive advertising in order to rescue the companies. Overall profits for both firms declined when measured over a five-year period incorporating the termination of advertising.

What can we afford

Budgeting techniques that address this question link advertising expenditure directly to some measure of profits or, more commonly, to sales. The most popular of these methods is the 'percentage of sales method', whereby the firm automatically allocates a fixed percentage of the value of its (say) quarterly sales of each of its products to advertising those products. It is assumed that increasing sales require additional advertising to sustain them. There are a number of advantages to the technique:

- It guarantees that the firm only spends on advertising as much as it can afford.
- Advertising effort becomes 'market led' in that resources are channelled primarily towards products that have genuine market appeal and which, therefore, are likely to do even better in the future. The percentage of sales approach prevents 'good money being thrown after bad'. Each product is given the advertising it deserves.
- Expanding markets are automatically developed.
- Periods of exceptionally high sales create windfall income that can be used to experiment with new media, fresh creative strategies and high-risk avant-garde approaches that otherwise could never be considered. A single successful experiment might lead to a promotional breakthrough with enormous long-term benefits for the advertising firm.

This method is particularly suitable for low-cost, high-price (and hence relatively lower sales levels) items, since here there is a large margin available for advertising, which should of course boost sales. The main disadvantage of the approach is that it ignores the possibility that extra spending on advertising may in fact be necessary when sales are declining in order to reverse the trend. Other problems are that:

- The technique cannot be used to launch new products or to enter fresh markets.
- Advertising costs can differ significantly from country to country, so that a greater level of expenditure may be needed to achieve a given level of performance in some markets than in others.
- The method's convenience and simplicity encourages management not to bother investigating the relationships between advertising and sales or to analyse critically the overall effectiveness of its advertising campaigns.

Choice of method

There are no simple criteria to apply when selecting a budgeting technique. It may be possible, however, to group together those foreign markets that exhibit similar characteristics in relation to advertising (importance of certain media, size of market segments, rules and regulations, media costs, etc) and apply an intuitively appropriate method to each group. If advertising in one group performs better than elsewhere the reason for this can then be analysed and applied to other markets. In choosing a budgeting method it may be useful to consider the following factors:

- **Marketing objectives**. Expanding a large existing market share usually requires far higher advertising expenditure than increasing a small share of the market. Advertising to narrowly defined market segments generally needs less resources than tackling broadly based consumer groups. The percentage of sales technique might be best in either of these situations.
- **Current market position**. The less satisfactory the current situation, the less useful is the simple percentage of sales approach.

- **Possible reactions of competitors**. Soaring sales accompanied by constantly increasing advertising could provoke competitors into an 'advertising war' not intended by the firm in question. The percentage of sales approach should not be used if this might happen.

Country allocations

Logical criteria are needed to determine which countries should be allocated the most amounts of advertising money. Basic considerations here include:

- the number of important, separate and independent market segments in each country;
- media costs per thousand prospects reached in various markets;
- intensity of local competitors' advertising;
- market share and the product's whereabouts in its life cycle in each country.

Brand and product development indexes

The brand development index (BDI) is a common and valuable indicator for deciding which markets should receive most advertising expenditure. Consider, for example, the problem of deciding how much of a firm's total European Union advertising budget should be devoted to a particular EU country. In this case the BDI is defined as:

$$\frac{\% \text{ of a brand's total EU sales in country X}}{\% \text{ of total EU population in country X}}$$

If, for example, 4 per cent of total EU sales are in Denmark (which has 5.1/342 = 1.5% of the Union's population), the BDI is:

$$\frac{4}{1.5} \times 100 = 267$$

suggesting high sales penetration in the Danish market.

   If the data is available it is useful to compare this number with the 'product category development index' (PCDI) for the total sales of the category of product to which the particular brand belongs. For the previous example the product category development index is given by:

$$\frac{\% \text{ of a product category's total EU sales in country X}}{\% \text{ of total EU population in country X}}$$

To illustrate this, suppose that a manufacturer of ink has figures on aggregate national expenditure on ink in each EU country. Assume that 1 per cent of total EC sales of ink occur in Denmark, so that the product development index is:

$$\frac{1}{1.5} \times 100 = 67$$

which indicates a relatively weak market for ink in this country.

Comparison of brand and product category development indexes tells the supplier how well its output is selling relative to market potential. A high brand development index in conjunction with a low product category development index implies a successful brand campaign in a weak market, and vice versa for high PCDI/low BDI. If both indexes are high, then the brand is doing well in a buoyant and competitive market. Low PCDI combined with low BDI suggests a poor market in normal circumstances. Clearly the analysis can be undertaken for any country in the world in relation to a particular regional grouping: Latin America, Eastern Europe, Africa, etc.

Note
Media such as television, newspapers, direct mail, etc, deliver advertisements, whereas 'vehicles' carry particular advertisements within each media category. Magazines, for example, are a medium, while individual magazine titles represent vehicles within the medium.

15

Below-the-line marketing communication

Below-the-line communications refers to anything that is not advertising. It encompasses public relations, corporate branding, and any other activities that do not involve a paid insertion of a message in an advertising medium. Below-the-line communications involve considerably more subtlety than advertising messages, so in the international context they present difficulties of their own.

INTERNATIONAL PUBLIC RELATIONS

Public relations (PR) concerns the creation and maintenance of goodwill. Note, however, that goodwill from some 'audiences' (consumers or governments, for instance) is more important than from others (eg competing businesses). Hence it is necessary for a firm to define the various 'publics' it needs to influence and the messages to which these publics will most favourably respond; and to decide how best to reach target groups (see Black, 1993, for a discussion of these matters). This may involve research into how the firm and its operations and products are perceived by outsiders and into the media seen most often by the company's leading publics (eg which newspapers are read by the people it most needs to influence). The objectives of an international PR campaign might be to:

- establish a brand image in foreign countries;
- create awareness among the general public of the existence of the enterprise;

- overcome prejudice against use of the product (religious or cultural prejudices for example);
- increase the number of enquiries;
- improve the ratio of enquiries to sales;
- reduce selling costs, especially the costs of distribution and/or of using sales people 'in the field';
- achieve a higher profile in the local press and on local television;
- minimize the damage due to the company's image following an accident or other disaster in which the company was involved.

Public relations techniques include the preparation of news releases, measures to attract the attention of television and radio companies, sponsorship and attendance at exhibitions. Other PR activities involve lobbying local and national politicians, opinion leaders and key pressure groups, and staging 'events' such as visits by celebrities, publicity stunts, competitions, etc.

in practice...

Banque Paribas

The Banque Paribas sponsors a variety of artistic and cultural activities in disparate countries and is typical of many other international businesses in that it adopts a customized approach to its local sponsorship operations. A major reason for the local customization of sponsorship activities is the difference in sponsorship traditions that exists between countries. In some countries (especially the United Kingdom, Ireland and Benelux), sponsorship is viewed as an integral component of the commercial marketing mix, driven by business needs with sponsors waiting to see tangible financial results from their investments. Arts sponsorship can indeed be used to increase sales, although not for every branded product. Hence sponsorship of niche rather than mass market products is most appropriate in countries where the commercial approach is paramount. Sports sponsorship, conversely, could be applied to the mass market. In certain other countries sponsorship by business has its roots in the philanthropic tradition. This is very true in France, and to some extent in Spain, Italy, Germany and Scandinavia. Money is given to the arts in these countries because the arts are perceived as worthwhile, not just to secure a return on investment.

Sponsorship based on the philanthropic approach is likely to be long-term in nature, in contrast with marketing-orientated strategies that normally are subject to constant review, and as such likely to take on short-term perspectives. A third model of arts sponsorship that has developed during recent years is founded on the supposition that companies have a civic responsibility to fund community services. The primary motivation here is that of 'enlightened self-interest': businesses benefit in the longer term via the creation of sound, more vibrant, and economically and culturally stable communities.

Increasingly, PR is seen as a major form of below-the-line promotion (see Note 1 at the end of this chapter) in all the world's main economic regions. Europe's PR industry is more than double the size of that of Japan but is still only a quarter the size of that of the United States, so there is obviously scope for further expansion (Hollis, 1994). A number of factors have contributed to the increased demand for PR services in industrialized countries, as follows:

- PR's ability to target precise groups of people whose attitudes are crucial for the well-being of the company. This can be done far more inexpensively than through general advertising, which reaches large numbers of individuals who are not remotely interested in the firm or its product.
- Large-scale privatization programmes in many countries (which boost the demand for investor, employee and consumer PR services). Mergers and acquisitions among companies also give rise to PR activity.
- Escalating costs of above-the-line advertising media in many countries.
- The general increase in demand for promotional services that has accompanied the continuing liberalization of world trade. Firms engaged in cross-border transactions need to establish favourable corporate images in foreign markets.
- Increasing expertise and standards within international public relations consultancies.
- The desire of increasing numbers of international companies to be seen as 'environmentally friendly', as a result of the huge rise in environment-related business opportunities currently occurring in many regions.
- The development of equity markets and wider share ownership in several countries not previously possessing a stock exchange, leading to increased demand for PR assistance with investor relations.
- The high cost of the damaging consequences of bad publicity, eg following catastrophes involving a firm's products or operations.

Structure of the industry

Help with public relations is available from three sources: special PR consultancies, the PR departments of the big advertising agencies, or from 'marketing communications' consultancy firms. The large PR firms are 'full-service' and undertake the complete range of PR functions: media relations, copywriting, events, political lobbying, news releases and so on. Large advertising agencies provide comparable PR services. Marketing communications consultancies see PR as part of the wider marketing communication field (which includes package design, display of products, merchandising, etc) and thus offer an integrated package of communications activities, including:

- media relations – press releases, seminars, briefing sessions for journalists;
- preparation of in-house leaflets, pamphlets and other copy, and the illustration and printing of such literature;

- obtaining publicity through devising newsworthy publicity stunts;
- communications audits, including checking the adequacy of existing investor and employee relations and suggesting improvements in these;
- media training – how to be interviewed on radio and television, how to answer journalists' questions;
- speech-writing for company executives who have to make important presentations to eternal audiences.

INTERNATIONAL DIRECT MARKETING

Direct marketing covers direct mail, telephone selling, catalogues and 'off-the-page' selling via cut-outs in newspaper and magazine advertisements, and is increasingly important as a selling medium throughout the world, especially in Western Europe and the United States (Baines, 1992). Indeed, the European Commission estimates that direct marketing today accounts for about a quarter of all commercial communication expenditure occurring within the EU. In the United States, direct marketing is the third largest marketing communications medium, after newspapers and TV. It is the case in all countries that a small number of product sectors dominate the industry's turnover, notably insurance and financial services, consumer durables, foodstuffs, credit cards and business-to-business promotions.

Printed direct marketing covers leaflets and circulars delivered door to door plus newspapers and magazine advertisements containing customer order forms or which invite customers to write or telephone to place an order. Telemarketing is today used both for consumer and business-to-business campaigns throughout the industrialized world. The telephone can be used both to obtain orders and to conduct fast low-cost market research. Telemarketing covers cold calling by sales people, market surveys conducted by telephone, calls designed to compile databases of possible sales prospects and follow-ups to customer requests for further information resulting from print and broadcast advertisements. Currently, the majority of cross-border telemarketing campaigns focus on business-to-business contacts, essentially because of the combined telephone/fax/telex/database facilities that an increasing number of companies possess and, in consequence, the greater reliability of business-to-business communications.

The administration of international telemarketing normally requires the use of a commercial telemarketing agency. Language skills are required, plus considerable skills and experience in identifying decision-makers in target firms.

Note that telemarketing agencies can be engaged to receive the incoming calls resulting from a multi-country 0800 number mail-drop campaign. Switchboard operators taking such calls have to be competent to respond in any of the languages involved and then to pass the call to someone sufficiently au fait with the caller's language to be able to follow up the enquiry. The major telemarketing agencies now have transnational arrangements enabling the local country processing of incoming calls.

Growth of direct marketing

Like sales promotions (see below), direct marketing campaigns have readily measurable outcomes and may be linked to wider marketing goals. It is a convenient and effective marketing tool: consumers' names and addresses may be easily assembled for repeated direct marketing use and perhaps sold to other parties. Importantly, profiles of particular customers can be built up using information from the firm's accounting and sales files in conjunction with data about their neighbourhoods, businesses (where appropriate) or socio-demographic characteristics. Other factors encouraging the rapid expansion of the international direct marketing industry include:

- development in mailing technology that have reduced the costs of distributing direct-mail literature;
- escalating costs of other forms of advertising and sales promotion in many states;
- the increasing availability of good-quality lists of prospective customers;
- developments in information technology (especially database technology and desktop publishing), which enable smaller companies to produce high-quality direct marketing materials in-house;
- the increasing availability throughout the developed world of interactive television facilities whereby consumers may order goods through a teletext system.

Direct mail

Direct mail offers a flexible, selective and potentially highly cost-effective means for reaching foreign consumers. Messages can be addressed exclusively to a target market, advertising budgets may be concentrated on the most promising market segments, and it will be some time before competitors realize that the firm has launched a campaign. Also the size, content, timing and geographical coverage of mailshots can be varied at will: the firm can spend as much or as little as necessary to achieve its objectives. There are no media space or airtime restrictions and no copy or insertion deadlines to be met. It is hardly surprising, therefore, that direct-mail activity is buoyant throughout the world. All aspects of the direct-mail process are subject to the firm's immediate control, and it can experiment by varying the approach used in different countries.

Direct mail is personal and selective, useful for informing customers of special discounts, credit packages, maintenance agreements, etc, and versatile since a variety of items and information can be included in the envelope, including any one of a number of possible response mechanisms. Freefone telephone facilities are available in most countries, and it is possible to quote an international 0800 freefone telephone number so that customers can ring free of charge in response to direct mail and other advertising campaigns. Further reasons for the industry's expansion include the increased number of independent households in many countries resulting from falling birth rates, higher divorce rates and increasing longevity, and fresh possibilities for the identification of distinct market segments among various types of family group.

It appears, moreover, that direct mail is also the fastest growing medium for business-to-business advertising. According to Royal Mail International (RMI), two-thirds of Danish companies, three-quarters of German companies and half of all Spanish companies use direct mail for business-to-business campaigns (RMI, 1994). Effective use of direct mail for business-to-business purposes requires the preparation of an accurate customer profile, including industry SIC, size of target company (measured, for example, by turnover, number of employees or market share), the people to approach in each business (purchasing officer, project development engineer, product manager etc), industry purchasing procedures and (where known) supplier selection criteria and the buying motives of prospective customers.

in practice...

Papermate

Around 150 billion pencils are purchased in Western Europe each year. The Gillette Papermate is an Italian 'non-stop' pencil designed for use in large firms that use large numbers of pencils. To introduce the product a mailshot was organized specifying:

- named chief executives;
- the 'Secretary to the CEO';
- the 'purchasing officer' in firms known to be big purchasers of office stationery.

The latter information was obtained from a database of office equipment buyers. Major stationery suppliers and distributors were also targeted. Each mail-drop contained a free sample, a high-quality reproduction full-colour illustrated letter in the national language of the relevant country, and a questionnaire offering incentives to recipients completing and returning it. The letters to the secretaries were written in shorthand. About 10 per cent of the questionnaires were returned. Key objectives of the (highly successful) campaign were to familiarize major users with a novel product, to 'push' initial sales through distributors, and to provide a basis for follow-up visits by sales people.

in practice...

Land Rover

A good example of the use of direct mail to sell a global brand is the firm Land Rover, which emphasizes the 'Englishness' of its product in its mailings throughout the world (even to the extent of insisting that English postage stamps appear on the envelopes carrying promotional materials). The image projected in foreign countries (which take 70 per cent of the firm's output) is that of

Land Rover vehicles being as English as Buckingham Palace, red telephone boxes, cucumber sandwiches, cricket on the village green and so on. This perceived Englishness is reinforced in all the company's promotional campaigns.

Mailings are based on a centralized international database linked by telephone and satellite to dealers in around 100 countries. Information gathered through the system is highly detailed and enables Land Rover to send, for example, a birthday card to a current or prospective owner, or information on new models and discount opportunities to existing owners at just the time they are likely to be thinking about trading in their current vehicle. Conversion rates have been high, reaching 8 per cent in some places. Indeed, a 'P G Wodehouse' style of language (suitably translated) is sometimes used in mailshot literature.

List broking

Commercial list brokers operate in all major trading countries. Information on list sourcing is available from national direct marketing associations and, in Europe, from the European Direct Marketing Association (EDMA), which operates a (chargeable) international list search and coordination service. List broking is expanding particularly rapidly in France, the Netherlands and Italy. Europe's worst countries for list availability are Spain, Portugal and Greece.

List brokers take their profits by charging commissions to list owners (the standard international rate is 20 per cent), so that they can offer their services to clients either free of charge or at low cost (depending on the amount of work involved).

Data protection legislation

This varies enormously from country to country. It is stringent in northern Europe and lax in Africa and the Far East. US laws on the matter differ between states (California has the strictest regulations). Important national differences relate to the following:

- Data collection methods – for example, in the Netherlands these must be 'lawful', whereas under British legislation they must be 'fair' as well as lawful. In France they must 'not be intended to deceive'.
- Whether and for how long personal data may be stored – this is severely restricted in, for instance, Denmark and Germany, but not at all in the United Kingdom or France.
- Whether the holding of personal data has to be registered with a central authority.

In Europe there is an EU Draft Directive on Data Protection intended to harmonize national data protection legislation and 'ensure the free and unfettered flow of data within the EU'. Under the proposals, data subjects (consumers) will have to give their express permission for the use by firms of data about them. The onus will be on businesses to seek the consent of data subjects and to provide them with full details of all intended disclosures. Paper records as well as computerized records will be subject to control (at present paper records are exempt from the Data Protection Acts of several EU countries) and, importantly, the profiling of consumers (ie deliberately collecting information on several dimensions of the lifestyles and activities of target groups) will be severely restricted (illegal in certain circumstances). The transfer of data to countries outside the EU that do not have equally stringent data protection laws will be forbidden, and blanket list swapping between organizations will not be allowed. Even if a data subject gives permission for their details to be used, that person will have to be notified the first time the data is passed on to a third party.

It seems that the only mailings that will be lawful under the proposed legislation will be (costly) untargeted mass mailings to names and addresses taken at random from public sources (telephone directories, electoral registers, etc). This will greatly expand the volume of junk mail distributed to consumers, as well as increasing advertisers' costs.

Robinson lists

Mailing preference schemes ('Robinson lists'), whereby individuals may register with a national list of people not wishing to receive direct mail literature, operate in the United States, Australia, Japan, Belgium, France, the United Kingdom, Germany, the Netherlands and many other countries. Usually they are operated by the direct marketing industries of the countries concerned on a voluntary basis and do not have the force of law.

INTERNATIONAL RELATIONSHIP MARKETING

Relationship marketing (RM) is an approach to marketing that seeks to establish long-term relationships with customers based on trust and mutual cooperation. It involves the establishment (where possible) of personal contacts and bonds between the customer and the firm's representatives; the eventual emergence of feelings within each party of mutual obligation, of having common goals, and of involvement with and empathy for the other side; and the integration of all the firm's activities (not just those of a marketing department) concerned with customer care (Bennett, 1996). Relationship marketing contrasts with conventional 'transactional' marketing, which has short-time horizons and focuses on securing a single sale. With transactional marketing there is limited customer contact and little emphasis on customer service. Quality is seen as a matter to be dealt with by the firm's production department rather than something that should concern the entire organization (Christopher *et al*, 1991).

Techniques of relationship marketing include the extensive provision of information on the firm and its products, personalization of communications with customers, free gifts and samples, attractive premium offers, and the careful monitoring of the relationship formed with particular customers. More fundamentally, RM is characterized by total commitment to customer care, openness, genuine concern for the delivery of high-quality goods and services, responsiveness to customer suggestions, fair dealing, and (crucially) the willingness to sacrifice short-term advantage for long-term gain. Suppliers attempt to create and strengthen lasting bonds with their customers; they shift from attempting to maximize profits on each *individual* transaction towards the establishment of solid, dependable and, above all permanent relationships with the people they serve. Customers are seen as partners in the marketing process, not as individuals to be influenced simply in order to make a one-time sale.

Repeat orders from existing clientele are much more profitable to the firm than new business, because there is no need to spend money on advertising, visits by sales people, etc. The practical implementation of RM has been greatly facilitated by recent developments in information technology that enable firms to hold large databases containing extensive personalized details of individual consumers. This has enabled suppliers to customize and target their promotions more precisely using differentiated messages based on known *individuals* in their own right. Technological breakthroughs have occurred regarding database capacity, interconnectivity, enquiry language and operational efficiency. Further reasons for current interest in RM include:

- the expansion of the Internet and the possibilities for direct interaction with geographically remote foreign customers that it provides;
- the huge expansion of international direct marketing that has occurred in recent years;
- higher customer expectations in relation to levels of service;
- the example of the successes achieved by large Japanese companies that place great emphasis on long-term commitment to customers and suppliers, on total quality management, and which pay meticulous attention to customer care;
- more extensive consumer protection legislation (eg on product liability, unfair contract terms, etc) throughout the world.

Closer relations between suppliers and customers (especially business customers, as opposed to end-consumers) have led to the proposition that many marketing situations can be analysed in terms of the theory of networks. A marketing network comprises a supplying company and other firms with which it has built a solid, reliable, long-term business relationship. The latter businesses may be customers, further organizations with which it has established links to provide mutual assistance and support (for example, a joint venture for distributing several firms' products), the company's own input suppliers, licensees or subcontractors, or partners in new product research and development. Within networks flows of *information* occur as well as exchanges of money and goods. Social interactions among the various parties can also influence outcomes.

INTERNATIONAL SALES PROMOTIONS

Carefully used sales promotions (see Note 2 at the end of this chapter) can be an extremely effective tool for marketing in foreign countries. They can be used to stimulate impulse purchasing, encourage consumer loyalty, shift slow-moving stock, increase the frequency of repeat buying, smooth out seasonal demand, and generally draw attention to the firm and its products. Company expenditure on sales promotions has grown rapidly throughout the world. In Europe, for example, the European Commission estimates that the rate of growth of spending on sales promotions doubled that for conventional advertising throughout the period 1991–94. Factors contributing to the expansion of sales promotion activities include:

- greater competition among retailers, combined with increasingly sophisticated retailing methods;
- higher levels of brand awareness among consumers, leading to the need for manufacturers to defend brand share;
- improved retail technology, eg electronic scanning devices that enable coupon redemptions, etc to be monitored instantly;
- greater integration of sales promotions, public relations and conventional media campaigns.

in practice...

Lea and Perrins

The Worcestershire sauce produced by Lea and Perrins sells in more than 130 countries. It is a homogeneous product made to a 150-year-old secret recipe. In order to strengthen its position in the European Single Market the company sought to devise a pan-European below-the-line promotional vehicle that would at once:

- stimulate point-of-sale impulse purchases;
- highlight the inherent versatility of the product;
- provide a means for coupon response;
- encourage mail-ins;
- generally induce higher sales.

The company's sales promotions advisor, AM-C London, came up with the idea of an international recipe book containing 'standard' recipes plus a number of specialist recipes appropriate for the culture of the particular country in which the book was distributed. Hence a 32-page full-colour book was produced in seven different languages. A variety of methods was used to distribute the book, depending on consumer preferences in the local market. In Italy and Spain, for example, the campaign focused on coupon response, in Denmark the book was sold at a low price in-store, while in Germany and the Netherlands the product carried a bottle 'neck-collar' that could be redeemed against the book either free or for a nominal charge.

Problems with international sales promotions

The basic difficulty for firms engaged in international marketing and wishing to employ sales promotion techniques in different countries is that disparate (and sometimes conflicting) laws apply in each state. For instance, a money-off voucher is legal in Spain but not in Germany; a 'lower price for the next purchase' offer is legal in Belgium, illegal in Denmark and could be illegal in Italy; cross-product offers (buy one item and get a big price reduction on something else) are illegal in Luxembourg, and free draws are illegal in the Netherlands. Coupons and door-to-door free samples cannot be used as easily in France as in most other states, while in Germany and certain other countries free gifts and premiums are forbidden if they constitute a genuine incentive to buy. The justification for banning free gifts is that they could represent unfair competition, ie their distribution can be interpreted as a form of 'dumping', undertaken merely to force rival companies into liquidation. Further criticisms of the use of sales promotions suggested by the representatives of governments that severely restrict or ban them are as follows:

- The true value of the promoted item is concealed, since consumers are improperly influenced (arguably misled) by the special offer (free gift, money-off voucher, entry to a competition, or whatever) accompanying the sale.
- Consumers cannot meaningfully compare the prices of similar competing goods because of the distortions and distractions that sales promotions introduce.
- Promotions encourage consumers to make unwise purchasing decisions, since they stimulate impulse buying, while deterring the critical and objective evaluation of the real worth of an offered product. The normal processes whereby consumers rationally relate quality to price are deliberately disrupted.
- Large firms that possess the resources necessary to plan and implement extensive sales promotion campaigns enjoy an inequitable advantage over smaller rivals. Competition between large and small businesses should be based (so the argument goes) solely on the quality and value for money of the principal product. Sweepstakes and lotteries are frequently singled out for particular censure in that they are said:
  - to encourage gambling;
  - to inculcate undesirable moral values in consumers' minds; and
  - deliberately to mislead the public (on the grounds that entry can never in fact be 'free' – the stake is necessarily embodied in the higher price paid for the promoted item).

The counter-argument to all these points is, of course, that in a free economy consumers are at liberty to decide for themselves whether or not to purchase products accompanied by premium offers, coupons, entry to competitions and so on. Increases in sales consequent to vigorous sales promotions can lead to unit cost reductions rather than price increases, and the intelligent use of promotions by small businesses can enable them to compete effectively against larger firms.

BUSINESS-TO-BUSINESS CAMPAIGNS

Business customers are usually far more discerning in their choice of products and supplying organization than are end-consumers. Usually they will investigate alternative items extremely carefully, and will establish rational criteria for their purchasing decisions. Thus, it is not surprising that business buyers tend to be avid readers of business, trade and technical magazines, the advertisements in which are likely to be scrutinized closely. Also, business-to-business (B2B) customers are less susceptible to emotive appeals than private individuals (they are accountable for their purchasing decisions to higher levels of management within their own organization), so that advertisements for B2B items typically need to involve a more technical and information-orientated approach than do advertisements for consumer goods. This is not to say that image advertising is unimportant, only that image creation has to be a *complement* to, rather than a substitute for, the provision of hard information. Such considerations have several consequences for international business-to-business advertising:

- The rational and objective approach to purchasing typically exhibited by B2B buyers means that their purchasing behaviour is essentially similar in all countries. Cultural differences between countries are far less important than for the marketing of consumer products. An automotive engineer (say) in Denmark will have purchasing motives comparable to those of automotive engineers in Germany or France. Moreover, the organizational climate of their employing companies is likely to be the same. Hence standardized approaches to advertising are often appropriate in the B2B field.
- There is a need for scrupulous attention to the detail of the translation of trade advertisements.
- Promotional messages should make it easy for buyers to establish logical criteria upon which to base purchasing decisions.
- It could be unwise to indicate a product's country of origin in the initial advertisement, since industrial buyers are usually looking for considerably more extensive after-sales service and customer support (possibly including training in the use of equipment) than the typical consumer goods purchaser. Creation of 'foreign' images for industrial products could evoke perceptions of potential unreliability, difficulties in obtaining spare parts, maintenance problems, etc, among B2B customers. Note that the availability and cost of customer back-up services (especially maintenance agreements) is often the determining factor in a B2B purchasing decision.
- Although trade journals are seemingly the ideal medium for business-to-business advertisements, great care is needed when selecting the trade journals to use in view of the lack of reliable circulation, readership and reach data for trade publications in many countries. (Professional and general management magazines might be more cost effective as they attract blanket business readership.)
- The size of the markets for certain types of industrial goods is likely to be small compared to markets for consumer products. Hence the precise targeting of market segments and careful choice of media vehicles is essential.

EXHIBITING

Trade fairs and exhibitions are among the oldest forms of promoting goods internationally (some European trade fairs trace their origins back to the fourteenth century), and no business-to-business advertiser can afford to ignore their potential. Exhibiting can enable a company to reach in a few days a concentrated group of interested prospects that might otherwise take several months to contact. The cost of exhibiting, moreover, is low compared to protracted above-the-line advertising. Exhibitions are especially useful for introducing new products to a market, since it is possible to obtain the initial reactions to new products of knowledgeable and attentive consumers, distributors, competitors, potential agents and other interested parties. Analysis of these first responses can be extremely valuable for deciding whether product modifications are necessary and/or how a full promotional campaign should proceed. Further advantages to exhibiting are that:

- Orders might be obtained on the spot.
- Small foreign firms without an extensive sales force have the opportunity to present their output to large buying companies on the same face-to-face basis as large local rivals.
- The acceptability of the product to local customers can be immediately assessed.
- The calibre of the competition can be estimated.
- Visitors' names and addresses may be used for subsequent mail-drops.
- Agents and distributors of the firm's type of product will be among the visitors.
- Although many technical specialists and company executives refuse to see or take telephone calls from outsiders who try to sell them things at their places of work, these same managers often do attend trade exhibitions. The customer goes to the exhibition in order to see the seller, and not vice versa.
- Products can actually be demonstrated in use in a wide range of specially created environmental situations.
- Customers attend trade fairs in a relaxed and receptive frame of mind. In certain industries a major annual trade fair effectively marks the beginning of a new sales year, with all competing businesses introducing their new models and product features at the one event.
- The majority of sales leads originating from exhibitions will be new ones, while existing customers are given the opportunity to communicate directly with the supplying firm.

Exhibiting plays an especially valuable role in promoting industrial goods in fields where there is much technical innovation, with new product features appearing at a rapid rate. Company buyers can examine and compare the outputs of competing firms in a short period at the same place. They can see the latest developments, and establish immediate contact with supplying businesses.

Local customer awareness of the firm's intended presence at an exhibition can be built up via advertisements in appropriate trade journals and/or by mailshots to selected firms. For introductions of completely new products it may be possible to attract advance publicity through press releases issued to local newspapers and magazines.

Thyssen

A successful exhibition stand does not necessarily have to be located within the main hall of an international exhibition. In 1995, the large German international group Thyssen created a telecommunications subsidiary, Thyssen Telecom, which it was keen to promote at the Telecom '95 exhibition in Geneva. These annual exhibitions are the telecommunication industry's largest event and attract much international attention (the 1995 exhibition was opened by Nelson Mandela). Hence space is booked long in advance, and no room could be found at short notice for Thyssen. Accordingly the firm's exhibition planning advisor, Park Avenue, arranged for the erection of a temporary structure alongside the main exhibition site. This structure had the substance and 'look' of a permanent building, as the aim of the exercise was to present Thyssen Telecom as a major force in the market. Hence it was felt that a large tent would not have created an appropriate image. The pavilion was constructed in only 10 days although it was fully air-conditioned and had a restaurant and full office facilities including a switchboard, ISDN lines and satellite communication systems, meeting areas, and a boardroom. Glass and steel figured prominently in the design of the building, emphasizing the company's heritage in steel and engineering. Four giant windows contained outward-facing video walls plus 30 video monitors featuring company promotional material. Two high-tech sculptures flanked the bridge leading visitors to the entrance. Despite the high cost of the project, Thyssen concluded that it was an enormous success. The company's image was considerably enhanced; leading politicians were attracted to the stand as well as the press and key commercial customers. So powerful was the strength of the corporate persona projected by the construction that the company used it again in subsequent major exhibitions, in preference to hiring space in the main exhibition area.

Durapipe Glynwed Plastics

Durapipe Glynwed Plastics is a UK-based company employing 400 workers in the manufacture of plastic pipes for use in the water and gas industries and for industrial processing. The firm sells in every region of the world; 40 per cent of its turnover comes from exporting. Exhibiting is regarded as an integral and important component of the business's marketing mix. The company participates in between four and six international exhibitions annually, focusing on exhibitions that concern building materials and gas and water industry equipment. Recently it has used exhibitions to enter the rapidly expanding Chinese market. Specific exhibitions are selected a full year in advance in order to prepare appropriate presentation strategies. Normally the firm will use an exhibition to lay the basic groundwork for subsequent marketing efforts. It does not expect to sell directly from its stands; rather it aims to influence knowledgeable potential customers who are already familiar with the applications of this type of product. Exhibitions are seen as an invaluable vehicle for explaining the benefits of Glynwed piping systems and their advantages over competitors' products. Management believes that the 'camaraderie' with people in the same line of business generated by a large international exhibition is an enormous benefit to an organization entering an unfamiliar market.

Problems with exhibiting

Exhibitions are a key device for promoting goods in world markets. There are, nevertheless, several problems associated with exhibiting, including the following:

- The cost, time and administrative effort needed to prepare an exhibition stand in a foreign country.
- Most consumers visit exhibitions to browse rather than to buy. How does the exhibiting firm obtain the names and addresses of those callers on its stand who, subject to a follow-up letter or telephone call, are actually likely to purchase its products? And how can the exhibitor identify important people who influence major buying decisions within their companies?
- Gimmicks may be highly effective in attracting visitors to a stand but can attract the wrong people. An audience may be greatly impressed by the music, dancing, demonstration or whatever it is that is provided, yet not be remotely interested in the product.
- What criteria will be used to determine how big a display to mount at any given exhibition?
- Having a large and attractive stand at an exhibition can induce competitors to do the same, thereby wiping out the benefits of exhibiting.
- How can the employees who staff a stand be prevented from treating the exercise as a holiday – paying more attention to the social aspects of their involvement with the exhibition than to finding customers? What specific targets can the staff be given and how can the attainment of targets be measured?
- How is exhibiting to be dovetailed into the company's general marketing plans? What marketing objectives does exhibiting seek to achieve?
- What is known in advance about the numbers and characteristics of the people who will visit the exhibition, their length of stay, needs and buying habits?
- How can the firm ensure that the proposed stand will be well located vis-à-vis the layout and illumination of the exhibition centre and the anticipated traffic flow?

At the time of writing, few *independently collated* research statistics are available concerning international exhibition audience sizes, visitor behaviour, the impact of attending an exhibition on purchasing decisions, etc. Exhibition organizers conduct such research for their own private use but will not release results that could result in exhibitors drawing detrimental comparisons.

Exhibition planning

Specific matters that need to be addressed when planning a firm's participation in an exhibition include:

- whether to undertake pre-exhibition promotions (eg mail-drops to people likely to visit the exhibition);
- visual presentation of the stand (colour scheme, headlines, staff uniforms, etc);
- the best ratio of staff-to-stand space;
- style and quantity of leaflets, brochures and other promotional literature;
- how to evaluate the effectiveness of the firm's exhibition efforts (eg how to measure the sales resulting from stand enquiries);
- budgetary control over exhibition activities (stand erection and removal, cleaning and insurance, printing of leaflets, hotel reservations for staff, hire of furniture, etc);
- booking of interpreters;
- deciding an exact position for the stand.

The typical visitor to an exhibition wants to learn how certain products can solve specific problems. They are seriously interested in what the firm has to offer and are looking for answers to questions that the exhibitor should easily be able to predict. However, it is essential to formulate the answers to anticipated questions in a novel, entertaining and engaging way, which requires devoting as much attention to designing an exhibition stand as to preparing the layout and body copy for an advertisement in (say) the trade and technical press. Examples of matters that require attention include:

- Emphasizing what the product can do, its unique attributes and properties.
- Showing the product in operation, using movement (dramatic wherever possible) against an attractive background.
- Devising stand literature to reinforce the chosen theme.
- Selecting the right sales people to staff the stand. Personnel must be fluent in the language of the country concerned, and technically knowledgeable about the product and the exhibiting firm. If senior managers from the exhibiting firm who are not fluent in the relevant language are to be present, then an interpreter needs to be on hand to deal with problems. Interpreters engaged in person-to-person 'on the spot' duties normally charge per day spent with the client. Note that face-to-face interpreting requires intense concentration (it is not possible to look up difficult technical words and phrases in a dictionary) and can involve substantial amounts of stress – especially if hostile discussions are involved. Thus, two interpreters may be needed for a full day's work, and both must be thoroughly briefed before the exhibition.

Samples

Samples distributed before, during and after an exhibition can be highly effective in ensuring that serious customer prospects actually experience the promoted goods. This is especially useful for items with features and benefits that cannot be described adequately using conventional media advertisements. Other advantages to sampling are that it:

- encourages the marginally interested prospect to try the brand;
- makes an impact on jaded buyers who have been bored and overwhelmed by approaches from suppliers at a large number of competing exhibition stands;
- can act as a 'stand-alone' form of sales promotion;
- is a fast and efficient means for gaining attention.

Problems with sampling include its cost, possible disinterest on the part of recipients, and the fact that if one supplier starts giving samples, then competing firms might feel compelled to do the same – leading to 'sampling wars' with increasingly extravagant gifts and no single firm gaining in the longer term. The following rules should be applied to the use of samples:

- They should demonstrate – clearly and *obviously* – the superiority of the brand.
- Samples must induce customers to try the item. They should not be distributed indiscriminately to people who may not be attracted to the product.
- Presentation of a sample needs to be carefully coordinated with the transmission of an advertising message promoting the item. The prospect should see or have explained the product's benefits, and then be given the sample to try out as soon as possible thereafter.

Selecting exhibitions

Not all exhibitions are worth attending, and for certain types of product there are so many international exhibitions that it is physically impossible to attend them all. The following criteria can be applied to deciding which to support:

- the degree of overlap between target consumers and likely visitors to the exhibition;
- whether the exhibition is well established (recently inaugurated exhibitions usually attract small attendances), and the track record of the exhibition organizers (their reputation, experience, etc);
- the extent of the availability of useful information on the composition of past audiences, and lists of attendees and previous exhibitors;
- how many orders are needed to cover the cost of exhibiting at the venue;
- whether the leads obtained from exhibiting can be easily followed up;
- the venue: whether it is likely to attract a large attendance, the availability of nearby hotels, parking space, etc;
- cost per square metre of stand space in comparison with other exhibitions, plus charges for ancillary services.

The more specialized the exhibition, the higher the probability that entry will be controlled in some fashion, eg by restricting admittance to holders of tickets previously distributed via mail-drops to appropriate businesses, inserts in trade and professional journals, etc. A nominal cover charge is imposed on other entrants, except perhaps for bona fide business visitors who present a business card on registration. Certain trade fairs reserve particular days for trade visitors, opening their doors to the general public for the rest of the time.

Notes
1. Above-the-line advertising is advertising in media that pay commissions to the advertising agencies that provide them with business. Examples are newspapers and magazines, television and poster site companies. Other promotional methods (such as PR or direct mail) are said to be 'below-the-line'.
2. Sales promotions include money-off coupons, competitions and free draws, free samples and premium offers (eg send in a certain number of packet tops plus a small amount of money and receive the offered item at a very low price).

16

Future developments in global marketing

Globalization is proceeding apace, with companies seeking to expand worldwide and with consumers becoming closer in their characteristics. Cultural differences are being eroded, and traditional differences between nation states are collapsing under the pressure of a desire to liberate trade. These changes are producing subtle differences in the way business is conducted. This chapter attempts to examine these potential changes, and to predict some of the possible consequences.

BUSINESS-TO-BUSINESS MARKETING

Most of the attention of marketers is devoted to business-to-consumer markets, but in fact business-to-business markets are much larger, especially in a global context. This is because all consumer goods pass through business-to-business markets first, and often do so several times, so the aggregate business-to-business turnover is vastly greater than that of the final consumer markets.

Business buyers are generally believed to be more rational than consumer buyers (although there is considerable doubt expressed about this). If business buyers are more generally concerned with practical, economic issues they are less likely to be affected by cultural factors. For example, a steel buyer in Japan will source steel from whichever country or factory is able to supply steel of the right quality, within the right time frame, and (presumably) at the lowest price. This is the same thinking a steel buyer in New York would have, or one in Buenos Aires.

In fact, the evidence is that this is not the whole story. Buyers are sometimes affected by the nationality of the supplying firm, because countries acquire reputations of their own, quite distinct from that of the companies within them (White and Cundiff, 1978). For example, Germany has a reputation for high-quality engineering, but this is based largely on the German car industry: it is entirely possible that some German engineering firms produce low-quality goods. Similarly, Eastern European countries have a reputation for poor-quality goods, yet Skoda produces exceptionally high-quality cars, and there is little doubt that Russian space engineering is of a high standard even if their consumer products are not.

In addition, some countries tend to be highly nationalistic. They will favour their own companies and products rather than foreign imports. For example, Swedish buyers show a distinct preference for local suppliers, even if the foreign companies can supply goods cheaper.

The main development in global business-to-business markets has been the emergence of deals between global companies. If both the supplier and the purchaser are global firms, the process becomes extremely complex, due to the large number of people who will be involved in the decision-making process. Industrial buying involves more than one decision-maker. Webster and Wind (1972) identified five groups of people who are involved in the process, as follows:

- **Deciders**. These are the people who make the actual final decision about purchase.
- **Buyers**. These are people who are given the task of sourcing suppliers, and negotiating with them.
- **Influencers**. These are people who are not directly involved in the purchase decision, but may be consulted by the decision-makers.
- **Users**. These are the people who will actually use the product. They often have a consultative role, and may well have a say in the final decision.
- **Gatekeepers**. These people control the flow of information to the decision-makers. They are often personal assistants, telephonists or secretaries who see their role as that of protecting the decision-makers from continual sales pitches from suppliers.

In a global context, these groups may be scattered across several countries, and therefore be subject to the cultural influences of several different regions of the world. If the supplying company is also global, the same is true of the sales representatives. For example, consider the position of a computer software company that has a system for handling international goods dispatch. The company will certainly want to market the product to global companies, but will need to deal with individuals in many different countries as a result. Although the global organization will need to use the same software throughout its operations (since there must be consistency), each subsidiary in each market will have its own autonomous decision-makers. Luckily, computers themselves have become fairly standardized, but each country will need the software to operate in the local language, and to be able to handle local differences in order procedures, product characteristics and communications infrastructure.

This type of sale is likely to involve negotiation, and considerable adaptation of the product to make it suitable for all the possible configurations. It will also involve price and delivery negotiations within each separate country, but with an overall coordination: sales people in each country will need to know what concessions have been granted by their colleagues elsewhere, and technicians will need to know what adaptations have been requested. These adaptations will also need to mesh with each other if the software is to function effectively.

For the supplier, the choice is between having one senior sales person who visits all the countries and all the decision-makers, and having separate sales people in each country and for each decision-maker. The former course of action requires a sales person who is able to speak many languages and is happy dealing across cultures: such a person is so rare as to be practically unobtainable. The supplier is therefore more likely to adopt a team approach, with regular contact between the members in each country and a single leader who coordinates their activities.

This type of sale would not have existed 30 years ago. Multinational corporations allowed their local subsidiaries to operate almost entirely independently because this was the only feasible way to conduct business in an era when travel was expensive and often slow, and international communications involved booking telephone or telex time on an undersea cable. In the intervening period, advances in telecommunications have not only made such deals between global firms possible, they have also made them essential.

ANTI-GLOBALIZATION MOVEMENTS

During 2001, major riots occurred at global summit conferences in Genoa and Seattle. These riots were the result of an anti-globalization movement, which has itself become global. Those who are opposed to the increasing globalization of business cite the power of the global companies, which after all are not accountable to any democratic process, and suggest that global firms are able to transcend national governments and impose their will on the rest of humanity. This accusation has a certain amount of truth in it: global firms often do have greater economic power than national governments, for example in terms of controlling exchange rates internationally, and can switch production between countries so as to maximize the tax breaks available. Of the largest 100 economic entities in the world, the majority are corporations: firms such as General Motors, BP and Microsoft are powerful enough to dictate terms.

Another objection to globalization is the erosion of national cultural values. Major firms are often accused of forcing cultural change on populations. This has been called McDonaldization, a reference to the well-known McDonald's practice of standardizing the product worldwide. For example, there has been an overall growth in tobacco smoking worldwide in recent years as the tobacco companies have targeted Third World countries, in effect exporting the vices of the industrial world.

A final objection is that global corporations have no allegiance to individual countries, and therefore have no compunction about causing environmental damage or economic damage in countries that represent sources of supply. For example, farmers in Africa are encouraged to grow cash crops to supply global corporations, while neglecting to grow sufficient food crops to feed the local population.

In many cases these accusations might be justified. Global firms will (unsurprisingly) seek the best deals they can for their shareholders when locating factories and distribution networks, without much regard for local needs. Equally, one might well understand that a corporation is more interested in its own survival and welfare than in that of the local population, and will negotiate accordingly. Erosion of cultural differences is likely to happen in any case, owing to increased world travel and more rapid communication of ideas – and there is little doubt that people will reject any incoming idea if it does not fit in with their own needs. Ultimately, global corporations are answerable to their customers, and frequently these corporations are boycotted by customers who disapprove of the corporation's behaviour.

Anti-globalization movements are likely to remain a feature of 21st-century life for some time, but are unlikely to have a major impact on the way global firms conduct business. The reason for this is that consumers indicate their support (or otherwise) for firms simply by choosing where to spend their money. If people in, say, France decide that they would prefer to eat at McDonald's rather than have the traditional two-hour lunch break, they will do so – and in practice, McDonald's has many home-grown imitators in France, including Quick and Buffalo Grill. The benefits of the globalization of products are likely to outweigh the drawbacks, and this in turn is likely to communicate itself to consumers, legislators and others. Having said that, efforts to maintain the cultural diversity of the world will also be welcomed.

GLOBAL REPUTATION MANAGEMENT

Global corporations have a problem in maintaining a reputation that has the same values across different cultures and national boundaries. The first problem is to establish a global voice. It is no longer possible to have substantially different messages for different audiences, since global communications are so rapid and all-embracing. In this context, the Internet has a strong role to play, since it is a powerful communications medium that is accessible by anyone with a computer and a modem – which in practice means anyone with the price of entry to an Internet café. Most global corporations have shadow Web sites carry scurrilous and occasionally libellous stories about the corporation concerned.

Public relations companies specialize, frequently along either industry lines or task lines, for example PR companies might specialize in parliamentary lobbying or in media relations. Obviously most specialize within their own countries. This means that the global PR firm is an unusual entity. In order to manage a global PR campaign, the firm would need to have good relationships with the media in many countries, and with governments and politicians, and with local organizations that might have an interest in the firm's activities. One firm is unlikely to have all these attributes, so the global company is forced to operate through many local PR agencies, each of which will need to be thoroughly conversant with the organization's global voice. In practice, this can be difficult to do, since PR is a subtle practice and what works well in one country is unlikely to work well in another. The global brand is likely to be contaminated by brand values relating to the country of origin: for example, a British firm might experience difficulties in some former colonial countries due to anti-British feeling, but benefit from Britain having a good reputation in others.

Identifying PR issues in different countries is also problematical. Issues are normally identified by monitoring the press, and preparing appropriate responses to PR threats and opportunities. In the global context, this means keeping up-to-date with thousands of different newspapers or TV stations, clearly an impossible task. A threat might be dealt with on a local basis, but care should be taken to ensure that the response is within the overall global voice. Opportunities are much harder to take advantage of, since they will often take the organization in a new direction, one that is unlikely to have been fore-seen within the global voice policy. Public opinion within countries is likely to be diverse, and difficult to monitor on a global basis: in many cases local conflicts between different groups mean that a global firm cannot possibly please everybody. For example, it would be virtually impossible to formulate a message that would appeal to both Israelis and Palestinians.

Fortunately for most PR people, leakage across national boundaries is relatively small, perhaps because the people who are in the best position to appreciate cross-cultural variations in voice are frequent travellers or Internet-sophisticated individuals. These people tend to be better educated and more attuned to the idea of cross-cultural differences. For example, a press release about a firm will only be read and understood by someone fluent in the language: for such a person to recognize a discrepancy in public statements, they would need to be fluent in several languages and also interested in the fact that a discrep-ancy exists. The net result of this is that, in most cases, PR people are able to operate with some latitude in the different countries in which a global firm functions.

WORLD FREE TRADE

Currently, the governments of the world are resting from the long round of tariff-reduc-ing discussions. The emphasis has shifted away from reducing tariffs worldwide, and towards creating trading blocs within which free trade is encouraged. However, these blocs are expanding. The European Union is set to grow over the next 20 years or so, to include Poland, Hungary and the Czech Republic. At the same time, other countries such as Turkey and Morocco are clamouring to join, which may open the door to other African and Middle Eastern countries to apply. MERCOSUR in South America is seeking both to expand until it covers the entire continent, and also to deepen its internal links by reduc-ing trade barriers to zero. The Asia-Pacific Economic Cooperation Forum has committed to establishing free trade amongst its members by 2010, and intends to extend this to developing countries within a further 10 years.

The thrust behind this thinking is to create powerful trading empires that can stand up to each other. No country wants to stand alone against the trading empires of the United States, Europe and Japan, so there will come a time when every country in the world is a member of one or other trading bloc. At that point, the logical next step is for each bloc to negotiate agreements with other blocs to create even greater empires. Already APEC and NAFTA are involved in talks aimed at scrapping tariffs, and APEC has invited the EU to join in. A refusal by the EU could mean that European goods will be shut out from half the world's markets, so there is strong pressure to accept the offer. Finally there might only be one world-spanning trade entity, with no barriers to trade whatsoever.

This will not happen soon, and of course may not happen at all: human history is one of conflict as much as it is one of cooperation. But the benefits of such an outcome are huge. Trade is always good: both parties are always better off as a result, so world wealth must inevitably improve and living standards rise.

MARKET RESEARCH

In most of the world's markets, research has proved to be difficult or impossible to under-take. Low literacy levels, poor infrastructures, and lack of government statistics have combined to make research expensive, slow, and unreliable. As wealth increases in the Third World, and as Eastern European countries become more liberalized, research is back on the agenda. For example, joint ventures between newly emerging Mexican research agencies and established US agencies are resulting in high-quality marketing information.

The third driver for this increase in research is the need for global firms to seek new markets in what were previously poor countries. Without clear market research, such expansion has been hindered in the past. With modern information-handling capabilities and an effective intelligence-gathering network, firms are able to generate information on a global scale regarding the most effective markets for the products. It is now possible for firms to develop a worldwide profile of their potential and actual customers, identify markets that are ripe for a new product, identify markets that transcend national bound-aries, and (perhaps most importantly) identify which markets are likely to prove most lucrative.

Global segmentation has always been hampered by firms' inability to generate compa-rable market research across the entire globe: with the changes inherent in the new market research, such segmentation will be as simple in future as national segmentation is now.

MARKETING THROUGH THE WORLD WIDE WEB

The World Wide Web is much touted as the most important marketing tool since the invention of television. However, most firms use their Web sites as if they were simply another form of billboard – in other words, they fail to make use of the potential of the system for interactive marketing.

Most Web sites provide information, and often do so in an entertaining and user-friendly way. A very large proportion allow potential customers to obtain quotes and even order online, although a frustratingly large number do not do this. However, very few allow customer-to-customer dialogue, and in almost all cases the marketers use the sites as one-way, mass-market type communications (albeit with a customer-operated search facility). In effect, most Web sites are little more than catalogues or brochures.

In fact, marketing has gone through two phases and is now entering a third (Schultz and Schultz, 1999). The first phase, in the 1950s, was characterized by manufacturers who found out (through market research) what customers wanted and then arranged for it to be delivered. During the 1970s and 1980s the retailers became dominant, telling manufacturers what to make. During the 21st century, consumers will be in charge, making their wishes known directly through the Internet. The rise in popularity of Internet auctions illustrates this. Consumers place bids for products, and if enough people bid for a product, even at a very low price, manufacturers will be prepared to supply the product.

In the global context, the world is still in Phase One. Global companies carry out research and decide (broadly) what to supply. Within a few years, however, customers will find it easy to obtain quotes from any firm anywhere in the world, whether or not that firm has a marketing presence in the country where the customer lives. This will inevitably bypass the role of the retailer, and also of the global firm, going straight to Phase Three, in which the customer is in charge of the process.

Again, these changes may not happen immediately, or even soon: the evidence from the Internet research that has been conducted is that the vast majority of customers still prefer to do business in the traditional way. However, the publicity given to the anti-globalization movement will certainly fuel a desire by customers to bypass the system and buy directly, and once the appropriate security and delivery systems are in place it seems almost inevitable that digital buying will become commonplace.

MARKETING PLANS

Given improvements in IT and telecommunications technology, marketing plans in the future will be a great deal more flexible. Software has already been developed that allows real-time adjustments in marketing plans, to take account of fluctuating demand. A simplified version of this is the booking system used by low-cost airlines: as demand for a particular flight picks up, the price rises. If demand falls, the price also falls. All this is triggered automatically by the software, which decides how fast seats are selling.

Inputs made at the customer's office will be integrated with inputs made at the firm in order to provide an instant, up-to-the-minute picture of the firm's current position. Global communications allow this to happen independently of location, so that the computer's virtual world is only a millisecond in diameter. As software improves, the computer will be able to integrate external environmental data to predict competitive responses, intermediaries' reactions, changes in the legal and political framework, and possible actions of other stakeholders to produce a real-time model of the corporate world.

Obviously such systems are only as good as the people who program them. For this reason, 21st century marketing will still need people who can think global, act local, and respond to customers' needs in an efficient and effective manner.

References

Abell, M (ed) (1991) *European Franchising: Law and Practice*, Waterlow

Alnasrari, A (1991) *Arab Nationalism, Oil and the Political Economy of Dependency*, Greenwood

Andersen, A (1993) *The Arthur Andersen American Business Sourcebook*, Triumph Books

Anholt, S (October 1993) 'Adapting advertising copy across frontiers', *Admap*, **28** (10)

Ansoff, H I (Sept–Oct 1957) 'Strategies for Diversification', *Harvard Business Review*

Baalbaki, I B and Malhotra, N K (1993) 'Marketing management bases for international market segmentation', *International Marketing Review*, **10** (1)

Baines, A (1992) *The Handbook of International Direct Marketing*, Kogan Page

Bangeman, M (1992) *Meeting the Global Challenge*, Kogan Page

Bartels, R (1968) 'Are domestic and international marketing dissimilar?', *Journal of Marketing*, **32**

Bartlett, C A and Ghousal, S (1989) *Managing Across Borders*, Hutchinson

Bennett, R (1993b) *Handbook of European Advertising*, Kogan Page

Bennett, R (1996) 'Relationship formation and governance in consumer markets: Transactional analysis versus the behaviourist approach', *Journal of Marketing Management*, **12** (6), pp 417–36

Besher, A (1991) *The Pacific Rim Almanac*, Harper

Blythe, J (2001) *Essentials of Marketing, Financial Times*, Prentice-Hall, Harlow

Booms B H and Bitner, M J (1981) 'Marketing strategies and organisation structures for service firms' in *Marketing of Services*, eds J Donnelly and W R George, American Marketing Association, Chicago Ill

Borden, N H (1965) 'The concept of the marketing mix', in *Science in Marketing*, ed G Schwartz, Wiley

Boyacigiller, N (October 1991) 'The role of expatriates in the management of interdependence, complexity and risk in multinational corporations', *Journal of International Business Studies*

Brooke, M Z (1992) *International Management: Review of Strategies and Operations*, 2nd edn, Hutchinson

Brown, L (1994) *Competitive Marketing Strategy for Europe: Developing, Maintaining and Defending Competitive Advantage*, Macmillan

Calof, J L and Beamish, P W (1995) 'Adapting to foreign markets: Explaining internationalisation', *International Business Review*, **4** (2), pp 115–31

Campbell, A and Tawadey, K (1990) *Mission and Business Philosophy: Winning Employee Commitment*, Heinemann Professional

Christopher, M, Payne, A and Ballantyre, D (1991) *Relationship Marketing: Bringing Quality, Customer Service and Marketing Together*, Butterworth

Cordell, V V and Wogtada, N (1991) 'Modelling determinants of cross border trade in counterfeit goods', *Journal of Global Marketing*, **4** (3)

Crabtree, J et al (1991) *International Sale of Goods*, Croner

Crawley, E (1993) *The Americas Review 1993/94*, Kogan Page

Diamantopoulos, A (1994) *Managing Pricing Decisions*, Chapman & Hall

Dore, I I (1993) *The UNCITRAL Framework for Arbitration in Contemporary Perspective*, Graham & Trotman

Dunning, J H (1993) *The globalisation of business*, Routledge

Engholm, C (1993) *The Other Europe*, McGraw-Hill

Ferraro, G P (1990) *The Cultural Dimension of International Business*, Prentice-Hall

Gates, S R and Engelhoff, W G (summer 1986), 'Centralisation in headquarters – subsidiary relationships', *Journal of International Business Studies*

Goldschmidt, A (1991) *A Concise History of the Middle East*, 4th edn, Westview, Oxford

Gronroos, C (1994) 'Quo vadis marketing? Toward a relationship marketing paradigm', *Journal of Marketing Management*, **10**, pp 347–60

Haigh, R W (spring 1992) 'Building a strategic alliance', *Colombia Journal of World Business*

Hofstede, G (1980) *Culture's Consequence. International Differences in Work Related Values*, Sage

Jobber, D (2001) *Principles and Practice of Marketing*, McGraw-Hill

Johanson, J and Vahlne, J E (1990) 'The mechanism of internationalisation', *International Marketing Review*, **7** (4), pp 11–24

Jorgenson J and Blythe J (2002) *A Guide To A More Effective Web-Presence*

Kapferer, J (1992) *Strategic Brand Management*, Kogan Page

Kwon, Y C and Konopa, L J (1993) 'Impact of host country market characteristics on the choice of foreign market entry mode', *International Marketing Review*, **10** (2)

Lancaster, G A and Massingham, L (1993) *Essentials of Marketing*, 2nd edn, McGraw-Hill

Levitt, T (May–June 1983) 'The globalisation of markets', *Harvard Business Review*

Lewis, J D (1990) *Structuring and Managing Strategic Alliances*, Macmillan

Lorange, P and Roos, J (1992) *Strategic Alliances: Formation, Implementation and Evolution*, Blackwell

Macrae, C (1991) *World Class Brands*, Addison-Wesley

Malhotra, N K (autumn 1988) 'A methodology for measuring consumer preferences in developing countries', *International Marketing Review*

Malhotra, N K (1991) 'Administration of questionnaires for collecting quantitative data in international marketing research', *Journal of Global Marketing*, **4** (2)

Mansfield, P (1981) *The Arabs*, Penguin

McCarthy, E J (1981) *Basic Marketing: A Managerial Approach*, Irwin

McEnery, J and Desharnais, G (April 1990) 'Culture shock', *Training and Development Journal*

Millington, A and Bayliss, B (1990) 'The process of internationalisation: UK companies in the EC', *Management International Review*, **30** (2), pp 151–61

Mintzberg, H (1994) *The Rise and Fall of Strategic Planning*, Prentice-Hall

Mintzberg, H (1983) *Structure in Fives: Designing Effective Organisations*, Prentice Hall, Englewood Cliffs

Moynihan, M (February 1993) 'How MNCs ease expatriates' return to home countries', *Business International*

Murdock, G P (1945) 'The common denominator of cultures', in *The Science of Man*, ed R Linton, Columbia University Press

OECD (1989) *Predatory Pricing, Organisation for Economic Cooperation and Development*, Paris

Olson, H C and Widersheim, P F (1978) 'Factors affecting the pre-export behaviour of non-exporting firms', in *European Research in International Business*, eds M Ghertman and J Leontiades, North-Holland, New York

Porter, M (1980) *Competitive Strategy*, The Free Press, New York

Porter, M (1985) *Competitive Advantage*, The Free Press, New York

Porter, M (1990) *The Competitive Advantages of Nations*, Macmillan

Rafferty, K and Bird, C (1993) *Asia and Pacific Review 1993/94*, Kogan Page

Reuvid, J and Bennett, R (eds) (1993) *Doing Business with the West*, Kogan Page

Schmitthoff, C M (1990) *Schmitthoff's Export Trade*, Stevens

Schultz D E and Schultz H E (1998) 'Transitioning marketing communications into the twenty-first century', *Journal of Marketing Communications* **4** (1) pp 9–26

Shiotani, T (August 1988) 'Outline of the Japanese distribution system', *Business Japan*

Stacey, R (1993) *Strategic Management and Organisational Dynamics*, Pitman

Stalk, G (1990) *Competing Against Time: How Time-Based Competition is Reshaping Global Markets*, Collier Macmillan

Stroud, A and Masters, C D (1991) *Transfer Pricing*, Butterworths

Turnbull, P W (1987) 'A challenge to the stages theory of the internationalisation process', in *Managing Export Entry and Expansion* eds P J Rosson and S Reids, Praeger, NY, pp 18–38

United Nations (1983) *Report of the Commission on Transnational Corporations*, UN, New York

US International Trade Commission (1993) *Potential Impact on the US Economy of the North American Free Trade Agreement*

Usunier, J C (1993) *International Marketing: A Cultural Approach*, Prentice-Hall

Wallace, H (ed) (1991) *The Wider Western Europe: Reshaping the EC/EFTA Relationship*, Pinter

Walsh, V (1992) *Winning by Design: Technology, Product Design and International Competitiveness*, Blackwell Business

Walters, P G (1989) 'A framework for export pricing decisions', *Journal of Global Marketing*, **2** (3)

Weigand, R E (spring 1991) 'Parallel import channels', *Colombia Journal of World Business*

Wells, L T (1972) *The Product Life Cycle and International Trade*, Division of Research, Graduate School of Business Administration, Harvard University

White, Phillip D and Cundiff, Edward W (January 1978) Assessing the quality of industrial products, *Journal of Marketing*, pp 80–86

Index